GRAY CAVALIER

GRAY CAVALIER

THE LIFE AND WARS OF
GENERAL W.H.F. "ROONEY" LEE

Mary Bandy Daughtry

DA CAPO PRESS
A Member of the Perseus Books Group

Designed by Trish Wilkinson
Set in 10-point Sabon by the Perseus Books Group

Cataloging-in-Publication data for this book
is available from the Library of Congress.

First Da Capo Press edition 2002
ISBN 0–306–81173–1

Published by Da Capo Press
A Member of the Perseus Books Group
http://www.dacapopress.com

Da Capo Press books are available at special discounts for
bulk purchases in the U.S. by corporations, institutions,
and other organizations. For more information, please contact
the Special Markets Department at the Perseus Books Group,
11 Cambridge Center, Cambridge, MA 02142, or call
(800) 255-1514 or (617) 252-5298, or e-mail
j.mccrary@perseusbooks.com.

1 2 3 4 5 6 7 8 9—06 05 04 03 02

Contents

Contents

Acknowledgments

I am indebted to many people who have helped me in writing this book. My first debt of gratitude is to my parents, Agnes Lassiter Bandy and Raymer Franklin Bandy. They nurtured, encouraged, and assisted me in all my endeavors my entire life. They were the first to say, "No limits." To their memory this book is dedicated.

Next, a huge thank-you to all my typists and computer gurus. Without you this book would not exist in its current form. My friends with typing skills are Janie Woodard, Mary Jane Holtoner, Kim A. Smith, Judy Wooters, Vince Beasley, Joan Brindley, and Sarah Wuntke. My colleagues Paula Waters, Sandra Jones, and Mary Jo Parker also proofread many of the chapters.

Fe Maria Finch prepared all the old pictures for publication and enhanced them with her artistic and computer skills.

The consummate artist, and my good friend, Pat "Devore" Wyatt, consented to portray Rooney Lee in oil. Before she started painting she studied her subject intensively and immersed herself in Civil War books as well as my manuscript to get the right feel for her subject and offered valuable advice.

Many of my relatives and friends have been "conscripted into service" to go with me to Civil War sites. Among these I would like to thank Martha Bandy Perry, Sam Lynn, Barbara Jordan, Jerry Hamrick, Janet Watson, Amelia Dees, and Mary Jo Parker. Lisa Wagner and Mary Jane Holtoner also have accompanied me to talk to many Civil War groups. Both of these friends could do my presentations as well as I.

My old dear friend Allan Gurganus was the first to read the entire manuscript and encouraged me through the publication process.

Bryce Suderow, a Civil War researcher extraordinaire, found countless resources for me to study and use. He also read portions of the book.

Others who have read chapters and aided me in many ways include Bud Hall, Chris Calkins, Gordon Rhea, Noah André Trudeau, and Pat Brennan.

I am indebted to the staffs of many universities and museums for aiding in my research. These include the Virginia Historical Society, the Museum of the Confederacy, the Virginia State Library, the University of Virginia, Washington and Lee University, Harvard University, Duke University, the University of North Carolina–Chapel Hill, the North Carolina Museum of History, and the University of South Carolina. The staff of the Wayne County Public Library was also very helpful. My research covered many years, and I thank all who helped in the past as well as the present.

I am also indebted to those who have been a part of preparing my manuscript for publication at Da Capo Press. Among these are Ted Savas, Robert Pigeon, Katharine Chandler, and Jon Howard.

I would like to thank my husband, Harry Daughtry, who has endured this process without a word of complaint even though he is not even remotely interested in Civil War history. He is one of the very few horsemen in the modern era who would have been good enough to ride with Stuart, Hampton, and the Lees.

CHAPTER 1

"There is not such another child"

William Henry Fitzhugh Lee, the second son and third child of Robert Edward Lee and Mary Custis Lee, was born at Arlington, Virginia, on May 31, 1837. The lengthy name was in honor of a man who had close connections to both sides of the family. William Henry Fitzhugh of Ravensworth had been a close friend and counselor to Robert's mother, Anne Carter Lee, and it was in his house on Orinoco Street in Alexandria that Robert Lee had spent his boyhood. Fitzhugh also wrote a letter of recommendation to support Robert Lee's application to West Point. In addition, he was Mary Lee's uncle, her mother's brother.[1]

Lieutenant Lee's first recorded mention of this son was to his friend Captain Talcott: "She [Mary] is very well and has got downstairs again. Her little limb is as ugly as ever, though she still thinks his nose is to subside, his mouth contract, eyes to open, hair to curl, etc.—and in fact to become a perfect beauty." Soon after he made this description of the baby, Lee left for Saint Louis, where a major engineering assignment waited for him. Once there he missed his family and inquired after the baby: "But how is the little one? I feel anxious to see him and to appreciate the great improvements that you say have taken place. Kiss them all for me." Lee was a natural as *père de famille* (father of the family) and expressed this to a friend later that year: "I am the father of three children . . . so entwined around my heart that I feel them at every pulsation."[2]

During the winter of 1837–1838 Lee was reunited with his family at Arlington. In the spring of 1838 he set out again for Saint Louis, but this time his wife and children accompanied him. The journey "was as

1

pleasant as could be expected in a country of this sort," and Lee reported "the boys stood it manfully and indeed improved on it." When they arrived in Saint Louis they lived temporarily with the family of Dr. William Beaumont. Here the Lee boys found some playmates, and their father described the ensuing play: "They have three interesting little children that are the constant companions of our two and as drumming was the mania at Old Point, riding and driving at Arlington, so steamboating is all the rage here. They convert themselves even into steamboats, ring their bells, raise their steam (high pressure) and put off. They fire up so frequently and keep on so heavy a pressure of steam that I am constantly fearing they will burst their boilers."[3]

By this time William Henry Fitzhugh Lee had received the nickname of "Rooney" by which he was known the rest of his life. It is not known what prompted his father to call him that, but the nickname was more lasting than those given to the other children. The young father's first impression of this baby had by now changed drastically. He urged Cassius Lee to "tell my cousin Philippa" some news and to "undeceive her on a certain point, as I understand, she is laboring under a grievous error. Tell her that it is farthest from my wish to detract from any of the little Lees, but as to her little boy being equal to Mr. Rooney, it is a thing not even to be supposed, much less believed, although we live in a credulous country, where people stick at nothing from a coon story to a sea serpent." In fact Lee had become such a doting father that he probably bored those with whom he corresponded with minute details of child-rearing. For example, he wrote Mr. Custis at length on Rooney's weaning and summed up with "Mr. Rooney has taken so kindly to bacon and bread that he does not feel the loss of his mother. He will not take tea or milk, and prefers a glass of this good Missouri water to all the tea you can make him." Lee's reports on the precocity of this child may be the only times in his life that he stretched the truth. When Rooney was little more than a year old, Lee wrote: "I was showing him a picture today of a woman and child and told him there was Grandmother and little Sister. He immediately turned round and pointed to his Ganny's portrait and tried to pronounce Gan-mother and then pointed to little daughter's. He walks all about, converts the chairs, books, etc. into steamboats and shoves them along puffing on the high pressure system." Mary Lee described her son about this time as "all about and is the most impudent fellow you ever saw. He knows nothing about Toms but is delighted whenever he sees a cow or horse. . . ." Apparently his love for animals, horses in particular, was evident from a very early age.[4]

Rooney Lee was an outgoing, active, boisterous child who claimed special affection from his parents from the beginning. About Christmas of 1838, Robert Lee wrote his brother Carter: "Both the boys are quite hearty. Mr. Rooney carries a wide row, and when offended struts about the room swelling like a turkey cock; the only person that he does not think himself called on to show defiance to is his 'Baba.'" His mother's opinion at this time was that "Mr. Rooney is considered the finest and handsomest boy in all the West. . . . He walks very well and says a great many words and is the most mischievous little creature I ever saw." He was into everything, and his parents had to keep a constant watch on him. Of his active nature, Mary wrote, "Today while I was sitting at my work not observing him, I turned around and saw that he had climbed on the table and was mounted on the top of Robert's writing desk." Robert Lee also did his share of babysitting during this period. While he wrote his brother, he described the scene around him: "Boo and Rooney with four of their little playmates have been keeping such a laughing, bawling, jumping 'rumpus and a rioting' around me that I hardly know what I have written, and Mr. Rooney is at this moment jerking the cover of my table with one hand and cracking me over the head with the broom with the other." It is interesting to note that there are ink splotches on this letter compared with Robert Lee's usually meticulous correspondence. The grandparents were kept abreast of their grandson's qualities by a very proud father: "As to Mr. Rooney I could write a book upon his beauties and merits though they might not be desirable to every eye. I am very anxious to point them out to you, Mother, for I know you would appreciate them. . . ." At this time Custis was old enough for his mother to begin her work as schoolmistress. However, it was "hard to induce him to sit to his lessons" while his wild little brother played around him. Mary wrote her mother that she wished she "had some of the little ones here to amuse Rooney all the time Kitty is washing; I find it rather tiresome to nurse all day such an unsettled brat." While she was writing the letter Rooney was "playing around me pulling my pens, paper and ink and is now trying to throw his Papa's hat out of the window. . . ." His father did not share her view and thought "there is not such another child in all Missouri and that he would not exchange him for the whole State."[5]

In May 1839, the Lees traveled back to Arlington so that Mary could have their fourth child at home. After a short stay in Virginia Robert Lee returned to Saint Louis. On the journey back the homesick father expressed his feelings for his children, Rooney in particular:

> You do not know how much I have missed you and the children, my dear Mary. To be alone in a crowd is very solitary. In the woods I feel sympathy with the trees and birds, in whose company I take delight, but experience no pleasure in a strange crowd.
>
> I hope you are all well and will continue so, and therefore must again urge you to be very prudent and careful of those dear children. If I could only get a squeeze at that little fellow turning up his sweet mouth to 'Keese Baba'! You must not let him run wild in my absence, and will have to exercise firm authority over all of them. This will not require severity, or even strictness, but constant attention, and an un-wavering course. Mildness and forebearance, tempered by firmness and judgment will strengthen their affection for you, while it will maintain your control over them.[6]

After being away from his family for seven months Lee obtained a leave during the winter and rejoined his brood, which now numbered four. For a while, at least, Lee could see to the discipline of his children himself. As usual he was as concerned about every minute facet of their upbringing as any engineering project he had ever undertaken. Also, as usual, he kept his friends updated on all domestic events. In the spring he wrote Colonel Talcott: "We have all been very well except our little boy with whom teething this warm weather has gone quite hard. He is much reduced though now tolerable well and as he has all but the eye and stomach teeth, which I hope he will defer till fall, I am in hopes we shall have no further cause of uneasiness." Lee spent much time playing with his children and became "a horse, dog, ladder, and target for a cannon by the little Lees."[7]

The Lee family remained at Arlington while the father pursued his duties as engineer, inspecting and repairing various forts on the East Coast. In 1841 he was given the task of updating and refitting the forts in New York harbor. This new assignment promised to be a lengthy one since both Fort Hamilton and Fort Lafayette were in poor condition. Consequently the Lees moved to Fort Hamilton and settled in a government-owned house there. Except for visits to Arlington the Lees remained in New York for five years. Lee described Rooney in 1842 as "a large hearty fellow that requires a tight rein." Rooney was more outgoing than his older brother Custis and also less inclined toward the quiet regimen of books. He wanted to be outdoors engaged in some activity, especially riding, at all times. His father described him at age six to his grandmother: "I am sure Mother you will be pleased with the proficiency of that Rooney. He is a smart fellow but does not confine his search after knowledge to books. He puts in requisition all objects that come within his reach and finds much to improve him in the savory composition of cakes, pies and such things, as well as in the productions of nature such as apples and peaches. He is charmed with the study of natural history, particularly with that of the horse and all belonging to him and will spend days in riding and driving that noble animal, without giving the least signs of weariness. I am sure he will profit by your instructions, Mother, but pray don't let him infect you with his zeal and lay yourself up." When Robert Edward Lee Jr. was born the father's love expanded to include yet another son. "No sooner was I conscious of his birth than all my affections were awakened. Perhaps it was from you telling me he resembled Rooney," he wrote to Mrs. Custis.[8]

During this period Lee spent a great deal of time with Rooney. Custis was away at school, the girls stayed at home with their mother, and Rob was still a baby. Rooney was the one who accompanied his father. On one particular excursion into the city of New York, Rooney went with his father in spite of complaints earlier that morning that he had some pains in his legs. Lee "laughed at and even indeed reproved him . . . , as it was not the first time he had made similar complaints during the week." The lure of the trip to the city caused the pains to disappear, and the two set off on horseback. Later while they were walking around the city, Rooney held his father's hand most of the way but did not complain. By the time Lee had finished his business, the little boy's discomfort became clear without him saying so. Lee hired a carriage to take them back to their horses and the ferry. Once home Rooney went to bed immediately. Lee then demonstrated his expertise as a nurse, trying hot baths, salts, and applications of camphor. Rooney remained in bed for five days while his nurse made him "flying visits" during the day and remained with him at night. Lee told his mother-in-law that he was the nurse because Mary was also sick, but "perhaps it was as well as he seemed to think my touch hurt him less than anyone else's." Although he feared an attack of "inflammatory rheumatism" he thought it might have been "a violent cold which seized upon his limbs." At any rate Lee was "truly grateful" for his son's recovery and felt "wretched" during his illness.[9]

In the summer of 1844 Rooney announced "that he intends to learn to swim this summer and wishes to commence at once." His swimming instructor was naturally his father. They practiced in the waters of New York harbor and were soon joined by Custis who was on vacation. By September Lee could report: "They have both become quite expert swimmers and Custis can go any distance. We go in bathing together every morning. . . . "[10]

By this time Rooney was "a big double-fisted fellow with an appetite that does honour to his big mouth" and with his brothers and sisters was "growing in mischief as well as size." His interests were still in active pastimes rather than studying. Lee wrote to Martha Williams: "Your Cousin Eleanor Rogers has been the occupant of your little room this summer, but she has now left it and Rooney has applied it to his study. It may therefore be considered vacant, so little time is he engaged in the most abstruse exercise. Boating, swimming, fishing, and riding occupy all his energies and in comparison with these the duties of the closet sink into insignificance and contempt. The tranquility of the sciences are therefore undisturbed by him." Mary Lee taught the children herself until they were old enough to go to a boarding school. Her first two were model students, but her third was more exasperating. Of her school and students she wrote: "[Mary] is always willing to take a lesson, Rooney as much averse to it as ever and his improvement but small. I hope this winter to get him to reading well. He is a good-natured fellow in the main but very unruly indeed and teases Wiggy almost out of her life. Rob is very fond of him and his rough ways."[11]

In November 1845 Mary made preparations to return to Arlington to await the birth of their next child. The departure was delayed for some time, however, because of an accident that happened to Rooney. He had been told not to leave the yard without permission and not to go to the stable unattended. However, the lure of the stable and horses was too much for him, and he "went down to the public barn where they were putting in some hay for the horses." He became fascinated by the workings of "one of those patent straw cutters, worked with great power by a crank" and tried to cut some hay. Instead he "took off the ends of the fore and middle fingers of the left hand—the first just at the root of the nail and the second at the first joint." Lee's orderly Jim carried him to the hospital inside the fort at once, but the post surgeon was in New York City. An hour and a half went by before a doctor arrived to tend the cut fingers. Then the ends of the fingers were reattached and dressed. "All that time he sat in the hospital with his fingers bleeding profusely, without complaining, and frequently scolded Jim for making a fuss about it," Lee later informed Custis. He added, "The officers who were present said they were astonished to see so young a boy behave so well, that they had seen many men under less trying circumstances behave worse." Mary Lee had been taking leave of the neighbors when the accident occurred, and Lee was in the city. The officers had taken Rooney home before Lee returned. Lee "found him sitting before the fire waiting for me, to take his supper."[12]

Rooney was cheerful as usual and "made light of the accident." Indeed he waited until his mother left them before he informed his father of the extent of the injury. Lee told a friend of Rooney's "firmness and self-possession" and that "it was not till he waked in the night and saw my distress as I watched by his bed that he shed the first tear." The anxious parents "watched day and night for fear of the hand being disturbed."[13]

Rooney tried to make up for his disobedience and carelessness by being "patient and submissive" and "never complaining." His father wrote Custis: "He has been more distressed at your mother's sufferings and mine than his own, and says he can do very well without his fingers, and that we must not mind their loss. Although he is at times obstinate and disobedient, which are grave faults, he has some very good qualities, which give us much pleasure." For a while it seemed that the ends of the fingers would knit and be saved. However, two weeks later it became obvious that the ends were not reviving, and they were removed. With his father as amanuensis, Rooney wrote to Custis describing the accident and the removal of the fingertips. He contritely wrote, "I hope neither of us will disobey our parents for the future." He then switched to a brighter subject—Christmas and the presents they would receive. Lee had bought Custis, the future engineer, a box of tools and Rooney, the animal lover, a pair of chickens that he wanted. Rooney also wrote to Custis about skating, a new game he had received, the holidays, and a playhouse. He adjusted quickly to the loss of the ends of his fingers, but his father was slower to accept the loss philosophically. He wrote that he was "deeply afflicted" by it but "thankful that it was no worse." He also hoped that it would be a lesson in obedience for Rooney and his brothers and sisters. During the healing process Mary was "in a constant state of watchfulness with Rooney whose great flow of spirits prevents his being quiet an instant."[14]

After Christmas Mary and the children traveled to Arlington as planned earlier. Rooney's fingers were healing, but the accident and his disobedience that caused it continued to weigh heavily on his father's mind. He wrote at length to Mary on the subject of disobedience: "A mother, indeed all parents, cannot begin too soon to form the habits of the child, and to habituate them to obedience is the first and most important lesson. If a mother lets pass the early years of a boy without establishing it, it is rare that she ever regains what she then lost. I am glad that William has been more docile and hope he will endeavor to continue in that respect. It is better now that he learned to control himself and to make himself useful and agreeable to those around him or the reputation he now acquires of a bad boy will stick to him till he is a man." Of course Lee was not blaming her for the accident, but he genuinely feared that their son's recklessness and high spirits, if left uncontrolled, could lead to other misfortunes. He also worried that when Rooney was away from him, he might not be given the firm discipline that he needed. He was well aware that even at the young age of eight, Rooney could use his charm to circumvent his mother's rules. Later Rob would write that this was possible and that he "at times took liberties with her orders, construing them to suit myself; but exact obedience to every mandate of my father was a part of my life and being at that time."[15]

This accident and Lee's reaction to it indicate that he was perhaps overly sensitive to any kind of disfigurement. He wrote to Mary: "I am glad to hear he uses his hand so well and hope that all may be for the best. Still the thought of his injury comes over my spirits like a withering blight and I feel as if I could have sacrificed my life to have saved that dear hand. Yet when I compare his affliction with those I see almost daily, I am filled with thankfulness it was no worse, and am ashamed of my still unreconciled feelings." As a fully mature man, Lee possessed a deep religious faith. But at this stage of his life he still questioned the justice of a divine will that later he would accept un-questioningly. He counseled her at length on the care of the fingers and having some "finger stalls" made by a glovemaker in Alexandria that would fit him properly. By summer the healing process was com-plete, and Lee was pleased to report to a friend: "Though Rooney has lost the use of his fingers he has the perfect use of his hand. They have healed up so well that the disfiguration is less than I anticipated. He is growing very fast and I hope into a fine boy."[16]

In the summer of 1846 Captain Lee took leave of his family once more and departed for his new assignment in Mexico and his first ac-quaintance with war. Mary and the children, now numbering seven, remained with the grandparents at Arlington. She ran the household, saw to the children's lessons, and tried to comply with her husband's wishes as to instilling an effort toward self-control in their sons. In his absence he wanted Custis to take a hand in directing and caring for his younger brother. He wrote to Mary on this subject: "And Wm. is at school. I am glad to hear that he is pleased with it and hope he will endeavor to learn a great deal before I return. Tell Custis he must act the part of a good brother towards him and advise and assist him in everything. And I particularly request that all their little quarrels be forever laid aside. Each must yield to the other. Wm. must give way to Custis for he is the eldest and Custis must make allowance for Wm., never get out of patience with him, or be too exacting for he is the youngest. They will now soon be men, will have a great deal to do and must grow up to love and respect each other. They cannot do this unless they learn to be wise and good."[17]

Lee's letters to Custis and Rooney during his absence are quite in-teresting. He described at length the countryside of Mexico, his horses, his daily routine, and his long rides. Only once did he actually describe combat. Even though he considered his sons almost grown, he avoided mentioning the gory aspect of war and preferred to tell them how much he missed them and wished they could be together. He gave Rooney lengthy advice on caring for his new colt and told him: "If you are kind to her she will love you and serve you well. You would be charmed to see how my mares greet me and prick up their ears and head whenever I approach them. The sorrel . . . generally greets me with a gentle neigh." He particularly missed his family at Christmas and wrote: "How often I have wished to be with you and how constantly I think of you while riding over this desert country but more particularly tonight how I long to be with you all. I hope good Santa Claus will fill my Rob's stockings tonight and that Mildred's, Agnes' and Annie's may break down with good things. I do not know what he will have for you and Mary, but if he only leaves for you one half of what I wish you, you will want for nothing. I have frequently thought if I but had one of you on each side of me riding on two nice ponies such as I could get you, I should be comparatively happy." Lee could not help preaching a little as was his custom. He admonished his sons: "You know it is the height of my wishes that you should be good, wise and true. You must therefore try hard to be all these, and when I come back give me the joy and satisfaction of finding you so." With Rooney he was more direct and more graphic in his sermon: "Your mother tells me that your teachers are much pleased with your conduct at school, both as regards your progress and behavior. This is delightful to me and I pray that you may always preserve your innocence and rectitude. Such horrid forms of vice meet one at nearly every step that I am sickened by its contemplation and would prefer a thousand deaths than to see the least practiced by any of my children."[18]

Robert Lee was away from his family for almost two years, and the reunion was a happy one. He wrote that he was surrounded by their "precious children" and that "the older ones gaze with astonishment and wonder at me, and seem at a loss to reconcile what they see and what was pictured in their imaginations. I find them, too, much grown, and all well." The initial shyness soon disappeared, and the boys went riding, swimming, and rowing with their father. They even took their turns at a high jump set up in the yard.[19]

The boys were growing into young men, and it was time to consider plans for the future. Rooney, in particular, was "growing wonderfully." His father wrote: "I do not know when he will stop if he goes on at this rate. His feet and hands are tremendous and his appetite startling." It is quite understandable that both boys wanted to follow in their father's profession as a soldier. In accordance with this wish, Custis entered West Point in the summer of 1850. Rooney was just as eager to join the army and follow his father and brother at West Point when the time came. Lee wrote to Custis in 1851 that Rooney's "ambition is still to go to West Point, and thinks there is no life like that of a dragoon. He thinks he might get through the Academy, though he would not stand as well as Boo. I tell him he would get 200 demerits the first year, and that would be an end to all his military resources." The reference to demerits was made as an indication that Rooney's high spirits and zest for the active life were still incompatible with his career as a scholar. His own mother (and schoolmistress) would even admit, "Rooney, I think, will never do for any of the learned professions." Although he was very proficient in both Greek and French, "his pronunciation is anything but pure Parisian," according to his father. Basically, though, the parents' concern for their son's future was due to his lack of self-control rather than any lack of ability. As Lee stated: "There is a great deal of good and energy in him, if it only gets the right direction. I strive hard to fix his attention and desires on what is good, but he is still of that age when he cannot appreciate all of its beauties." At fourteen, however, there was still time for improvement.[20]

The same year that Custis went to West Point, the rest of the Lee family moved to Baltimore so that Lee could work on the renovation of Fort Carroll. As usual, they all went home to Arlington for Christmas. Because Custis was unable to be present, Lee sent him the following verbal picture of the Christmas tradition at Arlington:

We came home on Wednesday morning. It was a bitter cold day, and we were kept waiting an hour at Baltimore for the cars, which were detained by the snow and frost on the rails. We found your grandfather at the Washington depot, Daniel and the old carriage and horses. Your mother, grandfather, Mary Eliza, the little people and the baggage I thought load enough for the carriage, so Rooney and I took our feet in our hands and walked over. . . . The snow impeded the carriage as well as us, and we reached here shortly after it. The children were delighted at getting back, and passed the evening in devising pleasure for the morrow. They were in upon us before day on Christmas morning, to overhaul their stockings. Mildred thinks she drew a prize in the shape of a beautiful new doll; Angelina's infirmities were so great that she was left in Baltimore and this new treasure was entirely unexpected. The cakes, candies, books, etc., were overlooked in the caresses she bestowed upon her, and she was scarcely out of her arms all day. Rooney got among his gifts a nice pair of boots, which he particularly wanted, and the girls, I hope, were equally pleased with their presents, books and trinkets.

Your mother, Mary, Rooney and I went into church, and Rooney and the twins skated back on the canal, Rooney having taken his skates along for the purpose. . . .

I need not describe to you our amusements, you have witnessed them so often, nor the turkey, cold ham, plum puddings, mince pies, etc. at dinner.[21]

Their return to Baltimore was delayed for about a week by an attack of the "grippe" or "influenza" that Rooney had, probably contracted while skating. Again his nurse was his father, who administered "a pill of blue mass and James antimonial powders, to be followed up by oil, syrup of ipicachuana, antimony, etc." according to the doctor's orders. His nurse reported the illness to be severe because "he is such a violent fellow that he has everything in a violent manner."[22]

In 1852 Rooney was fifteen years old and in the beginning of that worst of ages when one is expected to act like an adult without the privileges of adulthood. At the same time the sweet memories and pastimes of childhood are relished, and the aspirations of "being a man" are born. At times Rooney was perfectly content to be with his mother and the other children. His special favorites were the babies, Rob and Mildred. After a trip to West Point, Robert Lee gives the following description of his household on his return to Baltimore:

Day had broken, but I knew it was too early to expect admittance to the house at that hour, so I disposed of the trunk, and to wile away the time I walked leisurely up in the grey of the morning. I took the precaution to call by William's house and got his pass-key and let myself in, and had no difficulty in ascending to your mother's room. The door was locked and it took some time to rouse her, but instead of admitting me or opening the door, she prevented my entrance by saying that Emma Randolph was in there. So we had to make our salutations in the passage, and I determined to go up and see the children. I found both Mary's, who has moved to the front room, third story, and Rooney's door locked. After some loud knocks, Mary's was opened, and allowing sufficient time for the opener to get under cover, I asked if I could enter. There was no answer, so I walked in and found Mary sound asleep, some person by her side, buried in bed with her head completely covered. I saw it was too long for any of the children and having succeeded in waking Mary, she informed me that it was Cousin Cornelia Randolph. I had then to beat a retreat from there. I commenced applying at Rooney's door. After a little time it was opened, and stepping in there lay Rooney sound asleep in the middle of the bed, Mildred on one side of him and Rob crawling in on the other. Upon investigation I discovered that Rooney on coming up to bed had caught up the two little children from their room and put them into his bed, and fearful lest his mother when she came up might recapture them, had locked his door. I did not venture to examine farther into the house, so can't tell you what was going on in Cousin Brit's room all this time. I presume she was locked up, too.[23]

On other occasions Rooney felt obliged to "put away childish things," including his nickname. Of his many names he chose Fitzhugh to be called and apparently requested the family to do so. The one who gave him the nickname appeared the most reluctant to put it aside but acquiesced to his son's wishes. Robert Lee wrote Mary: "As he has had the name of Rooney long enough, we will now give it up, and call him by his own. As he was called after his uncle, a model of a perfect gentleman, both to perpetuate the name, and if possible, the character in the family, as well as to keep before us the noble original. I vote either for Wm. or Fitzhugh. I leave it to you and him to decide which. We have both a Wm. and a Fitzhugh in the family, but he must be the Atlas of the name, its personification and herald to posterity, and as he prefers Fitzhugh why let it be so. Unless you or he decide differently I shall know him by that hereafter." Lee tried to comply and addressed him as Fitzhugh in at least one letter, but in less than a year he was calling him "horse" and then Rooney again. A few years later when he married, he was called Fitzhugh by his wife and parents, but he was still called Rooney by his friends and other members of his family.[24]

The summer of 1852 brought another move for the Lees, this time to West Point, where Robert Lee had been named superintendent. In the fall of 1852 Rooney went to the boarding school of Mr. Peugnet in New York City. Robert Lee decided on this particular school after checking out all possibilities. One deciding factor was its proximity: "He requires to be near me and to feel that he is so," Lee informed Martha Williams. On his choice he added: "All things being equal I prefer a school in the country, though for certain considerations I have placed Rooney in the city of New York and shall keep him there this year. Young men must not expect to escape contact with evil, but must learn not to be contaminated by it. That virtue is worth but little that requires constant watching and removal from temptation. Still never uselessly place it in the way of temptation." Under Mr. Peugnet's instruction Rooney progressed satisfactorily in his studies. Except for a bout of rheumatism and a sprained wrist, which concerned his father considerably, his health was robust as usual. During this time his father characterized him as "a dear, affectionate boy—full of good impulses and kind wishes" and added, "We must not expect him to be exempt from the thoughtlessness and love of pleasure peculiar to youth." However, when Lee wrote to his son he could not refrain from his customary sermon. He told Rooney of some cadets who had to leave West Point because of their poor performance. He wrote: "See how cruel it is for young men by their neglect and inattention to bring upon their parents and friends the mortification and distress of their failure. Two nice lads, too, but they preferred their own ease and pleasure to their clear and imperative duty." At times it seems that Robert Lee went to extremes in lecturing to his son, but the incident of the straw cutter is evidence that from an early age Rooney was reckless and heedless of his own safety and well-being. He was sensitive, however, to the distress and pain that he caused his parents. His father knew this and tried to control him by playing on that sensitivity.[25]

In the spring of 1853 Mrs. Custis died unexpectedly, and the family was grief-stricken. Mary Lee arrived in time to make the funeral arrangements, tend to her father, and assume the role of mistress of Arlington. Her own grief for her departed mother must have been soothed in part by a letter she received from Rooney a few weeks later. It is the earliest letter written by him extant. In spite of the misspelled words, run-on sentences, and crossed-out letters, it is easy to see why a mother would keep and treasure this letter:

> My dearest mother,
> I received your sweet and affectionate letter: I think it did me more good than anything that I know of.
>
> I hope you are not overworking yourself in trying to do your duty, you must remember how many are dependant [sic] on you for their happiness, you have seven children who you know could not get along without you; you must judge them, in respect to their love for you, in their outward appearances, but if you could only see in to their hearts, you would see

there love that could not be removed, not even death, (the most fearful of all monsters to those unprepared, and the best friend to those prepared to meet their Saviour) can remove that love which is, and will be forever; there lies in the unfathomable depths of the heart an unquenchable love for a mother; I say this and I speak as I feel, Ma! I hope you believe me. Grandma is gone, but I hope it is all for the best. Certainly Great God would not have taken away one who contributed so much to our happiness, except for some good reason, and I am sure that her grandchildren will try and follow her example; the relations between man and man or woman and woman cease not in death. The dead leave behind them their example, their memory, and the effects of their life. Their influence still abides with us. Their names and characters still abide with us. We commune with them in their writings and we enjoy the benefit of their actions. Their image is impressed upon our dearest and most sacred hopes.

I think I have said enough about this subject at present. You must not grieve too much, you know she would rebuke you for it; walk about, and keep well. I only wish I was there to walk with you.[26]

Rooney spent the summer of 1853 at Arlington. His little sister Agnes recorded his arrival in her journal and described him as "perfectly enormous and just the same." In the fall he returned to Mr. Peugnet's school in New York. While there he kept a flower garden and went out with "the boys" on Saturday. But these pastimes were far from what he really wanted. Being away from West Point had not cooled his desire to be a cadet. Cousin Markie Williams had the same situation with her younger brother Orton and had written to Robert Lee about his attending West Point. Lee answered her at length:

In reference to Orton's coming to W.P.—his having had a brother here will make it more difficult to procure an appointment. The Reg'ns say there shall not be two brothers here at the same time. That is the only restriction. But I can advise no young man to enter the Army. The same application, the same self-denial, the same endurance, in any other profession, will advance him faster and farther. Nothing but an unconquerable passion for military life, would induce me to recommend the military profession. Notwithstanding my experience and advice, all my sons desire to enter the service. The tears stream down Rooney's cheeks, when I tell him of the almost insuperable difficulties to his procuring an app't to W.P. and of my disapprobation of his application. I have had, however, to give my consent to his making the attempt at the proper time, if he still continues to desire it.[27]

Rooney's desire to attend West Point was not fulfilled. Agnes Lee recorded in her journal: "Fitzhugh has not received his appointment after all his trouble. I am sorry it is *such* a disappointment to him. He is so anxious to enter the army in some way. I remember last summer when he used to stand watching dress parade he would involuntarily exclaim 'O if I was only one of them.'" He finished the term at Mr. Peugnet's school in such a manner that his father could report that he was "doing better now in his studies." The Lees went home for the summer vacation at Arlington after spending a few days with the Marshalls in Baltimore. The party must have presented an interesting sight at the train station. Mary had an injured foot and was carried by her father and Rooney. Annie was carrying her crutches, Agnes their heavy coats, and Rob the family dog. They did not lack for sympathetic helpers on the journey to Arlington.[28]

CHAPTER 2

"I could not excel for any but a practical life"

In the fall of 1854 Rooney Lee began his collegiate life at Harvard University. Although this was a very distant second choice for him, Harvard was at that time considered the preeminent university in America. Rather than just send his son to Cambridge, Robert Lee went with him and stayed long enough to see his son comfortably settled in. Mr. Custis was persuaded to leave Arlington long enough to make the trip also.[1]

In retrospect it seems that Harvard was an unusual choice of colleges for a young Virginian, especially considering the political climate of the time. In the spring of 1854 the passage of the Kansas-Nebraska Act into law caused angry demonstrations among the antislavery forces, especially in New England. In Boston Anthony Burns, a runaway slave, was taken by law officers under the provisions of the Fugitive Slave Act. Attempts were made to free him, and there were public outcries. When he was returned to his owner, many houses in Boston were draped in black mourning as a protest. A Harvard Law School lecturer served as the judge in this case, and there was an emotional turmoil at Harvard because of it. *Uncle Tom's Cabin*, in both book and theatrical form, was familiar to all the citizens of Massachusetts by 1854, two years after its initial publication. Such things as the sack of Lawrence, Kansas, by proslavery men and the atrocities of the abolitionist John Brown kept emotions in an uproar during Rooney Lee's first two years at Harvard. Much closer to home than "Bleeding Kansas," the attack on Senator Charles Sumner of Massachusetts on the floor of the Senate by South Carolinian Preston Brooks gave the antislavery movement a martyr. Sumner was a personal hero to many of Rooney Lee's classmates. In all it does not seem that Harvard would be the most comfortable place for a young man from a plantation in Virginia.

In 1854 there were approximately 400 undergraduates attending Harvard. Of the ninety-six in the freshman class, only thirteen hailed from states other than Massachusetts. Entrance exams were administered orally and emphasized classical languages and ancient history. The school year contained two terms, each twenty weeks long, with a vacation of six weeks in between. Commencement was traditionally held the third Wednesday in July. The curriculum was inflexible. For example, a freshman could expect to take Latin, Greek, mathematics, religion, and history. A sophomore would study Latin, Greek, French, Anglo-Saxon, mathematics, chemistry, botany, and rhetoric. Exams were administered by the Visiting Committee of Overseers rather than by the professors themselves. These were also given orally. Some of the more interesting courses were offered without credit. Among these were zoology by Agassiz and poetry by Lowell.[2]

Some students lived in the university dormitories while others chose more expensive lodging off campus. Rooney Lee occupied room 16 in Massachusetts Hall his freshman year. Tutors lived in the dorms to keep close watch on the students. James Mills Peirce, mathematics professor, lived in room 5 in Massachusetts Hall, only a short distance from the one occupied by Lee. Life was strictly regimented for the students. Prayers were held twice a day, and on Sunday attendance at church services was mandatory. The dress code required that students wear black coats at all times. A few students had servants who came in the early morning to bring coal and water, tend the fires, and fill the lamps with oil. It was not until 1855 that gas was first used in a dormitory.[3]

Class standing was decided by a "Scale of Merit" that incorporated points given for a student's academic performance and points taken for disciplinary infractions. Each theme, speech, recitation, and exam was graded on a scale of eight and multiples of eight. Any infraction of the rules brought deductions from the accumulated points on the same scale of eight. For example, being absent, tardy, or unprepared for class brought a deduction of eight points. A "private admonition" from the disciplinary committee of the faculty resulted in thirty-two points being taken away; a "public admonition" caused a loss of sixty-four points. Booklets were given to the students so that they could be aware of what constituted a "misdemeanor" or "violation of decorum." Some of these included playing games or smoking in the college yard and "carrying a cane or umbrella into the Chapel, recitation rooms, Library or any public room." Another infraction was "collection in groups around the doors of the College buildings, or in the yard, or loitering in the yard or entries, or sitting on the steps or lying on the ground." Some students intent on a high standing used a "pony," or translation of the text, rather than translating properly on one's own. Others preferred the honest way even though it meant a lower standing. According to a classmate of Lee's, to "squirt" was to perform well on a recitation, whereas "slump" signified a poor recitation and "dead" a horrible one.[4]

As his father would have expected, Rooney Lee's disciplinary record at Harvard was far from spotless, although he never was disciplined for any serious offenses. During his freshman year he received three private admonitions: one for absences from prayers, one for absences from Sunday church services and one for absences from recitations. His sophomore year he received one private admonition for six absences at recitation, then a public admonition for being absent twelve times. He was also "privately admonished for bringing his book to the mathematical exercise." During the six-week vacation he was required to study Anglo-Saxon literature and language twice a week. During junior year he received admonitions for twenty-five absences from prayers, seven absences from recitations, and "sleeping in church." Lee's rank for the first term of his freshman year was fifty-sixth out of ninety-one students. This was his best performance while at Harvard. From there he drifted downward—a far cry from his father's and brother's rank at West Point. "Rank at college is determined not by a uniform elegance of recitation or by a knowledge of the subjects in hand, but by a conformity to the college rules," a member of the class of 1858 opined. Rooney Lee probably agreed wholeheartedly with his friend, who confided the following in his journal:

My candid and true opinion is this: it is much preferable for a young man to study well, mingle sociably with his companions, enjoy himself as much as possible, take things as they come with cheerfulness, and take the chance of standing high, respected and liked by all, rather than study hard, become misanthropical, sorrow from day to day, take misfortune with grief, and run the risk of a very high rank not known or not cared for by his companions. The former leaves college with health, practical knowledge, with the friendship of the world, and at last becomes a great and good man. The latter goes into the world with learning merely obtained from books, without friends, in ill health, and at last becomes some obscure schoolmaster or author.[5]

In spite of the strict surveillance by the faculty, the young men at Harvard managed to have a good time. Traditionally there was a "football game" held on the first Monday evening of each college year. About 6:30 P.M. the freshmen and the sophomores lined up on the delta about one hundred yards apart. The sophomores got the first kick, and then it became a rough-and-tumble free-for-all. Some students prepared for this annual event by taking boxing lessons. A freshman reported in 1854: "My class fought nobly, but it was of no avail, the Sophs beat us. . . . After the first game the Juniors joined us and the Seniors the Sophs. We were again defeated." Later that year "some of the riot-stirring students exploded a mine before one of the college buildings: this was a signal for a regular stampede to see what was the matter." Gambling and drinking were commonplace, in spite of the religious overtones at the university. One of Lee's friends, Nicholas Longworth Anderson, had to treat seven others to a party because he lost a game of marbles. The winners "ate twelve dozen stewed oysters and drank six quarts of ale, besides much punch." Anderson concluded, "From the riotous singing which they made, I should think that the spree was a decided hit." For the Fourth of July celebration there were cannons firing, militia marching, and fireworks. On campus, window-smashing was a favorite sport among the underclassmen. Sometimes a fellow who had been hit by a water balloon retaliated by smashing the window of the perpetrator. Sometimes the faculty members had their windows smashed by disgruntled students. One particularly unhappy student wrote in his journal: "I have made good recitations . . . until this morning when that insignificant, miserable, mean scrub, James Peirce, compelled me to dead. If I don't smash his windows next term it will only be because there are no stones or other missiles in the neighborhood of Cambridge." Each morning a bell awakened the students. For fun, "Somebody . . . got into Harvard Hall and took the clapper out from the bell and upset the bell and filled it full of acid, and clamped all the doors in the building. Mills next morning had to ring the bell with a hammer." Other amusements were more commonplace—riding, boating, skating, billiards, dining out, and attending socials and theatrical presentations. Lee and his buddies also spent much time playing whist, a forerunner of bridge. Often they got together in each other's rooms for "sociables" and took turns providing the refreshments for these affairs.[6]

Clubs formed an important part of student life at Harvard. During his freshman year "Lee was the most popular and prominent young man in his class" and was elected president of the class. He was also chosen to be a member of the Anonyma Society, a group that flourished at Harvard during the 1850s but never gained official sanction from the university. A committee of the Anonyma chose the first ten of the group of freshmen, then turned over the society to these who in turn chose the rest. It was considered an honor to be chosen. One of the group recorded the proceedings in his journal: "A few evenings since on the delivery of the Anonyma Society to the Freshman class, we had a fine repast at the Fresh Pond Hotel. The champagne sparkled, roast ducks spluttered, and we ate. At a late hour in the morning all returned home, some drunk, some sober, some middling." When the selection of members was complete, Lee was elected president of this group also.[7]

Although very much in the swing of things at Harvard, Rooney had not given up on the possibility of attending West Point. He traveled to Washington between terms seeking an appointment as a cadet, but he failed in this attempt. His mother even wrote a letter to John R. Peters in support of her son's application in which she mentioned "the desire which has possessed him from boyhood to enter the army" as well as "his own ambition, peculiar fitness for the service" as his chief assets.[8]

With the idea of West Point out of his mind finally, Rooney returned to Cambridge. "He has borne up bravely, consoling himself with some sage remarks of Custis," Agnes Lee wrote in her journal. She also spoke of a trip to Baltimore about this time to visit her aunt. She added: "Cousin Anne Carter lives next door (to the Marshalls). She has a large family and crowds of cousins now staying with them. Charlotte Wickham, one of them, is not much older than I, is very pretty and sweet and I liked her very much." Rooney Lee also spent some time with his aunt on his trips back and forth to Cambridge, and it was on one of these visits in Baltimore that the romance between him and Charlotte Wickham began. As their love intensified, his dissatisfaction with Harvard grew.[9]

The freshman year ended on a light note, however, with the annual supper of the Anonyma Society. One of the members of the planning committee wrote: "Now since the society is an illegal one, and unchartered, of course the supper will be an infringement of the college rules, and I have since learned that if the faculty get wind of our proceedings, there is a likelihood of some severe punishment on the principal offenders." This threat did not deter the society members in the least, and the traditional dinner was held. The location was "kept a most profound secret lest it should get to the ears of the faculty . . . it being a most gross violation of the college laws." On June 21, 1855, "at eight o' clock a merry jovial set of students assembled at Brighton bridge, where they crowded into a couple of omnibuses . . . and rattled briskly off to Roxbury, enlivening the way by uproarious cheers and college ditties." The group arrived at the Norfolk House and "dispatched the substantials." There were many toasts while "the corks popped, and the champagne gurgled pleasantly into the wine glass, and thence into the throat." "Cheer upon cheer were given, and song upon song sung. Some were drunk, some tight, and some perfectly sober," one of the revelers remembered the next day. He described the return to Harvard: "At 5 we reached the college, drove into the green, gave three cheers, and ran like wildfire to escape, if possible, the lynx-eyed tutors." None of the students were caught and punished by the faculty. Some were unable to attend the commencement the next day, however. Those who did heard the speeches, joined in the singing of "Auld Lang Syne," and cheered for the individual classes and faculty members.[10]

With the freshman year completed, Rooney Lee returned to Arlington for the six weeks of vacation. His father was not with the family during this time. He had gone to his new post with the Second U.S. Cavalry. So he had to keep up with family matters by mail and from a long distance away. Apparently there was some doubt about Rooney even returning to Harvard. He wrote to Mary: "I am glad that [Rooney] is in such good health & spirits & hope he may pass his vacation pleasantly & profitably. After I hear from him, which I presume I shall do when he can spare sufficient time, & can better decide about his return to C—." Two weeks later he wrote that he had sent her a check to cover her bills and school expenses for the girls and Rooney and added, "I am afraid he is penniless."[11]

Mary served as an intermediary between father and son during this period. She knew well her husband's feelings on thrift and his hatred of debts. She could also understand her son's sensitivity to peer pressure concerning money matters. Robert Lee allotted $200 per term for his son's tuition, books, clothes, board, and personal allowance. Considering his small salary as an army officer and the many demands on it from a large family, this amount seems a generous one. However, Rooney's classmates were from affluent families who seem to have placed no limits on their sons' spending at college. One of Lee's classmates spent more than $700 in one term on hack fare alone. His friend Nicky Anderson congratulated himself in his journal for spending less than $700 in one term. Their amusements were expensive, and even the "sociables" in their rooms were lavish affairs. Rooney must have felt considerable pressure to keep up with his friends and in so doing incurred some debts. Besides, thrift and economy have never rated high on an eighteen-year-old's rank of priorities.[12]

Robert Lee corresponded often to Mary concerning their son's financial affairs. In September he wrote, "But I do not understand how Rooney was to get on to C—for the $5.00 you gave him will not be sufficient, & I did not want him to cash his draft until he reached C—." Actually Rooney asked his grandfather for the money for his return trip, and when his father found out, he was not happy: "I am sorry that the poor Roon is so poor a financier & particularly that he asked his grandfather for his expenses back. I wish you had furnished him with funds," he told Mary. He explained further: "I purposely restricted him that he might feel the inconvenience of his want of forethought, in the hope of converting him. I do not know any other way of working a reformation than by letting him both see & feel the effects of his errors. My letters I fear have but a small influence. There is something with him however that I like & which always disarms & mollifies one. He is ready to acknowledge his fault & take the blame & is frank & affectionate. God grant that he may in time get sufficient wisdom to see what is right & strength to do it."[13]

At the beginning of his sophomore year Rooney began to voice concerns that his education at Harvard was less than satisfactory. His father heard of this through Mary and responded: "In what respect did

(Rooney) despond of his success at Cambridge & what can I say to him more than I have? I see no reason why he should not succeed as well as others if he wishes to do so; & if he does not, he had better leave at once & go at something else." Rooney Lee was not the only one to feel the irrelevancy of the education they were receiving at Harvard. In particular, the students felt that they were not being prepared for any sort of professional life or career after college. Nicky Anderson confided this feeling to his journal: "I am tired, disgusted with Cambridge; I am weary of college life. Week after week rolls by in the same dull, unexciting manner. Day after day I seek into the roots of Latin, dig at the roots of Greek, and cut away at the branches of mathematics. Moment after moment I think of home, of friends, and of my separation from those I love. And what does the separation mean? What will Latin, Greek and higher mathematics profit me?" Anderson later decided to fill in the gaps in his education on his own. "I am going to put time into learning, not studying. I will try and get my money's worth of general knowledge, not mere book learning . . . ," he decided. Rooney Lee had come to the same conclusion and formed a group—an "eating table"—for the purpose of learning, discussion, and probing more relevant topics than those in the recitation halls. On receiving his invitation to join, Anderson declared it was "one of the nicest little assemblies in the city." Eight young men made up Lee's group. Rooney Lee and Jim May were from Virginia, William Elliott from South Carolina, Nicky Anderson from Ohio, and the rest were from Boston— Henry Adams, Benjamin Crowninshield, Hollis Hunnewell, and Josiah Bradlee. Politically this group encompassed some extremes. Anderson, for example, was a vehement supporter of the Know-Nothing movement, known for its anti-Catholic and antiforeign sentiments. Henry Adams, a Republican, believed in the antislavery crusade and considered Senator Charles Sumner a personal hero. Lee and May were products of the plantation society of Virginia. Elliott, the South Carolinian, left Harvard at the end of the sophomore year.[14]

Besides his own group, Lee joined two student organizations at Harvard his sophomore year. One of these, the Hasty Pudding Club, was considered by many to be the most exclusive society on campus. The initiates were in for considerable hazing, or "devilling," before becoming members of this fraternity, as well known for its ribaldry as its theatricals. The initiate was told to write "an essay of twenty pages" that was to be criticized by professors and members of the club. After toiling for days on "a literary production of unequalled merit," the initiate dressed in his best clothes and waited for his summons on the arranged day. Two members arrived and immediately stripped and blind-folded him. He was carried "up and down stairs, through mud and over fences, on grass and on pavement, until . . . utterly ignorant of his whereabouts." When the new member finally arrived at the destination, the old members were waiting. Their welcome included pinching, hitting, hissing, howling, and tossing in a blanket. Still blindfolded, the initiate was led into a room draped in black and decorated with "skulls, bones and rusty armor." When the blindfold was removed he could see "figures in white, horribly masked." One of these continued to "devil" him while another delivered a long lecture. Finally he was forced to kneel and was deluged with water. The carefully prepared essay was returned completely "matted with pudding and irrevocably injured." Then the members removed their masks and welcomed the new man into the club.[15]

The other fraternity that Lee joined was Psi Upsilon. According to Nicky Anderson, "It is the greatest honor to become a member. Eleven of the very best fellows, yes, the eleven best have been chosen from our class. It is a literary, social and brotherly society."[16]

These fraternities, socials, and entertainments continued to claim much of Rooney's time and consequently his academic performance suffered. From Texas Robert Lee told his wife, "You must encourage Fitzhugh to apply himself to his education and to endeavor to improve his present advantages, not to have to regret when too late opportunities lost." When Rooney corresponded with his father, apparently he painted a rosy picture of his studies and glossed over his other activities. In a letter to Mary, Lee wrote: "I have rec'd a letter from Fitzhugh, giving a very satisfactory account of himself. I hope he is not deceived as to his progress or his application. He is a cheerful, affectionate fellow, but I think he is easily satisfied as to his daily amount of study & learning. I trust he will always hold fast to correct conduct & gentlemanly feelings & bearing."[17]

Surprisingly Mary Lee was much more in tune with her son's feelings than his father was. She was his confidante. She spoke to him in concrete terms rather than in generalities. Her hopes and concerns for her son were expressed in simple terms that a teenager could understand. In the spring of 1856 Rooney wrote to his mother about her concerns: "I assure you that I respond to every motherly feeling that you have so affectionately expressed. On whom am I to rely, except on my mother? To whom am I to confide, except to her. Most willingly, dear Ma, do I accept your proposal & will willingly confide to you everything. At the same time you must not judge of me too hard, and must know that I am liable & exposed to all the temptations that others are." In this same letter he reported that his bills were for the time settled, but he said he could not promise her that he would never get into debt again. He did make one promise to her concerning tobacco. "A cigar, pipe, or tobacco of any sort has neither, nor will they, pollute 'these precious lips of mine' without your consent during my college course." He admitted that he had been to "one or two little dancing parties" since his last letter but stressed that he had been "studying very hard." Rooney was very straightforward with his mother regarding his shortcomings, his dissatisfaction with school, and his hopes for the future. He opened his heart to her, writing:

> I, as everyone else, am very fond of my ease & comfort but when I have anything to do which I take an interest in I am as persevering as any one & also as diligent. But never having had and not having a taste for literary pursuits I am totally unfit—I will not say totally—I mean that I could not excell for any but a practical life. I could be a lawyer, but both the study & practice of law would be as dry to me as a soldier's life would be to Bernard. And Grandpa having more land & servants than he knows what to do with I see no reason why I should not be a farmer.
>
> I tell you this because I wish you to know what I think.[18]

About this time Rooney became very ill. He had been under a doctor's care at times during the school year for "intermittent fever," and by the end of May it was decided by the doctor and the college faculty to send him home to recuperate. In the doctor's words he was not "severely ill considering the nature of the malady," but "the ordinary measures of precaution do not seem to be successful in warding them [the attacks] off." Of his son's illness, Robert Lee wrote, "I much regret also Fitzhugh's sickness, the necessity it was considered to impose on him to leave his college. I hope it was all right & may be for the best. It has broken into one of the best years of his education from which I hoped much & in which he seemed to be improving. Bilious fever seems like a strange disease for the latitude of Cambridge & I fear it was produced by his visit to A— & vicinity last summer & there seems to be a fair prospect of it being repeated thus." The disease known as bilious or intermittent fever in the nineteenth century is now known as malaria. The cause was supposed to be a miasm, or poisonous gas, which came from the decaying vegetation of a marsh or swamp. There would be periods of chills accompanied by nausea followed by fever and pain. Next would come the "sweating stage," and the fever would break. Cathartics and quinine were the drugs used to combat the illness. Rooney came home to Arlington with some "fine cousins," then went to the Virginia Springs with his mother, Rob and Mary, for three weeks to regain his health.[19]

By August he was ready to return to Cambridge. He left Arlington early so that he could spend a few days in Baltimore before proceeding on his way to college. By now Rooney and his cousin Charlotte Wickham were very much in love, but there is no record of family members having noticed. Their young age (he was nineteen, she was sixteen) probably was the reason for keeping quiet about their feelings. His early departure to spend some time with Charlotte caused him to miss the check that his father had mailed him from Texas. Robert Lee wrote to Mary: "I regret very much that Fitzhugh's check has missed its destination & I feel mortified that his creditors are kept out of their money. I fear all his affairs will be as loosely managed. He seems only to have time or thought for running about. If he could ever find time to learn the situation of things & let me know, it might be rectified." If Robert Lee had been at Arlington that summer instead of being in Texas, if he could have spent some time with his son, he very likely would have been more aware of his feelings and problems and less critical. Distance and lack of communication can cause problems in any family relationships, and the Lees were no different from any other family. A little later Robert Lee wrote: "There was no necessity of Rooney's leaving for Cambridge when he did. Had he stayed he would have rec'd my letter & you the one I wrote concerning him enclosing a draft for $200 & had plenty of time to reach his college. He thinks entirely of his pleasure & not of what is proper to be done." The letter that Rooney missed has not been saved, but Robert Lee wrote to Mary giving the gist of the letter:

I wrote him by the last opportunity giving my views as to his future course & him the option of either finishing his collegiate studies at

Cambridge—the Va. University or giving it up altogether. Although anxious & ambitious for his improvement, education, success & usefulness in life, I have no desire for his nominal standing, when he wants the reality. It is the *substance* not the *show* I desire for him. If he cannot, or will not, attain the former, I wish him to abandon the chase of the latter. He has to make his bread in the world, for I cannot aid him always, & must therefore make up his mind as to the means of obtaining it. All I can do for him, he can rely on. It is time he began to think of something else besides running about amusing himself, & I wish him to do it at once.[20]

Mary Lee, as usual, tried to smooth things over and wrote her husband, "I have urged very strongly upon him the importance of settling up everything at once & hope to learn soon that he has done so." One of Rooney's friends had paid his debts at the end of the term he did not complete, and Rooney had to pay him back upon his return and pay the next term's tuition. Mary Lee gave him the money to take care of all his debts.[21]

In November from his post at Ringgold Barracks in Texas, Robert Lee wrote his son a wonderfully warm letter that summed up his fears, hopes, and concerns for the future. It also contained good, solid advice for a young man who was not sure of his course in life. But most important it showed Robert Lee not as a cold, unfeeling man as he has been depicted by some but as a warm, considerate, loving father who wanted only the best for his son.

> Ringgold Bks. Texas
> 1 Nov. 1856
> Your letter of the 22nd Sept. my dear Son has just been handed to me by a courier from San Antonio. It was as unexpected as welcome, for I had not looked for so much pleasure until my return to San Antonio. I am very glad to find that you are again at your college, well & happy, & delighted to learn that you have determined to complete your course & are earnestly, faithfully & regularly studying. I think if you will persevere you will not only find your studies easy & agreeable, but also that it is entirely within your power to take a respectable if not a high standing in your class. You must not think me so unreasonable as to expect you "to be proficient in every branch of

literature," but I do expect you in graduating to have what you say you will have, "a good foundation for pursuing the studies of any profession, & of being also above the general run of educated men" as regards scholarship, gentlemanly deportment & virtue. Is that asking too much? I cannot believe you inferior, I am sure you do not wish to prove yourself so. You are right to defer making your final decision of a profession until you graduate & I would not recommend you to do otherwise for in the next two years, your tastes & feelings may undergo a great change. My only object has been to bring the subject to your consideration, to let you feel its necessity & to prepare you for it, that you might shape your course & studies accordingly. I regret as much as you can your disappointment in not getting to West Point. But it is solely because you wished it. I think you can be as useful & consequently as happy in other walks of life. You may have liked the life of a soldier, or as hundreds of others whom I know, had you been able to pursue it, become heartily tired of it. My experience has taught me to recommend no young man to enter the service. Those who prefer it, I am happy to see in it, but in the 5th Reg't. of Inf. now encamped near me, it is common even among the young officers who graduated under my superintendency, as well as among captains who were cadets with me to hear the wish constantly reiterated that they could earn their bread in some other way. You see therefore all do not love it who are in it & it must be acknowledged: it is a hard & thankless life. But should the life be so agreeable to you, it may not be impossible for you still to enjoy it. There are every year a number of young men from civil life appointed in the Army. There have been several this past June & must be so long as the yearly number of resignations continue as great. I see no reason why you should not get one of these appointments, if you desire & deserve it. None could present a higher recommendation than a distinguished graduate of Harvard University with a fair name, fair fame, health & strength. With the knowledge you may acquire there & with the devotion which you say you feel to the service & an earnest application to your duties, I will guarantee in a year or two, you will be as well qualified as the graduates of W. P. generally are.

I think therefore you are wrong "to curse the day you went to College" & trust it is in words, thoughtless words & not in reality, you do so. What could you have done more proper? Do not regret the past therefore, but look to the future. The coward looks back, the brave ahead. It is true, as you say, that your sojourn at Cambridge has separated us "by distance," but I feel no separation on my part 'in heart." If it has made you "cold & uncommunicative," it has but animated me with a more intense anxiety & yearning for your welfare & happiness. If by endeavoring to direct you to virtue & deter you from vice, to show you the beauty of wisdom & the evil of folly, to inspire you with a love of the noble characteristics of man & a detestation for the passions of a brute, is deserving of having my "opinions & love less valued," then am I rightly served. If you could hear the beating of my heart for you in the long, wakeful hours of the night, & feel the anxious throbbing of my brain for your future during the busy hours of day, you would find little cause to say that you had lost a "devoted father," whatever truth there may be in your assertion that I had lost "an affectionate son." An "undutiful" one I cannot say you have been: nor have I seen a lack of affection. I pray God I may never see it, never think it, never believe it. But that in His mercy I may first be cold in my grave & feel the green grass growing over my heart. I too enjoy the retrospect of our former life. I still feel the glow of your infant cheek as I carried you in my arms. I yet feel your arms clasping my neck as I swam with you on my back & I love to think of the many many times I have hugged you to my heart. Those days, as you say, have passed, but as happy ones may be before us. They may bring everything for our "approval" & produce nothing for our "disapproval." I trust they are not distant. I long for their arrival. I long to have you near me, with me. To see you, hold you, talk to you. But that cannot be now, for the duty of each keeps us apart. I cannot leave mine & you must perform yours. Let it then be done, so as to give us mutual pleasure. I can see no reason why your being at College should interrupt it. There can be but one right & wrong, there as here. I think I know the first, however prone I may be to follow the last. If you will pursue the first, you may feel as well assured of my approbation there, as if with me here. I fear this is not the letter you desired. But when I think of the momentous question before you, & that your present as well as future weal may depend upon its determination, I cannot treat it as if writing to a boy of nine, but must speak as if dealing with a man of nineteen. I can neither divest myself of my responsibility or exonerate you of yours. But I am done.

Very truly,

R E Lee[22]

Almost weekly during this period Lee wrote letters to Mary expressing his concern for his son. In one he said he had heard indirectly that Rooney was in Boston "with a party of his companions & well." He continued, "I hope he is doing well but I more frequently hear of him away from than at his College. He has never arrived at an age when he ought to know the value of his time & feel the responsibility of his acts." His love for his "dear son" and the frustration caused by his being apart from Rooney when his guidance was most needed are quite evident in a letter to Mary a week later. Lee wrote: "He gives me many anxious days & sleepless nights & adds more than years to the gray hairs in my head. Always affectionate & apparently disposed to do right, he is thoughtless & impulsive & is guided more by his feelings than his reason. Until I see that he has acquired proper self-control, & is guided by principles of duty, rather than the notions of others & feelings of pleasure, I can never feel assured of his conduct. Distance & my inability to watch & aid him, adds to my uneasiness. I hope, however, his increased years have given him increased wisdom & stability & that he now sees his proper course & steadily pursues it. I have seen so many young men throw themselves away before they were aware how fully they were bound in the chains of idleness & vice & when their eyes were opened, they were not strong enough to break them. It is therefore so important for the young to acquire habits of self-control & self-denial."[23]

By January of 1857 Robert Lee's letters had a tone of depression about them because Rooney had not written him since September. He asked Mary to send news of him. By March, however, he had received a letter from "the old Roon" that evidently charmed and delighted him. Once again he was "dear Fitzhugh," and Lee mentioned sending him money—this time with no advice or admonitions.[24]

In his junior year at Harvard Rooney continued to be content with a minimal amount of study, but he threw himself whole-heartedly into the amusements of the period. One of his chums, Benjamin Crowninshield, kept a diary of this year in which he noted the games of whist, the dinners, the "sociables" (one of which Rooney hosted on November 19), the sleigh rides, skating, billiards, "ice-creaming," and "oystering." Like all young men at college, they spent a great deal of time in the dorm rooms talking. The main sport that Lee and Crowninshield enjoyed was rowing. Both were on the crew of the *Harvard*, an eight-oar boat owned by the university. They rowed and trained nearly every day. Crowninshield actually trained in a gym to become fit. He noted in his diary that he "dumb-belled" and "packed myself in wet sheets, etc. for a sweat." He made no mention of Rooney Lee working out. Lee was always large and had inherited an enviable physique. The average weight for the crew of the *Harvard* was 149, but Lee weighed 175. One of his classmates considered him "the best oarsman I have ever seen." There were many practice sessions and races on the Charles River.[25]

In the spring of 1857 Robert Lee was still getting his news from his son in secondhand fashion. He complained that Rooney was "uncommunicative" in the letters he wrote to his father and feared that Rooney was "too much engrossed with his pleasures." When Mary suggested that he might live off "the land in the family," Robert voiced concerns that Rooney lacked initiative and maturity. He questioned, "If at 20 he is unable to be his own guardian how does he expect to be so at 21?" Robert Lee wanted his son to continue at college, but only if he desired to do so and could profit by it. Otherwise he had "no objection to his going to China, or anywhere else he can make an honest living."[26]

In May Rooney was laid up by some accident, probably a fall from a horse. When his father heard about it he wrote to Mary that he hoped it was not serious: "He is so uncommunicative to me that I presume he does not desire me to know of his problems & I can therefore only hope he is well & doing well." The possibility of Rooney being in debt still worried Lee a great deal. Lee feared that "he inherits much of that disposition from both branches of his family" and that he failed "to restrict his wishes to his circumstances." A week later Robert Lee wrote to Mary after receiving a letter from Rooney. It seems that even one letter from Rooney could make a decided difference in his father's attitude toward his son. Lee was ready to send money for the next term at Harvard. He reported that Rooney "seems to be well & writes hopefully & cheerfully. Says his course this year is very interesting & that he is reading French & Spanish." Lee hoped "he is acquiring wisdom & pray that he may be kept from all sin & harm." Lee ended by saying, "He mentioned nothing to me of his fall & I am truly thankful that he has escaped serious injury."[27]

As it turns out, a fall from a horse was not the only thing of interest that Rooney failed to communicate to his father. A commission as second lieutenant in the Sixth Infantry had been offered to him by General Winfield Scott. He had been recommended for the appointment by his uncles, Judge Marshall and Edward Vernon Childe, both of Baltimore. The commission was dated May 31, 1857, his twentieth birthday. Rooney wrote to his mother and acknowledged the debt he felt to his uncles for their recommendations and to General Scott for the appointment. It was the branch of service about which he had reservations. He wrote his mother, "If it was a cavalry corps to which I was appointed, I should not hesitate a moment in my decision." There were other considerations. He continued, "I think it would be showing but little respect to the opinion of Pa to accept without first consulting him. I feel as full of military ardour as I ever did & were I 2 years younger, I would accept an appointment to West Point. But I do not think it is very desirable to be settled down in a little post on the frontier, nor to be separated from friends & society would prove any great advantage to me. It is possible that I may get some more desirable appointment by waiting & I should then be able to finish my course here. I should much prefer the 2nd Cavalry." As for the first consideration, there was not enough time for a letter to get to Texas and a reply back before he needed to accept or reject the commission. The separation from society that concerned him was the separation from Charlotte Wickham. It is interesting to note that the appointment he really wanted was in his father's regiment, the Second Cavalry. His most important concern was for his parents' approbation. He left the ultimate decision for his future to his mother. Rooney continued, "My only object is your's and Pa's pleasure & happiness & will joyfully make any sacrifice that you wish. If you are pleased with the compliment & desire for me to accept, do not write for my approbation, but accept for me. On the other hand, if you feel indifferent or are unwilling for me to enter the army at this present time or at any

time, or think that it does not offer a sufficiently fruitful field for my
futile endeavors, just let me know." Knowing her son's dissatisfaction
with Harvard and his long-standing desire to be in the army, Mary Lee
advised him to accept. On a pragmatic note, she may have thought
that military discipline was exactly what he needed.[28]

General Scott had made the following recommendation for Rooney
to the Secretary of War on May 8: "I beg to ask that one of the vacant
second lieutenancies may be given to W. H. F. Lee, son of Brevet Col.
R. E. Lee, at present on duty against the Comanches.

I make this application mainly on the extraordinary merits of the
father, the very best soldier I ever saw in the field; but the son is himself a very remarkable youth, now about twenty, of a fine stature and
constitution, a good linguist, a good mathematician, and about to
graduate at Harvard University. He is also honorable and amiable,
like his father, and dying to enter the army."[29]

Rooney accepted the commission, or, as Henry Adams worded it,
"he gladly seized the chance of escape from Harvard." Rooney asked
his classmate Henry "to write his letter of acceptance, which flattered
Adam's vanity more than any Northern compliment could do." The
chums in Cambridge had one last blowout on June 24. They "went in
town to a supper at Parker's given in honor of Lee, Jones, Lowndes,
all of whom are going to leave the class." Crowninshield noted in his
diary that "the eatables were excellent." He admitted to partaking
"too much of the drinkables," and the next day he was "too sick to
get up till 2 o' clock." Rooney left the university about three weeks
before the end of the term.[30]

So ended Rooney Lee's three years at Harvard. It is truly doubtful
that he acquired the proficiency in Anglo-Saxon, rhetoric, or botany
that his tutors expected. Neither is the grammar in his few surviving
letters of the period what one might expect from a Harvard man. Like
all students in all ages he and his classmates complained about the rel-
evancy of the curriculum. But the sum and substance of an education
are not always found in the proficiency of subjects or class standing.
Rather, an education is the sum total of one's experiences, feelings,
and thoughts. It includes the people one meets, the successes, the fail-
ures, and the mistakes. It is hopefully a striving for self-knowledge
and maturity. In this sense Rooney Lee profited by his years at Harvard. He learned from his classmates and made some lasting friendships, which war put on hold for four years but could not break. He

was a natural leader of men, and in his college years he cultivated that "habit of command" that was to stand him in such good stead in the years to come. He learned to handle himself in difficult situations and to get along with others. The self-control that his father had stressed all his life became second nature to him. Henry Adams noted, "He was sober even in the excessive violence of political feeling those years; he kept his temper and his friends under control." So the equanimity and self-possession that marked him in his later years had already begun to develop while yet a boy.[31]

One of Rooney's classmates, Pasco of Florida, later remembered him as "well grown for his age, tall, vigorous and robust, open and frank in his address, kind and genial in his manners." Pasco thought he possessed "a more matured mind and a greater insight than the student usually possesses at the threshold of his career." In Pasco's mind Rooney Lee was well prepared academically and very prominent and popular throughout his stay at Harvard. Further, "He was of a friendly and companionable nature, and there were abundant opportunities . . . to develop this disposition, cultivate social intercourse, and strengthen the bonds of good fellowship." ". . . [A]n outdoor life in his Virginia home, and his manly training had given him an athletic frame which required constant and vigorous exercise. This he sought in active sports on the football ground and in the class and college boat clubs, where he was welcomed as a valuable auxiliary." Pasco declared that in retrospect the scholars of a class are often forgotten while "those who excelled in pleasant companionship, in kindly bearing, in generous conduct towards their associates, in outdoor games and sports requiring strength and dexterity are pleasant subjects to dwell upon." Rooney Lee "won the regard and confidence and respect of all his classmates and held a warm place in the hearts of those with whom he was most intimate."[32]

Another Harvard classmate who remembered Rooney Lee well was Henry Adams, one of the members of the eating table. Adams as a young man was physically delicate and small, a petty snob, and thought that a life as a politician would somehow be his simply because he came from a family of politicians. One of the highlights of his collegiate career was being elected "Alligator" of the Hasty Pudding Club. Henry did not join the Union Army as his brother Charles Francis Adams did but instead sat out the war in England. Consequently after the war he still considered the Confederates as traitors and thought that they should be hung as such. His depiction of Rooney Lee at Harvard was written after Lee's death, after the suicide of Henry's wife, and at a time when his skeptical, bitter, and cynical nature had reached a peak. So the portrait may be stained with the bile and animosity of time, whereas his opinion of Lee during the three years at Harvard may have been brighter and clearer. Some of the features and lines of the portrait still show through clearly, though. There were three Virginians in the class of 1858, Rooney Lee and two others, "who seemed instinctively to form a staff for Lee." Adams considered these three "as little fitted for it [Harvard] as Sioux Indians to a treadmill." But somehow Adams "liked" them and was drawn to their society, a "powerless friend of the powerful." In his autobiography Adams noted that "Rooney Lee had changed little from the type of his grandfather, Light Horse Harry. Tall, largely built, handsome, genial, with liberal Virginian openness towards all he liked, he also had the Virginian habit of command and took leadership as his natural habit." Then Adams belittled Lee for not being a scholar or an intellectual. It is interesting to note that Lee's class standing the first year was higher than that of Adams, with both being far from outstanding. Adams also sneered that Lee was "simple." If "simple" means guileless, unaffected, free from ostentation or duplicity, then Adams was right on target in his description of Lee. Most of the people who met him considered him simple in this connotation. For example, to one colleague Lee was a "simple, kindly, unaffected, modest gentleman." On the subject of simplicity, others remembered, "In him there was no manner of affectation; he pretended to be nothing but such as he was." "He admired frankness; he despised duplicity." "He was frank and open, plain and sincere, speaking only what he thought without reserve, and promising only what he designed to perform."[33]

Next Adams rambles about the vice and "low lives" of the Bostonian compared to the Virginian. "When a Virginian had brooded a few days over an imaginary grief and substantial whiskey, none of his Northern friends could be sure that he might not be waiting round the corner, with a knife or pistol, to revenge insult by the dry light of delirium tremens; and when things reached this condition, Lee had to exhaust his authority over his own staff." The culprit in this case was Jim May, a Virginian who was first scholar in the junior class and then president of the senior class. Nicky Anderson noted the event in his diary and wrote that May came by to borrow a pistol in order to avenge an insult. He was drunk, and his friends quieted him down. Anderson said, "May is a warm-hearted, noble fellow when sober, but he is killing himself by drink." At one point in his discussion on drinking Adams intimates that Lee also drank in excess, then contradicts himself. "Lee was a gentleman of the old school and, as every one knows, gentlemen of the old school drank almost as much as gentlemen of the new school; but this was not his trouble. He was sober even in the excessive violence of political feeling in those years." Lee certainly was around young men who drank, and probably joined in at times, but apparently not to excess. His classmates who kept diaries noted drinking on their part and on the part of others, but they never mentioned Lee in this regard. In fact, barely a year later there is a reference to Rooney's complete avoidance of whiskey. There is no record in his later life of drinking more than on a rare social occasion.[34]

It is interesting to note that during the war Henry was already disparaging of his former friend. In a letter to his brother, he wrote, "I see that you and everyone speak of Fitzhugh Lee as commanding against you. Surely this can't be my friend Rooney. I doubt whether Rooney would make a good cavalry colonel, though he might do well as a major or captain." On Lee's wounding and subsequent capture he wrote, "I exalt in the punishment of Rooney Lee." Adam's perception of their friendship may have changed over the years, but at any rate they were friends at Harvard, and Adams was happy to bask in a reflected glory of the big man on campus. Rooney Lee was the first to take note of Adams as an author when he asked him to write his letter of acceptance for the commission from General Scott. Adams wrote it and was flattered immensely.[35]

By the time Rooney Lee left Harvard he had reached a level of maturity that takes longer for most people. He knew that his niche in life would be a practical one. For the rest of his life he would be a soldier, a farmer, and a public servant. He knew that he wanted to marry his sweetheart, settle down, and start a family. In order to do that he had to make a living—"make his bread," as his father said—and he was ready to do just that. The end of the Harvard years also meant an end to the lack of communication that had sometimes marred the relationship between Rooney and his father. Their previous closeness was renewed and intensified in the years to come.

CHAPTER 3

"A lieutenant, USA"

The mail service from Arlington to Texas was quite slow, and it was more than a month before Robert Lee found out that Rooney had accepted the commission. As usual, Mary was the one to break the news. She was not sure that the commission was a "desirable" one, but Rooney's dissatisfaction at Harvard convinced her it was best to accept. She reported that Rooney had departed from Cambridge three weeks before the end of the term and had already ordered his uniform. She had sent him $300 to pay off his debts but was "uneasy at his disposition to spend money without being at the trouble of earning it." At times she could see through the charm, as when she wrote her husband, "He has a warm & affectionate heart but too careless & reckless a disposition . . . He always promises when I see him that he will do better." To a friend she confided, "Do you know that Roon is a lieutenant USA at last? Indeed he is; as large as life—6 feet 3—& now delighted. I hope his delight will continue, but expect one year at the western frontier will cure him of his ardor."[1]

Lee's reaction to Rooney's appointment was only slight surprise. He had planned to try to obtain a commission after his graduation from Harvard if he still desired an army life. Always the pragmatist, Lee reasoned, "If he enters now he will gain one year's rank, which may be a fair offset to the additional information he might gain by continuing at college." As to the branch of service, Lee thought that the infantry might be best, although he knew his son preferred to be on a horse. In his mind the infantry offered faster promotion, had "fine officers," was always needed in time of war, and spent more time at the post than in the field. If later Rooney wanted to transfer to the cavalry, Lee hoped it would be to his regiment "merely from selfish motives & from hope of having him with me." As usual, Lee trusted "it will be for the best & that he will be satisfied." Lee urged his wife to give him money for his outfit and travel expenses to his post until he could "come to his relief" financially.[2]

In July Rooney went for a short trip to Baltimore to see Charlotte Wickham. At that time he was in the army, but he did not have to report to his post at Governor's Island in New York City until August 1. His sister Annie described him at this time as having a mustache and imperial and so big that he made Custis look small. Brother Roon was "as funny as ever & as affectionate."[3]

Rooney was so busy with his courtship and getting prepared for army life that he did not write to his father during this time. In fact, he was never a prolific letter-writer and quite often depended on his family members, especially his mother, to relay news. Robert Lee, not sure of his son's whereabouts, also sent some very sound advice to Rooney through Mary. He hoped Rooney would "set himself to work diligently to prepare himself for his duties & endeavor to acquit himself honorably." Lee reasoned that Rooney had the advantage of one year's rank over those who had entered West Point at the same time he had entered Harvard. Again he counseled, "As he has gone into the Army, I wish him zealously to perform all his duties & to prepare himself for his station & not to trifle away his time or spend his energies in leaves of absence. A soldier's life I know to be a hard one. But those who enter it will consult their own interest as well as happiness by attending strictly to their duty." Custis was also at Arlington during this period, and Lee was sure that there would be a lively family reunion for all—all except him. "I fear the sight of them (the brothers) will seldom again gladden my eyes. I wish I could have seen them, if only to have had the pleasure of seeing that they were provided with everything that I could give them." Lee also had one last admonition about debt. He wanted to make sure that all Rooney's debts were settled and was "very much afraid that these habits of carelessness & improvidence will adhere to him through life. Still I hope in the end he may come out all right. He is very young yet." When Lee thought about Rooney's age (twenty) he was not sure of the year of his son's birth. He asked his wife to send him "a memo of all their ages" so he could be sure.[4]

The dust had barely settled from the first when Rooney dropped a second bombshell on his parents. He and Charlotte Wickham were engaged. He told his mother first and let her inform the rest of the family. Their love affair "had been going on for a long time," but they had waited until she had received her grandfather's approval before announcing the engagement to his parents. They still wanted it kept secret "not that he was ashamed of it but both being quite young it would give rise to much gossip." The young couple planned to wait a year or two before the wedding. Rooney hoped his choice met with their approval and begged his mother to write to Charlotte soon to welcome her into the family. Mary Lee had some reservations about the matter, one being that "the relationship is quite near." She seemed to forget that she and Robert Lee were also cousins, and marrying cousins in Tidewater society was an everyday occurrence. She resolved herself to her son's choice by thinking that "if she possesses the amiable qualities of her mother & grandmother she will be an acquisition." Also, knowing her son's reckless nature, she was certain that "a virtuous attachment is often a great safeguard to a young man."[5]

Charlotte Georgiana Wickham was three years younger than Rooney and had been brought up by her grandfather, William Carter of Shirley. Her father, George Wickham, had died before she was born, and her mother, Charlotte Carter Wickham, died while she was yet a baby. Both parents seemed to have died of tuberculosis.[6]

Robert Lee was only mildly surprised by this news. Indeed he was prepared for news of an engagement and surprised only by the young lady. He thought Charlotte "a sweet amiable child" but feared she was "ill calculated in health or from education to follow the drum over the Western prairies." He hoped that Mary had educated her about the hardships and privations that came with being married to a soldier. He joked that a lieutenant's lodging would not even be sufficient for her trunk. He also reasoned that "if their plans are to wait two or three years, both may change their minds half a dozen times before then. They are both mere children." He continued in a teasing manner that he knew "a kind of a widow" that he had planned to recommend to Rooney. It seems that this Texan woman had some designs on him. He continued, "I thought it incumbent on me to return her compliment by a call. I found the house & made myself as agreeable as I could for about 5 minutes, & when I rose to depart she took me out in her garden to see her corn & potatoes by STARLIGHT

. . . I told her I had no knowledge of horticulture & took no interest in agriculture in Texas. . . . Those are the kind of woman, tell Chass, a man wants in the army." Charlotte had already received her welcome into the Lee household by the bestowal of a nickname: Chass.[7]

Rooney's progress in learning how to carry out his military duties filtered down the army grapevine to his father in Texas. Robert Lee was "glad to hear such good accounts of Fitzhugh & that he contemplates seriously life and its duties." When he heard that Rooney's regiment was to be sent to Kansas he hoped that it would not be before he was "somewhat acquainted with his military duties." As Rooney began to show more maturity Lee began to refer to him more frequently as Fitzhugh, as did his wife and Charlotte Wickham. However, many of his relatives and most of his friends and acquaintances continued to call him Rooney throughout his life. One other sign of his maturity concerned the problem of debt. His father paid the last $104 that he owed in Boston and bought "a belt revolver pistol, a good double-barreled gun & equipments to take with him to the frontier." Other than that Rooney was to live off his army pay. Lee wrote to Mary, "He has made good resolutions & I hope will be able to adhere to them. If he does we need to have no fears. He tells me so far he has not violated them."[8]

One matter of concern for Robert and Mary Lee was the health of Rooney's fiancée. Lee wrote of his future daughter-in-law, "Charlotte I think a very sweet amiable person, but I fear her health is very delicate, though she looks rosy and rotund. Both her father & mother were constitutionally feeble, & I doubt whether she is calculated for an Army life, where you must endure physical privations & labour, neither of which she has known." Mary was more direct in discussing Charlotte's health. She had learned from a Lee connection in Baltimore that "Charlotte has entirely recovered from her scrofulous affliction & is in very robust health, that the physicians think the consumptive tendencies inherited from her parents may have gone off." Unfortunately tuberculosis does not go away.[9]

The only thing on Rooney's mind was marriage—and that as soon as possible. By October 1857 he thought that it would be unlikely that his regiment would go west that winter and saw "no reason his marriage should be delayed." His mother did not agree. To her husband she wrote, "I think they are both too young & it would be so well if he was sent away for a year or two. It would be a trial of their constancy." Mary needed some time to adjust to the idea of losing a son, but Robert Lee was ready to gain a daughter. From San Antonio he wrote the following letter welcoming Charlotte into the Lee family:

> I never thought, my dear Charlotte, when I held you a girl in my arms & felt rise for you the love I bore your mother, that you would ever be nearer or dearer to me than then. But you are now united in my heart with one who from infancy has been dearer to me than myself & whose welfare in manhood I value beyond my own. You can conceive then the grateful affection I feel for her who is willing to promote his happiness & smooth for him the rough path of life. I hope his love & devotion to you will make your part easy & that in return he will lighten your cares & bear your troubles. To me he has always been an affectionate son. To you I hope he may ever prove a tender & faithful husband. I feel very sensibly your kindness in consenting to enter our family. I fear you will find us rough soldiers. But I trust you will never have cause to doubt our affection. To me you will be as dear as my own daughter & if you will allow me I will guard & watch over you with the care of a father.[10]

On October 10, 1857, Mr. Custis died at the age of seventy-six. On his deathbed at Arlington he told his daughter that she "must do the best about Rooney's marriage." Rooney was at Governor's Island but came as quickly as possible upon receiving news of his grandfather's illness. He arrived the night of October 10, too late to see his grandfather before he died. Perry, a servant at Arlington, "met him at the door & told him." According to Mr. Custis's will, Arlington was to be Mary Lee's during her life and at her death would go to Custis. The White House plantation in New Kent County was bequeathed to Rooney, and Romancoke plantation in King William County was to be Rob's. He also left a legacy of $10,000 each to his four granddaughters. Other small pieces of property could be sold to make up the $40,000, and the revenue from the crops of the three plantations were to make up the balance. Robert Lee faced many problems as executor of the estate. Mr. Custis had accumulated debts, all three plantations were run down and neglected, and there was little operating capital. Moreover, the 196 slaves scattered all over Virginia were to be emancipated within five years of Mr. Custis's death. Lee took a leave of absence from his post in Texas and began the chore of straightening out the mess so that his daughters would have their legacies and his sons would have flourishing and prosperous farms. Apparently neither Custis nor Rooney was at the point in his military career when it would be advisable to take a leave.[11]

The winter at Arlington was brightened by visits. In January 1858 Charlotte came for a while. Robert Lee noted that he "never saw her looking so well & pretty." She was on her way to Baltimore to continue her lessons in music and painting. In February Rooney arrived from San Antonio unexpectedly. He had taken a group of recruits west, then returned east. He was "still bent upon an Army's life" and planned to go with his regiment on an expedition to Utah in April. His father agreed with his decision, saying, "Indeed it would not be proper for him at this time, his Reg't being on the eve of taking the field, to resign. He properly feels this & is somewhat embarrassed about his matrimonial projects, which in consequence must be for a time suspended. I think this better in any case for both parties though can understand it may not be the most agreeable to their feelings. He however is resigned & I have obtained Uncle Wm's concurrence." Lee had visited Williams Carter, Charlotte's grandfather, while on a trip to the White House to oversee improvements there. He explained the necessity for Rooney staying in the army until the regiment returned from the Utah expedition and Carter had agreed to postpone the wedding. Lee wrote to Rooney about the improvements at the White House in spite of $1,275 in debts there that he hoped to "work off" soon.[12]

Rooney came back to Arlington for a short visit in March 1858 before returning to New York, where he was to "accompany the last batch of recruits for the 'Relieving Army of Utah' to Leavenworth, and then join his regiment destined for that service." Rooney left "in buoyant health & spirits but with a sad heart." In the meantime Charlotte returned to her grandfather's, "where in the absence of her Roon she intended to devote herself to music & painting."[13]

Rooney was assigned to the battalion of Captain Henry Heth, who appointed him adjutant. Rooney's cousin Louis Marshall was the quartermaster, and the three were messmates on the campaign. Heth later remembered, "Lieutenant Lee showed many of the good qualities which make a good soldier, doubtless inherited from the great soldier, his father." It was no surprise that Rooney turned out to be a good soldier and a fine officer right from the start. Both his grandfather and father were excellent officers, and many of their attributes were passed on to him. Indeed what better role model for an army officer could there be than Robert Lee? Rooney had lived on army posts a good part of his life, and military routine and protocol were second nature to him. Furthermore his intense desire to be a soldier led him to study the military art from an early age. What others had to study in class he seemed to know intuitively. The leadership abilities that his classmates noted at Harvard made him a natural for a position of leadership in the army. [14]

Lee was pleased with this assignment and had some good advice for the young soldier:

> You are now in a position to acquire military credit, and to prepare the road for promotion and future advancement. Show your ability and worthiness of distinction, and if an opportunity offers for advancement in the staff (I do not refer to the Quartermaster's or Commissary Departments), unless that is not your fancy, take it. It may lead to something favorable and you can always relinquish it when you choose.
>
> I hope you will always be distinguished for your avoidance of the universal balm, *whiskey*, and every immorality. Nor need you fear to be ruled out of the society that indulges in it, for you will rather acquire their esteem and respect, as all venerate if they do not practice virtue. I am sorry to say that there is great proclivity for spirit in the army in the field. It seems to be considered a substitute for every luxury. The great body however do not carry it to extreme, while others pursue it to their ruin. With some it is used as a means of hospitality, and your col. Commanding used to value it highly in this way, and, perhaps, partook of it in this spirit. I think it better to avoid it altogether, as you do, as its temperate use is so difficult. I hope you will make many friends, as you will be thrown with many who deserve this feeling, but indiscriminate intimacies you will find annoying and entangling, and they can be avoided by politeness and civility. You see I am following my old habit of giving advice, which I dare say you neither need nor require. But you must pardon a fault which proceeds from my great love and burning anxiety for your welfare and happiness. When I think of your youth, impulsiveness, and many temptations, your distance from me, and the ease (and even innocence) with which you might commence an erroneous course, my heart quails within me, and my whole frame and being trembles at the possible result. May Almighty God have you in His holy keeping. To His merciful Providence I commit you, and will rely upon Him, and

the efficacy of the prayers that will be daily and hourly offered up by those who love you.[15]

The Sixth Infantry formed part of the expedition led by Colonel Albert Sidney Johnston against the Mormons in Utah Territory. The Mormons had settled in the Great Salt Lake Valley and set up an independent church-state under the leadership of Brigham Young. In the Compromise of 1850, Utah Territory was created by Congress, and Mormon lands came under its jurisdiction. At first there was harmony, but soon problems arose, including the practice of polygamy. In 1857 James Buchanan's administration decided to send in a military force to deal with the rebellious Mormons and restore order. The first military contingent arrived in Utah in the fall of 1857; Rooney's regiment—the Sixth Infantry—arrived in the summer of 1858 as part of a relief column. Johnston's men passed through Echo Canyon and on into Salt Lake City, which was nearly deserted. The Mormons had moved south and set up camp to avoid conflict with the soldiers. Johnston's force set up camp near Salt Lake City and began military occupation of the area, ready to move if the need arose. Ironically the Mormons were soon trading with the soldiers and were hired to help build suitable quarters.

When certain Mormons were to be tried in Provo, Captain Heth's company accompanied the judge and acted as provost. Heth was cautioned to keep his troops under strictest discipline so as not to alarm the citizens of Provo and provoke a confrontation. The mayor asked the judge to remove the troops; the judge refused. Armed Mormons soon arrived in town, and Johnston sent reinforcements to Heth. Conflict seemed imminent. Some of Heth's soldiers were stoned, but this was not repeated after Heth's threat to fire at the perpetrators. The futility of carrying on court in these circumstances was soon evident, so the judge adjourned the session; Heth's troops returned to the base camp. Their strict discipline had averted an armed confrontation with civilians.[16]

Aside from duties as peacekeepers, the Utah army was used to protect wagon trains and to find new paths west. All of these adventures Rooney relayed to his family at home. His father replied, "I was delighted, my dear son, . . . to learn that you were well, and so contented and happy in your new life. I know that, although there is much to weary and annoy in a campaign, there is much to cheer and excite, and I recognize in the expression of your feelings many of my own experiences." Although he may have been happy with army life, Rooney still had his mind on marriage. He mentioned the possibility of getting a leave of absence during the winter to come home and claim his bride. His father replied, "I thought that ceremony had been postponed two years! However, if you young people so wish it, I suppose it will have to come off earlier. About that you must determine." He playfully suggested taking leave when Rooney's regiment reached Oregon and taking Charlotte back there by way of China as "a wedding tour."[17]

Actually the Sixth had departed Salt Lake City and traveled through Carson's Valley to California. By December Rooney was at the Presidio, where Custis was also stationed. Lee sent New Year's wishes to his "Precious Roon":

I am delighted at you two being together, and nothing has occurred so gratifying to me for the past year. Hold on to him as long as you can. Kiss him for me, and sleep with him every night. He must do the same to you, and charge it all to my account. God grant that it could be my good fortune to be with you both. I am glad that you stood the march so well, and are so robust and bearded. I always thought and said there was stuff in you for a good soldier, and I trust you will prove it. I cannot express the gratification I felt in meeting Colonel May, in New York, at the encomiums he passed upon your soldiership, zeal, and devotion to your duty. But I was more pleased at the report of your conduct. That went nearer my heart, and was of infinite comfort to me. Hold on to your purity and virtue. They will proudly sustain you in all trials and difficulties, and cheer you in every calamity. I was sorry to see, from your letter to your mother, that you smoke occasionally. It is dangerous to meddle with. You have in store so much better employment for your mouth. Reserve it, Rooney, for its legitimate pleasure. Do not poison and corrupt it with stale vapors or tarnish your beard with their stench.[18]

By the end of January Rooney was back in Virginia, ready to work out details of a wedding. His sister noted his early-morning arrival at Arlington, saying, "I was clasped in the arms of a tall creature with a great deal of beard & a most shaggy outlandish coat, this terrific looking creature proved to be my own dear brother & when dressed is a very fine looking officer."[19]

Apparently Rooney had planned that he and Charlotte would live at his estate after the marriage. The White House, a 4,000-acre plantation on the Pamunkey River, had been the home of the widow Martha Custis before her marriage to George Washington. By 1859 it had fallen into disrepair, and, despite Robert Lee's improvements, was still not ready for occupancy. After visiting at Arlington for a while Rooney went down to Shirley on the James River to visit the Carters. At one point Williams Carter offered the young couple his Broadneck property and promised to build them a house there. This was later changed to a one-third interest in Broadneck after Carter's son Charles came to live there. Charlotte's dowry was a generous one, and Robert Lee was one of the trustees of the settlement. He traveled to Richmond to take care of the legal matters, then to the White House to make it ready for the bride and groom.[20]

The wedding of Rooney Lee and Charlotte Wickham took place on March 23, 1859, at Shirley. Mary Lee did not attend, but Robert Lee and the girls all made the trip. This marked the second union of the Lees and Carters ("Light Horse" Harry Lee had married Ann Hill Carter at Shirley sixty-six years earlier). The wedding was of the traditional Tidewater sort, with many guests who remained for days. After visiting for a while, the bride and groom stayed at Arlington until the White House was ready for occupancy. Rooney had submitted his resignation earlier, but the official date of the resignation was May 31, 1859, his twenty-second birthday. Officially he was in the U.S. Army for exactly two years.[21]

Robert Lee chronicled the events for Custis, who had missed the wedding. Lee described Charlotte to him: "She is a sweet thing, and affectionate, and you must love her as you do Fitzhugh. . . . Just now she is a little sick." In June Rooney and his father traveled to New Kent County to check on the repairs and improvements at the White House. The plan was for the newlyweds to move there by the first of the year and Rooney was to manage both White House and Romancoke. Lee wrote Custis, "I hope he will like it, and be successful in their management, for it will be a matter of importance to him and Robert. I have made the arrangement hoping it will be for his benefit. The sooner the legacies are paid off, the sooner he will get possession of his farm, and in the meantime can make arrangements and improvements that will result in his advantage and comfort. Charlotte seems much pleased at the prospect and is planning a great many improvements in their establishment."[22]

In July the young couple went to visit at Cedar Grove for two weeks, and in August they went to White Sulphur Springs. In a letter to her new father-in-law Charlotte reported from the Springs that "F. is the greatest beau there. Knows all the pretty girls, dances, etc." On that same visit, Mrs. Chesnut met Rooney and recorded in her diary, "Rooney Lee and his wife, that sweet little Charlotte Wickham, was there, I spoke of Rooney with great praise. Mrs. Izard said: 'Don't waste your admiration on him. Wait till you see his father. He is the nearest to a perfect man I ever saw.'"[23]

By January 1, 1860, Rooney and Charlotte were living near the White House, close enough so that Rooney could personally oversee the farmwork and the repairs. Robert Lee continued to give advice on plowing, fertilizer, harvesting, and sale of the crops. He stressed economy and personal supervision to details in all matters. He was pleased with Rooney's progress as a farmer.[24]

On March 9, 1860, Charlotte gave birth to an eight-pound boy, whom his grandmother called "a fine little fellow" and thought developed "new beauties every hour." It is interesting to note that Mary Lee made the trip to the White House to be with her daughter-in-law for the birth. She had her first baby on an army post away from family and proper care. For all the subsequent little Lees she traveled home to Arlington for the support and care she knew would be there. Certainly she did not want her new daughter to go through such a trial without the tender love and moral support only a mother can give. Robert Lee was sure that "the Mim must have rejoiced at another baby in the house, and have had all her former feelings brought back afresh." Robert Lee was delighted to be a grandfather. He wrote the proud father, "I sincerely congratulate you and my darling daughter, at his prosperous advent, and pray that his future career may give more happiness to his parents than even his present existence. You must kiss his dear mother for me, and offer my warmest thanks for this promising scion of my scattered house, who will I hope resuscitate its name and fame. Tell her I have thought much of her and long to see you both and your little treasure, who must, I think, resemble his papa."[25]

At first the new parents could not decide on the name—William Henry Fitzhugh Jr. or Robert Edward Lee? Finally they decided to honor the child's grandfather. Lee was truly pleased with the decision. He wrote, "You must teach him then to love his Grand Papa, to bear with his failings & avoid his errors, to be to you as you have been to me, & he may then enjoy the love & confidence of his father which I feel for you greater than which no son has ever possessed. May God guard & protect him through life." The baby was christened by a friend of the family who was visiting at the time. The rector of Christ Church in Alexandria performed the ceremony at St. Peter's Church near the White House.

In the spring of 1861 Charlotte and Rooney made a trip to Baltimore "for her health." They spent some time at Arlington, and the grandparents enjoyed some time with their grandchild. Robert Lee thought him "a sweet little boy" who reminded him "very much of his father when at his age." In his grandmother's eyes he was "the sweetest thing you ever saw." He was just learning to talk and could "say Robbie quite plain," but he was a little afraid of the house cat at Arlington.[26]

In little more than two years the White House had been changed from its rundown, neglected state into a prosperous farm. In spite of a large capital outlay for new livestock, equipment, and improvements to the main house and slave quarters, there was a profit of $5,064.22 for the year 1860. This profit went into the Custis estate. With less outlay and expectation for a larger crop the next year, there was promise of an even larger profit. In this way the girls' legacies would soon be paid off and the boys would have clear title to their farms. Rooney had even begun to look into alternatives for maintaining help when the time came to free the Custis slaves. The improvements begun by Robert Lee and continued and expanded by Rooney were turning the White House into a home of which any farmer would be proud. With his new wife and baby, Rooney had truly found his niche in life. At this moment in his life Rooney could not have been happier. But this idyllic scene was soon to be shattered.

The clouds of war were gathering slowly and inevitably into the storm that would soon burst over the nation. An American tragedy was about to open with the Lees as principal characters. Abraham Lincoln became president of the United States, and the Southern states began to secede. The Lees hoped "for the preservation of the Union" but felt the "aggressions of the North." They disliked the fire-eaters of both sides who rejected compromise and fanned the flames of war. Robert Lee wrote that he was "unwilling to do what is wrong, either at the bidding of the South or the North." He was very much opposed to "the renewal of the slave trade," which many in the cotton states proposed. Rooney Lee did not write down his views on the political events, but they were surely very similar to those of this father. Robert Lee wrote to one of his sons:

> The South, in my opinion, has been aggrieved by the acts of the North, as you say. I feel the aggression, and am willing to take every proper step for redress. It is the principle I contend for, not individual or private gain. As an American citizen, I take great pride in my country, her prosperity and institutions, and would defend any State if her rights were invaded. But I can anticipate no greater calamity for the country than a dissolution of the Union. It would be an accumulation of all the evils we complain of, and I am willing to sacrifice everything but honor for its preservation. I hope, therefore, that all constitutional means will be exhausted before there is recourse to force. Secession is nothing but revolution. . . . Still, a Union that can only be maintained by swords and bayonets, and in which strife and civil war are to take the place of brotherly love and kindness, has no charm for me. I shall mourn for my country and for the welfare and progress of mankind. If the Union is dissolved, and the Government disrupted, I shall return to my native State and share the miseries of my people, and save in defence will draw my sword on none.[27]

On April 12 the bombardment of Fort Sumter began. Lincoln called for 75,000 troops to put down the insurrection, and on April 18 the secession of Virginia was announced. The sons and grandsons of Light Horse Harry Lee shared his opinion: "Virginia is my country; her will I obey, however lamentable the fate to which it may subject me." Robert Lee resigned from the U.S. Army and a few days later offered his sword in defense of Virginia. He did not try to influence his sons' decisions. He wrote Mary, "Tell Custis he must consult his own judgment, reason, and conscience as to the course he may take. I do not wish him to be guided by my wishes or example. If I have done wrong, let him do better." Rooney traveled to Arlington to talk over matters personally with his father before making any decision. A lady who traveled on the train to Alexandria with Rooney the day after Virginia passed the ordinance of secession said that "she can never forget the contrast of his deep depression with the prevalent elation and jubilancy. He said the people had lost their senses and had no conception of what a terrible mistake they were making." Rooney must have had a clear realization of the North's overpowering man-power and resources as well as the absurdity of allowing a few hot-heads to tear a nation apart. Yet he, like thousands of others, was pulled into the maelstrom of civil war.[28]

CHAPTER 4

"Jine the Cavalry"

When he committed to the cause of Virginia, Rooney Lee wasted little time offering his services to his native state. He immediately placed under guard "all the vessels" on the river near New Kent. There were approximately 100 men with these vessels whom Lee was "anxious to send home, leaving their vessels and timber where they are." He wrote directly to Governor John Letcher, who directed him to retain the ships and their cargo and allow the men on them to go home (presumably in the North). Material was in short supply, and the captured timber and vessels might serve some purpose.[1]

Lee also organized a company of cavalry that became known first as the Virginia Rangers and then as Lee's Rangers. Lee's commission of captain was dated May 6, 1861. The company was organized in King William County and mustered into service in June 1861. The company marched from West Point in King William County to Ashland in Hanover County, where it was drilled in cavalry instruction.[2]

As soon as the company was mustered, Captain Lee requisitioned supplies for his men and mounts. He ordered seventy-two pairs of boots, jackets, pants, forage caps, and blankets. At that time there were sixty-four privates, four corporals, and four sergeants in the company for a total of seventy-two. The three officers provided their own uniforms and equipment. It is interesting to note that he also requested seventy-two overcoats and seventy-two horse blankets in June. Unlike many Southerners who believed that the war would be a thirty-day lark, Rooney Lee knew that it would be a long, drawn-out affair and thought ahead. When the uniforms came the invoice itemized the cost.

The shoes cost $1.75, jackets $2.75, pants $1.75, and overcoats $6.75. The price of the men's blankets ranged in cost from $1.50 to $3 and so, presumably, did their quality. He also requisitioned two "wall tents" and five "common tents" with tent poles and pins. There is no record of these being delivered. From the outset the young captain thought of his men and their well-being first.[3]

The two most important items in the cavalryman's equipage were left up to the men themselves. The weapons were an assortment of old rifles and hunting pieces that were totally unfit for cavalry service. The men soon learned to obtain the newer models from the U.S. Ordnance Department. As for the horses, the Confederate cavalrymen fared better. Although the practice of a man providing his own horse in order to be in the cavalry eventually caused many problems, initially it was a reason for the Confederate cavalry being the best in the history of warfare. The selection and breeding of prime riding horses was more than a hobby in the South; it was a passion and a way of life. Many Confederates rode off to war on the finest stock the plantation or vicinity had ever produced. Furthermore, they knew how to take care of their mounts. They knew how a horse should be shod, how and when it should be fed and watered, and how to recognize and treat illness and lameness problems. They took great pride in how well their horses were groomed and turned out. The Southerners learned to ride soon after they learned to walk and were always better riders and horsemen than their northern counterparts. Early in the war the Confederate cavalry could proceed directly to mounted drill while the Yankees were still learning the difference between a curb and snaffle and which side to mount.

Rooney Lee had finally found his niche in life, that of horse soldier. He had wanted to be a cavalryman all his life, and now he had the chance to be one. He was an excellent horseman and a fine rider in spite of his size. Generally speaking, a man who is six feet, three inches tall and weighs around 220 pounds is considered too big to look really good on a horse. But if the man is mounted on a large, high-headed horse and possesses the natural grace and posture that all good riders have, then the overall picture is one of power and elegance. One of his men remembered him: "He was of fine stature and commanding and handsome appearance. Though carrying more weight than was suitable to the saddle and the quick movements of the cavalry service, he was, nevertheless, a good horseman and an excellent judge of horses.

So well and wisely did he select them, that when mounted there seemed an admirable harmony between his own massive form and the heavy build and muscular power of his steed. A splendid iron grey, much of him nearly white, was his favorite amongst his horses, and when bestride this animal, at rest or in motion, he would have furnished no mean subject for an artist even though his portrait were displayed in the same gallery with those of Stuart, Ashby, Hampton, and Fitz Lee." Another young trooper later in the war was somewhat awed by the sight of Rooney Lee on horseback. He swore that he could make out Lee "in the darkest part of that forest at the darkest period of the night." "He was six feet three or four and weighed not an ounce less than three hundred pounds. He was mounted on his brown war horse, 'Frantic', a horse he always had his saddle changed to before going into a fight. The two together, man and horse, made one of the largest establishments I ever saw." A powerful man on a large horse can be a formidable and intimidating presence in combat, but the combination also offers a large target.[4]

The exercise and drill continued at Ashland for a few weeks, and Rooney came down to Richmond "in reference to business of his company." On this trip he briefly saw his father as well as Charlotte. Also during this period he was promoted to major and sent to the mountains of western Virginia with a small cavalry force. In this area the Confederate military was more like a patchwork of commanders and units rather than one cohesive army under a single general. There were important mountain passes to guard against Union attacks, railroads to defend, and plenty of reconnaissance to be done, but lack of organization threatened the Confederate initiative. Finally, R.E. Lee, now a military adviser to Confederate President Jefferson Davis, went to western Virginia to try to sort out the mess. Rooney's company was probably his only source of cheer during this entire campaign. He wrote Mary on August 9: "I have enjoyed the company of Fitzhugh since I have been here. He is very well and very active, and as yet the war has not reduced him much. He dined with me yesterday and preserves his fine appetite. Today he is out reconnoitering and has the full benefit of this rain. I fear he is without his overcoat, as I do not recollect seeing it on his saddle. I told you he had been promoted to a major in cavalry, and is the commanding cavalry officer on this line at present. He is as sanguine, cheerful and hearty as ever. I sent him some corn-meal this morning and he sent me some butter—a mutual interchange of good things." On one occasion Rooney was sent out with a flag of truce to the Yankee pickets to deliver a proposal on the exchange of prisoners. Possibly he was sent as a scout, but the Union commander was smart enough not to let him come any closer than two miles of the main camp.[5]

In August Custis took Charlotte and her son to the Montgomery White Springs in hopes that the baby's health would improve. The stay at the springs did not bring the expected improvement, so Charlotte returned to Richmond, then went on to Shirley plantation to visit her Carter relatives. It seems that Custis was the one who had to take care of the women in the family during the war as well as be personal quartermaster to the Lee men at the front. Robert Lee wrote to Custis in September that Rooney was "very well, hearty, and sanguine" but that he badly needed a "buffalo robe" that Custis was to have procured and sent to him. He prodded Custis by saying, "F. feels the want of it every night."[6]

On September 13 Rooney set out to reconnoiter one of the branches of Elkwater Fork and took a small contingent of troopers with him. Lieutenant Colonel John A. Washington, then a member of R.E. Lee's personal staff, decided to join the cavalry on the mission. Washington was a "long-time friend" of the Lee family and "a gentleman of the highest type and a true aristocrat." Rooney's orders were "to make a reconnaissance of the Federal position and to locate his camp." After having "successfully and satisfactorily" completed the assignment, Rooney was ready to return to camp with his squadron of cavalry. However, Colonel Washington, "who was full of life and spirit, protested against returning without having—as he termed it—a 'little fun' and proposed (to Rooney) 'to capture that fellow on the gray horse.'" Washington's proposal to capture or chase the vidette was "the result of a desire which prevailed at that period of the war—among [Confederate] officers especially—to see some sport in the way of a fight." Rooney acquiesced but realized that there could be danger ahead. He left his squadron "on a commanding position" and rode down into the valley with Colonel Washington and two couriers. The two officers left the two men "at the foot of the hills" and rode on alone. Rooney cautioned these two, "look out for us on our return which I felt would be sudden and rapid." Washington and Lee rode toward the lone sentry—Lee on a brown horse and Washington on a blood bay—and charged the final distance at a full gallop. Just before they reached the Federal on the gray horse a company of hidden Federals opened fire on them. "The Federals seemed . . . to raise up out of the bushes on the mountain side and deliver their fire at will." Colonel Washington "fell at the first fire and his horse immediately charged to the rear." Rooney, who was riding on the left of Washington and closer to the Federals, was not hit, but his horse was. At once he turned and "had to run the gauntlet going back" to his men. Rooney's valiant charger carried him quickly out of danger in spite of the horse's mortal wounds. When the horse finally collapsed, Rooney went with a flag of truce to reclaim Colonel Washington's body, which was subsequently interred at his plantation in Fauquier County.[7]

When Robert Lee moved to a position near Sewell Mountain in September, he regretted that he was not able to take Rooney along. But there was a surplus of cavalry in Governor John B. Floyd's area, and Lee was ordering them to be dismounted. Able officers in western Virginia were in short supply, and Lee could have used his son, who was quickly proving his capabilities as a cavalry officer. In fact, he wrote Rooney that he was "grieving over your absence." Although Rooney himself maintained good health, many of his men were out sick. The health problems of his men were a daily concern, so Rooney must have been privately distressed over his son's health. The baby had been sick for some time with short periods of improvement. By November Rooney was able to take a little time off and make a trip to Shirley plantation, where his wife and baby were staying. Mary Lee had also come for a visit, and the two ladies were planning to go on to the White House. Robert Lee wrote that he was "very glad Fitzhugh has got in to see his little wife and son and hope the latter will soon be well now since he has seen his Pa'a."[8]

Rooney's cavalry was ordered back east during the winter and was able to spend some time with the family at the White House. Agnes and Rob soon joined the family, and for a brief period a large part of the Lee family was together. Rob must have been afraid they would not recognize him as he announced that he was getting "to be a young man," "five feet ten, strikingly handsome, with a strong tendency to a moustache and whiskers." The main person missing from the family gathering was Robert Lee, now on duty in South Carolina. As usual, he corresponded regularly with family members. On one occasion he picked some violets and sent them in his letter to the ladies and added, "If F. is there give him some too." He also hoped that "the poor little baby has revived at the sight of his Papa." The baby was not improving, however. He needed attention "night and day" and was "too sick to play at all." The doctor attending him thought he could get well, but it would require "the most tender and careful nursing." His grandmother described him as "a poor little skeleton." Robert Lee wrote to Mary, "I am much pleased that F. has an opportunity to be with you all and will not be so far removed from his home in his new field of action. I hope to see him at the head of a fine regiment and that he will be able to do good service in the cause of his country." Rooney moved one step closer to making his father's hope a reality by being promoted to lieutenant colonel in December 1861.[9]

Robert Lee wrote to his son a letter extending wishes for a happy Christmas and new year and expressing his pleasure that the progress at the White House had continued. He could not help but include some advice. He told Rooney how to be the perfect husband: "You must do all she wishes. Dig her pits, plant her trees, and make her flower beds." As to military matters, Lee counseled: "You must apply to the service now all the energy of your character and have your command in a condition to be effective and creditable to you." Lee was particularly pleased that Rooney was stationed near home and hoped for a "more pleasant service" than he had in western Virginia. He also wrote a delightful letter to Charlotte, whom he addressed as "precious Chass." He sent her some violets he had just gathered and asked her to "kiss Fitzhugh . . . and the baby" for him, as he considered her kisses "the sweetest Christmas gift" he could send. He also chided her to go stay with Mary and "not run off with her son to Fredericksburg." Whenever possible Charlotte boarded near Rooney's camp so they could be together when he had some time off. According to Robert Lee, there were "too many young men there" and the area was too close to the enemy. He recommended that she visit only "the old men—your grandpapa and papa."[10]

Once back at school Rob wrote to his youngest sister, Mildred, about the Lee reunion during the holidays. This was to be the last peaceful gathering until the end of the war. He remembered: "I have just finished spending a delightful Christmas down at the White House, together with Ma, Fitz, Charlotte, Annie, Agnes and the baby. We had quite a family gathering. They were all very well and seemingly happy . . . The farm is lovely, the land, lying level near the river and breaking into beautiful hills as you go back inland. The house is small but very comfortable and very nicely furnished; the grounds around the house are being improved daily. . . . Fitz has a plenty of horses and we had some splendid rides and drives. . . . I suppose you have seen the promotion of Fitz in the papers. He is a Lt. Col. Of Cavalry and Col. [John Evans] Johnson is his Colonel. The regiment is attached to Gen. Holmes' brigade stationed near Fredericksburg."[11]

Rooney wrote to his father, informing him of the recent promotion, and received this reply: "I am very glad to hear that you are well and have attained such a bright position by your own merit. I hope you will strive hard to show you deserve it and go on increasing in honour and usefulness. Our country requires now every one to put forth all his ability regardless of self and I am cheered in my downward path of life by the onward and rising course of my dear sons." Lee was concerned by the problems of carrying out Mr. Custis's will. The slaves were to be freed within five years of his death. Lee was afraid of "what would become of them" if emancipated outright. If possible he wanted to hire some of them out and let the money mount up and then "apply the proceeds of their hire to their future establishment." His first priority was to act in a "way most conducive to the interests of his [Mr. Custis's] people and his heirs." The money due to the girls was to come from the profits of the farms and not from the sale of any slave. He thought it probable that Rob would have to sell his farm to come up with his share of the money and then make his own living. Because of the improvements Rooney had been able to make at the White House and the resulting profits, he could probably manage to pay his share and still retain his farm. This idea was feasible as long as the war did not interfere. Lee asked his son for comments and suggestions but was certain that the entire family had the same goal: "At any rate we must all do what is right and I know all will cheerfully unite in that effort," he told Rooney. Lee's own "private reserves" were cut off, and he was sure that his investments in northern stocks would be confiscated.[12]

Military affairs around Fredericksburg during the winter of 1861–1862 were not so hectic that Rooney was unable to write to his wife. He began by saying that there was "nothing of interest occurring in this quiet place" in spite of the rumors that a Yankee attack was imminent. He thought that any advance "may be put off until Spring." General Theophilus Hunter Holmes, the commander of the troops in and around Fredericksburg, had stopped all furloughs, but

Rooney cautioned Charlotte, "You must not be surprised at my dropping in, however, at any time." He enumerated all the ladies in the area whom he had visited and related all the gossip about the romances, engagements, and the like. He told Charlotte about one young officer's happiness and added: "You see I have not forgotten the times when I was in the same situation and I take great interest in all the young gentlemen's 'affaires de coeur.' Those were very pleasant times, with all the little obstacles which, then, I remember, I thought very great." He had sent her a japonica bush by way of Custis with the idea of planting it at the White House. He wanted her to do "great things this Spring" in the way of improvements on the farm. Uppermost in his mind, however, was "that precious boy." "I see little children 14 and 16 months old running all about and am very anxious to hear of my son stepping out by himself. You and he are always in my thoughts. I wish I could see you. I long for the time when Peace shall come and put an end to this unhappiness. God grant that the time may not be far off." These were the fervent hopes of the young father longing to see his family.[13]

Less than a week later he had figured out a way to see her. He wrote a quick letter with the proposition, "as I cannot get to see you, you should come up and pay me a short visit." He said he would try to meet her in Richmond, but if he could not leave, then Custis (as usual) would meet her and make arrangements. Much as he would have loved to see his son, he cautioned Charlotte to leave him at the White House with his grandmother because of a scarlet fever epidemic in the area. Charlotte came for a short visit, and it was during this time that their second child was conceived.[14]

As lieutenant colonel of the newly formed Ninth Virginia Cavalry, Rooney had a difficult task before him. Some of the companies recently brought under his command were not used to military discipline and drill. On March 19, 1862, Lee began to drill his companies twice a day and replace some of the antiquated weapons with new sabers and guns. Not all the weapons were updated, however. One seventeen-year-old trooper remembered that "not one company in ten had any arms that were fit to fight with." He had been given a Revolutionary War–era saber that broke off at the hilt when he swung it at a tree limb. They learned to man a picket line, scout, and do guard and courier duty. A trooper noted the change in a letter home, "We have to work very hard . . . all the time. . . . We are in a regiment and it is very different . . . no man is allowed to leave camp . . . sleep on the wet ground . . . corn bread and fried meat. . . . I think I shall become fond of it." Another wrote in his diary after being sworn into the Ninth: "A great day for all of us. Our spirits are high and we all look grand in our new gray uniforms. I was given a fine gray wool coat and pants with two cotton shirts. I am glad Captain Crutchfield told me to bring Pa's old rifle seein' as there are none of those fine muskets we have heard about for us . . . We are camped here (near Berea Church) for five days hoping to see some action but we drill and learn soldiering all day. There is a lot to learn and I am doing fine, our sergeant says, one day we may make passable soldiers."[15]

During this time the Ninth Virginia, a single regiment on paper, was in fact in two parts. Colonel Johnson with his part of the regiment was positioned north of Falmouth while Rooney had his part around Berea. It is not known exactly why this arrangement was made except that the relationship between Lee and Johnson was quite cool. Johnson was the only officer, either superior or subordinate, that Lee treated in this manner, and the odd balance of power lasted only a short while. It is also possible that this division of the regiment into two factions was ordered by General Charles W. Field, commander of the area, and had nothing to do with any strained relationship between Lee and Johnson.[16]

Around the middle of April Lee's command got a smell of gunpowder—the first for many of them. According to one trooper's report, Lee was out in a field to the east of the Berea Meeting House drilling a company when a picket rode up to him and reported "that the enemy were rapidly advancing and were nearly upon" the "Caroline Light Dragoons." Lee ordered them to proceed to their camp, which was "some several hundred yards up the road." There they were to break camp and move in an orderly fashion toward Fredericksburg and the rest of the Ninth. Before this could be accomplished the enemy came into view and began to fire into the camp. The Federal cavalry charged, and the last squadron to leave camp was "completely routed and squandered" with every man for himself the general rule. The men "in their flight . . . threw away their blankets, clothing, haversacks, and many of them their arms, and the wagons scattered the cooking utensils, rations and tents along the road." This stampede kept up "for at least two miles before Lee could get in front of the scattered troops, halt them and form a line." Meanwhile the Federals had stopped and Lee had time to throw up "a barricade across the road, which had fences on both sides." By now it was nightfall and the Confederates were reinforced by two infantry companies from the Fortieth Virginia, which had come from Fredericksburg. Lee positioned the infantry at the barricade with a company of cavalry on each side. In this position they waited until one o'clock. "The moon shone beautifully" when a lieutenant brought back the news that the Federals were getting ready to charge. The waiting troops were ordered to be quiet and steady and not to fire until the command was given. They "could see by the moonlight the flashing of drawn sabres." The Federals charged "right up to the barricade when the command 'fire' was given." After the initial barrage those who were able fled back up the road. "The road was filled with dead horses and men," but preparations for a second charge were being made. This charge met with the same fate as the first. Lee sent an officer to reconnoiter, and it was ascertained that the Federal cavalry was being reinforced by a large body of infantry. The barricade was abandoned, and Lee pulled back his forces. The next day the results were tallied: twenty-seven dead and a dozen wounded. Another trooper remembered it vividly as the first fight: "We had a nite shootout with some Federal horsemen just north of town. I hid behind a big stump and we all fired at once into them as they came into the clearing. This is the first I shot someone as I saw two of them fall and go down. They came back a while later and we shot at them again making them ride back in great haste. After they had gone I picked up a fine new rifle that loads from the back and a leather box full of bullets. This is finer than Pa's old rifle, shorter and easier to use ahorse." In a letter to Charlotte, Lee called the engagement a "brilliant fight" in which two charges of a "superior force" were driven back by his men. He also set the number killed at "some 30 of the enemy."[17]

In his official report Lee omitted the part about the "Dragoons" retreating in disorder at first. He reported that scouts had seen enemy cavalry approaching about 10 A.M. and that he had strengthened the picket line with the companies from Lunenburg and Lancaster Counties. "These companies held the enemy in check, retreating slowly, until 4 P.M.," he wrote. He set the Federal strength at a full regiment. The barricade was erected near Grove's Chapel about one mile from Falmouth with four companies from the Fortieth Virginia Infantry at the barricade with cavalry "on the right and left and in rear." About 1

A.M. Friday morning "the pickets reported the enemy coming down the Warrenton road at full gallop. We waited in silence until they came within 20 yards of the barricade, when the infantry poured a deadly fire into them and repulsed them. Within ten minutes they returned to the charge with a loud yell, and were again repulsed." Lee testified "with pride and gratification to the steady gallantry" of his men but acknowledged that the success was due mainly to the infantry reinforcements.[18]

The Union force consisted of four companies of the First Pennsylvania under Colonel George D. Bayard and seven companies of the Harris Light Cavalry (Second New York) under Lieutenant Colonel Judson Kilpatrick. Bayard reported that his men received a "galling fire" from the barricade and declared that he was facing "quite a heavy force." He stated his casualties at twenty-three men and many horses "in the trap which had been laid for us."[19]

The forward movement of the enemy forced the Confederates to withdraw from Falmouth and abandon the Northern Neck of Virginia. The bridges at Fredericksburg were burned after all had crossed to that side. A trooper remembered: "We were told to burn the bridge after crossin it so we soaked it with coal oil then set it alight. It sore die burn pretty." The Ninth was ordered "to remain and check any attempt of the enemy to extinguish the fire." Enemy artillery opened on them from a crest above Falmouth, wounding several men and killing a couple of horses. One unfortunate member of Company E accidentally killed himself at this time. They "stood without flinching, eliciting some praise from" their officers until the assignment was complete. Then they withdrew through Fredericksburg, where "all was hurry and confusion." Burning cotton and stores, fleeing inhabitants and other bodies of troops all added to this confusion. The rain fell in "copious showers" that night, and the troopers were without food and shelter. They were so exhausted, however, that they "gladly stretched themselves upon the earth and slept soundly." The next day they moved to Massaponax Church, then to Guiney's Station.[20]

On April 20, 1862, there was an election in the Ninth Virginia, and the regiment was reorganized. Throughout the Confederate Army it was usual for the privates to elect the company officers and the company officers in turn to elect the field officers. Obviously this procedure allowed men to become officers who were merely pandering to the wishes of others and who then turned out to be worthless in a role of leadership. Due partly to the large pool of officer material in the Confederate service, and also due partly to the good sense of the men who were voting, many excellent officers came to the front through this process. In the case of Rooney Lee, the "habit of command" that Henry Adams had despised at Harvard helped him to advance. From a modern perspective it is amazing that the one who had drilled them so mercilessly and demanded discipline and military bearing would be elected over one who had not. Still, Company C from Westmoreland County named themselves "Lee's Light Horse" in honor of Light Horse Harry Lee. So it is not surprising that they would want the grandson of the revered revolutionary hero to lead them into combat. A trooper from Company E summed up the election: "We elected Mister Lee as our Colonel today. He is a good man and knows what to do when it comes to fightin. Sargent Wright has been drilling us all afternoon and he has orders to keep it up until our new Colonel is satisfied that we know how to fight real good." The commission as colonel of the Ninth Virginia Cavalry was dated April 29, 1862. Lee was then twenty-four years old. His Lieutenant Colonel was R.L.T. Beale, a forty-three-year-old lawyer and congressman turned soldier.[21]

The Ninth Virginia was made up of ten companies, eight volunteer units, and two companies from militia groups. The majority were farmers, but some were professionals, businessmen, and students. Many were still carrying outdated guns and lacked uniforms and proper equipment for their horses. Stationed on the south side of the Rappahannock, they could see Yankees on the northern side near homes and loved ones. "The bitter thought of defenceless homes and helpless families brought more of sorrow than all the hardships of camp life and dangers of the field of battle" to the men. Sickness took its toll on many. Lee tried to make up for what his men lacked in material goods by steady drill for action to come. He found forage for the horses and held daily drills, dress-parades, and guard-mountings as well as routine picket duty. In spite of strict discipline, there were a few desertions. Near the end of May the regiment moved camp. They took the Telegraph Road and after three days' marching arrived at Yellow Tavern, about five miles from the Confederate capital of Richmond. Two days later they camped on the Brook Turnpike at Mordecai Farm. Private Charles R. Chewning noted the change in his diary: "We have been on picket duty for nearly a month now. We ride back and forth looking for Federals." Then on May 25, "We rode south in a great rush late last nite leaving patrol duties behind us. We are still in high spirits as we have been told there will be more action ahead." The regiment was at Ashland on May 26 and "rode hard for Slash Church" the next day but was ordered back before seeing any action. And still there was no action on May 31 as a great battle raged within earshot. Chewning continued: "We can hear a great battle to our front but no orders for us to join in. I never heart such a friteful racket all day and night. We all wish we could get in our licks but we just set and watch."[22]

The fighting they could hear was the battles of Fair Oaks and Seven Pines, in which General Joseph Johnston was wounded while trying to stop George McClellan's advance up the peninsula toward Richmond. On June 1 Robert Lee assumed command of the army around Richmond, an army that he would call the Army of Northern Virginia. A formidable task lay before Lee. McClellan's army was close enough to hear the church bells in Richmond, but his own army lacked cohesiveness and was doubtful about the new commander. He took time from his official cares to write Charlotte that he had been in Rooney's camp and that he was well. "You may have heard that a battle has been fought near Richmond, my darling Chass, and be uneasy about your husband. I write, therefore, to inform you that he is well. The cavalry was not engaged, and of course he was not exposed."[23]

On June 3 Rooney managed to write her a letter, which from him amounted to a lengthy epistle. He had time to write because he had been in Richmond since May 29, sick in bed at Dr. Conway's house. He had some type of food poisoning and had been "quite sick but expected to be able to return to camp in a day or two." He had been on a scout near Hickory Hill (her grandfather Wickham's home) during the battle of Hanover Court House (Slash Church). He wrote: "I made my way around and arrived on the hills back of H. Hill in time to see the enemy advancing up the lane. I rode to the house for a minute. Wms. was in bed, too sick to move. I saw the ladies. I heard that your grandpa was well." He passed on the news of the family. Custis was recovering from typhoid fever, Mary was in Richmond and had been by to see him twice, and various Custis relatives had taken part in the fighting. About his father taking command of the army, he wrote, "Pa has taken the field in person and we all expect has work this week" and "now that Pa has command I feel better satisfied." In fact, he thought, "Should victory be with us in this coming battle, I can see nothing to keep us out of Washington." He had heard some disturbing rumors from their home. The White House had been taken by McClellan as a supply depot for his campaign. Rumor had it that a man who had been left in charge there had been arrested for trying to communicate with Rooney, and the overseer had presumably been hung. He ended his letter by begging Charlotte: "You must make allowances for the paucity of my letters, my precious, as I am likely to have few opportunities of writing. You were always present in my thoughts, and I do long to see you. I suppose that boy, by this time, is a wonder-jackets & pants & walking. I suppose I will not recognize him. Kiss him for me every day & don't let him forget me . . . Good bye, my darling, may the Almighty protect us in this fearful struggle."[24]

The Peninsula Campaign was bringing the war to gigantic proportions with more men involved, more casualties, and less civility. It would not be long before the men of the Ninth and their colonel would see their share of action.

CHAPTER 5

"We're the boys who rode around McClellan"

Union commander George McClellan's huge army had moved up the peninsula of Virginia until it was within four miles of Richmond. Some of the Federals were close enough to hear the church bells of the Confederate capital. The position and strength of the left of this army, as well as the center, was well known to the Confederate commanders. But they did not know exactly how far the right extended or its strength. Furthermore, it was suspected that McClellan's entire army was being supplied by both railroad and wagon train from a supply base at Rooney's home, the White House. Its position on the Pamunkey, its existing wharves, and its proximity to the York River Railroad made it an ideal location for McClellan's main supply depot.

James Ewell Brown Stuart, better known as Jeb, had already made a personal excursion into this area and had also sent a scout named John Singleton Mosby into the Totopotomoy watershed to ascertain the positions and strengths of the Federals. Mosby learned that there was only a scattering of cavalry outposts in this region and that the supply line was virtually unguarded and open to attack. With Mosby's report in hand, Stuart rode to see his commanding general at headquarters. Stuart and Robert Lee met privately and devised a plan that would provide needed information about McClellan's right and possibly allow Stuart to wreck part of his line of communications and supply.[1]

For Stuart, the newly made brigadier general, this was his first major assignment. So that there would be no mistake in the plan and its purpose, Lee wrote out the orders himself. Stuart was to "make a scout movement to the rear of the enemy now posted on the Chickahominy, with a view of gaining intelligence of his operations, communications, etc." He was also to take the supplies he could carry and "destroy his wagon trains." Perhaps remembering Stuart's brashness as a student at West Point, Lee cautioned him "not to hazard unnecessarily your command."[2]

For the enterprise Stuart chose his ablest subordinates and best troopers. A force of 1,200 made up the raiding party. Colonel Fitzhugh Lee commanded the contingent from the First Virginia. Colonel Rooney Lee led the best of his Ninth Virginia. The Fourth Virginia was split between these two, as its commander, Colonel Williams Wickham, was sidelined with a recent saber wound. Lieutenant Colonel Jeff Martin commanded the Mississippians of the Jeff Davis Legion. Two pieces of the Stuart Horse Artillery under Lieutenant James Breathed also accompanied the cavalry.[3]

The news electrified the troops. "All were enthusiastic for action. The order to prepare rations was received with joy, and executed promptly." There was a good deal of "commotion in the camp" of the Ninth as haversacks were filled and ammunition distributed. No one, not even the officers, knew their destination, yet all were eager to go.[4]

At 2 A.M. on June 12 Stuart gave the command, "Gentlemen, in ten minutes every man must be in his saddle." Then he rode north up the Brook Turnpike and the line formed behind, each unit falling in as he went. Most of the troopers thought that they were going to the Shenandoah Valley to help Stonewall Jackson. As if to confirm this notion for any watching Union spies, Stuart moved off the turnpike and traveled northwest for a few miles, then turned back northeast and again to the north. Just south of the South Anna River the column turned to the east and finally went into camp on the Winston farm near Taylorsville. They had ridden a total of twenty-two miles the first day.[5]

Sometime after midnight Rooney accompanied Stuart to pay a courtesy call on the wounded Colonel Wickham at Hickory Hill. While Rooney socialized with his in-laws, Stuart napped in a chair; they returned to the camp after an early breakfast.[6]

Before dawn "several rockets were shot . . . making a whizzing noise and bursting into fiery flashes above the treetops." At this signal

the men and horses ate their breakfast and then, without bugles, resumed the march east toward Hanover Court House. One of Rooney
Lee's troopers thought that the raiding party was "a grand sight." As
for their position in the lead, he wrote, "Our regiment is given a great
honor as we ride in the lead. If there are any Federals we can get at
them first."[7]

At this point Stuart finally confided his plan to his colonels "so as
to secure an intelligent action and cooperation in whatever might oc-
cur." His scouts had returned with the news that there were no "serious obstacles" between his force and Old Church. When the column
reached Hanover Court House, it found Federal cavalry in position.
Stuart sent Fitz Lee with the First Virginia on a detour around the
Federals in order to come up on their rear and catch them between
the two parts of Stuart's command. Fitz ran into some swampy land
that prevented him from getting into position before Stuart advanced
on the Federals. The Federal force, approximately 150 troopers of the
Sixth U.S. Cavalry, escaped in the direction of Mechanicsville.[8]

The Ninth Virginia led the column towards Hawe's Shop with an
advance guard well out in front. Lieutenant W.T. Robins, the adjutant
of the Ninth, commanded the advance guard. As the Confederates
neared the Totopotomoy, Federal cavalry pickets that had been stationed there broke and ran for the single small bridge that crossed the
stream. The bridge was too narrow for all to cross at once, and many
were captured by the Confederates.[9]

A squadron of the Ninth under Captain William Latane immediately crossed the bridge and sped up the hill on the other side where a
portion of the Fifth U.S. Cavalry had regrouped to meet the charge.
One witness remembered: "Swords clashed, pistols and carbines
banged, yells, shouts, cheers resounded; then the Federal line was seen
to give back, and take to headlong flight. They were pursued with ardour, and the men were wild with this—to many of them—their first
fight." Captain William Latane engaged in hand-to-hand combat with
the commander of the Yankee squadron. Latane severely wounded the
Federal captain with a slash of his saber, but Union Captain W.B.
Royall killed Latane with a pistol shot. He was the only Confederate
who died during the entire raid. Latane's body was carried by some of
his men to a nearby farmhouse, where he was buried by the ladies and
slaves there. In his official report, Rooney Lee mentioned four privates
wounded in addition to the loss of Latane. Of the fight at Hawe's
Shop, he reported that his men "had a hand-to-hand conflict, and my

officers and men behaved with the greatest daring and bravery." He set the number of enemy killed at five and wrote that many were captured. He estimated the actual number of killed and wounded as probably higher, as many were killed in the nearby woods and many wounded escaped.[10]

A member of the Ninth recorded the day's events: "We made our first great charge here today. We formed up in the wood and charged across a large field. You should have seen them Federals run for home and mother. After the fight I took a fine pistol off a dead officer. He had a belt with a lot of small leather boxes full of caps and bullets and even one with a small powder flask. From a dead horse I got a nice blanket and saddlebags, now I can throw away my old ripped quilt and sleep warm these chill nites." Many of the troopers outfitted themselves as they went.[11]

In the advance toward Old Church, the First Virginia replaced the Ninth as the lead regiment. The Fifth U.S., a reorganized version of Fitz Lee's old unit, the Second Cavalry, had its camp at Old Church. Many Federals fled; several were captured by their former lieutenant. The Confederate troopers found "large supplies of boots, pistols, liquors and other commodities," which they "speedily appropriated." They burned everything they could not carry. The troopers hastily finished their plundering after hearing a report that there was gunpowder in one of the burning tents.[12]

At Old Church Stuart had to make a momentous decision: whether to return to Hanover Court House or to advance to Tunstall's and continue on a circuit around McClellan's entire army. He conferred briefly with the two Lees. Mosby overheard their discussion and noted that Rooney agreed with Stuart to go forward, whereas Fitz was in favor of going back the way they had come. By Stuart's reckoning it was fourteen miles back to Hanover Court House, where a pursuing Federal force was probably gathering. If they were forced to turn north, the South Anna River was impassable and would hem him in. But Tunstall's Station was only nine miles away. There Stuart could strike a real blow against McClellan's supply line and confuse the Union commander as to the actual purpose of his raid. This was the path least expected by the enemy, and Stuart felt certain that the Chickahominy was fordable and the path open in that direction. Stuart summed up his decision in his official report: "With an abiding trust in God, and with such guaranties of success as the two Lees and Martin and their devoted followers, this enterprise I regarded as most promising." He continued, "There was something of the sublime in the implicit confidence and unquestioning trust of the rank and file." Leaving Fitz to finish up at Old Church, Stuart moved on with the bulk of the raiding party.[13]

The Confederate column was now moving through a region that had been held by the Federals for some time. Consequently the civilians were overjoyed upon seeing the rebel horsemen. All along the way ladies were "rushing to the doors and windows and porches clapping their hands and waving their handkerchiefs in an ecstasy of patriotic joy." Some brought food for the hungry troopers, and others presented Stuart and his officers with bouquets of flowers.[14]

Stuart could only guess at the Federal pursuit being formed in his wake. Reports from those who had seen the column were grossly exaggerated. One lieutenant who had escaped from the Latane-Royall confrontation reported a large cavalry force with infantry to back it up. The Federal estimates of infantry alone ranged up to five regiments. General Philip St. George Cooke, Stuart's father-in-law, commanded the pursuing force. He was ordered to use caution and not to attack the supposed "superior forces of the enemy" with just his cavalry. Elements of the Fifth and Sixth U.S. Cavalries and the Fifth Pennsylvania Cavalry joined with a brigade of infantry commanded by Colonel Gouverneur K. Warren to try to catch up with Stuart. The pace of the pursuit was determined by the infantry, so the rebel cavalry could take their time and still stay ahead of Cooke and his men. Also, the Federals lacked the excellent scouts that Stuart had brought along.[15]

Stuart's brother-in-law, John Esten Cooke, remembered this ride to Tunstall's as "the gayest portion of the raid. From this moment it was neck or nothing, do or die." The Rebels were taking prisoners, confiscating anything they could use and burning all the rest. One ordnance wagon with its load of Colt revolvers was especially welcome to the men with substandard weapons. Others were delighted to find a wagon filled with champagne that some Union general would never enjoy.[16]

Before reaching Tunstall's, a force of the Ninth Virginia was sent to Garlick's Landing on the Pamunkey where the masts of two schooners could be seen. They found the vessels and many nearby wagons full of supplies for McClellan's army. All went up in flames.[17]

The advance guard of the Ninth Virginia, under Lieutenant Robins, led the way to Tunstall's Station. Suddenly at a bend in the road they met a force of Yankee cavalry. The Federals halted and drew sabers as if to charge. The advance guard also drew sabers, and the two units "stood, eyeing each other, about two hundred yards apart." When the rest of the Ninth came into view, the Federals beat a hasty retreat toward the White House. A messenger sent to warn those at the station "galloped through Tunstall's but never stopped, and when someone called to him, 'What's to pay?' he dashed along, calling out at the top of his voice, 'Hell's to pay!'"

They charged into the station with a fierce rebel yell. The Yankees scattered, and many were taken prisoner. One captain surrendered his whole company. The telegraph lines were quickly cut, and trees were felled to obstruct the railroad. Before they could adequately block the tracks, a train was heard as it approached the station. When the engineer saw the obstructions on the track and the Confederate troopers at the station, he bravely put on steam to force his way through. The train crashed through the makeshift barricade and sped on toward the White House. One of Stuart's scouts rode alongside the train and shot the engineer. Others fired at the Union soldiers crouching on the flatbed cars as they went by. Some were killed while others jumped off the train and were taken prisoner.[18]

McClellan's main supply base at the White House was a real temptation to Stuart, but he decided to go on. After all, there were plenty of wagons filled with materiel in the vicinity of Tunstall's to burn. One officer estimated that a field of thirty acres was filled with burning wagons. He wrote: "The roar of the soaring flames was like the sound of a forest on fire. How they roared and crackled!" Rooney also thought about how close he was to his home and how easy it would be to ride over and take a look. But duty came first, and the column moved on. Actually there was a force of six hundred at the landing backed up by gunboats on the river. So Stuart's rare show of prudence proved to be a wise move.[19]

The Ninth led the way to Talleysville, about four miles distant. The scouts were men who lived in the area and knew the land perfectly. Still, as they moved out in the dark, there was a tense moment when Stuart temporarily lost track of Rooney and his men. John Esten Cooke described what happened:

Meanwhile the main column had moved on and I was riding after it, when I heard the voice of Stuart in the darkness exclaiming with strange agitation:

"Who is here?"

"I am," I answered; and as he recognized my voice he exclaimed:

"Good! Where is Rooney Lee?"

"I think he has moved on, General."

"Do you know it?" came in the same agitated tone.

"No, but I believe it."

"Will you swear to it? I must know! He may take the wrong road, and the column will get separated!"

"I will ascertain if he is in front."

"Well, do so, but take care—you will be captured!" I told the General I would 'gallop on for ever till I found him,' but I had not gone two hundred yards in the darkness when hoof-strokes in front were heard, and I ordered:

"Halt! Who goes there?"

"Courier, from Colonel William Lee."

"Is he in front?"

"About a mile, sir."

"Good!" exclaimed the voice of Stuart, who had galloped up; "and I never heard in human accents such an expression of relief."[20]

Stuart's men passed by a large Union hospital and left it alone. They halted at Talleysville, a collection of three or four houses, and rested momentarily. Sutlers' wagons were not as fortunate as hospitals and were considered fair game for the exhausted and hungry troopers. The advance guard became "new men" after consuming "crackers, cheese, canned fruits, sardines and many other dainties dear to the cavalryman." One noted that they "helped themselves to such refreshments as the sutler had provided for his customers, without the usual ceremony of giving something in exchange." Such delicacies as "figs, beef-tongue, pickle, candy, tomato catsup, preserves, lemons, cakes, sausages, molasses, crackers and canned meats" delighted men who were used to fatback and cornbread when the Confederate commissary was having a good day. A New York reporter hidden in the bushes heard Stuart's men go by yelling "like a war party of Comanches." John Mosby considered it all "a carnival of fun."[21]

After an hour's rest and revelry the troopers moved on. They were exhausted, and many slept in the saddle. Those in the advance guard had to stay alert, however. One of these men remembered: "A beautiful full moon lighted our way and cast weird shadows across our path.

Expecting each moment to meet the enemy, every bush in the distance looked like a sentinel, and every jagged tree bending over the road like a vidette."[22]

At dawn the next morning Rooney Lee and the Ninth reached a little-known ford of the Chickahominy River. Lieutenant Christian had guided the column to this crossing on his family's Sycamore Springs plantation. Always before it had been "a safe, or at least a practicable, passage of the river." Recent rains had changed it into a torrent. The river was out of its banks, which made the tree trunks lining the banks an unseen labyrinth of treacherous traps. To make matters worse the desired exit from the rushing current was higher upriver than the point of entrance; so anyone trying to cross would have to swim upstream against the current. With the Yankees expected at any minute, it was a tense moment for all. Rooney wasted little time. He "determined on crossing the Chickahominy at this point at the peril of his life. After making a careful survey of the river and sounding the ford, he, with others, plunged into the flood with the heads of their horses turned upstream." In spite of being an expert swimmer, it was a struggle to reach the opposite bank. Some of the horses became ensnarled in the tangled roots and debris and were freed only with difficulty. Rooney did not want to be separated from his men, so he swam back across the flooded river. Most of the others apparently remained on the safe side. One trooper, who had left his horse on the other bank, swam back also. Much to his surprise his horse decided to join him. At midstream he heard its "heavy breathing" and "the sound of its feet like paddles in water." When he glanced back the horse was following him "like a dog" and dangerously close with his paddling hooves.[23]

John Esten Cooke found Rooney "cool and resolute" on the bank after swimming back. He asked: "What do you think of the situation, Colonel? 'Well, Captain,' was the reply, in the speaker's habitual tone of cheerful courtesy, 'I think we are caught.'"[24]

Other attempts to cross were made. First they cut down two pine trees, hoping that they would reach the opposite bank and form the basis for a foot bridge. But the trees were too short and were borne away by the current. Next a "long line made of bridle reins and halters tied together" was fastened from one side to the other, and a makeshift raft was thrown together. It was large enough to carry a dozen men with their equipment, but it nearly sank on the first try; the equipment was swept downstream.[25]

Stuart had come up by this time, and Rooney informed him that the ford was impassable. Stuart decided to move to the remains of Forge Bridge, about a mile downriver. There he placed his guns and threw out a rear guard to watch for Yankees. The Confederates' only chance of escape lay in rebuilding this bridge. Only the stone abutments remained. They found a skiff, which was placed midstream, and built a flimsy footbridge across. This enabled men to cross while carrying their equipment, the horses swimming across. But the guns were too heavy for this rude bridge. The troopers turned engineers and dismantled a large warehouse near the bridge. The main timbers were just long enough to reach from the bank to the abutments and from one abutment to the other. The planks from the warehouse provided the footing for the bridge, and soon it was strong enough for the men to ride the remaining horses over and for the two pieces of artillery to cross. The whole bridge-building venture took only three hours, and by one o'clock that afternoon the entire command was over. The Yankee pursuit finally caught up as the bridge went up in flames.[26]

The bridge had allowed them to cross the deep channel of the Chickahominy to an island in the stream. On the other side of the island the river was only a swamp full of trees. The water came up above the saddles. The guns were almost completely beneath the water, only the tops of the caissons showing. At this point the pole of one of the limbers was broken, and it had to be abandoned. The Union prisoners were riding double on the captured mules and had a rough time crossing the swamp. One, thinking the swamp interminable, swore, "How many d—d chicken-hominies are there, I wonder, in this infernal country?"[27]

Once out of the swamp the direction was toward the Charles City Court House. The raiders were still about thirty-five miles from Richmond and behind enemy lines. Once at the Court House, they rested briefly on the Wilcox farm. There they fed the horses and themselves and rested a while. Stuart turned over the command to Fitz Lee and rode on to General Lee with the information he needed. The rest of the column headed toward Richmond about 11:00 P.M. The men were silent as they rode. They knew they were still in enemy territory and did not want to attract attention. Besides, after three days of riding and little sleep, many were in a state of "drowsy unconsciousness as their weary horses bore them along." This night march was "by far the most taxing and exhaustive."[28]

Back in camp one of Rooney Lee's troopers described the last three days: "We are finally back very tired, sore, and hungry. We fought the Federals at three places and thrashed them soundly each time. We came back with full bags of good eats and a lot of badly needed equipment. Some of the boys found a Federal supply post and brought off all they could carry . . . We rested all day (the seventeenth) and sorted out our share of the booty, we are now ready for anything the Federals care to throw at us. I have a new pair of high boots, they are a little big but my old shoes had more holes than not." Like the others, he was replenished and confident in their ability to fight.[29]

The results of this raid were numerous. The tangible results—the captured weapons, horses, and mules—were speedily distributed throughout Stuart's command. The destruction and capture of materiel and the burning of one railroad bridge was a great loss to the Union Army, but in light of McClellan's enormous stockpile such a loss was not irreparable. The greatest results were intangible. As for the Southerners, morale among Stuart's cavalry and the entire army was lifted. After this exploit the men had explicit confidence in Stuart and the other officers who had performed so capably. This first raid set the scene for many others to come, but at the time it was accomplished it was unique in the annals of war. A Frenchman on McClellan's staff summed it up well: "They had, in point of fact, committed but few depredations, but had caused a great commotion, shaken the confidence of the North in McClellan, and made the first experiment in those great cavalry expeditions which subsequently played so novel and so important a part during the war." Stuart had humiliated McClellan, whether or not McClellan would admit it or even realized what had happened. The most important result of the raid was the information that Stuart furnished Lee on the position of McClellan's right. It was indeed vulnerable to attack. Consequently Lee sent for Jackson to come from the Shenandoah Valley and join him before Richmond for the attack that was to drive McClellan from the capital.[30]

In his official report Stuart praised his regimental commanders. He wrote that they "exhibited the characteristics of skillful commanders, keeping their commands well in hand and managing them with skill and good judgment, which proved them worthy of higher trust." He also hoped that General Lee's "sense of delicacy" would not cause him to "award to the two Lees (your son and nephew) less than their full measure of praise." (This plea fell on deaf ears, as the commanding general was careful not to mention either Fitz or Rooney in his

congratulatory general orders.) Stuart's praise of the two Lees continued: "Embalmed in the hearts and affections of their regiments; tried
on many occasions requiring coolness, decision, and bravery; everywhere present to animate, direct, and control, they held their regiments in their grasps and proved themselves brilliant cavalry leaders."
In a supplement to his official report, Stuart recommended both Fitz
and Rooney for brigade command. "Col. W. H. F. Lee, rivaling his
cousin in the daring exploits of this expedition, established a like
claim to promotion." Rooney's own report was a much shorter and
concise version of Stuart's, in which he praised his men for their bravery, in particular his adjutant, W. T. Robins. [31]

On June 22 Robert Lee took time from his preparations to attack
McClellan in order to answer a letter from Charlotte. He knew well
how lax Rooney could be about writing and did not want her to
worry about him unduly. Lee did tell her that Rooney had made "a
hazardous scout." He sent her an account of the raid and a copy of
Stuart's general orders to show her that "he conducted himself well."
He also wrote, "The General deals in the flowering style, . . . but he is
a good soldier, and speaks highly of the conduct of the two Lees, who,
as far as I can learn, deserve his encomiums." Lee ended his letter by
saying that he had recently seen Rooney "looking very well in a new
suit of gray" and sent a kiss to his grandson.[32]

Three days later Rooney wrote her himself, excusing his tardiness
by saying that he did not know exactly where she was. This was in
part true, because Charlotte and their son had been refugees since
leaving the White House. They visited with relatives and moved frequently. He told her that the battle was about to commence and that
"our army is in fine spirits and very confident of success." He assured
her that his health had been excellent since his "slight attack" a
month earlier. It seems that Rooney tried to spare Charlotte any grim
details in telling her the story of the raid. He began with "your husband has been on quite a little trip around McClellan's army." He laid
out the route by mentioning the homes of relatives and friends rather
than strategic sites. On his social visit to Hickory Hill the first night
of the raid, he arrived so late that he "woke them up after they had all
gone to bed." He relayed as much news of family and friends as he
did of military matters, although he did acknowledge that he had
charged with one of his squadrons "a very strong position." "After 5
minutes hard fighting, hand to hand, we completely put them to
flight," he continued. In summation he wrote, in characteristically

modest fashion, "Our trip was very successful & I suppose you have seen by the papers of the '9th' distinguishing itself." In closing he wrote: "I must now bid you 'good bye' my darling & have not said half that I desire to say, but I am just ordered to mount. May our Heavenly Father have us in his holy keeping. Kiss my darling boy for me & don't let him forget his Pa."[33]

At the time he wrote this letter the Ninth was camped at Mordecai's on the Brooke Turnpike. The orders to mount came after haversacks and cartridge boxes were filled and everything was ready. The new battle flag of the Ninth fluttered at its head as the column rode to Ashland by way of Yellow Tavern. On the way they passed the famous Stonewall Jackson, fresh from his victories in the Valley. One trooper found him "not imposing or graceful in the saddle," but his countenance indicated he "was intent on grave and momentous matters." They also rode by the camps of Jackson's men before bivouacking for the night near Ashland.[34]

Stuart had with him four other regiments besides Rooney Lee and the Ninth. The others included the First Virginia, the Fourth Virginia, the Cobb Legion of Georgia, and the Jeff Davis Legion. The Stuart Horse Artillery also accompanied the cavalrymen. His orders were to cover Jackson's flank on the extreme left of Lee's army in a concerted attack against McClellan's exposed right under Fitz John Porter.

On June 26 the cavalry mounted and moved out in advance of Jackson's men. When they reached the bridge over Totopotomoy Creek they found that it was impaired and there was an enemy force on the other side. The threat of artillery caused the Federals to retreat, and the bridge was quickly repaired. Felled trees also impeded their progress at times. They could hear artillery and small arms fire on their right during the afternoon. That night they slept with "bridles in hand" near the Pole Green Church.[35]

The Ninth resumed the march early the next morning and had reached the vicinity of Old Cold Harbor by afternoon. The progress of the cavalry was slow because they had to keep in touch with Jackson's infantry while scouting ahead and screening. On this day also Jackson was uncharacteristically slow and did not engage in battle as he should have. The men of the Ninth could plainly hear the sound of battle to their left. "The cannon fire became louder and more rapid," indicating that a great battle was in progress. For several hours the musket fire was "terrific in the rapidity and volume of its discharges." The rebel yell could plainly be heard, however, when the Confederates charged. The horse artillery opened on a road used by retreating Federals, and some answering "solid shot whizzed over the heads of the cavalrymen." The lessening roar of battle indicated that the Federals were retreating, and Stuart ordered his men to advance through part of the battlefield. The carnage left lasting impressions on the troopers. One remembered seeing a headless artilleryman, then a few paces farther, "a head entangled by his hair and heavy beard in the branches of a locust." They also passed a Federal hospital where "the smell of human blood grew dense and sickening." There were "wagons filled with hands, feet, arms and legs, and surgeons still busy with their amputating instruments." The Ninth slept on the battlefield's edge that night.[36]

At this point General Robert Lee was not sure of the direction of McClellan's army. McClellan's supply base was still at the White House on the Pamunkey, and there had been daily shipments of tons of supplies from this base via railroad to the Union Army of the Potomac. He decided to send Stuart to cut or destroy the line of communications and supply. This would force McClellan to retreat or fight without his daily means of supply.[37]

The White House, Rooney and Charlotte's home, just happened to be a strategic site in this war. To them it was the happy home of their short married life before the war and the place where their first child was born. Rooney had worked hard on improving the White House from its former neglected state under Mr. Custis's overseers. He had succeeded in turning it into a prosperous, flourishing farm by his own time and hard work. Certainly he felt justifiable pride in what he had already accomplished and had great plans for its continued improvement. Furthermore it had tremendous family importance. It had come to Rooney through the Custis family, and it had been the home of the widow Martha Custis before her marriage to George Washington. They also had lived at the White House on the Pamunkey when first married. There were existing wharves on the river and a railroad line only a short distance away, both of which aided a farmer in getting his crops to market. Unfortunately it was also an excellent location for receiving and dispensing war materiel to an invading army. McClellan realized its strategic importance and made it his base of supply for his campaign against Richmond.

One of the early arrivals at the White House thought it "must have been a very pretty place—a green lawn sloping to the river with trees." One Yankee found the Lee property "much the finest tract of land" he

had seen in Virginia and was in favor of "confiscating all their property and hanging them besides." A Federal officer found the house
"neat, comfortable and unpretending, with a verandah along the river
front, shaded by a beautiful grove." He also saw a "luxuriant growth
of a wheatfield of 100 acres," which was destroyed in a day by grazing horses and cattle. Inside the house he found that "it was richly
furnished, and many fine books were on the tables & in cases, and
some valuable paintings of the Custis family were in an upper room.
Ladies apparel lay just where taken off, as if the owner had left in
haste." Actually Mary and Charlotte Lee did leave in a hurry with
little time to pack or store valuables. Mary had tacked a note to the
front door: "Northern soldiers who profess to reverence Washington,
forbear to desecrate the home of his first married life—the property of
his wife, now owned by her descendants—A Grand-daughter of Mrs.
Washington." McClellan had placed a guard on the house, but still,
valuable items were stolen and the grounds were ruined.[38]

"The Lee house," according to another early visitor, was "a small,
neat cottage of modern style, with gothic windows, pointed gables,
and little balustrades, stood at the upper end of the ridge, overlooking
the river, and was surrounded by a green lawn in which there were a
few shade trees. A gravelled walk led to the front entrance. The
grounds were small, but laid out with considerable taste. Indeed,
everything about the cottage was neat and plain. There were also
flower and vegetable gardens near by, both under good cultivation. . . .
Then there were extensive fodder yards, barns and cribs, filled to their
utmost capacity with wheat, corn and other cereals. Below these there
was quite a village of negro cabins, stretching along the ridge and divided up into classes, with streets running between. The many colored
occupants of these cabins seemed well provided for and contented." In
two weeks time it was "transformed into a city of tents" of sutlers,
hospitals, storage, and correspondents. The wharves had also been expanded enormously, and a small navy of ships bustled into the area.
Wagons, artillery, and supplies were everywhere.[39]

On the morning of June 28 Lee ordered Stuart to attack McClellan's line of communications and supply. It was a march of approximately fifteen miles to the White House. Because McClellan's army
was actually withdrawing toward the James River and abandoning
the White House as a base of supply, the cavalry met only small scouting parties, which they dealt with quickly. Upon reaching the White
House they found infantry and gunboats still there. At Stuart's ap-

proach the Federals began to destroy everything they could to prevent
their capture. "After nightfall great columns of smoke and a bright il-
lumination announced that they were setting fire to the great town of
canvas and board houses that had sprung up at the place," one staff
member recorded. The fire continued all night, "and the country for
miles around was as light as day." The smoke and exploding shells
made the place resemble a battlefield. One can only guess what was
going through Rooney's mind as he watched the conflagration.[40]

The Federal preparations to evacuate had begun the day before. In
expectation of an attack (presumably by Jackson) the trees were cut
down, "even the grove in front of the White House." This was done
so that the range of the gunboats would be clear. Supplies were hus-
tled onto transports and sent down the river. On June 28, they received orders to stop sending supplies by train, as the railroad line had
been cut. When a telegraph operator received the message, "Go to
H—l, you d—d Yankees, we will be there in 20 minutes," he rushed
to headquarters "with his hair almost on end." The Federals soon began the destruction of the depot. They piled up commissary supplies,
covered them with hay doused with whiskey, and set a match to the
heap. Barges loaded with ammunition were fired, and locomotives
were destroyed. The sutlers' stores were burned. As the last troops departed, the White House itself went up in flames. One observer noted
that "many rejoiced at its burning." The house was burned by some
incendiary, probably a private of the Ninety-Third New York Volunteers, although in a regimental history the arsonists were named as
two captains and a sergeant. Many articles were stolen before the fire,
including books, a leather-covered box, and even the family bible.

One book was the only item ever returned to Rooney, and that was
four years after the war. He wrote to the Union officer who sent back
the memento: "I am very much obliged to you for sending it, as it is
the only relic of the past which has been restored to me. My house
and all it contained was entirely destroyed. Please accept my acknowl-
edgements for your consideration."[41]

"Before they left they burnt Colonel Lee's fine house to the ground
along with all the outbuildings. I do not know why they would do
such a terrible thing, Colonel Lee is a very fine man and comes from a
well respected family," one incredulous trooper confided in his diary.
Later in the war the destruction of private property became commonplace, but in 1862 the burning of the White House was a singular
event.[42]

Rooney's regiment moved in to take possession of the grounds early the next morning. There was still one gunboat threatening from the river, but it moved downriver after a short skirmish with Stuart's artillery. The destruction of supplies had been hurried, and some things were missed. Even the leftovers were unheard-of luxuries for the Confederates. They found all kinds of exquisite edibles and "liquors of every description." Roasted eggs, lemonade, canned meats, and cakes were washed down by various liquid refreshments. Before Rooney realized there was liquor everywhere, some of his men were drunk and had their own private stocks of liquor secreted away. To inspect each man and confiscate the liquor would have been a tedious, if not impossible, task. Always cool, Rooney thought quickly. A staff member recorded the scene: "Colonel Lee caused a report to be started that the enemy had poisoned all the liquor, leaving it there for us as a trap, and that one man had just died in great agony from the effects. As the report extended along the column, bottles of champagne and beer and whiskey went sailing through the air, exploding as they fell like little bomb-shells; while the expression of agony on the tipsy faces of those who had indulged too freely, as they held their hands to their stomachs, was ludicrous in the extreme." Sobriety and order were soon restored. The men of the regiment also found tremendous piles of carbines that had been thrown into the river.

The next morning the regiment moved down to the Forge Bridge on the Chickahominy. Federal infantry backed up by artillery waited on the other side of the river. John Pelham's artillery soon dispersed them. The regiment did not cross the river that day, but at night a squadron was sent across to reconnoiter. The next morning they moved twelve miles upriver to Bottom's Bridge, where they heard a rumor that McClellan's surrender was imminent. Upon reaching their destination they were ordered back to Forge Bridge. This time they crossed the river and marched to Malvern Hill, where they bivouacked for the night. Again they missed the fighting.[43]

The regiment stayed in the vicinity of Malvern Hill for about two weeks. Their duty consisted mainly of picketing and scouting while McClellan's huge army retreated to the James and withdrew. On July 10 they moved to a camp near Atlee's Station, where they remained for several weeks.[44]

As they were breaking camp at Malvern Hill, Rooney received two letters simultaneously from Charlotte. The news contained in them was devastating to a young father. Their young son, Robert Edward Lee III, had died on June 30 and was buried on July 5. The funeral service for the baby was held at St. Paul's Episcopal Church in Richmond, and the interment was in a plot belonging to the Wickham family in Shockoe Hill Cemetery. As soon as he could, Rooney wrote to Charlotte to express his overwhelming grief:

My precious baby—how his Pa mourns his loss!! I had no news of his being sick. I would, my darling, that I could be with you to share your grief!

As you say, it is God's will & I rejoice that "my boy" is happy in the arms of his Saviour. That he has been spared the trials, temptations & sorrows of this wicked world. I feel too that it is a just punishment for my many & daily sins. That is a thought which weighs heavily on my heart. It almost makes me feel that I am the murderer of my boy—

How I loved him! How I looked forward to see him walking and talking.

We must never forget him. Nothing can fill, in my heart, the place made vacant by his death. I loved my first born, as I can love no other. My hopes, pride were centered in him.

But it has pleased our Heavenly Father, with all our other afflictions, to visit us with this & we must bow to his will.

You must not let it bear too heavily upon you, my darling, especially in your present situation. Think of him as a bright Cherubim in the skies above.

Recollect that you are everything to your husband & you must take good care of your health for his sake.

Thanks to Almighty God, I have been brought in safety through the dangers of this last week.

Our house is in ashes & the whole plantation a wilderness. Hardly a servant left, I will write you more in time. My heart is heavy now.

He closed by expressing a desire for her to come stay with him for a while, as long as she did not run any risks to her health. (She was by this time four or five months' pregnant with their second child.) Their grief produced a great need to be together to help each other through this loss. Rooney had a deep abiding faith in God that helped carry him through this time of trial and others to come. He could mourn his loss but would always accept divine will. His feelings of guilt were natural, as all parents who experience such a loss feel that they are in some way to blame. In Rooney's case, his decision to go with his native state had caused him to lose his home and forced his wife and son to have to move from place to place. The ever-present *What if?* must have cut him deeply. If Charlotte and the baby had been able to remain at home, the youngster might not have contracted the illness that caused his death. Also, in the daily slaughter of mankind that war is, might not a vengeful God exact retribution? One can only guess at his thoughts, but his prayer was, "I hope that this summer will bring us peace."[45]

Almost as soon as he sent the letter to Charlotte he decided that he had to see her so that they could share their grief. Leaving his men at Atlee's, he rode into Richmond and arrived at his mother's house about 10 P.M. that night only to find that Charlotte had returned to Hickory Hill. Mary Lee wrote to her daughter-in-law that he was "much sun-burned but well & unhurt" and "very sad." The government had just placed a ban on moving coffins by railroad, and she was "rejoiced that our baby got here & is laid by his ancestors." She herself still mourned, "I cannot tell you how I still long to clasp him in my arms." She could not bear to think of "the scene of desolation at the White House." Mary also forwarded condolences from her husband. "I know what a void it will occasion in your hearts but when I reflect on his great pain we ought to rejoice. God grant that we may all join him around the throne of our Maker to unite in praise & admiration of the most High."[46]

By July 17 Charlotte was back in Richmond, but Mary Lee's rooms were so crowded that Charlotte had to look for other lodging. As soon as she arrived, Custis sent a note to Robert Lee, who in turn sent word to Rooney. This time he got to see her when he came to Richmond. For a short while military matters were quiet enough to spare some time for personal considerations.[47]

CHAPTER 6

"Follow the feather of Stuart"

Following the Peninsula Campaign there was a brief respite that one trooper described as "six weeks of the bright side of a soldier's life." There were drills and reviews that the ladies in the area attended. Some of the officers' wives took advantage of this peaceful time to visit their husbands. Charlotte traveled to her grandfather's house, Hickory Hill, near Hanover Court House to be with Rooney. Robert Lee wrote to his daughter-in-law, "I hope, too, Fitzhugh will be able to see a good deal of you, for I know he has been very anxious to be with you—has written to you several times in his mind if he has not been able to put his thoughts on paper—but the courier could not carry them." Mary Lee also visited for a time at Hickory Hill and reported to her daughters: "All Stuart's cavalry have been & are now stationed at Hanover C. House so we have had a great many visits. They have all gone this morning on a scout in the direction of Fredericksburg. Rooney had been here for two days. He is much sun burnt but looks well & in good spirits."[1]

There was a reorganization of the cavalry on July 28, 1862, in which Stuart became a major general in command of a division. Fitz Lee was promoted to brigadier general, and his command consisted of five regiments of Virginia cavalry—the First, Third, Fourth, Fifth, and Ninth. Rooney continued as colonel of the Ninth Cavalry, even though Stuart had asked for a promotion to brigade command for him as well as Fitz. Wade Hampton was named to command another brigade that included the First North Carolina Cavalry, the Cobb Legion, the Jeff Davis Legion, the Hampton Legion, and the Tenth Virginia Cavalry. A third brigade commanded by Beverly Robertson soon augmented Stuart's division.[2]

During this time there were drills daily in the camp of the Ninth. One particularly good musician in the regiment was ordered to familiarize all the buglers and men with the different bugle calls. One cavalryman thought the drills to be more than he could stand: "Would to God it was over . . . it certainly is a miserable life for a man to lead." Another trooper had more pleasant memories of this time. "We drill and parade but our camp is very nice beside a clear stream full of fat brown trout. There is plenty of big shade trees to be under when we come in tired and hungry." The drills may have been tedious and tiring, but the colonel of the Ninth knew that this was the only way to have a smoothly operating unit in battle. Attention to detail in instruction could lead to fewer losses and more effective firepower later on.

The "scout" toward Fredericksburg that Mary Lee mentioned began on August 4, 1862. The Ninth led Stuart's column as he went after some Yankee cavalry bent on destroying railroads. He found two brigades of infantry and attacked the rear guard. After bagging eighty-five prisoners and part of a wagon train, Stuart retired and returned to his camp.[3]

Even as McClellan was leaving the peninsula, a new threat was forming to the north. The Union Army of Virginia had a new commander, John Pope. One positive move that Pope made was to reorganize the cavalry at his disposal into three brigades. These he assigned to the individual corps of his army. Stuart's cavalry, by contrast, was more of a cohesive unit under one command.[4]

Pope's personality was an affront to Southerners. A braggart, he ordered his army to live off the land and carried war to the civilian population in a manner not yet seen. Even Robert Lee termed him a "miscreant" who should be "suppressed." Lee's army moved north to do just that.[5]

The Ninth headed out on August 15, marching to Louisa Court House. There they stripped down for action, leaving the sick, men without mounts, and all the baggage. From this point on their "sole reliance for rations for man and horse was upon the country." They crossed the Rapidan at Sommerville Ford and continued north. When they reached the Rappahannock near Richard's Ferry, a company of the Ninth led personally by Rooney Lee captured a Yankee officer and some privates who were carrying counterfeit Confederate currency. Realizing that Pope's army was on the northern side of the river, they retired a short distance and bivouacked for the night. At dawn the next morning they continued up the southern bank of the river. Because of the large infantry forces using the roads in the same direction, the cavalry often had to resort to the fields beside the road, making the march more difficult.[6]

While the Ninth and the rest of Fitz Lee's brigade marched, Stuart was having some problems. On August 18 Stuart was to move with his entire command to cut off Pope's line of retreat in a proposed offensive. However, due to a misunderstanding between Fitz Lee and Stuart as to the schedule and route the brigade was to follow, Fitz Lee's brigade would never make it to the rendezvous point on time. Stuart, unaware that Fitz was miles away, rode out to a place near Verdiersville to await his arrival. Stuart and those with him took this opportunity to unbridle their horses and nap for a while. Imagine their surprise when a cloud of dust that should have announced the arrival of Fitz Lee heralded the approach of a regiment of Union horses. Only expert horsemanship and a fine mount allowed Stuart to make his escape over a picket fence. He had to leave behind his favorite plumed hat and cloak, which became prizes for the Union troopers. A more important capture was that of one of Stuart's aides with detailed orders for the impending offensive in his saddlebags. This information allowed Pope to escape the trap that Lee had planned for him. When Fitz Lee finally arrived, his men and horses needed to rest. Consequently, Stuart's ride for the rear of Pope's army had to wait until August 20.[7]

Stuart's men crossed the river at 4 A.M. with Fitz Lee in advance of Longstreet's men and Robertson preceding Jackson. Both columns ran into rear-guard units of Pope's cavalry, but nothing major developed. Ever since his near capture Stuart had been thinking of a way to get revenge for his embarrassment. The way that suited him best was a raid to the rear of Pope's army.

At midmorning on August 22, Stuart started out with a column of approximately 1,500 men, including Rooney Lee and the Ninth Virginia. He went around Pope's right on a route that went first northward then eastward toward Warrenton. Warrenton had been under Yankee occupation for some time, and the townspeople greeted Stuart's men "with great demonstrations of joy." They were also more than happy to tell Stuart all they knew about Federal troop movements.[8]

That afternoon they headed east toward Catlett's Station, a major supply depot for Pope's army, which was situated on the Orange and

Alexandria Railroad. There was also a railroad bridge near Catlett's that tempted Stuart. If he could destroy the bridge, he would completely disrupt Pope's line of supply. This raid was hampered somewhat by a torrential downpour. One raider remembered "furious winds," "livid lightnings," and "reverberating thunders." It was so dark that it was impossible to tell friend from foe except when the lightning flashed. The Ninth, in order to maintain cohesiveness, devised a password system for identification. To the question "Who is there?" was given the answer "Colonel Lee!" with a countersign of "Draw sabres!"[9]

A quick scout of the camp revealed only a small picket force that was quickly captured. Another fortuitous capture was that of a "contraband" (at the time, the term used in reference to an escaped slave in Union-held territory) who had been impressed into service by an officer on Pope's staff. After getting over his first fright, he offered to guide Stuart to Pope's own headquarters. He was given the choice: "kind treatment if faithful and instant extermination if traitorous." Only one infantry regiment, the Pennsylvania Bucktails, guarded the place, and except for the picket force they were all in their tents on this miserable night.[10]

When the bugler sounded "Charge!" Stuart's men raced to their assigned destinations. Rooney Lee and the Ninth headed for the main depot and Pope's headquarters; the others made a dash for a camp farther down and the railroad bridge. Charging "at full speed," the Ninth let out a rebel yell that rose "above the howling winds and drenching rain." The Bucktails at the depot tried to make a stand, but the troopers fired "one withering volley," then "dashed among them with their sabres, leaping their horses upon the platform and crashing right into the freight room."[11]

Many prisoners were taken at the depot, and the command scattered to take other prisoners and rifle the tents and sutlers' stores they found. The biggest prize was John Pope's headquarters tent, where they found the general's personal items, dispatch books, and chests of money intended for army payrolls. Of great importance to the Confederates was Pope's daily reports of the location and strength of every outfit in his command. One of the raiders recalled the capture of a paymaster's wagon: "We found a wagon stuck in the mud . . . that was full of money chests. Colonel Lee himself came and took it back with him."

The excitement continued as the men charged up and down the streets laid out by the quartermasters and sutlers. One officer recalled that they were "scattering out pistol balls promiscuously right and left" and laughing "until they could hardly keep their saddles. Supper tables were kicked over and tents broken down in the rush to get out, the tents catching them [the Yankees] sometimes in their fall like fish in a net." The rain had subsided for a while, so the men burned many wagons and tents. They herded up droves of mules and prisoners and led off many fine horses belonging to Pope's officers. The telegraph wires were cut down in sections, and the general destruction continued for some time. By now the men of the Ninth were professionals at this kind of thing—they could tend to the task of destroying military stores while replenishing themselves at the same time. One officer was afraid they might "get drunk, for there was plenty of liquor in every tent, but the importance of restraint was appreciated, and none took more than they could carry."[12]

Officers as well as privates were busy plundering. Rooney Lee rode up to one man who was so busy with his thievery he did not recognize his colonel. Startled by Lee, he dove under a wagon and shouted, "I surrender." When Lee asked, "What regiment?" he replied "Ninth Virginia Cavalry." No one recorded Lee's reaction to this.[13]

Then the rain began again. It fell as if "poured from buckets," and the wind whipped it until "it was driven almost horizontally." In fierce storms like this, a horse naturally turns its tail to the blast for protection. Consequently "whole regiments of horses would rear and wheel around to get their backs to the storm." The fires were put out, and it was impossible to start others. Many prisoners took advantage of the storm and the darkness to slip away. Some of the mules that had been herded together ran off. The part of the raiding party charged with burning the railroad bridge found their task impossible.

Some of the escaped Yankees began to fire at the Confederates, and in the storm it was impossible to mount a charge to scatter them. Stuart considered that they had done all the damage they could and assembled his men for the return trip. Near daylight they withdrew and stopped for breakfast after a march of a few miles. The column contained hundreds of prisoners (one a woman dressed in men's clothing) and four or five hundred horses and mules. Lee was pleased with the destruction of the depot and the information contained in Pope's dispatch books. Stuart was delighted with the acquisition of Pope's uniform coat, which he offered to trade for his captured hat and cloak. The Yankees would not acknowledge his offer, so he sent the coat to Richmond for display as a prize of war. This second successful raid boosted the morale of the Confederate cavalry even higher.[14]

In his official report, Stuart praised Rooney: "[He] led his command boldly to within a few feet of the tents occupied by the convivial staff of General Pope and charged the camp, capturing a large number of prisoners, particularly officers, and securing public property to a fabulous amount." Stuart continued: "I feel bound to accord to the officers and men, collectively, engaged in this expedition, unqualified praise for their good conduct under these circumstances where their discipline, fortitude, endurance and bravery stood such an extraordinary test. The horseman who, at his officers' bidding, without questioning, leaps into unexplored darkness, knowing nothing except that there is a certain danger ahead, possesses the highest attribute of the patriot soldier."[15]

When Jackson began to move on August 25, Stuart and his cavalry followed. They eventually caught up with the famed "foot cavalry" by the next day at Bristoe Station. The next stop was Pope's huge depot at Manassas Station. This time the spoils were untouched, and the troops had a picnic at Federal expense. Shoes, clothing, saddles, and every delicacy in the way of food delighted and replenished the soldiers.[16]

On August 27, Fitz Lee and the Ninth and Fourth Virginia Cavalries marched toward Fairfax Court House "over fences, across ravines and through swamps." They reached the Court House at sunrise and took some prisoners. Then they proceeded to Centreville, where the Ninth ran into Pope's cavalry acting as rear guard. Rooney led the regiment in a charge, "driving them at full speed back upon the infantry." The regiment had four or five wounded and lost some horses but killed and captured several of the enemy. By now the horses were "nearly exhausted," so they camped for the night and found forage for their mounts.

During the battle of Second Manassas, Fitz Lee's brigade was assigned to guard Jackson's left and remained near Sudley's Mill "nearly inactive" while the artillery and infantry were engaged in bloody battle. When the battle ended, the Ninth moved with Stuart after the retreating Pope but, except for picketing and light skirmishes, were not engaged. They also were in support of Pelham's battery during the beginning of the fight at Chantilly. The march continued to Fairfax Station, then Drainesville, where the Ninth found its "long absent wagon train." They rested for a day and received word that the army was bound for Maryland. The news caused some officers to send their servants home, and the men with family and friends in the vicinity made quick trips to see them. Most all wrote letters to their loved ones on the eve of invasion.[17]

On the night of August 25 Rooney had found time to pay his father a visit. Robert Lee wrote to his daughter-in-law the next day to give her the latest news of her husband: "I arrived at my tent last night, my dear Chass, and to my delight found your Fitzhugh. It was the first time I had seen him since the battles around Richmond. He is very well and the picture of health. He could not stay very long, as he had to return to his camp about four miles distant. In the recent expedition to the rear of the enemy, (with a view of cutting off their R.R. communications) he led his regiment during a terrible storm at night, through the camp of the enemy to Catlett's Station, capturing several hundred prisoners and some valuable papers of General Pope. His cousin, Louis Marshall, is said to have escaped at the first onset, leaving his toddy untouched. I am so grateful to Almighty God for preserving, guiding and directing him in this war! Help me pray to Him for the continuance of His signal favor."[18]

After the day of rest on September 4, Stuart's horsemen rode to Leesburg, where he received his orders for the march into Maryland. The cavalry was to form a screen for the Army of Northern Virginia on the east. They were to make sure that the screen was not penetrated, and no Yankee was to know the location and strength of Lee's army. At the same time, they were to find out all that they could about the strength and position of McClellan's army, should this cautious general ever decide to pursue Lee. (Pope had been soundly defeated at Second Manassas, or Bull Run; McClellan was left with the job of pursuing Lee.)[19]

The Ninth forded the Potomac at Edward's Ferry and reached the little town of Poolesville, where some shop owners were convinced to accept Confederate currency for boots and other needed goods. One Northern war artist who saw Stuart's cavalry shortly after they crossed into Maryland described their uniforms as poor. Their horses were excellent, however, and they were well armed with guns "mostly captured from our own cavalry, for whom they express utter contempt." The Ninth spent the night at Barnesville and left a squadron there on picket duty while the rest of the regiment went on to New Market. There they spent two quiet days until word reached Rooney

Lee that the squadron at Barnesville had been attacked by a numerically superior force of enemy cavalry. Their objective was a signal station on Sugar Loaf Mountain, which at that time would give an extended view of Lee's army. At the base of the mountain the enemy
cavalry was repulsed, and the Confederates dismounted to fight. One
man remembered the odds as "three to one" in favor of the Federals.
Colonel Lee positioned his men on a wooded rise with some
squadrons dismounted as a skirmish line, and the remaining men
mounted. "The firing was very rapid and charge after charge was gallantly repulsed," recalled a Confederate trooper. The enemy artillery
began to fire into Lee's position, and one disheartened captain started
to retreat on his own. Rooney stopped him and asked if he was
wounded. "No," answered the captain, "but the enemy are in such
force we can't hold the position." He was promptly ordered back to
his place. The Ninth held its position until nightfall. The ground Lee
had selected provided good protection for the men, and casualties
were light compared to those of the enemy.

At night the regiment was pulled back to New Market, where the
men had time to cook some much-needed rations. They then returned
once more to the base of the mountain and were held ready for battle
until after midnight. From there they marched back over the mountain and at about 10 A.M. on Sunday morning stopped near a mill.
They enjoyed a short respite there while men and horses received rations. Here the ragged uniforms of the horsemen provided some
amusement for a group of women who were "as intensely hostile as
any blue stocking schoolmarm of Massachusetts."[20]

The sound of artillery fire could be heard from the battle of South
Mountain, but no one in the command was yet aware of the outcome.
About 4 P.M. the regiment was ordered to mount and rode for four
hours before arriving at Boonsboro. There they met the wagons, artillery, and units of infantry withdrawing through the village. To cover
the retreat, the Ninth moved with the rest of Fitz Lee's brigade toward
Turner's Gap. About one and a half miles from Boonsboro, they
waited for the enemy all night. At dawn the rebel cavalry began to fall
back. The enemy columns were already in sight "with their bright
muskets gleaming in the morning light." The Ninth brought up the
rear of Fitz Lee's brigade and "more than once" turned about to face
a supposed threat as they pulled back to Boonsboro.[21]

The pressure on Fitz Lee's brigade became more intense as the Union
forces increased in number. It became necessary for one regiment to

"make a stand" so that the rest could withdraw in an orderly fashion. That difficult assignment was given to Rooney Lee and the Ninth Virginia. Boonsboro at that time was a small village on the National Road that ran between Frederick and Hagerstown. The major intersection was the point at which Main Street crossed Church Street. Church Street was very narrow and built up on both sides as far as the school. Just outside of town it led to a covered bridge. The narrowness of this street made it necessary for Lee's regiment to operate in a column of fours. The squadrons were placed so that they could be used in succession in charging the advancing enemy. A squadron would charge, then retire to the rear of the regiment to reform while the next in line took its place. "By a rapid series of well executed attacks the 9th regiment thus covered the retreat" of the rest of Fitz Lee's brigade and gained time for a new position to be established to the west of town.[22]

Soon, however, the regiment began to receive fire from the civilians in the houses that lined the street. The enemy was not only approaching down the street but also coming by parallel routes. There was infantry in a cornfield outside of town that fired on their flanks and threatened to cut off the path of retreat. The withdrawal became disorderly as the regiment pulled out of town. Some piles of stone had been placed in the middle of the road for repair work. There, "amidst the impenetrable dust, many horses blindly rushed, and falling, piled with their riders one on another. Here and there in the pell mell race, blinded by the dust, horses and horsemen dashed against telegraph posts and fell to the ground, to be trampled by others behind."[23]

Just outside of town near the bridge, Rooney Lee's horse was killed and fell on him. The enemy rode by and did not notice him in the confusion. A squadron of the Ninth under Captain Thomas W. Haynes charged and retook this position. Some men pulled the horse off their colonel and called to him to rise and escape. He was "so stunned and bruised as to be incapable of moving hand or foot," however. Before the men could attempt further rescue, a new charge of the enemy pushed Captain Haynes's squadron back, and the colonel was left "to his fate."

Semiconscious and unable to move, Rooney lay beside the road for quite a while. He was completely helpless as the enemy forces "passed by within a few feet of him." None of the Yankees paid any attention to what they presumed was one more dead Johnny Reb, even if he was a colonel. Eventually, as his senses and strength returned, he thought of escape. Slowly and painfully he crawled to the nearby field and some woods. Fortunately there he found two Confederate soldiers who were separated from their units. They helped him to his feet and half-carried him to a nearby farmhouse, where they "procured" a horse. The group moved westward in the direction of Sharpsburg, staying clear of the roads and Yankee patrols. Before night Rooney was across the Antietam and "was soon afterwards in the hands of his friends, who welcomed him as one restored from the dead."[24]

Meanwhile the Ninth had rallied outside of town and continued to act as rear guard with the rest of Fitz Lee's brigade. They moved toward Sharpsburg but were not pressed again as they had been in Boonsboro. The Ninth had two officers and sixteen men killed in this engagement. A captain, whose horse was killed also, hid in the cornfield all day and made his escape that night, narrowly avoiding enemy sentries.[25]

Fitz Lee's brigade was posted on the extreme left of the Confederate line during the Battle of Antietam on September 17, 1862. They were in support of the horse artillery on Nicodemus Hill but were not actively engaged. They also made up part of the command that Stuart intended to use as a diversion on the left but called off. Their main job was to discourage straggling and to stop those who were leaving the front. Once back in Confederate lines, Rooney was sent to the plantation of "Ferry Hill Place," about three miles from Sharpsburg. This was the home of the Douglas family, who had a son on Stonewall Jackson's staff. Rooney had suffered many bruises, a badly sprained leg, and probably a slight concussion. The ladies of the house took care of him and some other Confederate officers.

There was little time to recuperate as the retreat back into Virginia began on September 19. Robert Lee's invasion of Maryland had come to an end. In the war's bloodiest day of fighting, the Army of Northern Virginia had fought seemingly overwhelming numbers to a standstill and had remained in line of battle the following day against any attack that McClellan dared to offer; none was forthcoming. Daunted but not beaten, they would regroup and fight again soon.[26]

CHAPTER 7

"And then we rode into Pennsylvania"

When the Ninth crossed back into Virginia and camped near Leesburg, there were less than two hundred men fit for duty. The colonel was one of those not completely fit, but he was sufficiently healed in a matter of days to be able to ride again. The low number was due to many conditions. Some had been killed, wounded, or lost during the Maryland campaign. Others had been left behind on the march due to the lameness of the horses. The macadamized roads of Maryland that were too hard for Lee's barefoot or poorly shod infantry were also hard on the horses. A horse cannot be ridden on paved roads for long without going lame. The concussion is just too great. Even those who were still sound needed time to recuperate from exhausting service. Further complicating the problem of rehabilitating the horses was a lack of good-quality feed. While the Ninth rested on the banks of the Opequon, the only fodder that could be found for the horses was green corn stalks. This soon "rendered very many of them unfit for service." Green fodder is usually too rich and can cause diarrhea or founder. The Confederate government's lack of a remount service was already beginning to be evident. Any cavalryman whose horse died or was unfit had to find his own replacement. Many times this meant going home to get another horse, and a man might be absent from duty for days or even weeks on such a mission.

Even so, the Ninth was called on to support General A. P. Hill as his infantry met a thrust of the enemy over the Potomac. After the Yankees were repulsed, the cavalry guarded the fords for another day, then returned to camp. For a few days everything was peaceful along the Potomac, and the men of both armies often fraternized midstream until ordered to stop.

Near the end of September, Fitz Lee was kicked by a mule and incapacitated for a while. Rooney, as senior colonel, took over command of the brigade. His picket line ran to the point near Shepherdstown, at the mouth of Opequon Creek, where it met that of Wade Hampton's brigade. On September 30 Lee and Hampton met and agreed on the procedure to follow in case of an attack. Lee planned to make a first stand at Williamston's crossroads if the pickets were driven in and a final stand at a stone bridge if forced to withdraw from the crossroads. If attacked, each was to inform the other.

At dawn the next morning Union General Alfred Pleasonton made a strong reconnaissance in the direction of Martinsburg. His force numbered 700 cavalrymen and included one battery of artillery. The picket of the Ninth was quickly overrun, and the Yankees advanced on the reserve squadrons at the crossroads. There one squadron was dismounted and waited in ambush while the other remained mounted. The Union cavalry "advanced rapidly and boldly" but "broke and fled precipitately" when fired upon. The men of the Ninth followed the Yankees as far as the main body of men who were waiting dismounted with artillery to back them up. The squadrons of the Ninth formed with the rest of the brigade and held their ground. Realizing that Lee's brigade was on this road, Pleasonton decided to head toward Martinsburg rather than renew the offensive in this direction. When attacked, Rooney sent one courier to Hampton to notify him of the enemy's advance. A second courier was sent after the Ninth fell back to the crossroads. Hampton made preparations to receive an attack but was surprised to see Federals entering Martinsburg. He drew up his brigade on the other side of the town and wrote to Rooney Lee that they "could retake the town." This message was not delivered.[1]

At this point Stuart rode up and held a brief conference with Lee and Hampton. He was evidently displeased with the turn of events and told his subordinates, "Gentlemen, this thing will not do; I will give you twenty minutes, within which time the town must be again in our possession." The brigade commanded by Rooney Lee "was advanced immediately," and Pleasonton pulled out of Martinsburg and began to retire along the Shepherdstown road. The Fourth Virginia made several charges on Pleasonton's rear while artillery shells burst over the heads of the pursuers. In the official reports, both sides claimed to have inflicted heavy losses on the enemy, but in fact casualties were light. On the Confederate side, "one lieutenant and several privates" were lost; Pleasonton admitted to losing twelve men. The affair ended at dark with Pleasonton recrossing the river.[2]

The official reports of this foray are quite interesting. Pleasonton's report verged on the fanciful throughout but became ludicrous when he claimed that "the ladies of the place had turned out and built up" the bridges that had been destroyed earlier so that his men could cross the river. Stuart was on the scene during most of the action, and his version is the one that the commander of the army sent to the inspector general's office in Richmond. This report is concise and basically presents the facts. However, General Hampton took offense at the wording and wrote a much longer report to indicate his actions and to erase any insinuation that his brigade had been driven back. For instance, he wrote, "I had been placed in the most critical position by the failure of Colonel Lee's pickets to communicate with me" in spite of admitting earlier in the report that Lee had sent two couriers when first attacked. The egos of many officers, North and South, were immense, and they took offense easily over what they considered to be a point of honor. Rooney Lee, by contrast, was much like his father in this respect. He was conciliatory when the occasion demanded and was more than willing to sacrifice pride for the greater good. In this case he took it upon himself to smooth Hampton's ruffled feathers. In Hampton's words, he "frankly . . . apologized to me for the failure of the plan of operations we had agreed on" in the presence of Stuart. This simple act mollified Hampton, and the two were able to work together throughout the war.

On October 8, Robert Lee sent Jeb Stuart the kind of orders the cavalryman loved. He was to lead an expedition into Maryland and Pennsylvania with a handpicked force of cavalry. His assignments were numerous: destroy the railroad bridge over the Conococheague River near Chambersburg; obtain information on the position and strength of McClellan's units; take or destroy government property, especially horses; and take into custody any civilian officials of the government so they could be held as hostages for the safekeeping of those Southerners that had been taken by the Yankees.[3]

Stuart decided to take six hundred men from each of his three brigades—Hampton's, Fitz Lee's, and Robertson's. These were selected as "the best mounted and most reliable men" from each command. Hampton would lead his own contingent, Rooney Lee that of Fitz Lee's brigade, and Colonel William C. "Grumble" Jones the group from Robertson's brigade. Pelham would bring along four guns from the horse artillery.

The selected troops received orders from Stuart that demanded "implicit obedience to orders" and the "strictest order and sobriety" in addition to their usual courage. Their destination was a secret known only to himself, but he promised success if all cooperated. Stuart also gave detailed orders for their conduct on the raid. Receipts were to be given for any horses or goods taken from civilians, and private plundering was "positively forbidden." One-third of each command was to be actively engaged in procuring horses and leading them afterward. The other two-thirds was to be "at all times prepared for action." The public officials taken as hostages were to be given kind treatment. Straggling was forbidden. Also in these orders, Stuart gave his recipe for success in cavalry operations: "The attack, when made, must be vigorous and overwhelming, giving the enemy no time to collect, reconnoiter, or consider anything except his best means of flight." This was to be "the most daring and brilliant affair" the Confederate cavalry had yet undertaken, a bold raid into enemy territory.[4]

The raiding party assembled at Darkesville and moved on to Hedgesville after dark so that they would not be seen from a nearby Federal signal station. "Every man was in the saddle" at dawn and crossed the Potomac at McCray's Ford after capturing the pickets on guard. They narrowly missed a brigade of infantry that had passed by only a short time before. Fog helped to conceal Stuart's movements, but they did not pass by without being seen. At 9:00 A.M. a small group of raiders went to secure a signal station, but two officers escaped. These two rode three miles and reported the column to superiors. They estimated the force at four regiments and four guns. So by 11:00 A.M. or noon at the latest, McClellan's army was aware that gray cavalry was heading into Maryland. A captain of the Twelfth Illinois Cavalry also observed Stuart's men and reported the activity up through channels. His estimate was 2,500 men and eight guns.[5]

The Rebels moved steadily on to Martinsburg. While in Maryland no property was seized, but as soon as they crossed the line into Pennsylvania they went to work. One officer recalled, "The men were wild with enthusiasm and eagerly watched for the line across which the fun would begin." At Mercersburg many obtained new boots and shoes from a merchant who was pleased with his volume of sales until he discovered that his customers only gave a receipt payable by the U.S. government. As befitted the courtly Stuart, orders were given not to take the horses from a lady's buggy. But all other horses were fair game. The weather aided Stuart's men immensely. There were occasional showers that kept the column from raising a dust cloud and also prevented the Pennsylvania farmers from going into the fields that day. Instead, they were all in their barns threshing wheat. The big draft horses were hitched to the threshing machines, so they were taken complete with harness. These huge horses were good for artillery and pulling wagons but were not the kind for the cavalry. The Rebels went out from the column in all directions to find horses. On one occasion a horse was returned to its owner. A little old lady came up to the Confederate officer in command of the detail and asked for her horse's return. She told him that the horse was too old for hard riding, but his sleek appearance made the officer doubtful. On closer inspection his gray hairs and almost toothless gums convinced the officer to return "her faithful and noble favorite."

Once the horses were secured, the raiders "inspected" the pantries of the Dutch farmers, where a tremendous display of good food usually awaited the starving men. One officer described their appearance as they returned to the column: "The returning party would present a vista of roasted turkeys, hams and rounds of beef strapped to the saddles, brown rolls peeping out from haversacks and crocks of cream and rolls of butter carried in the hand for the refreshment of friends in the column who had not yet gone out foraging." One member of the Ninth ran into problems while searching for food. He politely asked some women for whatever food they had, but they refused to give him anything. "Casting a wolfish glance upon the babies," he said he had never eaten human flesh but that he was hungry enough to eat a baby. He soon had all the food he could eat.[6]

The Confederates had ridden about forty miles that day and were now in the rear of McClellan's army. After dark they approached Chambersburg. Stuart sent in a flag of truce and demanded the surrender of the town. The officials of the town had fled, but a handful of citizens met the officer in charge of the flag of truce and told him there would be no opposition. General Hampton was appointed military governor, and his men moved in to take possession of the town. Nothing happened during the night, and the men got a few hours' sleep in the chilly rain.[7]

While in Chambersburg, discipline was strictly adhered to, and the populace was treated with great courtesy. The surrounding area was again gleaned for horses and provisions, with the officers giving receipts for any personal property taken. Public property was another matter. Machine shops and railroad depots were destroyed. The Rebels found army clothing and "about 5,000 new muskets, pistols, sabers, ammunition." They took all they could use or carry and burned the rest. One of their principal targets, the railroad bridge over the Conococheague, was not destroyed because it was made of iron.

Early the next morning the command rode out of Chambersburg in the direction of Gettysburg. This was only to confuse any pursuit, however, for Stuart soon turned south toward Leesburg. They narrowly missed two Union cavalry commands, one near Gettysburg and another later near Barnesville. The horse-stealing continued as long as they were in Pennsylvania and stopped at the Maryland line. Rooney Lee commanded the lead unit from the departure from Chambersburg until they reached Virginia. This march was long and tiring. From Chambersburg to Leesburg is a distance of ninety miles, and they halted only once for half an hour in the evening of the first day to feed the horses. The men rode captured horses to rest their own, and many dismounted and walked to offer their horses relief. The weather was clear, but the earlier rains again kept any dust clouds from forming that could be seen at a distance. The march that night was "terrible," one raider recalled. "The monotonous jingle of arms and accoutrements mingles with the tramp of horses' feet into a drowsy hum all along the marching column, which makes one extremely sleepy." The fatigue, the "uncertain light," and his "tortured imagination" produced a hallucinatory dream effect in which he saw "castles and beautiful houses along the road, which dissolved into thin air" as he approached. Others slept soundly and added their snores to the droning music of horses' hooves.[8]

The raiders entered Hyattstown at dawn on October 12. They had covered a distance of ninety-five miles in only twenty hours. However, safety in Virginia was still twelve miles off. As they continued on their steady march, Federal units were frantically trying to find them. Ever since they first crossed into Maryland the estimates of the strength of the Confederate force had risen, one putting it as high as 12,000, but most around 3,000. One rebel prisoner told Colonel Richard H. Rush, of the Pennsylvania Lancers, that Stuart had ten regiments of cavalry with him. It seems that Stuart's unwritten orders to his men included lying to anyone who asked about troop movements and strengths.

Those who could not lie convincingly just said nothing. The telegraph line was kept busy with reports and orders to move troops to catch Stuart. General-in-Chief Henry Halleck in Washington had wired McClellan that "not a man should be permitted to return to Virginia." McClellan wired back that he had made "every disposition . . . to cut off the retreat of the enemy's cavalry." Cavalry units under Pleasonton and General George Stoneman were in motion, the possible fords over the Potomac were guarded, and infantry on railroad cars were on standby to be transported in any direction needed. One observer with George Crook's infantry, when he heard about the orders for him to chase Stuart, thought, "They might as well send him after a flight of wild-geese." Pleasonton had made a hard march of seventy-eight miles in twenty-four hours to catch up with Stuart but, in so doing, had "crippled up" many of his horses and lost much of his effectiveness.[9]

When he left Hyattstown, Stuart moved to Barnesville, narrowly missing a unit of enemy cavalry, then on toward Poolesville. His movements could be seen from a signal station on Sugarloaf Mountain, and he wanted the observer to think he was going to Poolesville. On this road the Confederate advance guard ran into federal cavalry. Stuart's men were wearing blue overcoats taken at Chambersburg to ward off the early-morning chill. The Federals hesitated for a moment, which allowed the Confederates to draw nearer before charging. The advance squadron of Lee's brigade attacked and drove the enemy back to the main body of troops. "Quick as thought, Lee's sharpshooters sprang to the ground" and held back the federal skirmishers until Pelham could bring up a gun. The artillery fire then drove them back to an area beyond the Monocacy.

This allowed Stuart to move toward his intended crossing place. By holding this ground he kept a high ridge between him and the enemy that screened the movement of the gray troopers toward White's Ford. The continual fire from Pelham's guns convinced Pleasonton that he was blocking Stuart's path, but in reality the Confederates were turning off the main road and heading to the Potomac by another route. Pleasonton waited more than two hours before attacking so that reinforcements could come up.

Rooney Lee was in command of the lead unit as they approached White's Ford. Union infantry from the Ninety-Ninth Pennsylvania was drawn up in a strong position on a bluff near the ford. Realizing the danger of the situation, Rooney sent a courier to request Stuart to come. Stuart answered that he was busy and that the ford must be taken. Lee then began to make arrangements to attack. He planned to attack in front and on the left flank with support from the artillery. The cavalry would then have to attack a heavily defended infantry position while crossing a stream. While these preparations were being made, Rooney tried a ruse. He sent a courier with a handkerchief tied to his saber to the Federal commander with a note that said he was facing Stuart and his entire command. Further, the Federals' situation was hopeless, and to "avoid unnecessary bloodshed" he should surrender. Fifteen minutes would be allowed for the Federals to comply. At the end of this time, Lee ordered the artillery to open fire.

To the Confederates' amazement, the Federals pulled out of their strong position and began to retreat downriver, "with flags flying, drums beating, in perfect order." A wild rebel yell rent the air, and the crossing began. Lee sent one gun across to the Virginia side to command any approach from that side and kept the other on the Maryland side. Quickly the cavalry and the lead horses began to cross. Time was of the essence, so the horses were not allowed to stop and drink as they crossed. However, some stopped no matter what and "plunge[d] their heads up to their eyes in the water." It was very close, but soon all Stuart's men were again in Virginia. The Yankees stopped at the ford and did not continue their pursuit. They received a few warning shells from Pelham and could hear the cheers for Stuart as he galloped to the head of the column. After a brief rest they rode on to Leesburg, where they camped for the night.

This raid was quite a feat. Stuart's men had ridden 126 miles in all, most of it in enemy territory, and had completely encircled McClellan's army again. The last eighty miles were covered in only twenty-seven hours. Only one man was wounded, and two stragglers were captured. They had taken prisoner and paroled 280 soldiers in a hospital. They had taken or destroyed more than $250,000 worth of government property and seized more than 1,200 horses and thirty civilian hostages. Only one objective—the iron railroad bridge that could not be destroyed—was not attained.[10]

The effect on morale was even more important than any tangible result. The Confederate morale soared, and the cavalrymen began to think of themselves as invincible. Union morale was pushed even lower. One of the Union officers who chased Stuart wrote that "I regret very much that this second raid has been so successfully accomplished by Stuart's cavalry" but thought it was impossible for him to have done more. Another observed, "I am disgusted beyond measure."

In a letter home, Robert Gould Shaw wrote, "This raid of Lee's cavalry into Pennsylvania makes us feel pretty cheap; they must have had an exciting time of it." The reaction was much the same in higher circles. Secretary of the Navy Gideon Welles confided in his diary: "It is humiliating, disgraceful. . . . It is not a pleasant fact to know that we are clothing, mounting and subsisting not only our troops but the Rebels also." When McClellan tried to make excuses for his cavalry and said that the horses were worn out, an exasperated Lincoln asked, "Will you pardon me for asking what the horses of your army have done since the battle of Antietam that fatigues anything?" He continued, "Stuart's cavalry outmarched ours, having certainly done more marked service on the Peninsula and everywhere since." Later the raid became the subject of a Lincoln story. When asked about McClellan, Lincoln drew a circle and answered, "When I was a little boy we used to play a game, three times 'round and out. Stuart has been 'round him twice; if he goes 'round him once more, gentlemen, McClellan will be out!"[11]

In the final analysis, there is no doubt that the Federal pursuit of Stuart's men could have been better managed and more aggressive. Certainly the infantry who retreated from White's Ford without firing a shot could be blamed. But even if the cavalry had forced a fight with Stuart, it might have been as one trooper described: "It would have been a cold day for any force of their cavalry to have placed themselves in the way of men such as ours, fighting towards home."

Back in their camps the men got a little rest, and on October 15 the officers attended a grand ball. During this time Rooney Lee received a promotion to brigadier general. The actual date of the appointment was October 3, and the commission was to date from September 15. At this time he was twenty-five years old. The promotion preceded the actual command because during this period he was still in command of Fitz Lee's brigade while his cousin recuperated from the mule kick. By Special Orders No. 238, dated November 10, 1862, the cavalry division was reorganized into four brigades. Rooney Lee's brigade consisted of the Fifth, Ninth, Tenth, and Fifteenth Virginia Cavalries and the Second North Carolina Cavalry. Shortly, the Fifth moved to Fitz Lee's brigade, and the Thirteenth Virginia became part of Rooney Lee's brigade.[12]

During the last part of October Rooney had a little time to see Charlotte, who was expecting their second child soon. Robert Lee announced the visit to her: "I am going to send Fitzhugh down to see you. I know you will admire him exceedingly, especially now that he is a Genl. He will go as soon as I can make arrangements for his departure & if Fitz Lee was here he could go at once. But the wretched fellow got kicked by a mule & cannot walk. However, I think he can go soon. I shall send a great many messages by him & a great many kisses and you must make him give them all to you and tell about his expedition into Penna. & the nice things the Dutch girls gave him."[13]

On October 20, 1862, Rooney's younger sister Annie died of typhoid fever and its complications. She was nursed through her final illness by her mother and her sister Agnes. The burial took place in Warrenton, North Carolina, where the Lee girls had been visiting at Jones Springs. Rooney and Rob were notified of their sister's death by their father. They had not even known that she was sick. Rob wrote to his mother, "I could not then nor can I now realize that I shall never see her anymore in this world. . . . I never even heard of poor Annie's illness until I heard she was dead."[14]

When Rooney arrived in Richmond he was greeted with the news that he had a baby daughter, "a very fine pretty baby." She had been born "very unexpectedly" (possibly prematurely), and her mother was suffering from jaundice. He remained for a few days to look after his wife and baby. He made a quick trip to Hanover County to "bring a wet nurse" for the baby, as Charlotte was sick. This second child was named Charlotte Carter Lee to honor her mother and maternal family. Rooney left for the front reluctantly and only after getting his mother to promise to look after his family every day. He was back with his brigade by November 13 when Robert Lee wrote to his wife, "Fitzhugh is on the Rapp. I saw him today, tell Charlotte, on his gallant grey . . . I hope she continues well & that my grd. daughter is flourishing."[15]

In enlarging his staff as befitted a brigadier general, Rooney offered the position of aide-de-camp and rank of lieutenant to his younger brother Rob. Rob had seen hard service already in the Rockbridge Artillery since his enlistment in the spring of 1862. Of course they consulted their father before taking this action. Lee gave his youngest son "a horse and one of his swords." Rob visited his father at headquarters before assuming his new duties. While there he got his "first introduction to cavalry service" by being allowed to ride Traveller (Robert Lee's famous gray gelding) on a thirty-mile jaunt to Fredericksburg. Traveller did not appreciate the change in riders and refused to walk a step. Instead, he jogged the entire way, and his rider "could have walked the distance with much less discomfort and fatigue." Lee also gave his son money to buy a more appropriate uniform.[16]

On November 7 McClellan was replaced by General Ambrose Burnside as commander of the Union Army. Subsequently there was a change of front as Burnside moved in the direction of Fredericksburg for the winter campaign that Lincoln had wanted. On November 15 Robert Lee sent a message to Rooney telling him to order a nearby infantry regiment with artillery into Fredericksburg if the city was still unoccupied by Federal troops. Lee knew that Burnside was moving his army away from its position at Warrenton and thought he might be moving toward Fredericksburg. On November 18 Rooney was ordered to move to Fredericksburg with his brigade of cavalry and "to assume command of the cavalry and other forces now there." He was to "resist the occupation of Fredericksburg by the enemy" if possible and to picket the Rappahannock. Once it was ascertained that Burnside was indeed moving his army to Fredericksburg, Lee hurried the remainder of the Army of Northern Virginia there also. Once the army was assembled, Rooney's brigade picketed the river on both sides of Port Royal.[17]

While Burnside's army was waiting for his pontoons in order to cross the Rappahannock, the Confederate cavalry was active in maintaining their picket lines. About sixty volunteers from the Ninth Virginia, men commanded by Colonel R. L. T. Beale, made a foray by boat across the river and captured about fifty prisoners with horses and gear. On December 5 there was a lively fight between gunboats on the river and some riflemen on the banks. Rooney ordered Major Pelham to take two rifled guns and join in. The Confederates felt victorious as the gunboats steamed away after two direct hits.[18]

One private in the Second North Carolina wrote home of his adventures during this time. He mentioned one skirmish in which they took thirty prisoners as well as "7 wagons, loaded with coffee, sugar, flour, pork, crackers, oats." The "coffee sweetened with sugar" was a big hit with the North Carolinians. He bragged that he could name "several more instances, but they are too tedious to mention." In spite of officers' best efforts, fraternization occurred between the pickets. This Tarheel private wrote that they had "passed a law against shooting pickets" and that they talked "with each other while on post." Frequently the Rebels traded a "chew" for coffee. On one occasion Private Samuel M. Mason and a Yankee laid down their arms and met midstream. They "spoke very politely and visited," and many Federal soldiers swarmed down the bank when they found out he had tobacco.[19]

The baby girl that had been born that fall was never very strong, and on December 6 she died. The next day she was buried alongside her little brother in Shockoe Cemetery after a service in which the Reverend Charles Minnegerode of St. Paul's Episcopal Church in Richmond officiated. Her age was listed as seven weeks. The parents were, of course, devastated to have lost two children only months apart. One can only imagine the grief Rooney must have felt as well as the anguish of not being able to go to Charlotte to share her grief. Their letters have not been saved, but one exists from Robert Lee to his daughter-in-law shortly before the battle of Fredericksburg: "I heard yesterday, my dear daughter, with the deepest sorrow, of the death of your infant. I was so grateful at her birth. I felt that she would be such a comfort to you, such a pleasure to my dear Fitzhugh, and would fill so full the void still aching in your hearts. But you now have two sweet angels in heaven. What joy there is in the thought! I can say nothing to soften the anguish you must feel, and I know you are assured of my deep and affectionate sympathy." He had seen Rooney the day before and told her how much her husband wanted to see her. He also suggested a visit to Hickory Hill as soon as she had regained her strength. There they could possibly spend some time together.[20]

During the battle of Fredericksburg one regiment of Lee's brigade, the Ninth Virginia, was in support of Pelham's battery. Although not actively engaged, the brigade as a whole counted thirteen wounded men in the campaign. From their position many had a clear view of the battlefield as the artillery dueled and the infantry charged. They could see the impressive lines of blue as they marched up toward the city and the "motley disordered mass" as they retreated. By December 16, the Federals were gone after dismantling their pontoon bridges and slipping away in the night.[21]

In spite of the cold December weather, there was plenty of activity in the cavalry division. Another big raid was in the making. General Hampton had earlier made three successful raids on the Federal supply line. This time Stuart planned on enlarging the strike force and hopefully bagging bigger prizes. The number of men and guns were the same as in the Pennsylvania raid—1,800 men and four guns. Six hundred men from each brigade were selected for the mission. Wade Hampton, Fitz Lee, and Rooney Lee commanded the contingents from their respective brigades. On the day after Christmas the column crossed the Rappahannock and made camp for the night at Morrisville. Stuart's three-part attack plan went into effect early the next day. Hampton's target was Occoquon, the northernmost point. Rooney Lee was to move on Dumfries from the west, and Fitz Lee was to move to the same place from a southern route. The Lees had twenty miles to march before reaching their objectives; Hampton had an even longer distance to travel.

The Federal forces guarding the supply line had been increased since Hampton's earlier attacks. At Occoquon alone there was a brigade of infantry, almost two regiments of cavalry, and artillery. Other points along the supply line, the Telegraph Road, were similarly guarded. Rooney Lee's men first met the enemy at Wheat's Mill, a place where Quantico Creek crosses the Telegraph Road near Dumfries. A squadron of the Ninth Virginia charged and captured the picket. The squadron moved on toward Dumfries until being pushed back by a large infantry force. Lee pulled back to the southern side of the creek. One Federal cavalry squadron attacked but was repulsed. Stuart's artillery then opened fire on the position, and the enemy artillery answered. The Federals held a strong position on a ridge above the town. Meanwhile Fitz Lee's men had reached the Telegraph Road about two miles south of town. They captured some prisoners and wagons as they moved toward Dumfries. Once the two Lees were together, Stuart formulated a plan for attacking the town but abandoned the idea because the Union forces were in a strong defensive position and more numerous than supposed. Fitz Lee's men were ordered to skirmish with this Yankee force as a diversion so that the rest of the command could move on up Brentsville Road.

To the north Hampton fared no better. He split his force with an eye toward catching the garrison of Occoquon in a trap. However, one part of Hampton's trap closed too quickly, and the Yankees dashed by before the other could snap shut. The booty there was far less than expected. A disappointed Hampton rendezvoused with the others at Cole's Store late on December 27.[22]

Next morning, Stuart sent home the prisoners, the captured wagons, and two guns that were almost out of ammunition. The bulk of the raiding party moved on toward the Occoquon. Hunting on this day proved more rewarding. Fitz Lee and Hampton had engagements that netted prisoners and wagons. Then the Rebels marched toward Burke's Station, where they took the telegraph station by surprise.

Stuart's own operator took the key and read to Stuart all the messages concerning Federal troop movements to intercept him. In all his glory, Jeb then sent a complaint to the Union quartermaster-general in Washington: He complained of "the bad quality of the mules lately furnished which interfered seriously with our moving the captured wagons." Then the telegraph was cut and the rebel cavalry was on the march. They skirted a large infantry force at Fairfax Court House, then marched by way of Vienna, Middleburg, and Warrenton and arrived at Culpeper on New Year's Eve.

The tangible results of this raid were not as great as the earlier ones. However, 200 prisoners were taken, as well as "a large number of horses, mules, wagons, saddles, bridles, pistols, and sabres." The Confederates had moved quickly in poor weather conditions and had created havoc in the rear of the Union Army. Official Washington was probably aghast at finding out that Stuart and his horsemen had ridden within twelve miles of Washington. The Confederate loss was slight: one killed, thirteen wounded, and fourteen missing. Of these, there was one wounded and fourteen missing in Rooney Lee's command. In his official report, Stuart praised his subordinates: "The conduct of officers and men on this expedition deserves the highest praise, evincing patient endurance, heroic dash, and unflinching courage."[23]

This raid ended the year 1862, and the cavalry went into winter quarters and settled down into the routine of picket duty. For Rooney Lee's brigade this was a position on the Rappahannock. The most pressing need for the cavalry was forage for the horses. Nearly everything had to be shipped in, as the winter pastures were not enough for horses to subsist on. A few obtained furloughs to go home and visit with families and perhaps find a new horse to replace a worn-out one. The officers' wives moved close to the army to be with their husbands. Life in the Army of Northern Virginia would be relatively peaceful until the opening of the spring campaigns.

CHAPTER 8

"Like a shell burst in every direction"

During the relatively quiet winter, Charlotte and Rooney were able to see each other on occasions. Robert Lee wrote to his wife on January 8, 1863, expressing a hope that his son "had been able to visit Charlotte." If not, he suggested that "she had better pay him a visit." He was certain that Rooney could find "some kind neighbor to him who would take her in for a little while."[1]

He could also find some kind brother, his younger brother and aide, who could be spared from official duties long enough to serve as an escort. Because of the weather and a rising stream, Rob had a formidable task. It seems the mules pulling the ambulance balked midstream, and Rob had to enlist some aid from two gentlemen and a yoke of oxen to extricate the entourage from the stream. "Mrs. Lee's bonnet box, bonnet, cloak, furs, saucepan, Sallie's carpetbags" seemed a hopeless loss for a while as they were all "dripping water." They despaired of reaching their destination that night, and Rob thought of the "misery" he would endure when the others laughed at him "for not being able to take care of two females." He built a fire for his "sister" to warm herself by, and they ate a "wet lunch." He drove hard to make up for lost time, and they were met by "Rooney and staff just coming out to meet" them about dark. Charlotte stayed at the home of the Hunters, "very kind and considerate" hosts. For entertainment Rob took the ladies out to watch drill in a "hearse." He wrote his sisters that "Sister is delighted . . . with her hostess" and that she is "enjoying herself very much." There was a review of Rooney Lee's brigade on January 20. The commanding general attended and later reported to his wife that "they made a fine exhibition." He thought that Rooney "looked very well at its head on a noble black charger." Charlotte did not attend this review, as it was "too far" and her health was only "tolerable." As the disease of tuberculosis worsened, her good days in the spring of 1863 would far too often be interspersed with bad ones.[2]

During this time Rooney's brigade continued to perform picket duty along the Rappahannock from Port Royal to Urbana. A desire to strike at the Yankees led Rooney to formulate a plan for an attack on Gloucester Point. He assembled the brigade, issued orders, and proceeded "cautiously" to the target area. A reconnaissance party was sent out, and it returned with a report that convinced Lee to abort the mission and return the command to its camps. He was always ready to fight but never risked his men needlessly.[3]

On February 20 there was a skirmish of sorts with two Federal gunboats. These boats steamed up the river as far as Ware's Point and were ambushed by Lee's men and two pieces of the Stuart Horse Artillery. After receiving "a deadly fire," both boats were damaged and hurried downstream. The commander of these two gunboats did not soon forget this experience. Two months later Rooney Lee was ordered to make another foray up the river. He stopped short of Port Royal even though he had met no enemy fire. He was still "convinced that squads of the enemy's cavalry cross the river above." Without support, he feared "General W.P. [W.H.F.] Lee will laugh at us."[4]

The winter had brought yet another commander to the Army of the Potomac—this time Joseph "Fighting Joe" Hooker. Hooker at once began to reorganize his army, including the cavalry. As one Confederate officer noted, he "improved their heretofore worthless cavalry a great deal and from this time on we were to have more and more trouble with it. . . ." All the cavalry was placed into one corps commanded by General George Stoneman. This corps was made up of three divisions plus artillery and reserves. By the beginning of the spring offensive, the effective strength of the Union cavalry alone was 11,541. Furthermore, the cavalrymen were well-supplied and well-equipped. Besides their sabers, they carried usually a Colt revolver and a breech-loading carbine. Ammunition, rations, and forage for their horses were plentiful. The Federal government also managed to keep the army supplied with horses—a commodity that the Army of the Potomac used up profligately. The quality of these horses was not up to that of the Confederate service during the first two years of the war, but there seemed to be an endless quantity. In January 1863 the chief quartermaster of the Army of the Potomac reported: "The cavalry and artillery horses are in fair condition, considering that the quality of the animals never was first-rate. First-class horses have never yet found their way into this army. Many of them have been 'doctored up' by contractors, and sold into our hands, and the first service has discovered their unfitness." Unscrupulous horse traders knew that a few pennies' worth of laudanum could make a lame horse sound and a wild one docile long enough to pass government inspectors. A few dollars under the table to contractors could lead to deals worth thousands. Cavalry horses were worth $150 or more at that time.[5]

As both sides would soon realize, a parity in mounts was fast approaching. A mediocre horse that is in good condition and well-fed is approximately equal to a fine "blooded" horse that is skinny and run-down. A man who is mounted on even an average horse is worth much more to the cavalry than a trooper with no mount. The Confederate system of a man supplying his own horse had brought the effective strength of Stuart's cavalry down to a dangerous low in the spring of 1863. This problem was exacerbated by a lack of forage for the horses the cavalry did possess. A trooper from the Thirteenth Virginia wrote: "Horses are in very bad condition, forage extremely scarce. Out of 70 men [in Company A] we can turn out for duty about 30. Many horses have played out entirely." That meant that many men were either in "Company Q" (a camp for dismounted men) or on their way home to procure another horse. In Lee's brigade only the Second North Carolina was mounted on horses provided by the state. All the Virginians had to furnish their own. Good forage was almost nonexistent, and the cavalry had been dispersed so that food could be found for the horses. The brigades of W. E. Jones and Wade Hampton had been ordered to distant points to winter. Only the brigades of Fitz and Rooney Lee were with the army in the spring of 1863, and these were spread out over a large area. This spread was due to two reasons: to perform picket duty, and to subsist the horses. Rooney's brigade stretched miles to the right of the army. On February 23 Robert Lee mentioned to his wife that he had not seen their sons since the cavalry review in January. He continued, "They are down in Essex or Middlesex and I expect F. is exercised to get forage for his horses, etc. That is a great labour now, & I fear this hard weather will kill a great many."[6]

It seems that Rooney's dislike of letter-writing extended to official army business as well as to communications with members of his family. His reports were all short, concise, and businesslike and were on occasion mere notes or "memoranda" of troop movements. His bare-bones reports were quite a contrast to those of many Civil War field officers who seemed to be writing self-serving romance novels. He apparently saw no need to write at all when he had nothing to report, as shown by the following communiqué of March 4, 1863, to Stuart's adjutant: "Whenever I find that any troops are passing down, I always send the communication forward. If I don't send, you may know that no troops are passing down." His father joked about his son's reluctance to write in a letter to Charlotte about this time: "It is strange though that nobody writes to you now. You are both such good correspondents that I should think you would be overwhelmed with letters. Your mama says neither of you ever write to her. But I tell her it is the fault of the mails."

In March Charlotte was still staying with the Hunter family near Rooney's headquarters, and they were able to see each other often. Robert Lee wrote the following to his daughter-in-law during this stay: "I am glad you are so well and happy. Tell F. I know you 'look very well,' and more than that you look beautiful, and that he must answer all your questions, and R. must drive you out every day. You and that young bride must make fine company for each other. Affording each other so much time for fruitful thought, and when you do speak always on the same subject, your husbands. How deluded each must appear to the other. As to Fitzhugh, the Misses H. need take no credit to themselves for perceiving his condition. It is patent to all the world and requires no Columbus to discover it. Tell him that he must look at you as much as he can, for the spring is approaching and we have a great deal before us. I am glad you have had this opportunity to be together, and hope the war with all its baneful effects will always be removed far from you." Rooney's "condition" was his great love for his wife, made apparent to all by his actions and the look in his eyes. Charlotte returned this love. Since the death of their children, her husband had become her life. This "long stay with her husband" ended near the last of March. Rob took her to Hickory Hill to stay with her Wickham relatives and reported to his mother that "she was looking very well & seemed very sorry to leave."[7]

By April 1 the muddy roads had dried out enough for the armies to march on and resume the slaughter from the previous year. Like blue and gray giants that had been sleeping all winter, the armies began to stretch and flex their muscles and eye their opponents, looking for the best way to strike and kill one another. Rooney Lee's brigade struck their tents and marched to Orange Court House, where they camped for a few days. Then they crossed the Rapidan and moved on to Culpeper. Stuart's consolidation of forces was a necessity. Even so, he had only two brigades, Fitz Lee's and Rooney Lee's, numbering no more than 3,000 effectives, to face Stoneman's much larger cavalry force. On paper Stoneman had a four-to-one advantage.[8]

Hooker was already formulating great plans for his new cavalry corps, in spite of his earlier complaint: "Whoever saw a dead cavalryman?" On April 11 he issued orders to Stoneman for an offensive. The entire cavalry corps was to "move at daylight" on April 13, with each man carrying three days' rations and as much ammunition as he could carry "conveniently on his person." The cavalry was supposed to get between Lee's army and Richmond, cut off Lee's supply line, and block his path of retreat. Hooker thought Stoneman would run into Fitz Lee's brigade near Culpeper but was positive he would be able "to disperse and destroy" Lee's command "without delay" or "detriment to any considerable number" of Stoneman's troops. He was to destroy railroad bridges and equipment, cut telegraph lines, burn depots, and harass the enemy at all points. "Let your watchword be, fight, fight, fight," Hooker exhorted.

When Stoneman moved out on April 13, his command numbered 9,895 cavalry and 427 artillerists with twenty-two guns. They had wagons and pack mules carrying about nine days' rations. Facing Stoneman were three regiments of Rooney Lee's brigade and some guns from Stuart's horse artillery. The Tenth Virginia was detached and operating on the Virginia Central Railroad near Beaver Dam. The Fifteenth Virginia was still picketing the Rappahannock below Fredericksburg. Of the three remaining regiments, part of the Second North Carolina was detached, and the Ninth Virginia counted 750 effectives. Rooney Lee's entire force numbered approximately 1,350 men, including artillery. What they lacked in numbers they were prepared to make up for in pluck and courage. A member of the Thirteenth Virginia wrote, "Our cavalry is in poor condition, our horses are very poor for want of forage and constant use, but we will do our best, you may be assured."[9]

General Stoneman issued orders for General W. W. Averell to cross
the Rappahannock with his division on April 13. Simultaneously General John Buford was to cross with his brigade at the Rappahannock
railroad bridge. Once across and closed up, they were to march on
Culpeper. Gregg was to follow Averell. If they ran into enemy troops,
they would "be attacked at once and with the utmost vigor, pouring in
upon him every available man." The night before the proposed crossing was cold. Even so, Stoneman ordered no fires so that the element
of surprise might be maintained. However, Rooney Lee received word
that night of a heavy concentration of Federal cavalry across the river.
He sent a company of sharpshooters to beef up his picket at the ford
and then waited to see what might develop.

At Kelly's Ford about daybreak, the Federal cavalry attempted to
cross with the support of "a regiment dismounted as sharpshooters
along the bank." Lee's men, numbering about 150, opened fire. Lee reported, "They dashed back at the first volley from our sharpshooters."

Then, at the railroad bridge at Rappahannock Station, the Federals tried again. Lee's men were posted at the bridge itself, in a line of
rifle pits and in a nearby blockhouse. Two Federal companies forded
the river while three others charged over the bridge itself. They
forced the Confederates at the end of the bridge to pull back, leaving
those in the "rifle pits exposed to a flank fire." When gray reinforcements arrived, the Yankee troopers recrossed the river. "Firing was
kept up by the artillery and sharpshooters most of the day," according to the reports.[10]

During the ensuing artillery duel, Stuart and Rooney Lee had a very
close call. They, "with their respective staffs, had taken up their position, carelessly stretched on the ground, chatting and laughing and
watching the effect of the shells crossing each other over their heads,
as unconcerned as if there were no enemy within miles." Stuart's giant
Prussian aide, Heros von Borcke, was off to the right watching the
enemy movements with his field glasses. He saw the Federal officer
commanding the guns on the far bank focus on the group of Confederate officers with his field glasses. Then he began to "assist with his
own hands in pointing one of the guns upon them." Von Borcke yelled
a warning, which the group laughed at and ignored. "A few seconds
after, the shot was heard, and a shell fell plump in their midst, burying
in the earth with itself one of General Lee's gauntlets, which lay on the
ground only a few feet from the General himself, and bespattering all

who were nearest to it with earth and mud." It was now Von Borcke's turn to laugh as he saw his "gallant comrades stampede right and left from the fatal spot, chasing their frightened horses, followed by a rapid, though happily less well directed, succession of shots from the enemy's guns." That night it began to rain, and, without shelter tents, the Confederates spent a night of "wretched discomfort."[11]

After these repulses, Stoneman ordered a "vigorous demonstration" at Kelly's Ford and ordered his subordinates to "extend your pickets well down the river, so as to prevent the enemy crossing below and cutting you off." Apparently the Confederate cavalry was still capable of inspiring awe, for Stoneman was afraid Stuart and the Lees would cut him off even though he had a vast numerical superiority.[12]

On April 15 the Union cavalry tried again to cross at Beverly Ford and Welford's. They pushed back the picket force and moved downriver, where they recrossed. It had been raining heavily for hours, and the stream was running high. Just as the rear guard was recrossing to join the main Federal command, John R. Chambliss's Thirteenth Virginia came "charging at full speed under a rapid fire of rifles from the opposite side." "Many Yankees were drowned in attempting to swim" the swollen river. The Confederates also captured some prisoners who decided not to try to swim the river. Lee's loss was one man killed, two wounded, and four missing or taken prisoner. Twenty-four Federal prisoners were taken.[13]

Hooker forwarded the news to Washington that the advance of his cavalry had been stopped by swollen rivers. Lincoln's reaction was a feeling of "considerable uneasiness." He continued: "The rain and mud, of course, were to be calculated upon. General S. is not moving rapidly enough to make the expedition come to anything. He has now been out three days, two of which were unusually fair weather, and all three without hindrance from the enemy, and yet he is not 25 miles from where he started. To reach his point he still has 60 miles to go, another river to cross, and will be hindered by the enemy. By arithmetic, how many days will it take him to do it? I do not know that any better can be done, but I greatly fear it is another failure already." The president's prophecy of gloom was correct, and he would have been even more chagrined to learn just how few Confederates had stood in the way. Stuart certainly understood the odds and praised Rooney in his official endorsement: "The conduct of Brig. Gen. W. H. F. Lee, his untiring zeal, ceaseless vigilance, and intrepidity, united to fine military judgment displayed in his disposition [of troops] deserves the special commendation of the commanding general. His brigade was for days confronted with two divisions of the enemy's cavalry. His report will show how small his force was."[14]

The rains kept the river impassable and the Union cavalry immobile for two weeks. Robert Lee knew well the disparity in numbers between his cavalry and Hooker's. On April 19 he wrote Stuart, "I am aware that from the superior strength of the enemy he will be able to overpower you at any one point, but believe by your good management, boldness, and discretion, you will be able to baffle his designs." Hooker as well realized that he had the upper hand in numbers of cavalry. About the same time he wrote to Stoneman that Stuart had only "two small brigades of cavalry" opposing him and that these were "wretchedly mounted." However, in the coming campaign it was not the numbers of cavalry that would be the deciding factor but the leadership. The Confederates were bold and aggressive; the Federal generals were conservative at best and, in some cases, overcautious and timid.

Hooker's overall plan was to destroy Lee's army. To do this he proposed a grand flanking maneuver that would push the Army of Northern Virginia back on his cavalry, which would be massed in the rear. It was Stoneman's job to get into position by the time Lee's army was in retreat. Stoneman sent out reconnaissance parties to feel out the various fords. One brigade commander sent a report of a rumor "that at the fords the water has been filled with iron wirework, calculated to entangle the feet of horses, while the sharpshooters pop them off." Already, the Union mind-set was one of caution. The Confederate cavalry continued to picket the fords with the main body of troops at Brandy Station.[15]

On April 29, word came that the enemy was making preparations to cross the river at Kelly's Ford, and Rooney Lee ordered the Thirteenth Virginia to meet it. The Federal force was commanded by General Averell and consisted of three brigades of cavalry and a battery of artillery, "about 3,400 sabres and six guns." Rooney Lee fell back before Averell's advance, but skirmished as he fell back. The Ninth and the Thirteenth had hard work that day. When they reached the Rapidan, Lee drew up in line of battle. During one charge of the Ninth, two brothers named Wright were taken prisoner. One was shot after he surrendered; the other was interrogated by Averell. When asked about the Confederate strength, Wright answered that "there was no cavalry in front of him except W.H.F. Lee's brigade, but that the trains had been hurrying down all morning from Gordonsville crowded with infantry and artillery." In Averell's official report, he stated that he had found out that Stuart was waiting for him "with four brigades and fifteen pieces of artillery." He found some supplies at Culpeper Court House and took time to turn these over to "the poor people of the place." While there he heard that "General Jackson was at Gordonsville with 25,000 men." He also heard from his superior that the main force had been delayed and that he was to continue driving the Confederates toward Rapidan Station. The last word from Stoneman's staff was: "He turns the enemy over to you." This was a daunting assignment to one whose mind was already plagued by visions of vast gray hordes all around. When he reached Rooney Lee's position at the Rapidan, he stopped to study the situation. Averell had the opportunity to run over Lee and possibly destroy most of his command. But he lacked the drive and fortitude to do so and made only half-hearted attacks against what he called "strong and skillfully constructed" defenses with rifle pits full of sharpshooters and guns sweeping the entire area. Lee, by contrast, was prepared to fight against great odds and had retreated as far as he was going to retreat. He was effectively neutralizing a much larger force by a determined stand. By this time he was alone, as Stuart had gone with Fitz Lee's brigade to the main body of Lee's army. Finally Rooney received orders to burn the bridge at Rapidan Station, which he quickly did.[16]

By now the battle of Chancellorsville was raging, and Hooker, irritated by Averell's inactivity, ordered him to return his command to the United States Ford and report to Hooker in person. After losing only one man killed and four wounded, Averell withdrew. On May 3 he was relieved from command and replaced by Pleasanton. Hooker offered as a reason that he did not want units in his command "paralyzed" by men like Averell. He continued, "I could excuse General Averell in his disobedience if I could anywhere discover in his operations a desire to find and engage the enemy."[17]

Rooney then marched to Gordonsville, which he reached at 11:00 A.M. on May 2. He could now direct his attention to Stoneman and the rest of the Union cavalry. Stoneman himself did not make an auspicious start. He crossed at Raccoon Ford on April 30, and his command spent a miserable night as he had ordered no fires to be built and every man was to stand to horse. It was foggy and so cold that the mud froze overnight. Stoneman marched at daylight to Verdiersville,

crossing the path Stuart had taken to Chancellorsville. On the night of
May 1, Stoneman's command camped on the southern side of one of
the northernmost tributaries of the North Anna. Brigadier General
David M. Gregg's division, which had been detached the day before,
arrived at Louisa Court House early on May 2. Gregg met no opposition there and began to tear up the railroad. He was joined midmorning by Stoneman and the rest of the cavalry. As soon as Rooney Lee
arrived at Gordonsville (11:00 A.M. on May 2) he heard that there
was enemy cavalry at Louisa Court House. Stoneman sent a detachment from the First Maine toward Gordonsville an hour before
Rooney Lee sent the Ninth Virginia from Gordonsville toward Louisa
Court House. These forces collided, and the Yankees were driven
back, losing thirty-two prisoners. Rooney brought up the Thirteenth
Virginia to aid the Ninth and took up a position to await the enemy.
He learned then that Stoneman was at Louisa Court House with his
whole command, making preparations to move toward the James
River. His "men and horses being worried out by the four days fight-
ing and marching," Rooney withdrew to Gordonsville and sent out
the pickets.[18]

Stoneman detached small units to destroy bridges and railroads on
the North Anna and South Anna as he moved with the main column
and camped for the night at Thompson's Cross Roads. On May 3 he
could hear the artillery fire from the battlefield at Chancellorsville but
continued with his own plan. He met with regimental commanders
and explained his intentions: "I gave them to understand that we had
dropped in that region of country like a shell, and that I intended to
burst in every direction, expecting each piece or fragment would do as
much harm and create as much terror as would result from sending
the whole shell, and thus magnify our small force into overwhelming
numbers." He gave out several assignments. Colonel Percy Wyndham,
commanding the First New Jersey, was to destroy the aqueduct over
the Rivanna. The Second New York under Colonel Hugh Judson Kilpatrick was to destroy the railroad bridges over the Chickahominy.
Colonel Benjamin Davis and the Twelfth Illinois were ordered to
strike the Virginia Central Railroad at Ashland and Atlee's. General
Gregg's assignment was to destroy all the bridges on the South Anna.
Two other regiments, the Fifth U.S. and First Maryland, were sent out
with no particular target but with orders to burn and destroy. Stoneman would remain in camp with the remainder of the force and await
the return of the raiding parties.[19]

On Sunday, May 3, Rooney heard from his scouts that the Yankees were heading in the direction of Columbia, and he knew that their object was the aqueduct there. He went after them and arrived at night. Wyndham had already left, and Lee's command "pursued all night." By dawn they had traveled sixty to seventy miles. One trooper remembered the march as "very fatiguing." He wrote, "What a toilsome, painful march it was! As the hours passed in slow and wearisome procession, the soft earth seemed to woo with a tantalizing pervasiveness to pause and recline our aching limbs upon it, but in vain." The next morning Lee caught up with Wyndham. One squadron of the Ninth went out in advance, and soon those following saw "the men ahead . . . flashing their sabres in the morning light, and meeting a charge by a Federal squadron." There was a brief hand-to-hand struggle before the blue troopers retreated, leaving six killed, many wounded, and thirty-three prisoners. A captain of the Fifth U.S. thought that they were "engaged with at least 1,000 men." He reported that "the shock of the charge was so great that my foremost horses were completely knocked over." The Rebels charged with their usual blood-curdling yell. To the Federals this yell sounded as if it "must have come from at least a regiment." Rooney recognized Captain Wesley Owens of the 5th U.S. among the prisoners and talked with him a while. He found out that the force he was following belonged to Wyndham and that General John Buford's entire command was only three miles away. His own command was down to 800 men, and they were worn out. In his words, "I decided not to pursue." As for Wyndham, he had received "reliable information of General Lee's advance with a force of cavalry and artillery [and] thought it expedient to retire." They rested that day but sent out scouting parties. Lee "heard by telegram from Richmond that the enemy were everywhere." Rooney was probably frustrated by not being able to do more, but there is a limit on human endurance and capabilities. He sent word of his location and activities to General Stuart or General Lee by way of General Arnold Elzey on May 4, as he had no means of direct communication.[20]

After resting the men and horses for a short while, Lee headed toward Gordonsville. He had learned that Stoneman's men were returning by basically the same route they had used to advance and followed on their left flank. Stoneman's command crossed the South Anna at Yanceyville and then crossed the Virginia Central Railroad at Tolersville. It was a very cold night, difficult for both blue and gray riders. Buford was again detached from the column, this time with a hand-picked force to march

in the direction of Gordonsville. He was supposed to lead the Confederates into thinking that the entire command was going that way. About
two miles from Gordonsville he met Rooney Lee's men waiting for him.
He decided to head north and crossed the North Anna, which was rising
fast. Lee followed and took seventeen or eighteen prisoners. The last of
Buford's command had to cross the river by raft. With Buford out of
reach, Lee moved lower down upon hearing of another column (Stoneman). But by the time Lee arrived, the last Yankees were across and all
the bridges had been destroyed. The night of May 6, Lee's men
bivouacked three miles from Orange Court House. The next day they
went to Trevilian's in search of Yankees, but the scouts reported that
they had all crossed the Rapidan. At 3:00 P.M. Lee marched for Orange
Court House.[21]

Stoneman's raid was now officially over. None of the fragments of
Stoneman's "bursting shell" did quite as much damage as he had envi-
sioned. The raiders had done considerable damage but had failed to
destroy the aqueduct. Some of the key bridges had escaped harm, and
many were repaired quickly. In fact, the railroads between Fredericksburg and Richmond were open again on May 5, an interruption of
only two days. The raiders might have attacked Guinea's Station and
destroyed Lee's transport and supplies, which were virtually unguarded, but they bypassed that location. There was considerable
panic but no real damage in Richmond as Kilpatrick and Davis came
very close before seeking refuge in Union lines to the northeast. Kilpatrick's escape route led him to Gloucester Point, where he rested his
men for days. It was not until June 3 that he finally rejoined the
army.[22]

Offsetting Stoneman's accomplishments was the appalling loss of
horses. The Federal quartermaster of the cavalry corps reported:
"The horses were generally in fair condition when they started on this
expedition; they were all much exhausted and weakened by the
march." He estimated that 1,000 horses were abandoned and killed.
The orders were to kill all horses that could not keep up. This practice kept the Confederates from gathering them up and rehabilitating
them for future use. His estimate did not include Kilpatrick's contingent. The horses that were taken to replace them were generally
broodmares and workhorses that were not suitable as cavalry
mounts. Captain Charles Francis Adams, a former friend of Rooney
Lee's from Harvard and an officer in the First Massachusetts Cavalry,

left this impression: "On this last raid dying horses lined the road on which Stoneman's divisions had passed. . . ." Buford reported that many men were left behind as their horses were unable to proceed and substitutes could not be found. By May 13 only about half of Stoneman's cavalry was fit for duty; the rest were dismounted.[23]

Stoneman's raid was, after all, only a sideshow to the battle of Chancellorsville. Hooker sent off all his cavalry on what amounted to a wild-goose chase and left his army groping forward without its eyes and ears. He had hoped that General Robert Lee would be greatly vexed by reports of a large Federal cavalry force in his rear and might even retreat, but the Confederate commander paid almost no heed to this threat. The fact that General Robert Lee sent Rooney with only two regiments to deal with this threat indicates his lack of concern. He knew that Hooker was his main objective and used Stuart and Fitz Lee's brigade to screen and reconnoiter, which they did exceptionally well. Fitz was the one who found Hooker's flank "in the air" and led Jackson's corps on its flanking movement. Stuart was there to take over for the wounded Jackson at a crucial moment in the attack. In short, General Lee used his available cavalry to obtain the optimum result, whereas Hooker squandered his. If Hooker had kept all his cavalry with the army, there might have been a different outcome.

The *Richmond Sentinel* shared this opinion. In spite of the scare that Richmond had experienced with Union cavalry knocking at the gates of the city, many appreciated the effort of Rooney Lee and his small band of cavalry. The newspaper ran an account of their efforts during Stoneman's raid and ended: "This narrative is certainly one of great activity, gallantry and efficiency on the part of General Lee and his cavalry, with many important points to cover and with a force of only 800 to oppose a multitude, he yet checked and punished the enemy and escaped injury himself. Of what was transpiring around Richmond he had no means of knowing and did not know. As to the other portions of the cavalry, history will not take long to say which was the more important, to tear up a few rails at Ashland or to cooperate in the battle of Chancellorsville."[24]

In his official report, Stuart wrote that Rooney Lee's "memoranda" of his actions provided "evidence of sagacity and good conduct throughout, and of great efficiency on the part of his command." The commanding general echoed Stuart: "The small command of General Lee exerted itself vigorously to defeat this purpose (destruction by

Stoneman). The damage done to the railroads was small, and soon repaired, and the canal was saved from injury. The details of his operations will by found in the accompanying memorandum, and are creditable to officers and men." To President Jefferson Davis, Lee sent an appeal for more cavalry: "I hardly think it necessary to state to your Excellency that unless we can increase the cavalry attached to this army we shall constantly be subject to aggressive expeditions of the enemy similar to those experienced in the last ten days. . . ."[25]

At the end of this campaign Rooney Lee's command camped near the village of Orange Court House. On June 12 the men heard the news of Stonewall Jackson's death. A trooper remembered: "The effect of the announcement wrought a change in every man's expression, and threw a solemn gloom over the camp." This news also prompted Rooney to write his father and beg him not to expose himself recklessly to enemy fire: "I hear from everyone of your exposing yourself. You must recollect, if anything should happen to you, the cause would be very much jeopardized. I want very much to see you. May God preserve you, my dear father, is the earnest prayer of your devoted son."[26]

He also wrote his mother, expressing concern over her health, which was steadily declining: "I think of you, my dear Mother, very often & I pray God that he may restore you to health." He urged her to take care of herself, as she would "have a plenty to do" when she returned to Arlington. His father had sent him an early birthday present, and he told his mother he was "much obliged" for the "handsome" gift. After asking about the news of the traveling Lee clan, he wrote of the casualties of the last campaign in which several of their friends and family connections had been killed or wounded. In a prophetic way, he wrote, "We are gradually being thinned out. Whose turn next?"[27]

CHAPTER 9

"It was his day of glory"

For a short period after Chancellorsville, there was time for rest and refitting. The commanding general's orders to Stuart were to get his "cavalry together, and give them breathing time, so as when you do strike, Stoneman may feel you." During this time many men returned to their commands with new horses, and the lush spring grass in the pastures was beginning to fill out some of the lean flanks of the cavalry mounts. By late May Rooney Lee's old regiment, the Ninth Virginia, boasted a strength of more than 1,000 officers and men. The brigade was camped near Welford Ford for about a month between campaigns.[1]

Charlotte took advantage of this "breathing time" to visit her husband. She arrived at his headquarters near Culpeper Court House on May 16. They were together as often as he could manage to be away from his official duties, and Charlotte met some interesting people while visiting. One of these was Justus Scheibert, a Prussian officer who was attached to Stuart's headquarters as an official observer. He was something of an artist and made many sketches of the Southern cavalry operations. Charlotte had studied art and did some painting herself. Hearing of his talent, she asked him to touch up some of her work. She was boarding at a house in Culpeper, and Scheibert went there one afternoon to finish a small portrait she had done of a lady. Stuart and some of his staff just happened to be sprawled on the grass outside the house, enjoying the spring sunshine. An observer noted that Scheibert "was dressed in a very short jacket and white trousers in which his fat person looked as if it had been melted and poured in."

When they had completed the portrait, they laid the canvas on a chair so that the oil could dry. Scheibert had many odd ways, one of which was to jump up, wave his arms in conversation, and "then pop down on any chair that happened to be nearest to him." During one of his "fits of enthusiasm" he popped down on the wet canvas without noticing it. When it was time to go, Charlotte thanked him and turned to get the picture for one last perusal. She could not find it. The good captain exclaimed, "Oh! the wind must have blown it under the piano!" Down on all fours, he went to search for the missing canvas. "Here it is," Charlotte cried, "screaming with laughter as she pulled the unfortunate picture from the broad seat of Scheibert's white trousers." The lady's face had been transposed onto his derrière. Scheibert "bolted" out of the house without saying goodbye or gathering up his hat and gloves. Stuart and his staff saw him "waving his arms wildly and roaring like a bull with laughter." He flopped down on the grass and rolled "over and over" laughing. Every time his rear was up, the officers enjoyed the view of the lady's face on the seat of his pants.[2]

On May 23 Robert Lee wrote to his wife: "I am glad you heard from F [Fitzhugh] and R [Robert] & that Charlotte is so well accommodated. I hope she will be able to spend a little time with F." However, he could not help but tease his children a little. He wrote to Rooney: "I wrote you a few lines the other day and also to daughter Charlotte. Tell her she must talk quick to you. Her time is getting short and the soldiers complain of officers' wives visiting them when theirs cannot. I am petitioned to send them off." He offered one remedy to the situation by adding, "Kiss Chass for me and tell her that daughters are not prohibited from visiting their papas. It is only objected to wives' visiting their husbands."[3]

Stuart ordered a review of the cavalry assembled near Culpeper for May 22. This included the brigades of Wade Hampton, Fitz Lee, and Rooney Lee. Charlotte was able to attend and was thrilled at the sight of her husband at the head of his men. She described the event in a penciled note to her father-in-law, who in turn relayed the news to Mary Lee in Richmond: "I have received a letter from Charlotte. She was at Culpeper Court House very comfortable & happy. Had seen the review & all the Genls. & had much to say about Fitzhugh. . . . Fitzhugh & Robert were both well & according to Charlotte looked uncommonly handsome at the review." Robert Lee also predicted future action: "I think we shall hear from Genl. Stoneman next week. I hope we may be able to frustrate their plans in part if not in whole." This prediction came true in just nine days, but with a new cavalry chief.[4]

During the month of May the Confederate cavalry was engaged in "incessant drilling" in preparation for the impending offensive. The horses enjoyed the rich pastures around Culpeper, and the ranks were growing daily as men came in with new horses from home. The men had time for fishing and swimming in the nearby streams. It was a beautiful camping spot, and the cavalry was "in the highest spirits."[5]

Stuart's cavalry command had been greatly enlarged by the arrival of two more brigades for the upcoming campaign. Beverly Robertson's command (at least two regiments of it) had been ordered up from North Carolina, and William "Grumble" Jones's brigade had just come in from the Shenandoah Valley. This brought Stuart's command up to five brigades, totaling approximately 9,500 men.[6]

The massing of gray cavalry did not go unnoticed by the Federal scouts. On June 1 General Alfred Pleasonton, who had just recently replaced Stoneman as the cavalry commander of the Army of the Potomac, received a warning that Stuart was up to something. "I have every reason for believing that Stuart is on his way toward Maryland," warned G.S. Smith. Pleasonton at first dismissed this by saying "any performance of Stuart's will be a flutter to keep us from seeing their weakness." The brass in Washington was more concerned, however. From there, Halleck warned Hooker: "Prisoners and deserters brought in here state that Stuart is preparing a column of from 15,000 to 20,000 men, cavalry and artillery, for a raid." General Robert Milroy advised "that the militia of Maryland, Pennsylvania and Ohio be called out at once, as doubtless there is a mighty raid on foot." Brigadier General John Buford, with the best of the Yankee horse soldiers at that time, sent Pleasonton information he had obtained "that all of the available cavalry of the Confederacy is in Culpeper County. Stuart, the two Lees, Robertson, Jenkins and Jones are all there. . . . My informant . . . says Stuart has 20,000; can't tell his instructions, but thinks he is going to make a raid."[7]

Meanwhile Stuart—blissfully unaware of the rumors of his plans burning up the Yankee telegraphs—was making plans for an even larger and grander review. The plains near Culpeper proved to be a ready-made parade ground for cavalry, complete with a hill for a reviewing stand. Invitations were sent to several distinguished guests, including the commanding general of the army, the former secretary of war, George Randolph, and many admiring young ladies. New uniforms for officers were ordered, and everything was polished and shined. The night before, there was a ball in the town hall that turned out to be a "gay and dazzling scene."[8]

June 5, the day of the review, was "beautiful, sunny." Stuart and his staff rode from Culpeper to the parade ground, being greeted by the "enthusiastic cheers of the populace." The various brigades were already drawn up in a long line. Stuart, followed by his staff, galloped down the front of this line, then circled around to the rear of it and on to his spot on the hill. As he went, the generals with their respective staffs joined him so that a band of nearly a hundred officers made the final gallop to the reviewing stand. Next, the individual commands passed in front of Stuart, the dignitaries, and the ladies. They each started out at a trot at one end of the plain. About a hundred yards from Stuart's hill, they broke into a gallop and charged past at full speed, the rebel yell piercing the air and the brilliant sun flashing from hundreds of brandished sabers. The horse artillery fired several blank rounds, adding their own thunder to the drumming of horses' hooves and bugle calls. For the spectators it was a thrilling sight, like being in a battle except there were no casualties and no enemy. "It would make your hair stand on end to see them," declared one viewer. Many young ladies with escorts fainted from the excitement; those without escorts managed to stay on their feet throughout the spectacle. To top off the day there was another ball, this time out on the grass near Stuart's headquarters. Bonfires were lit to provide light to dance by. Also that night there was a dinner at Afton, Samuel Bradford's home. A total of thirteen Confederate generals dined there, including Stuart, Rooney Lee, and other generals from Longstreet's and Ewell's infantry corps.[9]

The day after the review, Buford sent the following report to Union cavalry headquarters: "Yesterday cannon firing was heard toward Culpeper. I suppose it was a salute, as I was told Stuart was to have had that day an inspection of his whole force." The *New York Herald* carried the story of the review on June 8: "It is reported that there was a review of the forces of Fitzhugh Lee and Wade Hampton by General Stuart at Culpeper yesterday. They numbered from twelve to fifteen thousand. By this time General-in-Chief Halleck in Washington was so convinced that Stuart was going on a raid that he detached engineers to Pittsburgh to prepare the defenses of the city."[10]

The only thing that kept the review of June 5 from being perfect in Stuart's mind was the absence of the commanding general. Robert Lee

had been detained and could not attend. When he sent Stuart word
that he would be able to review the cavalry on June 8, a repeat performance was ordered. This would prove to be a quieter affair, not the
social event of the earlier review. Most of the ladies had gone home,
but there was an appreciative audience. John Bell Hood had answered
the invitation to bring "any of his friends" by bringing his entire division to watch the spectacle. Again the brigades rode by, this time under the watchful eye of the army commander. They walked, then trot-
ted, and finally galloped as they went by, then pulled down to a walk
again to avoid wearing out the horses. One hot-blooded horse was
convinced that the charge was a real one, however. In spite of a heavy
hand on the curb, "She shot out like an arrow, overtaking the
squadron in front, made a rear attack upon it, and broke it in two."
Hood's infantry made a sport of catching and appropriating all the
hats blown off during the review. In spite of the grumbling on the part
of some of the participants over the work involved, all had to agree it
was "a grand sight to behold this splendid pageant."[11]

From his position as aide to his brother, Robert Lee Jr. observed
that the "efficiency, confidence, and morale (of the cavalry) were never
better." Of the review he wrote: "We had been preparing ourselves for
this event for some days, cleaning, mending and polishing and I remember we were very proud of our appearance. In fact, it was a grand
sight—about eight thousand well mounted men riding by their
beloved commander, first passing him in a walk and then in a trot."[12]

Robert Lee Sr. wrote his wife the next day to tell her of the day's
events: "I reviewed the cavalry in this section yesterday. It was a
splendid sight. The men & horses looked well. They had recuperated
since last fall. Stuart was in all his glory. Your sons & nephews well &
flourishing. Fitz Lee was on the ground not in the saddle tell Sis Nan-
nie [Fitz's mother], but sitting by some pretty girls in a carriage. He
says he is afflicted by an attack of rheumatism in his knee. I fear it is
so, but he is getting over it & expects to be on duty in a few days.
Fitzhugh was on his black charger tell Charlotte & Rob by his side.
. . . I am very sorry Charlotte had left. But understand from Fitzhugh
she was very well." To her he stressed the upbeat aspect of the review,
but his careful eye had noticed some details that needed improving.
The day of the review, he wrote to Colonel Josiah Gorgas, the chief of
ordnance in Richmond, to complain of the carbines and saddles he
had noticed. The saddles made in Richmond "ruined the horses'
backs," and the Confederate-made carbines "were so defective as to

be demoralizing to the men." He acknowledged the problems of the Confederate supply system but suggested that changes be made. He thought it better "to make fewer articles and have them serviceable" than to manufacture a large quantity of shoddy goods.[13]

To answer the threat of an imminent raid by Stuart, Hooker had the following orders hand delivered to his cavalry chief: "From the most reliable information at these headquarters, it is recommended that you cross the Rappahannock at Beverly and Kelly's Fords, and march directly on Culpeper. For this you will divide your cavalry force as you think proper to carry into execution the object in view, which is to disperse and destroy the rebel force assembled in the vicinity of Culpeper, and to destroy his trains and supplies of all descriptions to the utmost of your ability." The same day Pleasonton declared that his "people are all ready to pitch in."[14]

For this endeavor Pleasonton's cavalry command was strengthened by two brigades of infantry temporarily under his command. These brigades came from the Fifth Corps and were commanded by Brigadier General Adelbert Ames and Brigadier General David A. Russell. These infantrymen would add a strength of 2,800 men to the cavalry. The Union Cavalry was divided into three contingents under Brigadier General John Buford, Brigadier General David Gregg, and Colonel Alfred Duffié. Pleasonton's strength totaled 11,000 men and twelve cannons.

Pleasonton's force outnumbered Stuart's by 1,500 men, but Stuart had a slight advantage in artillery. Stuart's command was spread out in the order that they would march as they crossed the Rappahannock on the morning of June 9. Their goal was not a raid but to screen the movements of the entire Army of Northern Virginia as it marched north. Fitz Lee's brigade, temporarily led by Colonel Thomas Munford due to Lee's attack of rheumatism, was posted above Hazel River, nearly eight miles to the northwest of Stuart's headquarters, located on Fleetwood Hill near Brandy Station. Rooney Lee's men were next in line. They were camped near Welford (Farley), a house owned by the Welford family that Rooney used as headquarters. This position was almost due north of Brandy Station. A battery of the horse artillery under Lieutenant James Breathed was also bivouacked with Rooney Lee's brigade. Jones's brigade was nearest to Beverly Ford. It was camped at St. James Church, west of the main road that ran from the ford to Brandy Station. Wade Hampton's men were posted south of Brandy Station between Stuart's headquarters on Fleetwood Hill and the village of Stevensburg. His pickets were out to Kelly's Ford and beyond. The two regiments of Robertson's brigade were watching Kelly's Ford and two other fords from their location between Jones and Hampton. Stuart's pickets covered a line ten miles in length. The majority of the men were resting in their camps, packed and ready to move the next morning.[15]

While the Confederates slept, the blue troopers began to move toward the fords. Pleasonton had made his plans based on incorrect information. A scout had informed him that "the two Lees are at Culpeper" and "Hampton's Legion and almost 1,000 infantry at Brandy Station." So he ordered his subordinates to move in two columns. John Buford was to lead the First Division, the reserve brigade of cavalry, and Ames's infantry brigade across at Beverly Ford. A second column under Gregg was to cross at Kelly's Ford six miles downstream. This force consisted of Gregg's own Third Division, the Second Division, and Russell's infantry. Once across, the forces of Buford and Gregg were to converge near Brandy Station, then proceed together toward Culpeper, where they expected to catch the bulk of the Confederate cavalry unaware. Because of Pleasonton's faulty reconnaissance, his plan called for the two wings of his command to meet squarely in the middle of Stuart's strung-out brigades.

To keep the element of surprise, Pleasonton ordered no bugle calls, no fires, and as little noise as possible in the ranks. The horses were unsaddled but not unbridled, and the men ate their food cold. There was little rest for these men, as the order to move out came at 2:00 A.M. Through the night they rode on to the fords.[16]

Buford's column reached Beverly Ford exactly according to the established timetable. At dawn the first troopers splashed across and took out as many of the pickets of Jones's Sixth Virginia as they could. The dense woods and the roar of water spilling over a nearby dam helped to muffle the sounds while fog obscured vision. The pickets who did escape made record time in sounding the alarm, and Jones's men scrambled onto their horses to meet the Yankee column. Reveille had awakened them only shortly before the reports of Yankees at the ford reached the camp, and few were completely dressed as they pounded off to meet the blue column approaching from the river. There was plenty of confusion in the camps of the Sixth Virginia and Seventh Virginia, but there was also quick reaction and response to the unexpected threat. A battery of Stuart's prized horse artillery—for some unexplained reason parked between the ford and Jones's main camp—experienced a wake-up call much worse than reveille. "Just as we were rounding up the last sweet snooze for the night, bullets fresh from Yankee sharpshooters came from the depth of the woods, and zipped across our blanket beds," recalled one artillerist. They jumped up, threw the harnesses on the horses, limbered up, and drove to a safer location.[17]

The first Union troops across the ford belonged to Colonel B.F. Davis's First Brigade. As they pushed toward Brandy, they met Jones's Confederates, "strongly posted in the woods and behind barricades." The Federals charged through the woods that lined the river and into an open field on the other side. From there they could see the gray artillerymen frantically trying to move their guns. Immediately Davis mounted a charge to take the guns but was counterattacked by elements of the Seventh Virginia striking from the right and the left. In the melee that followed Davis was killed. By this time Buford himself had crossed the ford and rode to the fighting to see for himself "how matters stood." He positioned his First Division on the left side of the road that ran from the ford to Brandy Station and the reserve brigade on the right side. For the moment he posted the infantry on both sides of the road out of sight in the woods. Buford was a thirty-seven-year-old West Pointer and Indian fighter, a career army officer. He was solid, usually smiling and smoking a pipe as he rode his favorite gray. One of his men thought "it was always reassuring to see him in the saddle when there was any chance of a fight." On that day he had come to do just that. The fighting escalated as Jones ordered successive charges by his regiments. These were met by Buford's men. Jones's line finally stabilized with the artillery near St. James Church and the remainder running almost due north.[18]

When word of Yankees crossing at the ford first reached Stuart early that morning, he had sent couriers galloping off to his brigade commanders with orders to come to the fighting. The men of Rooney Lee's brigade were already up. "Boots and Saddles" had sounded at 6:30 A.M. on June 9. (The Confederates ruefully called this bugle call "Saddle Up" because of a scarcity of boots.) Their plans for the day included a twenty-mile-march to Fox's Spring on the Rappahannock, but this was not to be. Lee had already ordered all the men with sorebacked horses to remain behind as the cavalry headed north. Stuart's frantic orders to come immediately changed all this. Orders were now to "mount every man" as "To Horse-Lead Out" sounded at 7:00 A.M. Quickly the men formed platoons, and as soon as they turned into the road leading toward Beverly Ford they began to move at a gallop. For more than a mile they rode hard, most of them unaware of what lay ahead. As they rode out of a section of woods, the column turned left. They could see Federal artillery on the Cunningham farm between Dr. Green's house and the river. Rooney Lee's three Virginia regiments and the Second North Carolina took up positions quickly to oppose Buford. The North Carolinians took a position behind a knoll on which two guns of Breathed's battery were placed. All the men who had "long range guns" were ordered to fight on foot and were soon "hotly engaged with the enemy." Lee had reacted quickly to Stuart's call and moved aggressively. In positioning his men he used the terrain to great advantage. He established contact with the left end of Jones's existing line and extended his line along Yew Ridge, which rose near the western end of Fleetwood Hill and ran north. A courier was sent dashing off to Jones to notify him that Lee was on the left. Rooney Lee now had high ground from which he could easily confront Buford. Wade Hampton had similarly reacted quickly and moved into position on the right of Jones's line. Now Buford faced a semicircle of three full Confederate brigades. Their deployment was so fast that Pleasonton notified Hooker at 7:40 A.M. that there had been a "severe fight" and that "they were aware of our movement, and were prepared."[19]

Buford decided to attack in the direction he had started—along the road toward Brandy Station. His left had been "severely pressed by the enemy's skirmishers and artillery" from Jones and Hampton, and he thought the best way to alleviate this pressure was to crush it. He ordered a charge that was made by the Sixth Pennsylvania and the Sixth U.S. Cavalry "almost up to the mouths" of the Confederate artillery. It was a gallant charge into a veritable "hornet's nest" of flying lead. The Rebels proved too strong for these two regiments, which were forced to retreat. The support that was supposed to come did not, and the blue troopers were almost cut off and had to fall back in what one called "a race for life." It was "a fearful ride, full two miles of ground covered with dead and wounded men and horses, wide ditches . . . all the time pursued and fired at by those grey bloodhounds." This attack somewhat relieved Buford's left. In his mind it "drew the enemy to my extreme right, where they moved, and threatened to overwhelm me." Actually the Confederates had not moved, as it was a different force altogether—that of Rooney Lee.[20]

Buford then turned his attention to his right, the Confederate left. Devin's First Division remained on the eastern side of the Beverly Ford

Road confronting Hampton. Two infantry regiments, the Eighty-Sixth New York and 124th New York, were positioned in the woods to the north of St. James Church facing Jones. The remainder of the force was directed toward Rooney Lee's strong position along Yew Ridge. At the base of the ridge was a stone wall manned by dismounted cavalrymen. Two guns commanded by Lieutenant P. P. Johnston were on the ridge with a good field of fire. The troopers who were not at the stone wall were held ready to attack on horseback.[21]

About 8:30 A.M. Buford began a series of attacks with his cavalry supported by artillery. "In this position there was very severe work for the skirmishers and artillery, for several hours," Buford recorded. Rooney Lee had a close call during this part of the battle. He was standing with some staff members near a big hickory tree and just a few feet from one of Lieutenant Johnston's guns. A Federal shell hit the tree "and threw pieces of it over them." Also, a group from "Company Q" had chosen a spot about a half-mile behind Lee's line as an observation post. Another shell in their direction scattered these onlookers. The Second North Carolina and Tenth Virginia mounted at least one counteroffensive to the many attacks on their position. A contingent of the Eighth Illinois attempted to flank the defenders at the stone wall but met a "fire too severe to admit of his turning their flank as easily as had been imagined." Buford called on the infantry as well. "Do you see those people down there?" Buford asked an officer of the Third Wisconsin Infantry. "They've got to be driven out," he insisted. The captain figured that he would be outnumbered, but he might be able to move through the wheat field to the far end of the wall. From there his men could deliver an enfilading fire down through the Confederate defenders. Buford allowed the captain to take responsibility for the attempt by adding, "I don't order you; but if you think you can do it, go in." Stevenson led his men through the wheat to the far end of the wall. Once in place they fired "with terrible accuracy." Simultaneously other infantrymen charged, yelling to give the appearance of a larger force. The surprised Confederates pulled back, losing several prisoners from the Second North Carolina and Tenth Virginia.

At almost the same time that his left flank was dislodged, Rooney Lee observed that Jones and Hampton were withdrawing, leaving his right flank uncovered. Jones and Hampton had not been pushed out of their line but rather had been summoned by Stuart to meet another threat. The second wing of Pleasonton's attack force under Gregg had finally made it to the battleground. In Buford's words, "Gregg's guns were heard and the enemy began moving." Stuart had stripped the line at St. James Church to defend Fleetwood Hill against Gregg's attack. Buford's men were incredulous as they saw the rebel guns pull away from St. James Church. Devin, commanding the force in front of Hampton, thought they were going to charge "when suddenly the Rebel line wheeled into column and began to work to the right."[22]

Rooney Lee began to pull back from his position on Yew Ridge. This was accomplished "in full view of the enemy" and without hindrance. A new line was formed on the northern end of Fleetwood Hill, on even higher ground than the adjacent Yew Ridge. Lee deployed his regiments in a fishhook or question-mark pattern that would be much more difficult to turn than if it were in a straight line. At the point of the hook was the Thirteenth Virginia under Colonel John Chambliss. Next in line and in the curve was R. L. T. Beale's Ninth Virginia, then J. Lucius Davis's Tenth Virginia, and his last regiment, the Second North Carolina under Colonel Sol Williams. One of Jones's regiments, the Seventh Virginia under Lieutenant Colonel Thomas Marshall, had been left behind when Jones hurriedly departed to defend the southern end of Fleetwood Hill. This regiment consequently acted as if it were part of Rooney Lee's brigade.[23]

By 11:00 A.M. Gregg's guns could be heard as he approached the southern end of Fleetwood Hill. Buford decided to press on in Gregg's direction. "Gregg's cannonading becoming more distinct and furious, I resolved to go to him, if possible," he later reported. Taking all his force except the Fifth U.S. Cavalry, Buford attacked Lee's position "under a tremendous artillery fire." The reserves were also committed. As one Union officer commented on Buford's attack, "There were to be no fresh troops in waiting. Every one was needed at the front." He called the Rebel resistance "stubborn" and wrote, "Both sides charged repeatedly with the sabre, and at times dismounted to fight." Buford reported that ammunition ran low, so "out flew the sabres and most handsomely were they used." In the "hand to hand" fighting, he thought his enemy was "vastly superior in numbers," but this was not so. Rooney Lee's total effective strength in his four regiments as of May 25 only numbered 1,529, and his fifth regiment, the Fifteenth Virginia, was on detached duty picketing the lower Rappahannock. Moreover about 600 men in the Union cavalry possessed the Spencer seven-shot repeating carbines, and most of these were in Buford's First Brigade. As early as 12:30 P.M. Pleasonton sent word to army headquarters that he was engaged with 30,000 of Stuart's cavalry, had "lost heavily," and asked for part of the Fifth Corps to be sent toward Beverly Ford just in case.[24]

Pleasonton may have been thinking of lines of retreat by midday, but Buford and Gregg were apparently still full of fight. All through the early afternoon the fighting continued between Rooney Lee and Buford's forces, largely by dismounted men and artillery. Simultaneously at the southern end of Fleetwood Hill, Stuart's and Gregg's cavalry were fighting almost a separate battle for control of Fleetwood. Although Stuart had been surprised a second time by the arrival of this second column in his rear, quick reaction by Stuart's staff and subordinates had saved the day. A series of dashing charges with regiment meeting regiment, pistols, and sabers used in desperate hand-to-hand combat developed as Stuart fought to retain possession of the hill.

About 3:30 P.M. the fighting between Lee and Buford escalated into mounted, regimental charges and counterattacks. At almost the same time, Pleasonton sent a staff member, Captain Frederick Newhall, to find Buford and order him to break off the engagement and withdraw. It was some time, however, before Newhall could find Buford. When he started out he could see "Buford's troops engaged on high ground at the extreme end of the valley, in the edge of a wood . . . some two miles or more from the river." He could also see the wounded moving back to the ford. He continued his search for Buford.[25]

Buford had worked his way around to his right until he had "entirely enveloped" Lee's left. From an elevation southwest of Dr. Green's house he attacked. Again he used infantry—segments of the Second Massachusetts and Third Wisconsin—to open the way for a mounted charge. The infantry managed to dislodge a section of the sharpshooters behind a stone fence under the command of Colonel Chambliss. Into this breach came the Sixth Pennsylvania, making its second major charge of the day. They "pushed forward in fine order, bearing down upon the line of sharpshooters behind the stone fence, putting them to flight and making some captures." Lee's mounted regiments were in line just over the top of the hill. As the Sixth Pennsylvania came up the hill, the Ninth Virginia "assailed them with the sabre, breaking them into confusion. . . ." This charge by the Ninth remained "vividly impressed" in the mind of one of the participants. He remembered: "Our colonel W. H. F. Lee, had been promoted to brigadier-general, and my regiment was in his brigade. About 4 o'clock in the afternoon, Lee put himself at the head of my regiment

which was at the foot of a hill out in the open field, standing in column of fours, and gave the order to charge up the hill, he riding at the
head of the regiment. I was very near to the head of the column and
could see all that took place. When we got to the summit of the hill,
there, some two hundred yards away, stood a long line of blue-coated
cavalry. Lee did not hesitate an instant but dashed at the center of this
line with his column of fours. The Yankees were of course cut in two
at once, but each of their flanks closed in on our column, and then a
most terrible affray with sabers and pistols took place." The Pennsylvanians were forced back, not exactly in the direction they had come
but "directly on the stone fence through which there was but a narrow opening." There was a pileup of men and horses at this opening.
The Ninth pursued them past the fence to the woods, where Federal
artillery opened on them. Many of the prisoners taken earlier were
freed by this action.[26]

Just as the Pennsylvanians were driven back, the Second U.S. Regulars hit the Ninth Virginia in the flank and forced "them back in a severe hand-to-hand encounter." During this fight Captain Wesley Merritt (later major general) of Pleasonton's staff was riding with the
regulars. He rode up to a tall "prominent Rebel officer" and pointed
his saber toward him. "Colonel, you are my prisoner!" he audaciously commanded. The officer responded with a saber blow that, if
Merritt had not parried quickly, would have taken off his head instead
of just his hat. The Rebel then opened a gash in Merritt's leg. In "the
dust and smoke and steam from the heated horses making the air dark
and obscuring the vision," the officer disappeared, and other officers
went after Merritt, who barely managed to escape. The captain
thought he had crossed swords with Wade Hampton, but most likely
it was Rooney Lee. He still wore the three stars of a colonel, even
though he had been a brigadier general for months. Only two men—
Lee and Beale—would have been on that part of the field at that time
wearing a colonel's gray uniform. Furthermore Lee, not Beale, would
have been prominent for his height.[27]

As the Ninth Virginia was pushed back, Lee committed the Tenth
Virginia and the Second North Carolina to the fray. A member of the
Second North Carolina remembered Colonel Sol Williams giving the
order to form by squadrons, then "gallop, march." As the North Carolinians came over the hill they could see the Ninth Virginia and Thirteenth Virginia being driven back in their direction. When the Tenth
reached a point that it could fire into the enemy without hitting their

comrades in the Ninth and Thirteenth, they "halted and opened fire."
Colonel Williams ordered his regiment to oblique to the right, and as
they went around the Tenth he ordered a saber charge. The North
Carolinians went in with a yell, and the Federals began to pull back.
The Second followed with the colonel well in advance. He was about
to leap his horse over a wall, calling for the Second to follow him,
when he turned to go back to the regimental flag and collect his men.
He was calling on them to fall in when he was shot "through the head
and died immediately."[28]

In this last fighting Rooney Lee, "seeing the enemy in retreat, commanded 'Forward,' and was at the same instant wounded." A lieutenant remembered: "General Lee directed in person the counter-
charge, and as his mounted men swept over the hill . . . , a bullet
passed through his leg, in the moment of victory. Directing a soldier to
notify the next officer in command that he was wounded, after passing his sword over to an orderly, he was assisted from the field."[29]

Just as the last of these charges was made, Colonel Munford arrived with three of Fitz Lee's regiments. He sent in riflemen from three
squadrons and ordered the artillery with him to open fire. The Federal offensive was over at this point, as Captain Newhall had finally
found Buford and delivered Pleasonton's orders. Whether Buford
agreed to the necessity to withdraw or not, he complied with his superior's orders. In his report he merely stated, "By this time Gregg's
firing had ceased and I was ordered to withdraw." An "abundance of
means was sent to aid" Buford, and the withdrawal was carried out
with little harassment from the Confederate forces. With Rooney Lee
wounded, the leadership on that part of the field devolved on Colonel
Chambliss and Colonel Munford. In Chambliss's words, "About half-
past four o'clock P.M. Brigadier-General W. H. F. Lee was wounded,
and Colonel Sol. Williams, 2d North Carolina Cavalry, was killed,
and I assumed command, having previously been in charge of three
squadrons, dismounted as sharpshooters. Only a few shots were fired,
and the action was virtually over when I assumed command." From a
vantage point near the Welford house Munford could see "a division
of cavalry, a brigade of infantry, and two or three detachments of dismounted cavalry." Munford followed Buford's withdrawal but considered it "impracticable at any time to engage them in a hand-to-
hand fight." If Lee had not been wounded, the Confederates might
have made a more vigorous pursuit of Buford, but this was not so.
The rest of Pleasonton's command was already across the river when

Buford's men began to cross unhampered. Thus ended an engagement that had "lasted near 14 hours" for the Union forces. The exhausted, dirty, and often bloody troopers rode slowly on to a camping spot about three miles to the east of the Rappahannock. The horsemen in gray were left to clean up the battlefield and prepare as best they could to move out in advance of the Army of Northern Virginia as it headed north.[30]

As the greatest cavalry battle of the war came to a close, the losses were tallied. On the Confederate side 485 officers and enlisted men had been lost. Union casualties totaled 866. In his official report Buford noted that his losses were "heavy" and thought that "the enemy suffered equally." Buford's losses were heavy—more than 500 for the day, with the Sixth Pennsylvania suffering the most (108 casualties). However, Rooney Lee's brigade lost a total of ninety officers and men. Although Lee's losses were not equal to Buford's, they were commensurately high considering the disparity of numbers between the forces at the outset. These numbers indicate "that on no part of the field was the contest more bloody" than the area where Lee and Buford fought. Stuart remained in possession of the field and counted three artillery pieces, six flags, carbines, sabers, horses, and the like as won in battle.[31]

The intangible results were great and mixed as to the outcome. The Confederates claimed victory on the grounds that they held the field while the Federals retreated. They had kept the Yankees from penetrating their gray curtain in front of Lee's army. The cavalry had fought alone in spite of having infantry to call upon if needed. A segment of Major General Robert Rodes's division was held ready to the west of Fleetwood but was never called upon. In fact, Stuart's entire cavalry command was not engaged that day. Only fifteen Rebel regiments were in the fight compared to twenty-four regiments of cavalry and ten regiments of infantry on the Union side. Stuart, although surprised, fought magnificently and did everything he could have to meet the threats and to counter them. His subordinates, at least Hampton, Jones, and Rooney Lee, carried out their roles in admirable fashion. The Confederate cavalry on the whole fought well, as usual. General Robert E. Lee, who watched the last scenes of the battle unfold from a position at the Barbour house, "Expressed great admiration of the grit and courage manifested by the soldiers on both sides."

For their part, the Federals did not feel defeated and could on this account call it a victory. Pleasonton did not accomplish what Hooker had ordered. He had not destroyed the Confederate cavalry. So he conjured up alternative missions in his mind that he thought he had accomplished. He claimed first to have thwarted an impending raid by Stuart and then to have captured Stuart's headquarters and papers that divulged Lee's plans. Finally he fabricated a different purpose altogether for that day, a mission of reconnaissance only rather than of forcing Stuart to fight. As overall chieftain, Pleasonton was defeated that day. Two of his subordinates, however, fought well and stubbornly. Buford and Gregg both deserved great credit for their part in the battle. The most important victory won that day was a mental and moral victory won by the blue troopers. As one of Stuart's staff officers judged: "One result of incalculable importance certainly did follow this battle,—it made the Federal cavalry. Up to that time confessedly inferior to the Southern horsemen, they gained on this day that confidence in themselves and in their commanders which enabled them to contest so fiercely the subsequent battlefields of June, July, and October."[32]

Other subsequent actions may also have been the results of the battle of Brandy Station. The hours of savage fighting and the lives expended in trying to move Rooney Lee's men from the high ground of Yew Ridge and later the northern end of Fleetwood Hill may have left an indelible impression in Buford's mind. Three weeks later, as he watched Major General Henry Heth's infantry trudge toward Gettysburg with only his division between Lee's army and the high ground behind him, he may have seen visions of Fleetwood Hill in reverse. At any rate, he committed his men to a last-man defense of the good ground until Major General John Reynolds's men could relieve them. Likewise, the knowledge gained on June 9—that the Yankee cavalry could fight, too—may have influenced Stuart's actions. Prior to this he felt comfortable in raiding in any direction with a comparatively small force—1,500–1,800 men—as he was certain that they could ride over any Federal cavalry that got in their way or could quickly outmaneuver any infantry force they encountered. After Brandy Station he knew that he would need a much larger force to counter the Yankee cavalry. As he broke away from Lee's army later in June, he took with him three full brigades, those of Wade Hampton, Fitz Lee, and Rooney Lee (now commanded by Chambliss). If he had left any of these three with the main army to provide a screen and serve as scouts, the army would not have groped along blind. Any of these three would have been competent and would have had the confidence of the army commander.

As to Rooney Lee's conduct during the battle there are several points to consider. First, he reacted quickly to Stuart's orders to move toward the fighting. He wheeled his regiments into line and galloped off as fast as possible to his position. When he arrived he intuitively took in the lay of the land and effectively used the terrain in positioning his troops. He placed the artillery where it would have a good field of fire over the entire plain. Although in command of cavalry, he did not hesitate to dismount a portion of his men as sharpshooters, who used the protection of existing stone fences at the base of Yew Ridge and later at the second position on Fleetwood Hill to maximum effectiveness. When the time was proper, he used his mounted men in spirited, decisive charges. He personally led his men and was oblivious to danger as the assaults were made. He followed military protocol in all matters, as indicated by his sending a courier to notify Jones that he had taken a position on Jones's left. In the second position, on Fleetwood, his extreme left followed the contour of the ridge and was, in essence, refused, which made his flank more difficult to turn. In all, he performed solidly and decisively, always cool under fire. Stuart realized how efficient Lee had been, even though he was not under Stuart's eye the entire day. Stuart praised him in his official report: "General W. H. F. Lee engaged the enemy in a series of brilliant charges with his regiments, alternately routing the enemy, and, overpowered, falling back to reform." Also he wrote, "Brigadier-Generals Hampton, W. H. F. Lee, and Jones were prompt in the execution of orders, and conformed readily to the emergencies arising." Finally, Stuart reported, "Brig. Gen. W. H. F. Lee's brigade was handled in a handsome and highly satisfactory manner by that gallant officer, who received a severe wound through the leg in one of the last of the brilliant charges of his command on the heights. . . . I deplore the casualty which deprives us, for a short time only, it is hoped, of his valuable services." In a letter to his wife, Stuart again praised Lee: "General William H. F. Lee, with his whole Brigade, distinguished themselves, fighting almost entirely against regulars." A chaplain of the Tenth Virginia wrote that "each command acted nobly" in what he considered the "most hotly contested cavalry battle of the war." He continued: "The forces under W. H. F. Lee, that worthy descendent of 'Old Light Horse Harry,' bore no mean part in the fray. We have to regret the temporary loss of our general." Stuart's Prussian aide Heros von Borcke later commented that Lee had "demonstrated outstanding initiative" and, furthermore, that "it was his day of glory." He wrote that in the last charges Lee's men moved "forward to the attack in such magnificent style that an enthusiastic shout of applause rose along our lines on the heights whence the conflict could be plainly witnessed."[33]

The newspapers carried accounts of the fighting at Brandy Station almost immediately. While the Richmond papers sharply criticized Stuart, the Northern press lauded Buford. On June 11, the *New York Herald* reported that Buford had fought "one of the most obstinate cavalry fights that has occurred during the war." It was "of the bloodiest character, mostly hand to hand with sabre and pistol," the reporter continued. He also amazingly reported that "the force of the enemy cavalry alone is estimated at 50,000." On June 14 the *Herald* carried a reprint from a Richmond paper that said "General Fitzhugh Lee is severely wounded." By June 16 the paper had sorted out the difference between the two "Fitzhugh Lees" and correctly stated that "at the cavalry fight near Kelly's Ford . . . Brigadier-General Fitzhugh Lee, a son of Major-General Robert E. Lee, was very severely wounded." Unfortunately for Rooney Lee, the news of his wound and the place of his convalescence soon became known to the Union command. He would soon have another "battle" to fight, one entirely different from that fought on Fleetwood Hill.[34]

CHAPTER 10

"Nine long, weary months"

Late in the afternoon on June 9, 1863, Rooney Lee was brought from the battlefield of Brandy Station to Culpeper. He was met on his way from the front by his father. Rooney's concern was more for his courageous officers and men who had been killed and wounded that day than for his own prospects for recovery. The nature of his wound was severe, but it could have been worse. The ball passed through the thigh, missing the bone and the main artery. His youth and robust health were factors that prompted his father to hope for "a speedy recovery." Once in Culpeper, Lee was taken to Hill Mansion, where he spent the night. Later, on the night of the battle, with his official duties concluded, the commanding general took time to visit his wounded son and make arrangements to send him to a place where he could be nursed back to health. According to Hill family tradition, the young daughter of the family held Traveller's reins in the yard while the general spent some time with his son.[1]

The following day, Rooney Lee traveled to Hickory Hill, the Wickham home in Hanover County. Lieutenant Robert Lee now became his brother's nurse instead of his military aide. In spite of his need to oversee the movement of the gray legions heading toward Pennsylvania, the commanding general found time to write to his son:

My dear son:
I send you a dispatch received from Custis last night. I hope you are comfortable this morning. I wish I could see you, but I cannot. Take care of yourself and make haste and get well and

return. Though I scarcely ever saw you, it was a great comfort
to know that you were near and with me. I could think of you
and hope to see you. May we yet meet in peace and happiness!
Kiss Chass for me. Tell her she must not tease you while you
are sick, and let me know how you are.

God bless you both, my children.

Truly your father,

R. E. Lee[2]

To his daughter-in-law Charlotte, he wrote confidently of her ability to nurse her husband back to health and philosophized that as
"some good is always mixed with the evil in this world" she would be
able to spend some time with her husband during his convalescence.
He asked Charlotte to join him in "thanks to Almighty God who has
so often shielded him in the hour of danger for this recent deliver-
ance" and to "lift up your whole heart in praise to Him for sparing a
life so dear to us, while enabling him to do his duty in the station in
which He had placed him."[3]

Three days later Lee wrote Mary requesting further information on
his son. He had not heard from him since he left Culpeper and feared
that he might have gone on to Richmond. Lee wanted him to go
"where he can get good medical attendance and escape the infected
air of cities." He also confided, "My heart is . . . tortured by the condition of my poor Fitzhugh."[4]

At this time the father need not have worried, for Rooney had indeed arrived at Hickory Hill, where the number of nurses increased
considerably. In addition to Rob, he had his wife, mother, and sisters
to wait on him. For convenience he occupied one room in a small
two-room "office" near the main house, and his chief nurse, Rob,
slept in the other. The wound began to heal, and for two weeks the
Lees enjoyed a period of comparative peace and happiness.[5]

This idyllic quiet was broken in a most unexpected manner. With the
Army of Northern Virginia threatening Pennsylvania, there was an
open stage for Union cavalry operations in Virginia. Colonel Samuel
Perkins Spear, of the Eleventh Pennsylvania Cavalry, commanded an
expedition that disembarked from the White House on the Pamunkey
River and proceeded along the southern side of that river with destruc-
tion of the railroad bridges and track north of Richmond as his goal.
With a force of approximately 1,050 men, Colonel Spear moved first to

Tunstall's Station, where he captured and destroyed some Confederate commissary goods, then on to Hanover Court House, where he found a quartermaster's depot. He also destroyed the railroad bridge over the South Anna river after defeating a small force of the Forty-Fourth North Carolina Infantry. Sometime during the fight at the bridge, Colonel Spear received word that Rooney Lee was convalescing at Hickory Hill, only a short distance from Hanover Court House. At once he sent Lieutenant Tears with a detachment of Company F of the Eleventh Pennsylvania Cavalry to take General Lee, "if he could ride."[6]

The first indication that the people at Hickory Hill had of any Union troops in the area was the sound of shots being fired near the outer gate of the plantation. Mrs. Wickham, thinking that someone was shooting at the squirrels in the yard, sent Rob to stop the trespasser. Before the young lieutenant reached the grove of trees near the gate, he saw a small group of Union cavalrymen. Fortunately they did not see him because of thick foliage. Rob raced to the office and informed his brother that there were Union cavalrymen close by. Rooney ordered his brother to get away at once. He did not believe that a wounded man would be harmed by the enemy, but young Lieutenant Lee would be another matter. Besides, if he could avoid other parties of Federal cavalry and reach the nearby plantation of North Wales, he could keep their horses from being taken. Rob slipped out of the office and hid behind a hedge at the same moment that another, larger group of cavalry rode into the plantation yard. Rob reached a place of relative safety and saw a large group of cavalry on the main road from the courthouse. He could also see the smoke from the burning quartermaster depot at Hanover Court House. Lieutenant Lee waited until he thought "the coast was clear" and made his way back to Hickory Hill using the shrubbery in the gardens as a screen. He got as close as twenty yards from the house when he saw that there were still Federal cavalrymen around it. From his hiding place he saw his brother carried out of the office on his mattress and put into the Wickham carriage. With horsemen in blue around it, the carriage wheeled out of the yard.[7]

Lieutenant Tears brought his prize to Colonel Spear at the moment that the fight for the South Anna bridge ended. Colonel Spear had served in the regular army as an enlisted man and was a first sergeant in the Second U.S. Cavalry in 1860. The historian of the Eleventh Pennsylvania Cavalry records that "Lee and Colonel Spear had known each other in the old army (one as an officer and the other as an enlisted man). General Lee asked to be paroled, saying that he had captured thousands of Union prisoners and expected to capture thousands more, but he always paroled his wounded prisoners. Colonel Spear replied that he would have to go to White House, and that ended their intercourse." The same historian was of the opinion that "Colonel Spear would have been justified in granting his request, for it was usual at that time for both sides to parole their wounded prisoners. . . ." The fact that Rooney Lee was denied parole seems to indicate that he may have been a major target of the raiding party from the outset, even though this is not mentioned in the official orders to Colonel Spear. The Lee family certainly believed this to be true; as Robert Lee Jr. stated, "This party had been sent out especially to capture him." Lieutenant Colonel Arthur Fremantle records that in a conversation with General Lee on July 7, 1863, "He told me of the raid made by the enemy, for the express purpose of arresting his badly wounded son (a Confederate Brigadier General), who was lying in the house of a relation in Virginia. They insisted upon carrying him off in a litter, though he had never been out of bed, and had quite recently been shot through the thigh." Even the New York Herald, in reporting the news of the expedition, felt it necessary to offer some justification for this denial of parole. Under the headline "Why General Lee was not paroled," a reporter stated, "Colonel Spear might have paroled General Lee . . . but the dastardly tone the rebel leaders have taken toward our own officers captured in actual conflict, and their refusal to surrender certain ones on account of this, and account of that . . . still prevented him from displaying too much charity."[8]

As Rooney Lee was being carried away, two other "prisoners" were taken by the raiders. Lee's faithful servant Scott had taken his master's best horse out for a little exercise, oblivious of any danger. Before he knew what had happened, both man and horse were captured by the Yankees. The blue troopers saw no need to guard Scott—after all, to them he was a slave that they had liberated. Why wouldn't he cheerfully go with them to freedom? Scott did not have the same view of the situation, however. He waited for his chance to escape and headed to North Wales, the plantation where the rest of the Lee horses were being kept. Just ahead of a Union party of troopers on a horse-hunting detail, Scott took the others to safety. The loss of his favorite horse was certainly a cause for vexation to Rooney Lee. A cavalryman's horse is, in a sense, an extension of himself, a faithful companion, even a close friend. To know that this companion would be used, or even possibly abused, by enemies would be a sore trial indeed.[9]

Newspapers on both sides were quick to pick up on the capture of Robert E. Lee's son. The Richmond Daily Dispatch carried a report of the raid on June 27, the day after Rooney Lee was taken prisoner. The Daily Richmond Enquirer reported details of the capture, including eyewitness accounts that "General Lee, whom the Yankees were carrying along, was said to be suffering very much." Colonel Spear's expedition merited front-page headlines in the New York Times on June 29, 1863. The rest of the page was devoted to speculation as to the destination of the Army of Northern Virginia. On June 30 the New York Herald carried the following report from their correspondent at White House, Virginia: "He was shot through the thigh, but is doing well. He came in a very comfortable carriage and four which belonged to his friend. He has all the bearing of a refined and courteous gentleman. He is firm looking, and calculated to produce the most favorable opinion of his abilities as a leader. . . . To the many questions that were asked him he gave the most courteous answers, and I assure you he made no small number of friends by his manners. He goes down on the Thomas A. Morgan to Fortress Monroe this morning." Apparently the humiliation of capture and the physical ordeal had not lessened Lee's equanimity and poise.[10]

These headlines raise an interesting question that will probably never be answered: At what point did Robert E. Lee know of his son's capture? He told Colonel Fremantle about it on July 7 and wrote the following to his wife on the same day: "I have heard with great grief . . . that Fitzhugh has been captured by the enemy. I had not expected that he would have been taken from his bed and carried off. But we must bear this additional affliction with fortitude and resignation and not repine at the will of God. . . . I am particularly grieved on your account and Charlotte's." The news was in the Richmond papers as early as June 27 and in the Northern newspapers on June 29. During the entire Gettysburg Campaign, those at Confederate headquarters were "informed by the new Northern newspapers brought through by the scouts every day." So it is possible that some men at headquarters knew. Whether or not they passed along the information to the commanding general before or during the battle of Gettysburg is impossible to know now. Lee may have learned first through private or official correspondence from Richmond, but it is not known exactly when he heard of the capture. Although it is impossible now to prove or refute the hypothesis, there may have been one other reason that Lee "lost the matchless equipoise that usually characterized him." "In the days at Gettysburg, this quiet, self-possessed calmness was wanting" in Lee perhaps because of personal reasons as well as the many official cares. If Lee's heart was "tortured" by concern for Rooney after he was wounded, might not he have been even more so by his son's capture and the possibility of the wound being worsened by the move?[11]

When Rooney Lee arrived at the White House on the Pamunkey, he was examined by Major General John A. Dix's medical director. Dix then ordered him to be sent on to the Chesapeake Hospital at Fortress Monroe and seemed certain "that he will not be injured by the movement." On June 27 Lee was admitted to Hampton Hospital at Fortress Monroe with "a flesh wound, thigh." He was soon transferred to the Post (Chesapeake) Hospital. Confederate prisoners were usually treated at the Hampton Hospital, whereas the Chesapeake was a hospital customarily reserved for officers of the Union Army. The Chesapeake Hospital was located just outside the fort itself and had a capacity for seven hundred patients. On July 1 William H. Ludlow sent the following dispatch to army headquarters in Washington:

> I have the honor to acknowledge the receipt of the telegram of the General-in-Chief directing that the officers captured by Major-General Dix be not exchanged.
>
> No exchanges of Confederate officers have been made since the order of the 25th of May last forbidding paroling or exchanging such officers.
>
> Brigadier General W. H. Fitzhugh Lee, wounded, is in hospital here on the certificate of the medical director that he required hospital treatment. General Lee has given his parole to confine himself to the hospital and make no attempt to escape. As soon as he can be moved he will be sent to Fort Delaware, as we have no place of confinement here. His retention settles all questions about hanging our officers.[12]

Ludlow's dispatch to Major General Henry Halleck contains the first mention of Lee as the solution to the problem of "hanging officers." This problem had begun four months earlier and several hundred miles away. In April 1863 Captains William F. Corbin and Jefferson McGraw were captured in Kentucky while recruiting for the

Confederate Army. Although they were at first assured that they would be treated as prisoners of war, they were executed as spies. It seems that General Ambrose Burnside wanted to make an example of them and refused any leniency. Recriminations were called for in Richmond. By order of Provost-Marshal General John H. Winder, two Union captains were to be chosen to be executed in retaliation. This was still just a threat on the part of the Richmond authorities when Ludlow wired Halleck on July 1 that Lee's "retention settles all questions about hanging our officers." The threat became closer to reality on July 6 when the actual selection of the two captains to be executed was made. All of the Union captains in Libby Prison were ordered to form a hollow square in a room on the lower floor of the prison. At first the captains thought that they were about to be exchanged and were hopeful of a speedy trip home. These hopes were soon dashed when the captains learned the true reason they had been assembled. The commander of the prison, Major Thomas P. Turner, read aloud the order from General Winder. Then the names of the captains and their respective commands were written on slips of paper and put in a box. A Federal chaplain drew the names from the box. The first name to be drawn was Captain Henry Washington Sawyer, First New Jersey Cavalry, and the second was Captain John M. Flinn, Fifty-First Indiana Infantry. These two were taken to Winder's office, where they were informed that their execution would be carried out in a matter of days.[13]

Sawyer asked for and was granted permission to write his wife. In his letter he explained the situation and wrote: "My dear wife, the fortune of war has put me in this position. If I must die, a sacrifice to my country, with God's will I must submit, only let me see you once more and I will die becoming a man and an officer; but for God's sake do not disappoint me." The letter was sent through channels, and Captains Sawyer and Flinn were put in a dungeon in Libby Prison to await execution. Mrs. Sawyer received the letter on July 13, but instead of submitting to the tragedy she took a positive course of action. Her husband had asked her to come to Richmond with the children so that he might see them once more. Instead, she traveled to Washington with a friend, Captain W. Whelden, and Representative J. T. Nixon of New Jersey. On July 14 they were granted an interview with President Lincoln, who asked them to come back the following day, only one day before the two Federal captains were to be executed.

Lincoln conferred with Major General Halleck and other advisers before coming up with a solution to this problem. Captain Flinn was not
without his own champion, although he knew nothing about it. O. P.
Morton, governor of Indiana, wrote to Secretary of War Edwin Stanton on July 11 that the execution of one of his constituents and an officer of Indiana volunteers "would be deliberate murder" and that he
trusted that the War Department would "notify the rebel Government
that if it is done strong retaliatory measures will be adopted." Ludlow,
the Federal agent for the exchange of prisoners, offered his own advice to the brass in Washington when he wired the news that Sawyer
and Flinn had been selected for execution. He recommended "that
two Confederate officers now in our hands be immediately selected
for execution in retaliation for the threatened one of Sawyer and
Flinn" and that he "be authorized to communicate their names to the
Confederate authorities."[14]

All who voiced an opinion seemed to agree that "an eye for an eye"
was the course to follow. The ultimate decision was Lincoln's. This
little drama concerning the lives of two men must have seemed almost
insignificant at first to Lincoln considering the ghastly loss of life at
Gettysburg just days before. On July 14 the mental and emotional
stress had probably pushed Lincoln's patience to the breaking point. A
measure of this can be seen in Halleck's message to the victorious Major General George Meade that day. "I need hardly say to you that the
escape of Lee's army [i.e., from the Confederate defeat at Gettysburg]
without another battle has created great dissatisfaction in the mind of
the President." On the morning of July 14 Lincoln's secretary, John
Hay, described the president as depressed. Lincoln received the news
that Lee was across the Potomac just as the Cabinet was about to meet.
He called off the meeting because he was not capable of deliberating
the matters before the Cabinet. Secretary of the Navy Gideon Welles
confided in his diary that he had rarely "seen the President so troubled,
so dejected and discouraged." Robert Lincoln found his father "in
tears, with head bowed" later that day and told Hay that "the Tycoon
is grieved silently but deeply about the escape of [Robert E.] Lee." For
Lincoln the victory at Gettysburg was a hollow one. Lee had been allowed to withdraw, to regroup, and to carry on the war. In a letter that
he wrote to Meade but never sent, Lincoln put his feelings into words:
"I do not believe you appreciate the magnitude of the misfortune involved in Lee's escape. He was within your easy grasp, and to have

closed upon him would, in connection with our other late successes, have ended the war. As it is, the war will be prolonged indefinitely." Robert Lee may have escaped the Union grasp, but his son had not. For whatever reason, Lincoln decided on the night of July 14 to up the ante in the captain-for-captain game. The next morning, Halleck sent the following order to Colonel Ludlow:

> The President directs that you immediately place General W. H. F. Lee and another officer selected by you not below the rank of captain, prisoners of war, in close confinement and under strong guard, and that you notify Mr. R. Ould, Confederate agent for exchange of prisoners of war, that if Captain H. W. Sawyer, First New Jersey Volunteer Cavalry, and Captain John M. Flinn, Fifty-first Indiana Volunteers, or any other officers or men in the service of the United States not guilty of crimes punishable with death by the laws of war, shall be executed by the enemy, the aforementioned prisoners will be immediately hung in retaliation. It is also directed that immediately on receiving official or other authentic information of the execution of Captain Sawyer and Captain Flinn, you will proceed to hang General Lee and the other rebel officer designated as herein above directed, and that you notify Robert Ould, esq., of said proceeding, and assure him that the Government of the United States will proceed to retaliate for every similar barbarous violation of the laws of civilized war.

Ludlow immediately informed Robert Ould, the Confederate agent of exchange, of the Union's position on retaliation.[15]

Rooney Lee received the news of his imminent hanging while still in the Chesapeake Hospital. He was carried within the fort itself and put in a casemate on July 15. It is not now known which particular casemate he occupied, but it was at least similar to the one in which Jefferson Davis was imprisoned after the war. In this one the thick walls have one small window fitted with iron bars that allows the prisoner a view of the moat surrounding the fort. There is a fireplace at the other end. Heavy doors open into a room for guards that has a ground-level entrance to the interior of the fort. Lee was held in this casemate in solitary confinement the entire time he was at Fortress Monroe.[16]

The official Confederate reaction to the Union threat of retaliation is not known, but Sawyer and Flinn were never executed. They remained in the dungeon at Libby until August 16, when they were moved upstairs and treated the same as other Union officers. The Richmond papers continued to demand the deaths of the Union captains, and the fate of the four men was in doubt for some time. On August 20 Ludlow wrote Stanton: "I am satisfied, as I have been from the first, that Sawyer and Flinn will not be executed. This was settled by the prompt and significant selections of Lee and Winder." As late as December 1863, the situation was still the same, although some of the public furor had died down. On December 5 Stanton sent Lincoln a general summary of military operations and a report on the status quo of prisoners of war in which he noted: "Two prisoners, Captains Sawyer and Flinn, held by the rebels, are sentenced to death, by way of a pretended retaliation for two prisoners tried and shot as spies by command of Major General Burnside. Two rebels officers have been designated and are held as hostages for them." Robert E. Lee's views on retaliation were expressed privately in a letter to Custis on August 7, 1863.

I had seen in the papers the intention announced by the Federal Government of holding him [Rooney] as a hostage for the two captains selected to be shot. If it is right to shoot these men this should make no difference in their execution, but I have not thought it right to shoot them, and differ in my ideas from most of our people on the subject of retaliation. Sometimes I know it to be necessary, but it should not be resorted to at all times, and in our case policy dictates that it should be avoided whenever possible. The opportunities as well as the desire of our enemies are so much greater than ours, that they have the advantage, and I believe it would be better in the end for us to suffer, keep right in our own eyes, the eyes of the world, and the eyes of God, and that justice would thereby be sooner done us, and our people would thus suffer less, than if we took the opposite course. My grief at the intention of the enemy, as regards Fitzhugh of course, was intensified . . . I am however powerless in the matter and have only to suffer.

Lee never interfered in this matter of retaliation, not even for his own son.[17]

Correspondence for prisoners of war was usually censored both coming and going. Rooney wrote to his wife, his mother, and his brother Custis and they to him, but only one letter from this period exists. Therefore what is known of him during the time he was imprisoned comes from other sources. The family also obtained news from Rooney from those who had seen him or heard from him. Robert Lee and his son did not communicate with each other during this time. Rooney's letters were passed on to his father from the other members of the family. On one occasion Lee wrote to his wife: "I have read with much interest the affectionate notes of Fitzhugh and Markie. About the former I grieve daily." He also wrote, "I now long to see him more and more and wish I could communicate with him without affording to his jailers the opportunity of rejoicing in his misery." Probably if Lee had written, the letter would have been plastered on the front page of every Northern newspaper. Also, the expressions of affection and sympathy that Lee might have sent would have strengthened the belief on the part of the Union authorities that holding the son and threatening his life grieved the father.[18]

Fortunately for Rooney Lee, the leg wound continued to improve despite the frequent moves and imprisonment. On July 12 Robert Lee wrote that he was "very glad to hear that Fitzhugh suffered but little by his removal." Lee tried to reassure his daughter-in-law about her husband's well-being. He wrote to her: "I can see no harm that will result from Fitzhugh's capture except his detention. I feel assured that he will be well attended to. He will be in the hands of old army officers and surgeons, most of whom are men of principle and humanity. His wound I understand had not been injured by his removal, but is doing well." In early August Lee informed his wife: "I have heard of some doctor having reached Richmond that had seen our dear Fitzhugh at Fort Monroe. He said his wound was improving and that he himself was well and walking about on crutches." Later that month he sent her the latest news: "Custis has heard from him by some late arrival. He is reported doing well—walking about and as having everything he wants except his liberty." In September he reported "nothing new from F____ except reports from returned prisoners saying he was doing well and well treated and a great favorite with the Yankees." A few days later he wrote to Mary: "His wound is nearly healed and he is able to walk about though his leg is still stiff. His keepers are kind to him and give him all that is necessary. I understand some ladies have obtained the privilege of sending him a basket of supplies once a week and that they are very bountiful in their provision."[19]

From this it appears that Rooney was treated better than the average Confederate prisoner of war. Still, he was kept in solitary confinement while at Fortress Monroe. To a gregarious and sociable person like Rooney Lee, this may have been harder to bear than physical privations. Confederate prisoners of war passed through Fortress Monroe on their way to prisons in the North and came back that way when they were exchanged. But Lee was the only one ever kept there for any length of time. Indeed, when he was captured, the Union commissioner of prisoners reported that there was "no place of confinement" at Fortress Monroe. A place had to be made for him in a casemate of the fort that was away from any other Confederates. As the furor of retaliation abated somewhat, Captains Sawyer and Flinn were removed from the dungeon at Libby Prison and put back with the other prisoners. At Fortress Monroe Rooney Lee continued to be held in solitary confinement months later. In October Rooney Lee made a formal request for less restriction through Robert Ould, the Confederate agent of exchange, as follows:

> Brig. Gen W. H. F. Lee, C.S. cavalry, Fort Monroe, states that he has been informed that Captain Sawyer, for whom he is held as hostage, is not closely confined like himself and if so he asks that he shall receive the same treatment.

[Endorsement]
October 9, 1863
Respectfully returned to General Meredith, agent of exchange.
    Captain Sawyer is treated like all the other officers who are prisoners of war. He associates with them and is in the same room As far as treatment is concerned he is under no ban or disability. I have so informed General Meredith before.
R.O. Ould
Agent of Exchange

On November 14, Ould informed Meredith that neither Sawyer nor Flinn was being held in "close confinement" but that "it will not long be the case unless our officers and soldiers in your custody are relieved from their close confinement." These formal requests were ignored, and Rooney Lee continued to be held in solitary confinement.[20]

Difficult as the capture, imprisonment, and threats of hanging were on Rooney Lee, they were worse on his wife, frail Charlotte Lee. It seems that the horrors of war often affect those who wait and watch at home as much as or sometimes more than those who fight. Only a year before, their son had died, followed shortly by their infant daughter. Their home, the White House on the Pamunkey, had been in Union hands most of the war and had been burned in 1862. So Charlotte had been forced to move from one place to another, sometimes staying with relatives and, whenever possible, taking a room near cavalry headquarters to be close to her husband. Indeed, he had become her whole life. Robert Lee described her love for her husband: "She was so devoted to Fitzhugh. Seemed so bound up in him, that apparently she thought of and cared for nothing else. They seemed so united, that I loved them as one person." Barely over the shock of her husband's wound, Charlotte was forced to stand by helplessly with the other family members and watch her husband being carried off as a prisoner. Then came the threat of hanging this wounded man, and Charlotte Lee's already tormented state of mind must have become a nightmare. She lived each day wondering whether he might die from some complication concerning the wound or be hung because of the warring governments' sense of justice. It is no wonder she became physically ill. She went with Mary Lee to the mountains of Virginia in July with the hopes of recovering her health. A Virginia lady who saw her at this time wrote in her diary, "As I looked at the sad, delicate lineaments of her young face, I could but inwardly pray that the terrible threats denounced against her husband by Yankee authority might never reach her ear: . . . the mere suggestion would be enough to make her very miserable." This trip did no good, as Mary Lee wrote Mildred that she hoped Rooney would be exchanged "on Charlotte's account as her health is very delicate. She has been quite sick ever since she came to the mountains and has had a Dr. attending her." Robert Lee encouraged his daughter-in-law to take care of her health. He chided:

You must not be sick while F. is away or he will be more restless under his separation. Get strong and healthy by his return that he may the more rejoice at the sight of you. . . . I can appreciate your distress at F.'s situation. I deeply sympathize with it, and in the lone hours of the night I groan in sorrow at his captivity and separation from you. But we must all bear it, exercise all our patience, and do nothing to aggravate the evil. This, besides injuring ourselves, would rejoice our enemies, and be sinful in the eyes of God. . . . Nothing would do him more harm than for him to learn that you were sick and sad. How could he get well? So cheer up and prove your fortitude and patriotism. What, too, should I do? I cannot bear to think of you except as I have always known you—bright, joyous, and happy. You may think of Fitzhugh and love him as much as you please, but do not grieve over him or grow sad. That would not be right, you precious child.

Charlotte wanted to travel to Fortress Monroe to see her husband, but Robert Lee sent word that he thought "it very doubtful whether they would allow her to visit him. The only way of accomplishing it is to get permission from Mr. Secretary Stanton in Washington through Mr. Ould to take the flag of truce boat to Old Point." Because others had been refused permission, he doubted that it would be granted in her case. Furthermore, anyone who obtained permission was obliged to take the oath of allegiance to the United States. So Charlotte continued to be "weak and sad" and wanted to return to the springs in the Virginia mountains to find some cure. Her pathetic condition prompted Custis Lee to offer himself in exchange for his brother. He was to be a hostage for him for a period of forty-eight hours or longer, but "this request was curtly and peremptorily refused." Mary Chesnut noted in her diary that "Custis Lee offered himself to the Yankees in place of his brother, as he was a single man with no wife and children to be hurt by his imprisonment or made miserable by his danger. But the Yankees preferred Rooney."[21]

Exchange then was the only way in which Rooney Lee could return home. Officers on either side had not been exchanged since May 25, 1863. Robert Lee explained to his wife that the exchange had been suspended "owing to some crotchet or other." Actually it seems that the commissioners for exchange on both sides had agreed to disagree. Each refused to make any concessions that might aid the other side and quibbled over technicalities. This bickering and threats of retaliation and hostage-taking only caused the prisoners to remain in captivity for longer periods of time. Petty squabbles caused untold days of misery for those unfortunate enough to be captured. Robert Lee was greatly distressed by his son's imprisonment but did not interfere with the workings of the bureaucracy. In October he wrote to Mary: "I have no idea when Fitzhugh will be exchanged. The Federal authorities still resist all exchanges because they think it is to our interest to make them. Any desire expressed on our part, for an exchange of any individual, magnifies the difficulty, as they at once think some great benefit is to result to us from it. If you want a person exchanged, the best course is to keep quiet about it." Later he expressed a wish "that some general officer of cavalry might fall in our hands with whom he might be specially exchanged." The Reverend T. V. Moore, a former pastor of Richmond's First Presbyterian Church, told of a Federal officer in Libby Prison who wanted Lee to obtain his release. In return the officer was certain he had the connections to ensure Rooney Lee's exchange. Moore relates that Lee "respectfully but firmly declined to ask any favor for his own son that could not be asked for the humblest soldier in the army." The self-control of the commanding general won out over the tender feelings of the father, who once said that it was through his children that he was "most vulnerable, most sensitive." This was true even in December 1863, when General Meade bypassed the commissioners of exchange and offered to exchange outright Confederate prisoners for the Union prisoners in Richmond. Lee declined his offer, saying, "The cartel having been agreed upon by both parties to regulate the exchange of all prisoners I do not consider myself at liberty to depart from its provisions."[22]

The Union bureaucracy made one error in its hostage selection that seems almost comical now, although it was deadly serious in the summer and fall of 1863. At the time Rooney Lee was named to be hanged if the Confederates executed Captains Sawyer and Flinn, another rebel officer, not below the rank of captain, was also to be selected. In much of the official correspondence and all of the newspaper accounts of the proposed hanging, this officer was called "Captain Winder." This man was supposed to be the son of General John H. Winder, the provost-marshal general of the Confederacy. So the Yankees believed they had two generals' sons as hostages. Actually Captain Robert H. Tyler of the Eighth Virginia Infantry was the man in question. On July 16 he was placed in close confinement in Old Capitol Prison in Washington. In October Colonel William Hoffman, the Union commissary-general of prisoners, began to speculate on the "whereabouts of Captain Winder." He asked William Ludlow, the former Union commissioner of exchange, where Winder was imprisoned. Ludlow replied that he did not know. When he was ordered to place Rooney Lee and an officer not below the rank of captain in close confinement, there were no captains in his department. Later he heard that "Captain Winder" had been chosen and assumed that he was imprisoned in some other department. Meanwhile, Captain Tyler, also believing that there was a "Captain Winder," wrote to Robert Ould that he could not ascertain the reason for his close confinement. He urged Ould to present his case to the Union authorities. He wrote, "I am extremely anxious to know why I am held" and stated that the superintendent of his prison had "tried in vain to find out." It took a month for Tyler's letter to go through channels. By this time Hoffman had realized his mistake and loftily replied that "Captain Tyler is in error in his reference to Captain Winder as having been held as a hostage for Captains Sawyer and Flinn. We hold no prisoners of war by the name and rank referred to." Almost four months after he was first put in close confinement, Captain Tyler was informed why.[23]

As the bloody conflict continued, feelings of hatred and mistrust escalated on both sides. The lists of casualties and prisoners of war increased to unimaginable proportions. The families could bury their dead with appropriate honors, cherish their memories, and get on with their lives, but the prisoners of war became a cancer that ate at the hearts and minds of families and friends. With thousands of prisoners on both sides, there were not many families who were not touched directly or indirectly by their plight. Conditions in the prisons were abysmal—of that there is no doubt. Those with a father or brother or friend in enemy hands were made painfully aware of the conditions by the newspapers of both sides. For example, in the New York Times of November 6, 1863, a returned prisoner described in detail the "cries of mortal suffering and anguish coming . . . from the poor fellows who have had the misfortune to fall into rebel hands in Virginia." Among the "barbarities" he included cramped quarters, poor food, theft, and murder. He described "our poor shivering Union soldiers now held in utter wretchedness, naked and famishing, and subject to all the dire diseases." He ended his harangue with a "remedy for the gross and disgraceful abuses, the inhuman and barbarous treatment." This remedy was "retaliation, then, strict, stern and unflinching, and that on Virginia rebels only." In Richmond the newspapers spoke of "hoisting of the Black Flag" and "war to the knife" while declaring that "all this forbearance and chivalrous courtesy on our part—all this Christianity and civilization . . . has been thrown away upon such an enemy." Both sides were guilty of not being able to admit to gross inhumanity on their own side. During the summer of 1863 Hoffman, Union commissary—general of prisoners, had already begun to place restrictions on Confederate prisoners. Officers were not permitted to buy clothing except in case of dire necessity. He decreed, "One suit of outer garments and a change of underclothes is all they require, and if they have this they will not be permitted to purchase anything more." Clothing had to be of "gray cloth . . . with plain buttons, without trimmings." They were not allowed to purchase boots, only shoes of inferior quality. Furthermore Confederates were "not permitted to receive clothing from their friends, nor . . . permitted to send for it except so far as may be requisite to supply their absolute wants." In November 1863 General Neal Dow wrote to Secretary of War Stanton describing conditions at Libby Prison. He said: "Our officers are robbed of everything when captured, if not then, when taken into prison. . . . We sleep on the floor without blankets except as we obtain them from our friends. Only one of our rooms has glass, all the others . . . have open windows." Although he attributed the "starvation rations" to the "extreme poverty of the rebel Government" he asked that "[rebel] officers may at once be subjected to the same treatment that we suffer." On the same day a delegate of the U.S. Christian Commission echoed Dow's proposal by calling for retaliation—"treating their officers as they treat ours." These suggestions found favor with the high command in Washington. In a report on prisoners of war to Stanton, Halleck declared the treatment of Union prisoners "barbarous" and Libby Prison as worse than "the Black Hole of Calcutta." He piously stated that "Rebel prisoners held by the United States have been uniformly treated with consideration and kindness. They have been furnished with all necessary clothing and supplied with the same quality and amount of food as our own soldiers while our soldiers . . . have been stripped of their blankets, clothing and shoes, even in the winter season, and then confined in damp and loathsome prisons and only half fed on damaged provisions or actually starved to death." Halleck believed that retaliation was "fully justified by the laws and usages of war."[24]

The Union authorities were ready to impose harsher restrictions on the Confederate officers held as prisoners. Another step in this direction was the removal of William Ludlow as the Union exchange agent. His Confederate counterpart felt that he was replaced because of his wish "to be fair and humane." Brigadier General S. A. Meredith was chosen to take his place. Meredith's base of operations was at Fortress Monroe. Apparently Rooney Lee was receiving too much

attention and not suffering enough to suit Meredith's idea of a prisoner of war. At any rate he wrote to Washington on November 8,
1863, to "suggest that General Lee be removed from this fort to Johnson's Island or to some point where he will not be lionized as he is
here." He further stated, "No prisoner of ours, whatever his rank, receives such treatment in Richmond." It was not in keeping with the
Union desire to make Confederate officers suffer to have one of high
rank enjoying any comforts. It is not surprising that Lee was considered a celebrity of sorts—almost a local tourist attraction. After all, he
was the son of the great Rebel commander and a lieutenant of Jeb Stuart, the *beau sabreur* (fine swordsman). Both connections imparted to
him an aura of the hero worship that surrounded Lee and Stuart.
Even their Union opponents, especially the ones who had been surprised and defeated by them, felt both respect and awe for the Confederate generals. So it was natural that there was a certain amount of
curiosity concerning the younger Lee. Besides, his youth, looks, courteous manners, and considerable charm drew people to him all his
life—why should his captors be any different? It is also likely that
some of his friends from the regular army, Harvard, and his prep
school in New York were stationed at Fortress Monroe and unwilling
to let their old chum suffer too much. At any rate Meredith took a
dim view of this and wanted him moved. Secretary of War Stanton
agreed and recommended "that he be sent to Johnson's Island, where
he can be placed on a footing with other prisoners of war on that island, and if the Government orders the rebel officers to be subjected
to special treatment corresponding to that which the rebels extend to
Union prisoners in Richmond prisons General Lee will be in a right
position for sharing it." Orders were sent immediately for Lee to be
taken to Johnson's Island by way of Baltimore, then overland by train,
in the care of one officer and three men with "particular instructions
to insure that he shall not escape." Before the orders could be carried
out, news of a possible "attempt to release the prisoners at Johnson's
Island by armed steamers from Canada" was received in Washington.
The orders were countermanded, and Colonel Joseph Roberts, commander of Fort Monroe, was told to "send him to Fort Lafayette,
New York Harbor." When General Benjamin F. Butler heard of the
move and that officers and men from his corps were to form the escort, he wired Washington and asked that the request be sent to him.
Washington complied, and Butler wired back, "General Lee will leave

tonight." While all this was transpiring, Rooney Lee wrote the only letter extant from the period of his imprisonment:

> Fort Monroe
> 12 Nov. 63
> Dear Custis-
> Fort Lafayette
> I leave this evening for Sandusky, I believe. Please cause my letters to be directed to that place. I am ignorant of the cause of the change, but will write you on my arrival. I am very well.
> Yours,
> W. H. F. Lee

This letter was evidently read by General Butler, as he wrote across the bottom, "Col. Lee was removed by order of Commissary Gen. of Prisoners at Washington." Lee must have written the letter when he was informed that he was to be moved to Johnson's Island. After the change in orders, he merely crossed out "Sandusky" and wrote in "Fort Lafayette." It is interesting to note that Butler referred to him as "Col. Lee" when he must have known that his rank was that of brigadier general. This reference is probably due to the fact that Rooney Lee always wore the three stars of a Confederate colonel, even when he was a major general. This was in imitation of his father. When Robert Lee learned of his son's transfer, he wrote to his wife: "Any place would be better than Fort Monroe with Butler in command. It is probable he will be sent to Johnson's Island where the rest of our officers are. . . . I hope he has recovered of his wound. His long confinement is very grievous to me."[25]

Fort Lafayette was located on an island in New York harbor and was part of the network of defense that included the larger Fort Hamilton. It is ironic that Rooney Lee was imprisoned first at Fort Monroe, then in Fort Lafayette. Both had earlier, more pleasant memories for the Lee family. Robert Lee was stationed at Fort Monroe soon after his marriage to Mary Custis, and their first child was born there. Lee was stationed at Fort Hamilton from 1841 to 1846. Lee taught Rooney to swim during that time in the waters near the fort. He once recalled that memory to his son: "I yet feel your arms clasping my neck as I swam with you on my back." This tender memory was probably all but forgotten by Rooney Lee as he entered the fort, now a prison, on November 15, 1863. Fort Lafayette was not originally intended to be a prison, and the prisoners that were sent there were put in casemates and battery rooms. A prisoner there described the casemates as fourteen feet wide and twenty-four feet long. The arched ceilings were about eight feet high at the highest point. The floors were planked, and there was a fireplace in each casemate. The prisoners were "without bedding or any of the commonest necessities. Their condition could hardly be worse on a slave ship on the middle passage." Besides Confederate officers, the prisoners included blockade-runners and various political prisoners.[26]

Most of what is known of prison life at Fort Lafayette comes from extracts of the *Right Flanker*, an underground newspaper "circulating among the southern prisoners in Fort Lafayette, in 1863–64" and published in 1865. On the title page this publication was "dedicated to them generally, and especially to the Confederate Officers whose autographs are here given, as among them were contributors to the *Right Flanker*"; eleven signatures follow; the first is of "W. H. F. Lee, Brig. Gen., C.S. Cavalry." Others include Captain Tyler, Major General Franklin Gardner, and members of his staff. The purpose of this newspaper was "to instruct and amuse" and to create "the spice of excitement which the risk of such a contraband undertaking affords." The departments of the paper included agricultural, nautical, local news items, and, of course, editorial. The first edition was published in October 1863.

The arrival of Rooney Lee in Casemate No. 3 was duly recorded by the reporter, who called him "a worthy representative of him whose name alone attracts the attention of those who can appreciate true patriotism and chivalry, wherever the cause of the South is known." To welcome him there were "bouquets, marks of appreciation on the part of a lady residing in sight of the Fort, of the newly-arrived rebel general." The reporter also noted that there was one junior officer "who takes pleasure in making it evident that he is expert in the duties of a jailer" and that "the idea of bouquets to rebels is mortifying to his feeling." Apparently Lee was still a celebrity in spite of the move.

Thanksgiving and good weather made the last week in November fairly pleasant for the prisoners. However, the *Right Flanker* noted that "the newspapers clamoring for retaliation on rebel prisoners," the arrival of more prisoners, and the posting of more guards were indications that "there is going to be a tightening of the screws." Soon the

prisoners were forbidden to buy or receive any goods other than tobacco and writing utensils from the outside. Other restrictions included
clothing. The prisoners were allowed "one change of under and over-
clothes, and a pair of laced (not long-legs) boots." Food was also re-
stricted to "tough beef, dry bread, beans and bad coffee." When
Colonel Martin Burke, the commandant of Fort Lafayette, received
word on the restrictions he was to impose on the prisoners in his
charge, he asked if they were to be allowed to receive "donations from
friends." The reply was that prisoners had to have relatives in New
York to supply their needs. Upon receiving this news, the editors of the
Right Flanker defiantly wrote, "Let it come, many of us have done
marching, and successful fighting, on still shorter rations: and vowed
not to complain." "The old campaigners" showed "those not accustomed to roughing it" all the ways to fix the plain food so it was more
edible. The editors also noted that with the exception of the commandant and one "Irish Lieutenant" the officers at Fort Lafayette "would
prefer that they should not be required to have charge of any prisoners." Apparently most were humane in their dealings with the prisoners
in spite of the harsh restrictions they were supposed to enforce.[27]

In Casemate No. 3 an inmate from Maryland whose daughter visited weekly was the link between the prisoners without relatives in the
North and the outside world. He was the "caterer" for the group and
obtained both food and clothing for others. He and his daughter even
managed to pass a letter to a wife in the South from her imprisoned
husband without it being perused by Federal officers. They also cir-
cumvented the rules concerning clothing by the daughter bringing her
father clothes, which did not fit him but did fit others in the casemate.
The prisoners would send out worn-out clothes under the guise that
they needed alteration to fit the father. New clothes would be brought
in as the altered articles. It seems that the "Maryland friend could not
be fitted until after several trials." The daughter also smuggled money
to her father. This was used to bribe the guards to provide food and
other articles desperately needed.

Life in the casemates was dreadfully boring for the prisoners, with
little to break the monotony. They were allowed outside during the
day and locked up at dark. In the winter months that meant that they
were locked in for approximately fifteen hours a day. The *Right
Flanker* noted, "We lose patience with every kind of games which it is
in our power to engage in." The Northern newspapers provided some

interesting points to ponder, especially the demands for peace from Fernando Wood and the exploits of the Alabama. Fresh arrivals, including Rooney Lee's cohostage, Captain Tyler, brought in news but added to the already crowded conditions. Even during the day when they were allowed outside, exercise was limited due to the ice covering the yard. The officers of the garrison frequently invited ladies over to visit, and some of these were curious to see the "appearance Rebels in prison make, especially . . . young, good-looking Generals." When the officer of the day called for the Rebel general, frequently other prisoners went out also. This was especially so when the band was playing. Sometimes the band played "Dixie" for the prisoners, then changed to "Yankee Doodle." The Rebels retaliated by singing "The Bonnie Blue Flag" and "I Love Old Dixie, Right or Wrong" for the "Yankee Lady Visitors." One form of excitement came from a report that the New York harbor defense system was threatened by a steamer trying to get in without being searched. As a result the prisoners were locked up under close guard. Another scare in which Rebel rams were supposed to be attacking New York to free the prisoners caused the prisoners to be locked in with howitzers at the doors of the casemates. Searches sometimes caused a stir among the prisoners. On these occasions the greenbacks were stuffed in a rat hole, and the *Right Flanker* was hidden. Other than these episodes, prison life was a matter of existing and enduring day by day in ever more crowded surroundings. Concerned about this overcrowding, Colonel Burke informed Washington that there were "more prisoners at Fort Lafayette than can be accommodated there without interfering with the work of remounting the batteries" and that he could not "conveniently accommodate any more."[28]

Charlotte Lee, her frail physical health worsened by mental distress since the imprisonment of her husband, became desperately ill a few days before Christmas 1863. In her distress she called for her absent husband: "I want Fitzhugh, oh, I want Fitzhugh." Mary Lee tended her in this final illness and wrote to a friend that she was "unconscious for nearly twenty-four hours prior to her dissolution and I hope suffered but little in comparison to what she would have done had her brain been unclouded." She died on the morning of December 26 and was buried beside her two children the next afternoon. Mary Lee wrote to her son to inform him of Charlotte's death and confided to the same friend, "It will be a terrific blow to him, so unexpected, for he has not known how ill she has been the whole summer." Robert Lee also thought of his son at this time. He wrote to Mary: "I grieve for our lost darling as a father can only grieve for a daughter. I loved her with a father's love, and my sorrow is heightened by the thought of the anguish her death will cause our dear son, and the poignancy it will give to the bars of his prison. May God in His mercy enable him to bear the blow He has so suddenly dealt, and sanctify it to his everlasting happiness!" A few days later he wrote, "I grieve only for ourselves and particularly for our dear son, whose sorrow under the circumstances will be inexpressibly grievous." Lee's mind was still in the same vein when he wrote a friend, "How keen will be his anguish and how bitter to him his captivity." It is difficult to envision the emotions that must have swept over Rooney Lee upon reading his mother's letter. To lose two children and his wife in a period of eighteen months was a crushing blow. Of Charlotte Lee, a Virginia lady said, "Greater beauty and sweetness rarely fall to the lot of woman." There is no doubt that he loved her deeply. To combat the disbelief, shock, anger, guilt, and numbness that accompany grief, Lee had only his own deep faith to support him. There were no close friends, no family to lend him support, and no work to occupy his time and thoughts. His despair must have been apparent when he wrote back to his mother. Of this Robert Lee wrote, "I have read Fitzhugh's letter with much interest. Poor fellow, he has nothing to draw his thoughts from his deep sorrow and I fear it will wear him down." Three weeks later he wrote Mary, "I am glad to hear that some kind people at the North think of poor Fitzhugh—God grant that he could be released but I trust He will permit that in his own good time." When Robert Lee wrote this on February 14 he undoubtedly still considered it unthinkable for him to meddle with the bureaucracy of exchange to obtain his son's release.[29]

For someone else in Richmond this was not the case, however. Several days before Robert Lee wrote to his wife that he hoped their son could be released, the forces had been set into motion that would finally obtain Rooney Lee's exchange. It is possible that the impetus came from Custis Lee, then an aide to Jefferson Davis in Richmond. Some Confederate officer went to Libby Prison to tell Union Brigadier General Neal Dow that it might be possible to arrange his exchange for Rooney Lee. He told Dow "that if the United States government would make the proposition the Confederate authorities would accede to it, but that the latter would not take the initiative." He also told Dow that he could write freely to his relatives and friends about the proposed exchange and that these letters would pass the examiners and be sent. So

Dow wrote to his son on January 28, 1864, "I have reason to believe that if the government will propose to exchange General Lee for myself, the only Federal general here, and equivalent officers for Captains Sawyer and Flynn . . . , the proposition will be favorably entertained and the exchange effected." Dow had been captured on June 30, 1863, and, as the highest-ranking officer held by the Confederates, was something of a celebrity himself. He also had friends in high places, including the vice president, Hannibal Hamlin. Hamlin and the senators from Maine saw to it that the proposal for exchange was made as suggested. On February 8, 1864, Washington ordered General Benjamin F. Butler to propose the exchange. The details were agreed upon, and by February 20 Rooney Lee had been informed by letter, "from a gentleman direct from Washington, that a proposition had been made . . . to exchange Brigadier-General Neal Dow and Captains Sawyer and Flynn for himself and any two captains whom the United States Government might designate." Captain Tyler requested that he be one of those captains, as he had also been held as a hostage. On February 25, 1864, orders were sent from Washington that Lee and Tyler were to be sent under a suitable guard to General Butler at Fort Monroe.[30]

Before the two left Fort Lafayette, there was a banquet of sorts given in their honor. The Right Flanker described in detail the celebration at the "Lafayette Bastille": "The company present on the occasion included the most notable and fashionable of the sojourners at that celebrated establishment." The food and drink were the usual fare of the prison except for some "old rye." There were many patriotic toasts to "our glorious cause" and "the Southern Army, a band of patriots struggling for liberty," with another lifted to "our Chairman, the worthy son of one of the most famous in upholding the honour of the Old Dominion in the greatest rebellion of ancient or modern times." There were also numerous musical selections, including "The Bonnie Blue Flag." "Stonewall Jackson's March," "Up with the Stars and Bars," "Maryland, My Maryland," and, especially for Lee and Tyler, "Home, Sweet Home." In the next issue of the newspaper it was noted that "the two hostages have left for Fortress Monroe to be exchanged. . . . May all the happiness they wished for attend their arrival home."[31]

Lee and Tyler left Fort Lafayette on March 1, 1864, and on March 3 Lee was listed as a prisoner on parole at Fort Monroe. By the terms of the parole, he was limited to the Hygeia Hotel. The Hygeia had once been a fashionable resort hotel just outside the main gate of Fort Monroe. During the Civil War it was temporarily used as a hospital. It is not known why Lee was kept in a hospital for more than a week, but at least he was not kept in solitary confinement this time at Fort Monroe. Probably he was physically ill, at least exhausted and drained emotionally. His captors may have wanted him in better shape before he returned home. It was not until March 11 that his name appeared on a list of prisoners sent to City Point, Virginia, on a flag-of-truce boat. Soon he was in Richmond, finally reunited with his family after "nine long, weary months" of imprisonment.[32]

On March 15, 1864, Mrs. Chesnut recorded in her diary that she had seen "General Lee, Smith Lee and Rooney go by." She had heard the general say of Rooney, "Poor boy, he is sadly cut up about the death of that sweet little wife of his." The general himself "had tears in his eyes when he spoke of his daughter-in-law just dead." Mrs. Chesnut also wrote: "Rooney Lee says Beast Butler was very kind to him while he was a prisoner. And the Beast sent him back his war-horse. The Lees are men enough to speak the truth of friend or enemy, unfearing consequences." After spending just a short time in Richmond, Robert Lee had to return to the army to prepare for the spring campaign. He was still very concerned about his son and wrote to Mary that he wanted "especially to see more of dear Fitzhugh to whom my heart was so full I could say but little." He wanted Rooney to come to see him at headquarters so they could spend some time together. Again he wrote his wife: "I hope Fitzhugh is well and will soon be strong again. Tell him he must come up and see us when he is ready. Stuart wants to see him."[33]

Jeb Stuart did indeed want to see his very capable subordinate. In September 1863 he had written to Agnes Lee, "I hope Rooney will be back soon—I miss him much—He will no doubt be promoted upon his release." Stuart had the reorganization of his cavalry corps on his mind long before Rooney Lee was exchanged. Soon after Lee's arrival in Richmond, Stuart wrote to him:

My Dear General—
Words can not express the joy your safe return to us caused me, and I assure you I have never failed to improve every thing tending to effect your rescue from a position the most galling a soldier is ever called to endure.

I am extremely anxious to greet you and as I can not leave the front, beg that you will come and spend a few days with me as soon as you are enough restored.

I shall return to my Hdqts tomorrow. I wish to have something to say relative to your assignment to duty and hope you will not encourage any proposition till you can confer with me. Your sincere friend

J. E. B. Stuart[34]

Near the end of March Rooney Lee went back to the army and spent some time with his father and with Stuart. On March 30 Robert Lee wrote to Mary that Stuart and Rooney had gone to hear Governor Zebulon Vance deliver an address to the North Carolina troops and that "they are to be back to dinner." Lee and Stuart, among others, gave Rooney Lee what he needed most after his imprisonment and the loss of his family: support and a purpose for life. In April Robert Lee wrote his son a masterful letter that also carries some indication that Rooney was more resigned to his loss and ready to resume his place in the war.

Camp, Orange County, April 28, 1864
I received last night, my dear son, your letter of the 22nd. It has given me great comfort. God knows how I loved your dear, dear wife, how sweet her memory is to me, and how I mourn her loss. My grief could not be greater if you had been taken from me. You were both equally dear to me.

My heart is too full to speak on this subject, nor can I write. But my grief is for ourselves, not for her. She is brighter and happier than ever—safe from all evil, and awaiting us in her heavenly abode. May God in His mercy enable us to join her in eternal praise to our Lord and Savior. Let us humbly bow ourselves before Him and offer perpetual prayer for pardon and forgiveness.

But we cannot indulge in grief, however mournfully pleasing. Our country demands all our strength, all our energies. To resist the powerful combination now forming against us will require every man at his place. If victorious, we have everything to hope for in the future. If defeated, nothing will be left us to live for. I have not heard what action has been taken by the Department in reference to my recommendations concerning the organization of the cavalry.

But we have no time to wait, and you had better join your brigade. This week will in all probability bring us active works, and we must strike fast and strong. My whole trust is in God, and I am ready for whatever He may ordain. May He guide, guard and strengthen us, is my constant prayer.
Your devoted father,
R. E. Lee

Just a few days after receiving this letter from his father, Rooney Lee returned to the Army of Northern Virginia, this time for good. Robert Lee informed his wife: "Fitzhugh got up safely and looks better than when I last saw him. He is preparing for his work." Rooney Lee was now physically and, in a great degree, mentally healed and ready to do his part against "the powerful combination" of U. S. Grant and Philip Sheridan now threatening Virginia.[35]

CHAPTER 11

Major General, C.S. Cavalry

For almost five weeks Rooney Lee was in a kind of military limbo. When he was exchanged from prison he was, in essence, a brigadier general of cavalry with no brigade to command. He spent much of this time in Richmond interspersed with trips to the army to visit his father and to spend some time with Stuart. One of Stuart's staff officers described one of his visits to the Wigwam, Stuart's headquarters. He was "enchanted to see him" as he considered "the whole Lee family are delightful people." About the Lees, he wrote, "I take to them as kin." About Rooney in particular he continued, "He is a charming person: grave, but cheerful, and fond of a joke." It seemed the current joke for April Fool's Day concerned the scarcity of "drawers" among Stuart's staff. When Lee returned to Richmond, the officer wrote that he had enjoyed the visit "greatly," then added: "I sympathize greatly with General Rooney for his wife's sake, whom I always liked much. Poor fellow, he bears his loss manfully." After nine months as a prisoner of war, Lee needed this time to heal physically and emotionally before resuming any official duties.[1]

During this same period the cavalry of the Army of Northern Virginia was reorganized. This was not a spur-of-the-moment action but rather one that had been in progress for some time. As early as May 27, 1863, Stuart had recommended a reorganization in which each brigade would have only three regiments so that they could "be kept in higher state of efficiency and be more easily handled." These smaller brigades would be grouped into divisions under Fitz Lee, Wade Hampton, and Rooney Lee. Writing familiarly to his commanding general,

Stuart continued: "I know your natural disinclination to promote those so near to you but I beg you in this instance to allow me to be the judge, from long and intimate official relations showing them by all odds to be deserving this distinction over all others. I beg to refer you to the condition of Brigadier General William H. F. Lee's brigade in Captain White's inspection report forwarded today." Quite pragmatically, Lee responded that the emphasis should be placed on improving the effective strength of the regiments. The promotions would be meaningless if the size of the commands could not be enlarged.[2]

After the Gettysburg Campaign, Lee himself proposed a reorganization of the cavalry. There were to be four regiments to a brigade with a total of seven brigades. Fitz Lee and Wade Hampton would be made division commanders with the rank of major general. His plan was carried out with minor changes on September 9, 1863. In Rooney Lee's brigade, now commanded by John R. Chambliss, there were four regiments: the First South Carolina and the Ninth, Tenth, and Thirteenth Virginia Cavalries. The Second North Carolina had been placed in an all–North Carolina brigade under the command of Brigadier General L. S. Baker. The Fifteenth Virginia, which formerly had been in Lee's Brigade although often on detached duty, was assigned to the brigade of L. L. Lomax. Robert Lee objected to the First South Carolina being separated from the Second South Carolina, and soon it was back in Young's brigade. This left Colonel Chambliss in command of only three regiments—the Ninth, Tenth, and Thirteenth Virginia—in Rooney Lee's brigade.[3]

Chambliss had capably led the brigade since Brandy Station, and on October 23, 1863, Stuart asked that he be promoted to brigadier general. Stuart had not forgotten Rooney Lee, however. In the same letter he wrote: "Repeated efforts have been made by me to obtain the release of Brigadier General William H. F. Lee, now a prisoner of war at Old Point Comfort, but I fear that no efforts will avail for some time to come. I need him very much to command his brigade, but am also anxious for his exchange in order to be promoted, for no officer of my command more richly deserves it than he, and none would bring more ability, zeal and patriotism to such a post than himself." Stuart felt that the promotion he requested for Chambliss was due and that when Rooney Lee was exchanged he would also be promoted. Chambliss, a thirty-one-year-old West Pointer, was promoted to brigadier general on January 27, 1864, to date from December 19, 1863. In Special Orders

No. 35 dated February 6, 1864, Chambliss was still "assigned to the temporary command of W. H. F. Lee's brigade."[4]

Because of these actions, Lee was temporarily without a command when he was exchanged. Almost immediately Stuart asked Richmond for him to be promoted: "Brig. Gen'l. W. H. F. Lee having been exchanged I have the honor to recommend his promotion to the rank of Major Gen'l. and assigned to the command of a Cav. Division to consist, for the present of [Thomas] Rosser's and Chambliss' brigades of Virginia Cavalry. . . . I beg leave to submit to the Dept. and Executive the claims of this modest but no less deserving officer for promotion, who, but for having been in the enemy's hands would have received this recommendation six months ago. The history of the Cavalry of the Army of Northern Virginia furnishes the illustration of those qualities of a cavalry commander possessed in so eminent a degree by this officer, whilst his conduct at Fleetwood where he was severely wounded was heroic, as his skill was masterly. The best interests of the service will be served and a meritorious officer rewarded by the promotion recommended." Stuart's recommendation was forwarded to army headquarters for Robert Lee's approval. The next day he laconically added: "If the Cav. is increased as the prospects now indicate, it will be better to organize it into three divisions. Each of the Virginia brigades will number about 2,000 men; the four will amount to 8,000, too many cav. for one man to handle or care for in a country and service like ours. I would recommend then that two divisions be formed out of the four brigades. Gen'l. W. F. Lee is the Senior Brigadier at present in the cav. in this army and I think his services have been as efficient as the others. I therefore concur in the recommendation of Genl. Stuart."[5]

Rooney Lee was promoted to major general on April 23, 1864, to date from the same day. He was at that time twenty-six years old. His next birthday would be on May 31. This made him the youngest Confederate to hold the rank of major general. For this distinction, he narrowly beat out Robert Hoke, who was named major general also on April 23, 1864, with the commission to date from April 20. Hoke would turn twenty-seven on May 27, 1864. In the Confederate service youth was not a factor in determining rank. Regardless of age, Lee was a veteran cavalry commander who would never be called a "boy general" due to rashness, inexperience, or impulsive action. His rise in rank was a steady climb based on merit and achievement, as compared with some who jumped from staff captain to brigadier by currying favor. If any of his officers or men ever thought about his age, they guessed him as older than he was. One who first saw him in May 1862 thought he was twenty-eight years old, four years older than his actual age at the time. They knew his background and assumed that because he had been to college, then pursued a career in the regular army, was married and had children, and had been a farmer for a while before the war he must be older than he really was. Moreover, his calm, reserved manner, equanimity, and poise made him seem much more mature than one would expect of a man his age.[6]

The reassignment of units as ordered on paper was not carried out immediately in reality. Rooney Lee took command of only one brigade of his division in late April, and it would be many days before he was actually in personal command of the second brigade. He rejoined his old men of the Ninth, Tenth, and Thirteenth Virginia that now constituted Chambliss's brigade. The Ninth was, as usual, in good condition. As one trooper reported, the "men were greatly recruited and our horses in good order." The regiments were brought together at Hamilton's Crossing for about ten days near the end of April. Rooney Lee also regrouped his staff at this time. His younger brother Rob had first reported to Chambliss in the summer of 1863, then was assigned to the staff of Fitz Lee. There he remained until Rooney's exchange and promotion. As Rooney Lee once again gathered up the reins of command, there was little time for preparation or organization before the battle was renewed. Lee was present for an inspection of Chambliss's brigade on April 30. One trooper remembered: "It is the first time we have seen him since he was released from prison. He was greeted with loud cheering." Another wrote, "His appearance was greeted with tremendous applause from the Brigade particularly our Reg't which he commanded for so long."[7]

The military situation in the spring of 1864 was quite different from what it had been in June 1863, when Rooney Lee was wounded and captured. The Army of the Potomac and the Army of Northern Virginia were on opposite sides of the Rapidan in early May 1864. The Union force comprised roughly 120,000 men of all arms with another small army of support personnel including commissary, medical groups, transportation, engineers, and huge wagon trains. On the Confederate side, Lee waited with half that many men. While George Meade continued as head of the Army of the Potomac, Ulysses Grant was now commander of all Federal forces and would personally direct the latest offensive to crush the rebellion. This time, however, Grant would move without the shackles of constraint that Washington had imposed on all the previous commanders. He would be his own man and introduce to Virginia the concept of total war. Grant summed up his plans to Meade: "Lee's army will be your objective." In all previous attempts to take Richmond, the Army of the Potomac had advanced, been defeated, and then withdrawn to regroup for another try under a different general. This time would be different given Grant's particular brand of bulldog tenacity. This time it would be war to the hilt.[8]

To aid him in his task, Grant had brought Phil Sheridan with him from the western theater. He assigned this bantam rooster of a general to the cavalry because he was "dissatisfied with the little that had been accomplished by the cavalry so far in the war." Sheridan commanded more than 13,000 men, including horse artillery. There were three divisions of the cavalry. The first was commanded by Alfred Torbert, replacing John Buford, who had died of typhoid. David Gregg continued in command of the second, and the third was given to James Wilson. Sheridan was almost immediately at odds with Meade over their ideas on the proper use of cavalry. Meade wanted them to guard his trains and picket his front, whereas Sheridan wanted to concentrate his men and go after the famed cavalry of Jeb Stuart. Stuart waited with little more than 8,000 troopers who would have to try to make up the difference in numbers with spirit and courage. The scales were also tipped in favor of the Federal cavalry by widespread use of the Spencer repeating rifle. Most of the blue troopers carried these .54-caliber breechloaders, which used brass cartridges loaded in a clip holding eight rounds.[9]

The entire Union Army was spread out around Brandy Station until May 1864. They had wintered on the ground of the cavalry battle of the previous June. The Confederates were on the other side of the Rapidan and could view the enemy from the signal station on Clark's Mountain. They knew that the officers' wives and sutlers had been sent to the rear, and with good spring weather and dry roads the offensive was about to begin. Robert Lee called on Richmond to send every man that could be spared from other fronts. Lieutenant General James Longstreet and his corps returned to the Army of Northern Virginia just in time for battle. There was a review of Longstreet's men in April that was more like a "military sacrament" than a parade. One observer noted of Robert E. Lee that "the old gentleman looks as well and pleasant as ever, he was accompanied by his son Gen. Lee, who was so long a prisoner." Many ladies and citizens also attended, and the generals "were very pleasant and chatty, smiling and talking with ladies." From his position north of the Rapidan Grant could strike to the west and maneuver Lee's army out into the open. This would take Grant away from his supply lines and leave the road to Washington open for a counterattack, however. Another alternative was to move to the east and cross the Rapidan in a more direct route to Richmond. This way Grant's army could be more easily supplied by river. The major obstacle in this direction was the Wilderness, an area approximately twelve miles long and six deep. This was an area of forest that in many places had once been cultivated. The soil was poor and the land was allowed to grow up again. The underbrush of vines and briars was dense, and there were occasional boggy places. There were few roads through this tangle of trees and brambles, and if a man got off the paths it was like hacking through a dark, impenetrable maze. Lee predicted that this was the way Grant would choose. On May 2, from a vantage point on Clark's Mountain, Lee pointed in the direction of Germanna Ford and Ely's Ford and said "Grant will cross by one of those fords." As an open invitation, the fords were left unguarded. The day before, in a rare quiet moment, Rooney had gone to church with his father and stayed for dinner. Afterward Lee wrote to Mary to tell her that their sons were well and to ask her to send a new pair of gauntlets that had been given to him so that he could give them to one of his sons.[10]

On May 4 the Federals began to cross. Lieutenant General Gouverneur K. Warren's V Corps crossed first at Germanna Ford followed by Major General John Sedgwick's VI Corps. The II Corps under Major General Winfield Scott Hancock crossed six miles to the east at Ely's Ford. For the moment, Ambrose Burnside's IX Corps stayed behind to protect supply lines. The Federal forces began to move at midnight, and by 9 A.M. the following morning Lee was aware of their movements. He ordered the three corps of his army to march east to intercept the Federals. Lieutenant General Richard S. Ewell and Lieutenant General A. P. Hill were to move by parallel roads, the Orange Turnpike and the Orange Plank Road. Longstreet was to follow the Catharpin Road farther to the south. All three lines of march would cross the roads taken by the Federals. Stuart's cavalry was spread out from one side of Lee's army to the other. Rooney Lee's Virginia brigade was on the extreme western edge of the army. When the Federals began to cross south, the brigade crossed the Rapidan going north and then moved eastward downriver and bivouacked near Morton's Ford. On May 5 Captain William M. McGregor's battery of horse artillery received new horses and orders to report to Rooney Lee as soon as possible. It is not known exactly when they reported, but Lee was expecting them by May 6. Lee's brigade was then in the vicinity of Culpeper, and he reported "everything so far in my front and left is quiet." There were reports of Yankee cavalry in the area, but no contact was made. In this report Lee added, "Please impress upon the general Stuart the necessity of sending me my other brigade as soon as it can be spared."[11]

The battle of the Wilderness was fought on May 5–6 as the two armies collided amid the brambles and thickets. The very nature of the Wilderness made this battle different than all others. A year earlier Chancellorsville was fought on part of this ground, and soldiers often spotted white skeletons, the skulls grinning as the forces moved toward one another. Sometimes the remnant of a blue or gray uniform marked the victims' former allegiance. Smoky, eerie confusion reigned often as units floundered through green thickets and mazes of briers. As the battle died down at night, the moans of the wounded often turned to screams as the woods caught fire and the flames engulfed them. Lee's losses were at least 7,500, including Longstreet wounded, while Grant's were closer to 18,000. In spite of this, Grant sent word to Washington "that whatever happens, there will be no turning back."[12]

Rooney Lee's brigade was still posted at Morton's on May 7 when Lee reported, "All quiet on my front." He repeated his request for Gordon's brigade and wrote, "If you see Stuart jog his memory." Removed from the battle front, they had heard rumors "that General Longstreet was wounded" and that the Confederate troops were "driving the enemy." On the same day Hampton wrote to Stuart that he preferred to retain Gordon's brigade, although it had already been assigned to Rooney Lee. Also on that day, Grant ordered his army to move toward Spotsylvania Court House to the southeast. Therefore Rooney Lee's brigade was ordered from one side of the Confederate Army to the other. Once Grant's direction was known, all available cavalry would be needed there.[13]

Lee's brigade moved out on May 8. They passed through the area where Grant's army had spent the winter and saw "large stores of army materiel and numerous tents unstruck." They crossed at Ely's Ford and took some stragglers as prisoners. Soon they reached Wilderness Tavern, where two Federal field hospitals were set up. Amputated limbs were piled up near the tents where "some poor fellows who had died under the amputation of their limbs still lay stretched on the surgeon's tables." Some wounded Confederates begged to be taken along and were put in the brigade ambulances. As they crossed the actual battlefield the ground was "thickly dotted with the dead, who lay as they had fallen under a burning sun, many of them with their faces to the sky, and quite black from incipient decay." The next day the brigade prepared for action several times as they marched but did not actually fight. They went into bivouac on the road from Spotsylvania Court House to Massaponax Church. During the fierce fighting at Spotsylvania, Lee's brigade was posted to watch the enemy's left flank. One trooper of the Ninth Virginia wrote home after seeing the Union dead at Spotsylvania, "Grant would be willing to sacrifice his whole army if he could only take Richmond."[14]

Even before the fighting at Spotsylvania had ceased, Robert Lee became apprehensive about the movement of the Union Army and ordered the cavalry "to picket every road from the Ni to the Rappahannock." On May 11 Rooney Lee reported, "There is evidently a general move going on. Their trains are moving down the Fredericksburg road, and their columns are in motion." He further noted that the trains were in motion "all night" and the wounded were being moved to Belle Plain, a small hamlet on the Potomac that became Grant's supply base for about two weeks in May.[15]

Sheridan had also started out on a new mission while Grant and the infantry were fighting at Spotsylvania. After a heated round with Meade, Sheridan boasted that he could "thrash hell out of Stuart any day." When Meade repeated this to Grant, the Union commander asked: "Did Sheridan say that? Well he generally knows what he's talking about. Let him start right out and do it." On May 9 Sheridan set out at the head of 10,000 cavalry and thirty-two guns. He moved to the Confederate supply depot at Beaver Dam Station, where the guards torched a three-week supply of rations for Lee's army. The Yankees began to destroy track and railroad cars. When Stuart heard of Sheridan's move, he divided his force. Probably remembering the censure at Gettysburg, this time he left both Hampton and Rooney Lee with the main army and took only Fitz Lee's division and Gordon's brigade from Rooney Lee's division. By doing this he left half of his men with the main army and took only 4,000 troopers—not nearly enough to stop Sheridan. Stuart raced to get in between Sheridan and Richmond and set up a defensive position. In the ensuing fight Jeb Stuart, the beau sabreur of the Confederacy, was mortally wounded. Fitz Lee and Gordon, backed by infantry from Richmond, stalled Sheridan and continued to push him as he withdrew. In one of the last attacks against the Federal rear guard, Gordon also fell mortally wounded. The news of Stuart's death was a shock to the cavalry. One officer of the Ninth Virginia recalled: "No information could have been to the men who had long followed him more startling, astounding or painful. He had seemed to them to lead a charmed life not to be cut short by any fatal bullet. They now looked at each other in mute wonder, and their faces bespoke the bitterness of disappointment and grief. It was the morning of May 14, 1864, and they felt it to be the gloomiest one that had ever dawned on the cavalry corps of Lee's army." In the absence of a cavalry commander, Lee ordered that "until further orders, the three divisions of cavalry serving with this army will constitute separate commands and will report directly to and receive orders from these headquarters of the army." Stuart's staff was also reassigned with Major Charles Venable, now reporting to Rooney Lee.[16]

The men of Rooney Lee's division did not have much time to mourn their fallen leader. McGregor's battery and part of Chambliss's brigade were posted on the Myers farm near a house known erroneously in reports as the Gayle house. The artillery had been engaged off and on for two days, losing three men. A portion of Brigadier General Romegn Beck Ayre's Union brigade was ordered to occupy McGregor's position. Two Federal batteries moved into position near the Beverly house approximately three-quarters of a mile from McGregor's position. At 8 A.M. Rooney Lee reported to army headquarters: "Everything is moving up toward Beverly. Heavy columns of infantry and their artillery, which has been parked, are now moving forward. I will open my rifles." The artillery on both sides opened, and a courier was sent galloping to bring up the rest of the brigade. As soon as they arrived the troopers dismounted and prepared to go into action. They formed a line of battle and pushed close to some outbuildings near the main house. They slowed briefly when they received heavy musket and artillery fire, yet they charged on. Finally, the heavy Federal firepower compelled them to retire, leaving their dead on the field. Meade was on the field himself and ordered the Federal position to be strengthened. Two southern infantry brigades advanced at this time, Ambrose R. Wright's Georgians and the Mississippians of Brigadier General Nathaniel Harris. As they charged, the cavalry of Chambliss's brigade opened fire on the flanks. An officer from the Ninth Virginia recalled: "The opportunity of charging with infantry never had fallen to our lot before, nor had we been pitted against infantry; but there was no shrinking on the part of our men. They were filled with an ardor it is not easy to restrain. They were mourning for Jeb Stuart who was that day being borne to his burial, but his spirit seemed to hover near them and to beckon them on with his own intrepid and dauntless courage." The Federals got off a couple of rounds then "fled from the hill in a tumultuous rush." General Meade himself narrowly avoided being captured as his men retreated. He then ordered Wright to retake the former position even if it took his whole corps. By late afternoon, after firing more than 200 rounds of artillery, the Federals finally noticed that the Confederate force had withdrawn.[17]

Grant had determined to outflank Lee's army. As Grant moved his army it was imperative for Lee to find out where, when, and in what strength he was moving. The Confederate cavalry was out on picket in many directions, alert for any movement. It rained for two days, but on May 16 the skies were clear and the roads began to dry out. Rooney Lee's men under Chambliss were picketed in the vicinity of Stanard's Mill on the Po River. On that day Rooney reported on Federal activity to headquarters. He wrote that Chambliss was in "a good position at Stanard's Mill" and that he had driven the enemy pickets and been in turn driven back. He reported other activity but did not think it was "a general advance." Later the same day he reported again on his lines and added, "I have sent scouts out and hope to hear from them in the morning." On May 17 the pickets collided again near Stanard's Mill. "The enemy advanced with more force and courage and for half an hour or more there was quite lively firing of Arty. and small arms," an engineer observed. Finally two squadrons of the Tenth Virginia charged, capturing some prisoners and losing two killed. At 3:30 P.M. that day Robert Lee sent a courier to Rooney with orders "to push out and ascertain where the enemy were." The courier arrived "in midst of engagement" and left before Rooney Lee could respond verbally in spite of being told to wait. Rooney sent another report that "all roads from Massaponax to Rappahannock are

scouted and picketed." Furthermore he stated, "There is no movement of the enemy in this direction or toward Bowling Green." He
could hear "heavy firing" in the distance, away from his sector. The
lines continued to move, with the cavalry scouting and probing for
the enemy and screening the movements of Confederate infantry. This
type of service was hard on the horses as well as the men. One
trooper of the Ninth Virginia wrote about this time that his mount
had not been unsaddled in two weeks and had received "only three
ears of corn to eat during a period of four full days." He was not concerned for himself, however, "I will cheerfully submit to ten times this
much . . . for my country's sake."[18]

On May 20 at about 2:30 P.M. Lee's pickets were pushed back by
Federal infantry at Smith's Mill. These troops were part of Hancock's
II Corps, leading off Grant's next move to get around the Southerners'
right flank. Portions of Lee's cavalry found themselves in tight situations as their picket posts were overrun. One example was that of
Lieutenant George Beale and one company of the Ninth Virginia.
They were positioned near Guinea's Station, and their main assignment was to watch a road that ran parallel to the railroad. The lieutenant posted his most trusted men at intervals along the road. These
men were ordered to fire a warning shot when the Federals came into
view, then race to the regiment's headquarters. The next picket was
placed a quarter-mile down the road with the same instructions. After
midnight the company heard the report of the first picket's rifle. They
were barely mounted when they heard the second. They moved on to
a bridge where they removed some planks and waited in ambush.
When the Federals started across the bridge they fired a volley. After
withdrawing some distance down the road, they did the same at another bridge. By then it was nearly light, and they "could see a long
line of cavalry" as it approached. This time the Federals sent out
sharpshooters as well as a dismounted party that waded across the
river and attacked the Virginians in flank. "There was then some
lively running to get to our horses," the lieutenant remembered. From
a safe hill south of the river, they could see the infantry of Hancock
and Warren as they marched toward Bowling Green. Before they rejoined the regiment they had another close call. After dark they saw
some campfires. Two men were sent to verify that it was the encamp-
ment of the Ninth Virginia, but the answer to "What regiment is
this?" was "Fourth New York Cavalry." After more night riding, they

reached the Telegraph Road but did not know which direction to take. Presently two soldiers rode by and gave them the information they needed. This was Robert Lee riding with a single orderly through the night. He gave directions to the brigade, and the company rejoined them by dawn. The rest of the brigade was trying to slow the advance of another of Grant's corps with both artillery and dismounted men.[19]

Another contingent of the Ninth Virginia had a similar experience near a bridge. One trooper wrote in his diary on May 21: "We went down to the bridge and the men with the long range guns were put out for sharp shooters. We saw the 2nd U.S. Corps passing down on the opposite. Some of our squadron went over and captured several prisoners and pack mules. The Yankee infantry soon came up and made us leave by a flank movement on our right. We had a long run." The next day they were almost surrounded by Federals "but managed to keep them off of us." Not all of Rooney Lee's men were fortunate enough to escape. Union Colonel George Sharpe reported on May 21 that the prisoners who were cavalrymen were from the Ninth, Tenth, and Thirteenth Virginia of Chambliss's brigade. He had interrogated an officer and erroneously decided "that William Henry [Rooney] Lee is in command of the above and Rosser's brigades, which are all the cavalry with the enemy." The Confederate cavalry had done its job well, for Sharpe continued, "The enemy were apprised of the movement of Hancock as early as 2 o'clock this morning." Rooney Lee's cavalry did important work during this period in probing for enemy movement and keeping his father apprised of the changing situation. Reports were sent or signaled to army headquarters every fifteen minutes. Ironically, the Army of the Potomac's system of corps and division insignia made it easier for the Confederates to ascertain the identity of forces. For instance, if a flag bore a blue trefoil, it represented the Third Division of II Corps. If the flag was of a red Maltese cross, then the men carrying it were from the First Division of V Corps.[20]

By noon on May 22 the Confederate Army had crossed to the North Anna's southern bank. Chambliss's brigade was reunited, and Rooney Lee was with this part of his command. The whole brigade supported two artillery pieces under Captain Breathed in an attack on Federal infantry. The troopers fought dismounted. They disengaged and withdrew to a spot where they could shell the Federals as they emerged from some heavy woods. The enemy force they had attacked was the head of a corps that could now be seen "moving forward, regiment following regiment." That afternoon the brigade crossed the North Anna, camped for the night near the Central Railroad, then recrossed the river the next day. The next two days (May 24 and 25) were spent picketing the North Anna.[21]

On May 24 Grant made an assault on Lee's strong lines at Ox Ford. When it failed, he decided to move again to the left on May 26. As he moved he chose as a new supply depot on the Pamunkey River the White House—Rooney Lee's home. Lee's army moved by a shorter route than Grant's circuitous one and was camped at Atlee's Station by May 27.[22]

On May 27 Rooney Lee was finally in personal command of his other brigade, the North Carolina Brigade. The Third North Carolina Cavalry had just arrived from the Old North State "in splendid condition." It joined the First, Second, and Fifth North Carolina Cavalries in this brigade. Colonel John A. Baker of the Third was the senior colonel, and command of the brigade devolved on him temporarily. A member of this brigade wrote of the assignment, "The brigade was placed in Gen. W. H. F. Lee's division, whose past gallant conduct has won for him our most implicit confidence."[23]

On May 28 the Federal infantry began to cross the Pamunkey River on pontoon bridges. The Yankee cavalry moved out in advance. Robert Lee ordered his cavalry to make a reconnaissance in force to verify the crossing. Wade Hampton, as senior major general of the cavalry, was in command of the Confederate force. This included his own division, Wickham's brigade from Fitz Lee's division, and Rooney Lee's division. They headed in the direction of Haw's Shop, so named for a blacksmith's shop at this important intersection on the way to Richmond. The Federal cavalry forces in this area were from Gregg's division. The land was densely wooded, and the men fought dismounted generally. The rebels met Gregg's pickets two miles from Haw's Shop and drove them in. Soon they were "heavily engaged" with the main body. While Hampton's and Fitz Lee's men fought in front, Rooney Lee's division went down the road to the left with the intention of turning Gregg's flank. However, he was unable to accomplish this for two reasons. First, Gregg received reinforcements from Brigadier General George Armstrong Custer's brigade; and second, the infantry seen massed behind the cavalry could have flanked and overwhelmed Lee's men. He did manage to get into a good position to protect the left of Rosser, and his artillery "did good service." Also, Lee sent out the North Carolinians as skirmishers "who engaged the enemy hotly, driving them back some distance." The Federals made several assaults on the main line. Their repeating rifles and infantry support gave them a decided advantage, but they could not force back the Confederates. Finally, Hampton ordered a withdrawal in view of the numerical superiority of the Federal forces and because he had obtained the information Robert Lee wanted. Among the prisoners were infantrymen from V and VI Corps. Lee now knew the direction and strength of Grant's move.[24]

After the engagement at Haw's Shop, the Confederate cavalry was posted with Hampton at Atlee's Station, Fitz Lee on the right and Rooney Lee on the left of the army. Lee's division remained near Fair Oaks for two days, keeping an eye on Federal infantry near Hanover Court House. There were a couple of skirmishes with their rear guard. On the afternoon of May 30 Rooney Lee reported to Hampton that the enemy force in his front was withdrawing and moving toward Cash Corner. He added that he could "see the flag of Sixth Corps very distinctly."[25]

On May 31 there was "a sharp skirmish" at Hanover Court House between Rooney Lee's division and Wilson's division of Federal cavalry. Lee's North Carolina Brigade was in advance that day. All four regiments fought dismounted and "double quicked in with as much élan as old veteran infantry," one trooper remembered. He thought "the scene was grand," as the Tarheels, "jaded and worn, rushed over a hill and saw long black lines of the enemy sweeping over a wide plain." Infantry moved in on both flanks, and the line was pulled back. They held this position until dark, and there was no further Union advance that day. At night the entire command was withdrawn except the First North Carolina, which remained in the saddle in line of battle all night.

The next morning Wilson advanced, and the gray horseman could see "his long lines of cavalry . . . moving out." Lee's pickets fell back along the Ashland Road. About noon they stopped at Ashland, and Wilson pressed the attack. Hampton had come up by this time with Rosser's brigade and met Rooney Lee on the Telegraph Road near Ashland. They conferred and decided to attack. Rosser came in on the left flank and "pressed the enemy vigorously." The North Carolina Brigade made a dismounted attack in which M. B. Young, temporarily in command of the brigade, was severely wounded. Because of this the charge faltered. Then "Lee immediately formed the troops for another attack" while Hampton led the Tenth Virginia and squadrons of the Third North Carolina and Seventh Virginia in an attack on Wilson's right flank. According to Hampton, "These combined assaults were completely successful, the enemy giving way at all points & he was pursued until night forced us to halt." Wilson had to leave his dead and wounded behind and lost several prisoners. A private in the Thirteenth Virginia considered "June 1st . . . the hardest day's work I ever did." He continued, "We had to double quick a great deal and marched altogether several miles. The day was immensely hot in addition."[26]

Just before the battle at Ashland, Rooney Lee added a young aide-de-camp to his staff who had previously served with Jeb Stuart. Theodore Stanford "The" Garnett was returning to duty with the army when he happened to ride by a group of riders and recognized his old friend, Robert Lee Jr. Garnett rode with them for several miles. When Rooney Lee had first returned from prison and visited Stuart at his winter quarters, Garnett had hospitably shared his tent with him. During their conversation Lee found out that Garnett was planning to return to his old company in the Ninth Virginia as a private, as his commission had expired upon the death of Stuart and the dissolution of his staff. Lee told him, "No, that will never do; I will write a letter to the Secretary of War at once, asking that you be commissioned and assigned to duty on my staff with your same rank." He also told Garnett, "You had better stay with me; you know all my staff, and you will be welcome here." When the column bivouacked that night, Lee wrote the request. Garnett carried the letter to Richmond and returned with the commission the next day. So began his connection with Rooney Lee's "military family," which he considered "from the first always of the most pleasant character." The remainder of Lee's staff at this time was as follows:

1. L. Tiernan Bryan, Major and A.A. General
2. John M. Lee, Major and Inspector General
3. Albert G. Dade, Major and Commissary Officer
4. James S. Gilliam, Chief Surgeon
5. Joseph Walters, Captain and A.Q.M.
6. Frank S. Robertson, Lieutenant and Engineer
7. Thomas W. Pierce, Captain and Ord. Officer

8. Robert E. Lee Jr., Lieutenant and A.D.C.
9. Beverly B. Turner, Lieutenant and A.D.C.
10. Philip Dandridge, Lieutenant and A.D.C.[27]

A new trend in cavalry fighting and tactics was emerging during these fights in the spring and early summer of 1864. In most of these engagements most of the men fought dismounted because of the heavily wooded terrain. A North Carolina officer later wrote, "In fact, as the war advanced, the sabre grew into less and less favor, and the policy of the great Tennessee cavalry-man N. B. Forrest was adopted, of using the 'revolver on horse and the rifle on foot.'"[28]

The battle of Cold Harbor, especially savage and bloody, was fought on June 3 as Grant assaulted Lee's fortifications and lost heavily. According to one rebel staff officer, this battle was "perhaps the easiest victory ever granted to the Confederate arms by the folly of the Federal commanders." For three more days the armies fired at and shelled each other from a distance, and the dead were not buried until June 7. While this battle raged the cavalry went on reconnaissance and fought again at Haw's Shop. Rooney Lee sent in the Second and Fifth North Carolina dismounted. One trooper remembered "driving the enemy steadily and rapidly before us, our artillery opening furiously upon their lines." They pressed on "with deafening yells" and took the first line of entrenchments. Just at that moment the Federals were seen moving on the left flank at the double-quick. Lee immediately ordered them to retire, which was done slowly and in good order. Afterward Lee "issued a congratulatory order for their gallant conduct." According to Hampton, the North Carolinians "carried the works in handsome style" and "to the entire satisfaction of the division commander and myself." The following day Robert Lee wrote to his wife, "Our boys in the field are well. Fitzhugh with his division was engaged at Ashland evening before last, & last evening near Old Church. On both occasions doing well." Again on June 7 he wrote: "I saw Fitzhugh yesterday. He was very well. I am full of gratitude to our Heavenly Father for His preservation of all of our sons and nephews."[29]

The North Carolina Brigade received its newest commander on June 7. Rufus Barringer was a forty-three-year-old former lawyer and politician with no formal military training. However, he had risen steadily through the ranks due to his ability and leadership on the field and his organizational efficiency. Part of the cavalry got a much-needed respite in June while a constant watch was maintained for Grant's next move. A private from the Thirteenth Virginia wrote home about this time: "We are getting the greatest quantity of bread and bacon, & occasionally draw Sugar and Coffee. Tobacco rations were issued to us the 1st of this month." His spirits were high, as he added, "Everything is going gloriously for us and I think this campaign will close the war." Part of Lee's division was camped near the battlefield of Cold Harbor, where the stench was still sickening. A trooper from the Ninth Virginia wrote home: "The flavor, part horse, part Yankee & several other varieties is not very pleasant . . . such slaughter, such wholesome murder has never before taken place on this continent. It is enough to make one shudder to think of it." On June 9 Rooney Lee reported to army headquarters: "I am just riding out on the picket line. Everything quiet here this morning so far. Scouts are out north of the Chickahominy, and, as I wrote you, Chambliss moved to the left last night." Chambliss was on that day at Chesterman's Crossroads, the intersection of the Hanover Court House Road and the road to Haw's Shop. Barringer's brigade was near Bottom's Bridge and picketing down the Chickahominy. Also at this time McGregor's battery, which was attached to Lee's division, managed to trade two worn-out Napoleons for two three-inch rifles that would serve the horse artillery better.[30]

Grant made his next move on June 12. His sledgehammer blows so far had only dented the steel of the rebel army, but they had not broken it. His men pulled out of their earthworks and began to swing to the southeast. His plan was to cross the James and strike at Petersburg, an important rail hub and supply line only twenty-two miles south of Richmond. The only cavalry with the Army of Northern Virginia at this time was Rooney Lee's small division, as the men of Fitz Lee and Hampton were following Sheridan on his way to the Valley. On the same day that Grant began his movement, Robert Lee wrote to his wife Mary, "I saw Fitzhugh and Rob yesterday on their way from one wing of the army to the other." This could possibly indicate a point to ponder. Was this movement only Rooney's incessant riding of the established picket line, or had Robert Lee already guessed Grant's direction and sent him to scout for any movement to the southeast?[31]

Rooney Lee reported to headquarters on June 13 that Barringer's pickets had been driven in at Long Bridge and that a pontoon bridge was being built. As the Federals crossed "in heavy force" the cavalry retreated toward White Oak Swamp. Then they moved to Malvern Hill, where they were on the left flank of the Federal position. Rooney Lee led the North Carolina Brigade on a reconnaissance, and they skirmished with the blue cavalry and took thirty-seven prisoners. The next day there were three skirmishes, one near Malvern Hill and the others below there. At one point they were shelled by gunboats on the James. Rooney Lee sent three reports to army headquarters on June 15. He reported that all the prisoners taken were from Wilson's cavalry division and thought "it was merely a reconnaissance." In the third he wrote, "I am pushing the enemy back on all the roads."[32]

The next two days were spent scouting for Grant's army. At 3:30 P.M. on June 17 Robert Lee sent a telegram to his son that read: "Push after the enemy and ascertain what has become of Grant's Army." He could not know that Rooney already had the information he needed and had sent a courier galloping with the news. Lee had ridden to the home of Dr. Wilcox, from which he could see the movement of Grant's army across the river. On the afternoon of June 17 Rooney Lee wrote to headquarters: "I am in sight of the enemy's pontoon bridge at Wyanoke Neck. Their infantry and artillery was principally crossed at this point in transports. Their cavalry left Charles City Court House this morning. No troops crossed at Berkeley. The rear of their infantry column left this place last night." He continued: "Can see no opportunity of doing anything as the Peninsula is flanked by large number of gun boats. There are ten in sight from this place." He rode back to his camp, where that night he reported again: "Grant's entire army is across the river." His men had captured about thirty prisoners "of different corps."[33]

The North Carolinians marched on June 18, crossing the James River on a pontoon bridge near Drewry's Bluff. After marching twenty-seven miles, they camped four miles from Petersburg. The next day they marched through the city and camped one mile south. "Picket firing was kept up day and night," one trooper recorded.[34]

The cavalry movements and placings of the next few days were directed by Robert Lee. As he informed Jefferson Davis: "Genl. William F. Lee I have ordered to Petersburg with Barringer's NC brigade leaving John Chambliss to cooperate with Hampton if practical in striking at Sheridan, who is apparently making for the White House. If he can not cooperate with Hampton, I have ordered him to follow Genl.

William F. Lee to Petersburg. Genl. Hampton will continue to watch Sheridan and endeavor to strike at him, but if the latter escapes and takes transport at the White House, Hampton is ordered to move as rapidly as possible to Petersburg. The enemy having transferred Wilson's division of cavalry to the south side obliges me to call over Genl. W. H. F. Lee."[35]

Grant wanted to try to envelop Petersburg. He was not ready, however, to settle into a siege until he had exhausted other options. Petersburg was an important rail hub with lines to areas of the Confederacy still able to supply Lee's army. One line ran directly south to Weldon, North Carolina, and then on to the open port of Wilmington. The Southside Railroad ran to Lynchburg in western Virginia. This line also connected with a third—the Richmond and Danville—about fifty miles west of the city. If Grant's cavalry could destroy either or both of these lines, then supplies to Lee's army would be virtually cut off.[36]

For this task he chose James H. "Dandy" Wilson, a twenty-six-year-old graduate of West Point and another "boy wonder" of the Union Army. He had been a member of Grant's staff, and his appointment by Grant as the head of the Third Division had caused unrest among some of the subordinates. Wilson jumped at the chance to show his ability in independent command when Grant explained the assignment. For this raid Wilson's force would be his own division and another smaller division from the Army of the James under August Kautz. Together they totaled about 5,500 men. Two batteries of horse artillery, each with six guns, would also accompany the raiders. His orders were to hit the rail line "as close as practicable to Petersburg and destroy it in the direction of Burkeville and the Roanoke River." Two special targets were the High Bridge on the Southside line and the Roanoke Bridge on the Richmond and Danville line. Once his mission was accomplished he was authorized to escape to North Carolina or return to Grant's lines. He opted for the second and received assurance from Meade's staff that his point of return would be covered. Major General A. A. Humphreys, Meade's chief of staff, informed him that "the Army of the Potomac should cover the Weldon road the next day, the Southside Road the day after." Furthermore Hampton and the Rebel cavalry were off chasing Sheridan, and he "need not fear any trouble from him."[37]

The only trouble would come from Rooney Lee and his North Carolina Brigade. He also received reinforcements from a new brigade under the command of James Dearing. Dearing had departed from West Point when the war began and had served conspicuously in the artillery. He had just been promoted to brigadier general on April 29, 1864, at the age of twenty-four. In his small brigade were the Sixty-Second Georgia, the Fourth North Carolina Cavalry, and the Seventh Confederate. Lee's force numbered about 1,500.[38]

The Tarheels were guarding a portion of the Weldon Railroad below Petersburg on June 21 when they saw a "large Yankee force of infantry" approaching. These men were from Brigadier General Barlow's division. Barringer dismounted three regiments while holding one mounted in reserve. The heavy undergrowth concealed his men along the rail line. The first skirmish line fired when the Federals were less than a hundred yards away. They then retired slowly to the second skirmish line, where "the real fight was to be made." A battery of four guns also opened on them. As the Federals were being driven back, one regiment charged after them, taking several prisoners. Barringer's loss was "twenty-seven killed, wounded and missing," while the Federals lost about sixty killed and taken prisoner. This infantry attack may have been planned as a diversion to screen the departure of Wilson's raiders. It certainly held their attention as Wilson made his final preparations.[39]

Wilson's raiders headed out at 3 A.M. on June 22. His men each carried five days' rations and a hundred rounds of ammunition. The advance was commanded by Colonel Samuel Spear of Kautz's division. This was the same colonel whose Pennsylvania regiment had captured Rooney Lee a year earlier. The historian of the Eleventh Pennsylvania remembered the incident well. He surmised, "Doubtless, General Lee was anxious to meet Colonel Spear, that he might even up the score when he was captured at South Anna." Soon after daylight the Federals reached Ream's Station and destroyed some track, the depot, and thirteen rail cars. Barringer later recalled: "Early on the 22nd, Gen. Wm. H. F. Lee put his picket lines in charge of Chambliss' brigade and one of my regiments, the Third, and with my other three, First, Second and Fifth and Dearing's small brigade, he started in pursuit of the raiders." They caught up with Wilson's rear guard at Ream's Station and attacked. "Sharp skirmishing was kept up till the rear arrived at the South Side road," Wilson reported. Colonel George Chapman, in command of the rear guard, wrote that "the enemy follows the rear of the column closely, keeping up a continual skirmish until a couple of hours after nightfall." Chapman had to re-lieve the regiment in the rear because it was "exhausted with the work" of holding off the Confederates. Meanwhile Kautz, who was in command of the advance, made a detour because he had been told by captured pickets that "two brigades of cavalry, under W. H. F. Lee, were stationed at the Six-Mile House guarding the railroad." He turned south and followed Boydton Pike for "four or five miles," then turned west to Dinwiddie Court House. There he went north and reached the railroad between Sutherland's and Ford's Depots. They reached Ford's Depot about 6 P.M. and began a night of destruction. One of the raiders remembered: "The weather was in the most favor-able condition for the destruction of the railroads; clear skies, a burn-ing sun, and several weeks of drought had rendered all wood materi-als intensely burnable. The work of destruction was kept up until midnight, when the tired men were allowed a brief rest." The Confed-erates "could plainly see the light of the burning houses at the station during the night."

By daylight they could see that "the track of the invaders made one complete scene of desolation." The track had been torn up, with the crossties making huge bonfires. The iron track was then placed on the fires. The result was a twisted mess that could not be reused for rail-roads. Scouting parties went off from the main column in all direc-tions to seize provisions and horses.[40]

Kautz's detour had caused a gap between his force and that of Wil-son. By a forced march Lee managed to get in between the two com-mands near a small station known as Blacks and Whites (now Black-stone) not far from Nottoway Court House. He had taken "a detour through a country road" that the Federals did not know was there. His men were "annoyed" by the smoke from the burning railroads as well as the usual dust of a hot June day. They were also "fired with a spirit of revenge, at the sight of these burning ruins, and the tales of woe the frightened ladies eagerly poured into their ears," and were "eager to overtake the 'robbers' and put an end to some of them, and if possible all." Wilson's raiders had not only destroyed military tar-gets and seized horses; they had stolen personal items and destroyed private property for sport. Many farm families were left destitute. Also, many slaves followed Wilson in hopes of finding freedom.

At Blacks and Whites there was an intersection between the railroad and the public road that crossed it at right angles. The Federals were in the railroad cut, some engaged in destroying the tracks while others rested. Wilson had expected Lee to come from the same road he had taken and had thrown up some earthworks along that road. However, Lee attacked the railroad cut from the direction of the intersecting road. General Dearing made the initial attack with the Seventh Confederate Cavalry leading under the command of Lieutenant Colonel Thomas D. Claiborne. They were soon "hotly engaged." McGregor's battery kept up a hot fire as well from its position to the left of the road. Dearing's force, however, was "not equal to the work at hand and was pushed back." Lee immediately called on the First and Fifth North Carolina "to come to the front fast." They arrived just in time, for Dearing's retreat had left the battery open for capture by Chapman's Federals. The North Carolinians passed the guns, "wildly yelling and firing furiously." On their right was Major W. Roberts in command of the Second North Carolina. He was an officer whose "courage never failed" and who "saw everything in battle." He had seen the bluecoats massed in the railroad cut and knew there was an opportunity for a flanking movement. He had pointed this out to Colonel C. M. Andrews, his superior, but could not persuade him to attempt the maneuver. When Andrews was wounded and the command of the regiment fell to Roberts, he immediately ordered the attack. Chapman withdrew to the railroad cut, and the battle continued until night. "Whole trees and saplings were cut down with shells and minié balls," one officer remembered. According to Chapman, the fighting "at times was quite severe." Toward daylight the Federals pulled out and followed Kautz's path down the railroad in the direction of Hungarytown and Keysville, leaving their dead and wounded behind.[41]

Lee reported the events on June 24 by saying, "My command has behaved in the most creditable manner." His loss was between sixty and 100, including Colonel Andrews of the Second North Carolina, who died from having his leg amputated, and Lieutenant Colonel Claiborne of the Seventh Confederate Cavalry, feared to be mortally wounded. He sent back some of his artillery because it was out of ammunition. Lee ordered a short rest that morning because the men and horses were exhausted. General Dearing had sent his wagons back to Petersburg, so his men had been without food for nearly two days. Lee's scouts had been busy tracking Kautz and Wilson, and Lee could report to army headquarters their direction. He also accurately guessed their path of movement: "I think it probable that the two bodies may unite somewhere in the vicinity of the railroad bridge over the Staunton River and return by way of Stony Creek, so as to damage the Weldon Railroad as much as possible." He decided to separate his command. Dearing was to move on the Federals' left flank while Lee followed them directly with Barringer's two regiments. On the afternoon of June 24 they resumed their march toward the Staunton River bridge, a key to Lee's line of supply. That same day Wilson caught up with Kautz near Burkeville, and the destruction of the railroad and the plundering continued. Wilson left a trail of dead horses. One of his men wrote, "We shot on the average one horse every quarter of a mile." The Yankees would kill even a temporarily lame or exhausted horse to keep the enemy from getting it and making it useful again.

Shortly after dawn on June 25 Wilson and Kautz marched toward the Staunton River bridge, destroying track, sawmills, and small bridges as they went. The main bridge was defended by artillery and an assortment of junior reserves, old men, disabled soldiers, and a few officers. Kautz made several attempts to take the bridge but was unsuccessful, losing about sixty killed and wounded. Rooney Lee also made "a vigorous assault" on Wilson's rear at the same time. By this time Wilson had had enough. He "determined to withdraw to the eastward and march back to the James River." He headed back to Grant's line by way of Stony Creek, as Rooney Lee had predicted. Lee continued to follow the raiders but selected only the men and horses able to make the march. Barringer's brigade had approximately 1,200 effectives at the outset, but because of the hard marching, incessant fighting, and intense heat the number was reduced to "less than 300 men and animals equal to the task of further pursuit." A trooper wrote, "We were formed into line and closely inspected and every horse found unfit to stand a forced march was ordered to be sent back to Petersburg." These men walked and led their horses back to Petersburg. They walked on parallel roads so that they could obtain food and forage. With the handful he still led, Rooney Lee continued to annoy Wilson "with dogged determination."[42]

Wilson was headed back to Grant's lines, moving through several small towns to his destination of Stony Creek. Wilson's men were now subsisting completely off the land. Another impediment was "the great mob of contrabands who followed, despite the warnings of the commanding officers." Also, they were losing horses at an appalling rate.

"The rear guard was kept busy killing exhausted horses," a Pennsylvanian wrote. He also said that the "whole population seemed to have vanished from the country" except for some slaves willing to risk all for freedom. Wilson had every reason to believe that the Union Army had taken the area to which he was heading and that Hampton and Fitz Lee were north of the James. He was in for a surprise. Based on Rooney Lee's prediction of his movement and current scouting reports, forces had been moved to intercept Wilson. At Stony Creek Rooney Lee's other brigade, under Chambliss, was waiting. Hampton was moving into position at Sappony Church while Fitz Lee was covering Ream's Station. Wilson was riding into a trap. Wilson engaged Chambliss's brigade, and the fight went on into the night. Wilson then ordered Kautz to move in the direction of Sappony Church and Ream's Station. Many men of his rear guard were captured by Chambliss's men as the main body withdrew. Wilson dispatched a trusted aide to break through the gray lines and ask for aid from General Meade. Meade ordered Wright's infantry corps to move toward Ream's Station. However, by this time Wilson was beyond help. Pummeled by Hampton and almost surrounded, Wilson thought only of escape. He destroyed all his wagons and abandoned his wounded and all his artillery. The two parts of the command became separated, and Kautz's men slipped away in the woods and swamps following a pocket compass and a map of Virginia. Wilson and his main body of troops were then routed by Fitz Lee and some infantry under General William Mahone and had to run for the safety of Grant's lines "in scattered and fugitive parties."[43]

The results of Wilson's raid were mixed. He had destroyed miles of track, depots, and other railroad gear, which took the Confederates about two months to repair. Yet he had considerable losses in men, horses, and materiel. In the two commands of Wilson and Kautz, there were 71 killed, 262 wounded, and 1,119 missing or captured for a total of 1,452. (One of those killed was Lieutenant Tears of the Eleventh Pennsylvania Cavalry, who had been in charge of the squadron that captured Rooney Lee in June 1863.) Many of the wounded were abandoned by Wilson's orders, with some surgeons volunteering to look after them and be sent to prison. The losses of horses exceeded 1,000. One Confederate counted 127 dead horses along a twenty-seven mile stretch of road that was not the main one Wilson had followed. In addition, Wilson lost all his artillery, as well as wagons and ambulances.

Kautz himself referred to the raid as a "disaster," and his sentiments were echoed by other Union officers. George Custer confided to his wife Elizabeth his views on the "court favorite": "You cannot imagine what a blow this humiliation is to our esprit de corps."[44]

Perhaps the most salient aspect of the Wilson-Kautz raid was the effect on the civilian population. Wilson apparently lost control of his men as they pillaged, burned, and stole profligately and in general terrorized the inhabitants of several counties. John Tyler reported that the Yankees "ravaged the whole country through which they passed, robbing the inhabitants of their last morsel of food and last article of clothing, and of their last servant, horse and mule, burning and destroying as they went." Other witnesses reported that Wilson's men abandoned "stolen vehicles of all kinds . . . crammed with books, bacon, looking-glasses and ladies wearing apparel." Other stolen items included a silver communion service from St. John's Church, Cumberland Parish, Lunenburg County. One of the Confederate cavalrymen wrote home: "I wish they were nearly all dead for they have done us a good deal of damage. In their camps yesterday we found all kinds of ladies apparel that the rascals had stolen on their raid." One resident who still had a little food and shared it with a trooper in Barringer's brigade whittled twigs into the shape of forks so they could eat. The raiders had stolen all his cutlery. The Southerners were not the only ones outraged. The provost-marshal of the Army of the Potomac, Marsena Patrick, described Wilson's raid as "one continuous scene of plunder & burning."[45]

Without question the most tragic aspect of the raid was the hundreds of slaves who followed in Wilson's wake in hopes of obtaining freedom. The Union officers told them not to follow, but they had to make the attempt at liberty, even if it was a forlorn one. Most of them were "sent back home." There were men and women of all ages, from infants to oldsters in their seventies. A member of the Ninth Virginia was amazed that "one woman actually gave birth to a child nearby the battlefield." War has many faces that no list of facts and figures can realistically depict.[46]

Rooney Lee throughout the days of the raid demonstrated quickness, determination, and his own certain brand of bulldog tenacity. He read the overall topography of the land, including key military targets, and was correct in his surmise of Wilson's path. This enabled the Confederates to set the trap that led to Wilson's eventual rout. He asked the full measure of his men but did not sacrifice them needlessly. He and his men deserved great credit for their part in the pursuit of the raiders. They also needed a break to rest and refit for further battles. As for the Federals, they knew that in spite of their superiority in numbers, armaments, and supplies they could not take lightly the continuing threat of Confederate cavalry.

CHAPTER 12

"The line must be held"

After the Wilson-Kautz raid, Rooney Lee's division occupied positions in Dinwiddie County with Barringer's men on Hatcher's Run and Chambliss's brigade on Gravelly Run. They were on the right flank of the Army of Northern Virginia. They could now finally rest a little and refit their mounts and equipment as well as keep up a constant watch on picket. The scouts traveled far past the picket line into Federal territory. McGregor's battery of horse artillery was also camped with the division on Armstrong's Farm. The officers did not slack off on drill during this time. In Barringer's words, they were able to turn their "attention to the vital work of organization, drill and discipline—a work always essential to cavalry success." Many men received new weapons taken from Wilson's raiders. In the First North Carolina "more than half . . . were armed and equipped from the foe."[1]

On July 2 Robert Lee asked Jefferson Davis to appoint Wade Hampton as the overall cavalry commander. Since Stuart's death each of the three division commanders had reported separately. In any joint action the senior division commander assumed command. Lee felt that this was an awkward situation that would be ameliorated by putting one man in command who would be "permanently and solely responsible." Three days later he wrote again to Davis about his concerns for the recruitment of his cavalry force. "The enemy is numerically superior to us in this arm, and possesses greater facilities for recruiting his horses and keeping them in serviceable condition," he pointed out. In spite of the losses inflicted on the Federal cavalry in recent engagements, there were Confederate losses as well, "which we were less able to bear." Lee concluded with a warning that on an increase in the "supply of horses and recruiting our cavalry" depended "the issue of the campaign in Virginia."[2]

The period of rest had returned some men and horses to active service. On June 30, 1864, Rooney Lee's division counted 190 officers and 2,677 men present for a total of 2,867. Only ten days later, on July 10, 1864, the field returns for the army indicated 247 officers and 3,957 men in his division present for a total of 4,204. Hampton's division remained constant during this time while that of Fitz Lee decreased by almost 200. Rooney Lee's division was the largest, as Hampton's total was 3,570 and Fitz Lee's only 1,725 in July. The number present did not reflect the actual number of men and mounts ready and able for combat, however.[3]

Around July 1 Rob Lee was absent from his staff duties for a time. He was ordered to report "at once to the commanding general" without any explanation. Some of his young friends teased him that he was to be "shot for unlawful foraging" while others surmised that he was to be sent to Europe as an emissary seeking recognition of the Confederacy. The real mission was to carry a letter to General Jubal Early, then menacing Washington. The commanding general told Rob what orders were in the letter so that he could verbally relate the contents if necessary. He was told to destroy the letter itself if capture by the Federals was imminent. The mission was a secret one, and Rob did not divulge it to his mother and sister in Richmond, whom he saw for a moment while waiting for a train; neither did he tell his companions in the cavalry until long after his return. He rode day and night until catching up with Early in Maryland, then rode back to Petersburg to report to his father.[4]

There exists a pen portrait of Rooney Lee from this period. John S. Wise, just seventeen years old, had recently been allowed to join the Confederate service. He was ecstatic to see his heroes in person and compared his feelings to a boy who had just closed the Iliad or the Odyssey and was allowed to see his "heroes in the flesh, and performing the valorous deeds which immortalize them." In the Army of Northern Virginia they were all about him. He described how he felt: "A house, or a tent by the roadside, decorated with a headquarters flag, guarded by a few couriers, was all that stood between their greatness and the humblest private in the army. They were riding back and forth, and going out and coming in at all hours, so that everybody saw them." The defeat of Wilson and his raiders was a hot topic of conversation during this time, and Wilson had become "the laughing-stock of Lee's army." Those who had contributed to his defeat were near-celebrities in Petersburg. Wise described many of the generals of the army, including Rooney Lee. Here is how he appeared to a young Rebel in the summer of 1864:

General William H. F. Lee, familiarly called "Rooney," had lost much time from active service. He was captured early in 1863, and detained in prison until about May, 1864. Upon his return to active service, he quickly reestablished himself by energetic work; and the manner in which he attacked and followed up General Wilson fixed upon him anew the affections of the army. He was an immense man, probably six feet three or four inches tall; and, while not very fleshy, I remember that I wondered, when I first saw him, how he could find a horse powerful enough to bear him upon a long ride! In youth, he had figured as stroke-oar at Harvard. Although of abstemious habits, his complexion was florid. His hands and feet were immense, and in company he appeared to be ill at ease. His bearing was, however, excellent, and his voice, manners, and everything about him bespoke the gentleman. Speaking of cavalry, a horse simile is admissible. "Rooney" Lee, contrasted with Hampton, suggested a Norman Percheron beside a thoroughbred; General Fitzhugh Lee, a pony-built hunter. I have known all the Lees of my day and generation,—the great general, his brothers, his sons, nephews, and grandsons,—and General "Rooney" Lee I regarded and esteemed more highly than any of the name, except his father. Yet he was the least showy of that distinguished family. This gentleman—a gentleman always and everywhere—would have made a more conspicuous reputation in the cavalry, if the war had not ended so soon after his return from long imprisonment. He had not much humor in his composition, although keenly appreciative of it in others. He was a widower in 1864, and nothing of a society man, although a gallant admirer of women. . . . He had none of the tricks which gain popularity, but somehow he grappled to him the men of his command with hooks of steel, and is remembered by his veterans with as much affection as any officer in Lee's army.[5]

While the cavalry south of the James enjoyed their breathing spell, Union and Confederate forces were being moved about on the chessboard of Virginia roads and towns. General Jubal Early had led his infantry to the outskirts of Washington in an effort to cause the recall of

some of Grant's forces around Richmond and Petersburg and to con-
tend with Union raids on the Shenandoah Valley's vital supplies of
food. Wade Hampton's cavalry also moved in the direction of the
Shenandoah Valley. Grant decided on an offensive north of the James
to try the Confederate lines near Richmond. He wanted Hancock
with his V Corps and two cavalry divisions to attack in the vicinity of
Deep Bottom.

The area known as Deep Bottom encompassed a loop in the James
River and the area north of the loop. It was approximately five miles
southeast of Lee's lines at Richmond. From Richmond three roads
came into the area: the New Market Road, or River Road, closest to
the James; the Darbytown Road a mile north of that; and the Charles
City Road farthest from the river. Another important topographical
feature was Bailey's Creek, or Bailey's Run. It fed into the James from
the north and contained a mill known as Fussell's.[6]

Hancock began his move on July 26 and ran into an unexpected
Confederate line behind Bailey's Creek the next morning. Sheridan's
cavalry also was blocked by the Rebels, and their attempts to flank
the line were unsuccessful. This threat caused Lee to bring up reinforcements, among which was Rooney Lee's cavalry division from
south of the James. They moved out at 2 P.M. on July 28 and marched
twenty miles that night. They moved again "at an early hour" the
next morning and crossed the James River at Chaffin's Bluff. Lee's division and the cavalry brigade of Martin Gary took up positions on
the left of Major General Joseph Kershaw's men.

General Richard Anderson, the Confederate commander, prepared
for an attack on the morning of July 30. The pressure on the Union
line mounted during the day, and in the afternoon Anderson moved
on Riddell's Shop. Kershaw, with three brigades in the center, attacked
Fussell's Mill. To Kershaw's left Rooney Lee moved down the Charles
City Road in the direction of Riddell's Shop.

The Ninth Virginia led Lee's division and ran into the First Maine
Cavalry about 5 P.M. Soon the men of the Ninth "were engaged in a
spirited action with the enemy on the classic field at Malvern Hill."
The regiment lost ten or fifteen wounded and a few horses. The
Union cavalry brought up some reserves, and the Confederates were
pushed back. Lee remained in front of the Federals until 9 P.M. Then
he went into bivouac at Deep Run. At nightfall Hancock began his
withdrawal.[7]

On July 30 the Federal mine was exploded under Elliott's Salient, and there was a terrific battle in the resulting crater in the Petersburg trenches. One of Rooney Lee's men recorded that he could feel the shock of the explosion: "Next morning at five o'clock the mine . . . was sprung, and as I laid on the ground under my tent over 20 miles away I plainly heard the explosion and felt the shock of the ground."[8]

Rooney Lee's division remained north of the James until July 31. At 10 P.M. they saddled up and rode south, crossing the James at Chaffin's Bluff near dawn, and marched to their old camp south of Petersburg. They continued to hold the picket line there for about two weeks. The fact that Lee's division of cavalry was still north of the James on July 31 was noted by George Sharpe, Grant's chief of spies and scouts, in a report to Federal headquarters. The position of each command on a day-by-day basis was extremely important to the high command of both armies. Lee and Grant took seriously the movement of each pawn and knight in their bloody chess match. Sharpe's report was also interesting in that he referred to Lee as "Rooney Lee" rather than as "W. H. F. Lee."[9]

Division headquarters was in Dinwiddie County about eight miles from Petersburg, and the young men of the staff took what respite from war that they could. Rob Lee wrote his sisters about life in camp on August 12, 1864: "You must not imagine that we poor Rebels are entirely destitute of the delicacies of the season." He told of eating apples and cantaloupes for breakfast and lunch and of "2 large watermelons cooling for dinner." There was also a stream nearby where he had enjoyed "a delightful bath." Life there would have been fine were it not for "the flies, yellow jackets & hornets" that gave "neither our horses nor ourselves a chance to fatten." Rob also mentioned his father: "I saw Pa the other day; he is very well & in good spirits. The ladies around the country keep him supplied with everything nice, which he always shares with his sons when they come to see him."[10]

August brought movements of key players in other areas of operation. Grant sent Sheridan with two divisions of cavalry to consolidate the Federal commands in the valley of Virginia. His orders were twofold: to destroy Early, and to lay waste to the Shenandoah Valley. As usual, the Federal movements were as much politically as militarily motivated. On the same day as the Crater battle raged, Early had audaciously moved into Pennsylvania and torched the town of Chambersburg. With elections a little more than three months away, to the electorate of the North it seemed that the Republican president and his generals were not much closer to winning the war, and the Democrats—with George B. McClellan as their leader—were quick to point out the military reverses.

Lee had to counter this move in order to aid Early and protect his largest source of supplies. In spite of his lines at Richmond and Petersburg being paper-thin, he sent Fitz Lee's division of cavalry and a division of infantry from the I Corps to Culpeper under the command of Richard Anderson. Wade Hampton was also ordered to march to Culpeper. Grant's scouts knew of this move but thought it might involve more manpower. Grant was afraid that the force en route to the Valley would be enough to defeat Sheridan. As a result, Grant concluded, "I had to do something to compel Lee to retain his forces about the capital." The plan Grant devised was almost a duplicate of Hancock's earlier drive into the Deep Bottom area. This time it would have to be stronger and quicker in order to succeed.[11]

Hancock was again in charge of the move. He commanded his own II Corps and two divisions from X Corps as well as a division of cavalry under Gregg. Grant also devised a canny ruse this time. The cavalry crossed the James below Deep Bottom while the infantry of X Corps crossed above Deep Bottom. Hancock's II Corps, however, embarked on transports and moved downstream, away from the intended target. After dark, they were to reverse direction and proceed to the Deep Bottom area. The Federal troops fell for the ruse at least. They were delighted to be moving out of the trenches; they were not much concerned about the destination as long as it was not Petersburg. The first problem for the Federals was that it took so long to load the troops on the vessels at City Point—more than seven hours. The boats were crowded, and the men suffered intensely from the heat and insects. They moved downstream approximately five miles and at midnight reversed their direction and headed upstream to Deep Bottom. The troops began disembarking while the cavalry crossed on a pontoon bridge that had been covered with hay to muffle the sound of the horses' hooves.[12]

On the morning of August 14 Hancock began his attack. The Confederate fortifications proved to be more than expected, as was the number of troops manning them. Grant had expected this part of the line to be weakened greatly by Lee sending men to the Valley. To Grant's surprise the prisoners taken indicated that only one division had departed. Immediately Lee ordered up his cavalry to the threatened area. He sent a telegram to Hampton to return and ordered Rooney Lee's division up from the south side of the James. Lee's troopers packed up and started north about noon and camped for the night between Petersburg and Richmond on the Telegraph Road after crossing the James on the pontoon bridge near Drewry's Bluff. The commanding general sent a telegram after midnight on August 15 to Charles Field, commanding the Confederate troops in the Deep Bottom area, that reinforcements were on the way. He further directed Field to send a staff officer to meet the cavalry of Rooney Lee with instructions to move "where he is most required."[13]

Chambliss's brigade of Rooney Lee's division moved down the Charles City Road past White's Tavern on August 15 before meeting any enemy resistance. The Federals "retired slowly" while skirmishing was kept up between Lee's advance line and the rear guard of the retreating Federals. With little loss they pushed the Yankees some distance past White Oak Swamp, taking prisoners and gathering up the wounded left behind. As it grew dark they withdrew to the eastern side of the swamp. The Thirteenth Virginia remained on picket in works that commanded the swamp's passage while the rest of Chambliss's brigade camped for the night at White's Tavern. The men "suffered terribly for water there being none within less than 2 miles and but little that near." Every well in the vicinity was dry.[14]

In the same manner, Lee's North Carolina Brigade under Rufus Barringer, the former lawyer, drove the Federals across White Oak Swamp. They found a "strong party" near Fisher's Farm, and Lee ordered Barringer "to drive them off." Barringer's Tarheels attacked vigorously and pushed the pickets of the Thirteenth Pennsylvania back to the main body of the regiment. They continued to drive back this regiment, as well as the Eighth Pennsylvania, and were stopped only by abatis that the remainder of the Second Brigade of Gregg's division had hastily thrown up. At midnight the Carolinians withdrew a short distance to regroup.[15]

The morning of August 16 was still and hot even by southern standards, and many men looked vainly for water. Nevertheless the Federals advanced up the Charles City Road in the direction of Rooney Lee's pickets. Near Fisher's Farm three regiments of Federal infantry deployed to the left of the road while two regiments of cavalry took the right. About 6:30 A.M. the skirmish line moved out and crossed

Fisher's Run. The infantry took the pickets of the Thirteenth Virginia in flank and pushed them back. Then the Virginians were hit by a column of fours from the Sixteenth Pennsylvania Cavalry followed by three more regiments of cavalry. The Confederates fled for the cover of some close woods about a half-mile to the rear. The brigade commander, General John Chambliss, had ridden out early that morning to his picket line with orders for the other two regiments to follow him. The Tenth Virginia moved up quickly, but the Ninth tarried, waiting for men to return from their futile search for water.[16]

The area of engagement was in many places "a veritable jungle of small bushes and underbrush." Visibility was poor. Chambliss rode up to the front in an effort to stop his men and became separated from his staff. The advance detail of the Sixteenth Pennsylvania came around a bend in the road and spotted "a fine looking man in grey— well mounted" less than 200 yards away. They called on him to halt, but he wheeled his horse around to escape capture. The lieutenant in charge yelled "Fire!" and the Federals' Spencer carbines hit their target. General Chambliss had vowed never to be taken prisoner and died in his attempt to avoid capture.[17]

Chambliss's death added to the "great confusion" of the Virginia regiments. When the Ninth Virginia finally got in the saddle to comply with Chambliss's earlier orders, they went only a mile before coming under enemy fire. This regiment dismounted and formed a battle line at a right angle to the road. A fight ensued that lasted until it appeared that the Rebels were about to be flanked. They then fell back to the crest of a hill. A witness reported that "General Lee came up with our brigade and by his great personal courage rallied the Virginians."[18]

At this point the Federals smelled victory. If they could continue to push up the Charles City Road, Richmond was only a short distance away. Robert Lee telegraphed to Jefferson Davis at 10:35 A.M. that "Lee's pickets at the swamp have been driven back and that the enemy in heavy force are advancing up the Charles City Road and are nearly at White's Tavern." He further recommended for the "works at Richmond to be manned." Rooney Lee's division, however, quickly put up breastworks, and Lee placed a battery of horse artillery in support. He formed a line strong enough that Gregg, with his advancing cavalry, thought he was encountering infantry. Lee positioned Barringer's brigade to the left of the road and the Virginia Brigade on the right

with the Tenth Virginia closest to the road, then the Ninth and the
Thirteenth. They linked with Brigadier General Martin Gary's brigade
of cavalry and a brigade of Texan infantry.

About noon Gregg ordered his dismounted cavalry forward
against the Confederate line across the Charles City Road. Their first
volley killed a few men, but the line held. An hour later the Rebels in
turn attacked Gregg and his infantry supports. This infantry broke
for the rear at the first shots, leaving Gregg and the cavalry to deal
with the advancing Confederates. Some of the remaining cavalrymen
bunched in a shallow depression to the right of the road from which
they could see the Rebel soldiers moving through the woods to the
left of the road. The Confederates were from the Ninth Virginia and
had unknowingly overlapped part of Gary's men to their left and received a volley from them. This friendly fire disrupted the men of the
Ninth, who naturally thought that they were being flanked by unseen
forces in the woods. When Colonel R. L. T. Beale got to the scene, he
saw "a body of our men in confused order." In his words: "A heavy
fire of musketry was opened on us from the slope of the hill which
bounded the bottom in our front. Our line hastily ran back to the
ravine about fifty yards behind us, and the troops in the rear mistook
the movement for a panic."[19]

Apparently Rooney Lee also perceived that his former regiment
was retreating in panic and disorder. Furthermore it was retreating
from a key position in his line, a line that if broken could leave the
road to Richmond wide open. Barringer remembered that "Gen.
W. H. F. Lee, in person, rallied the Virginians and formed a new line
with the First and Second North Carolina in front." The First North
Carolina moved into line on the right, and Rooney Lee sent his staffer
Major John Lee for the Second North Carolina "to hurry to the
front." Colonel William P. Roberts wrote later, "In a short while I reported to the Major-General. My orders were to relieve the regiment
to my front, the Ninth Virginia, I think it was, and he further said to
me: 'Roberts, you know what to do, but the line must be held.'"[20]

No one recorded exactly what Rooney Lee said when he saw that
the Ninth Virginia was retreating in confusion, but it must have been
forcefully worded and delivered, for Colonel Beale wrote that "the
conduct of the regiment, which created a momentary apprehension of
a panic, called forth bitter denunciation from our Major-General." Lee
realized the gravity of the situation and was further mortified that the

break in the line was caused by a panic in his old regiment. In the heat of battle his usually calm, gentlemanly demeanor no doubt changed to that of a warrior, and his reaction to the situation exploded in harsh words. One diarist in the Ninth Virginia recorded a couple of days later that Lee had been "very severe in his remarks" about the conduct of the regiment. To make matters worse the North Carolinians had heard the remarks and delighted in repeating them to the Virginians later. The diarist continued, "As we returned to camp Barringer's Brigade which we passed through commenced joking our men and repeating Lee's remarks—which enraged the men very much and it came near ending in serious difficulty." The temper of the Lees could flare up on occasion in spite of the heavy-handed self-control that was usually apparent. Furthermore the true caliber of a leader in battle is not to be judged as a popularity contest but to get winning results.[21]

The Confederate attack gained momentum as the first Federal line was driven back to the second line, which ran along a knoll on either side of the Charles City Road. A third line was also formed a half-mile behind the second near Fisher's Farm. A trooper of the Second North Carolina, W. A. Curtis, described the action in his diary:

It was known to our officers that the Yankees were in line of battle across the road a few hundred yards in our front, and preparations were made to advance and attack them. Gen. W. H. F. Lee was in command and he formed his line at right angles with the Charles City Road with the centre resting on the road. After the line was formed and all necessary instructions given to the officers and men along the lines, a pistol shot fired at the road by Gen. Lee was the signal to advance the whole line. At once the line moved forward knowing a heavy line of Yankee infantry was in front concealed by the bushes. We were instructed to reserve our fire until we came in view of the enemy. Forward the line moved, peering through the bushes for the first glimpse of the enemy. About two hundred yards was passed over when the blue line was discovered and about one-third of our men fired as they had been instructed to do, the others reserving their fire so as to make three volleys of a few seconds intervals. On our first fire the enemy gave us a heavy volley with but little damage. We now knew their guns were empty, and raising the "rebel yell" we immediately charged their line which promptly gave way. Then commenced a hot pursuit. We kept pressing them and forcing them back, advancing against shot, shell, grape-shot and canister, as well as minie balls. We kept up the charge for over a mile, continually firing our Sharpe's rifles, the only arms we had. Reaching a field just beyond a thicket of pine bushes, the Yankees set fire to the leaves and attempted to make a stand. Reaching the fire, Major Roberts' loud voice was heard giving the command to charge through the fire, which was done without faltering, and as we reached the edge of the field we were within a few steps of the Yankees who had attempted to make the stand, but their backs were toward us now and they were running headlong through the open field. At the farther side of the field near the road were two pieces of artillery that gave us a couple of charges of grapeshot, when the yell was raised "Capture the artillery." Our line moved steadily and rapidly on and came near capturing the guns before they could limber up and retreat.

The Federals retreated before both brigades. The North Carolinians pushed down the Charles City Road after "an obstinate and bloody struggle" until they ran up against the last line of defense, which was secured with artillery. There they were aided by Gary's cavalry and the Texas infantry brigade that "came up fast from the direction of Fuzzle's [sic] Mill and struck the Federal left." By now it was a rout. A member of the Second North Carolina described the action: "After an hour of desperate fighting, the Yankee line began to waver & with a yell we charge them. . . . They in utter confusion fly before us, leaving their dead and wounded in the field and many of them rushing head-long into the muddy bottom of the famous old White Oak Swamp, from which uncomfortable position they were extracted by our men." A reporter on the field noted that the "enemy's dead was strewn far and wide on the route."[22]

The Virginians also forged ahead, taking a Federal position behind a barricade of pine rails. There the exhausted men, almost out of ammunition, were "ordered to lie down and rest." "The day was the most trying our regiment had ever experienced," the colonel recorded. "Not one drop of water could be had, the heat was intense, and the wood was dense and tangled."[23]

General Hampton arrived on the field midday on August 16 and noted: "Consulting with Maj. Genl. Wm. Lee, it was determined that a portion of my command should gain the right and rear of the enemy while he made an attack in front. Gary's brigade was also on the right of his line & it was ordered to participate in the attack. These dispositions

made, Lee moved his line forward, & in a gallant charge not only regained the ground he had lost, but drove the enemy in confusion across
the White Oak Swamp. Quite a number of prisoners, chiefly Infantry,
were captured, & the fight ended most creditably to our arms. My men
were but slightly engaged being held in reserve, & I found Lee quite able
to maintain himself."[24]

Elsewhere on the line the Confederates were pushed back early in
the day, but they rallied and successfully attacked the Federals later.
Almost no fighting took place on August 17. Rooney Lee sent a flag of
truce to Gregg's lines with a request for the return of General Chambliss's body. The body was exhumed by the Federals and returned
through the lines. Upon opening the rude coffin, Chambliss's brother
identified the body. Also on the general's chest was an envelope con-
taining two gold buttons and his West Point class ring, which had
been returned by his old classmate, Gregg, the Federal cavalry general. Upon the death of Chambliss, Colonel J. Lucius Davis assumed
command of the Virginia Brigade.[25]

Among the wounded in the engagement of Second Deep Bottom
was Rob Lee. On August 15 he was "shot in the arm and disabled for
about three weeks." He himself wrote that the wound was severe
enough to get him a furlough but not painful enough to keep him
from enjoying his sick-leave.[26]

On the night of August 17 the Ninth Virginia held the picket line
along White Oak Swamp. One trooper recalled it as "a miserable rainy
night and very dark." He wrote: "I can hear the Yankees talking very
distinctly just opposite me on the other side of the swamp and was
startled several times by tremendous splashing and fearful groans—
proceeding evidently from something in the swamp which afterwards
proved to proceed from several horses which the enemy in their retreat
the day before had abandoned, they having become mired in the
swamp and left to perish but many had during the day been rescued by
some of our men at the risk of being shot by the enemy—but we had
many among us that would risk at any time their lives for a horse."[27]

Robert Lee ordered a concerted attack all along the Deep Bottom
line for August 18. Hampton's plan for the cavalry included Rooney
Lee attacking on the Charles City Road while Butler, of his division,
crossed the swamp and attacked the right flank of the enemy. There
was a delay in positioning the commands so that the attack did not
begin until late in the day. Hampton was with Lee's command and

saw them drive "the enemy some distance in the front" while Butler attacked on the right. The Confederates captured 167 prisoners in this movement.[28]

Hampton reported the day's action to army headquarters: "General William H. F. Lee made a very handsome and successful fight yesterday. He drove the enemy two miles and a half, killing many and capturing 110 prisoners, representing two brigades of infantry, in addition to Gregg's division of cavalry. I have not witnessed a more gallant affair with our cavalry this campaign than the one of yesterday." In his report Hancock wrote that his men on the Charles City Road were "pressed back . . . by a superior force of infantry." This was indeed a compliment to the Confederate cavalry fighting dismounted.

An interesting sidelight to the fight at Second Deep Bottom was the fact that some in the Federal high command were still confused as to the identity of Fitz and Rooney Lee. Winfield Hancock, commander of II Corps, in several reports mentioned the cavalry on the Charles City Road as belonging to the division of W. H. F. Lee. About midday on August 16 George Meade sent Hancock the following communiqué: "There is some confusion about the cavalry in your front. As I understand it, W. H. F. Lee is sometimes called Fitz Lee, the other Lee is Fitzhugh Lee. I suppose the former is in your front; the latter was at Reams Station yesterday." The very capable Hancock was more thorough in his study of opposing generals and immediately wired back a lesson to his superior: "This division of cavalry is General W. H. F. Lee's (Rooney Lee), General Lee's son, not Fitz Lee's, who is the oldest division commander, but the one who was in Fort Lafayette. They are both named Fitz Lee, but one is known as Fitz Lee and the other as Rooney Lee among their companions. This command left Reams Station day before yesterday at 11 o'clock and arrived here yesterday morning." Hancock was smart enough to know that being aware of the difference in the Lees would allow him to know whether there was one or two divisions of cavalry in his front.[29]

There was no rest for the troopers of Lee's division. That same rain-soaked night they marched again to the south side of the James to meet another threat on another portion of the line. They recrossed the James on a pontoon bridge and marched to Petersburg. While the fighting was still in progress at Deep Bottom, Grant had prepared his next strike at Lee's lines. The Federal V Corps was pulled out of line into a reserve position while others covered their part of the line. Next they moved to their left toward the Weldon Railroad. This move brought up several possibilities. First, if Lee had weakened this part of his line to send men to Deep Bottom, then a strike could do real damage. Or if Major General Gouverneur K. Warren (commander of V Corps) managed to take possession of at least a part of the Weldon Railroad, then Lee's supply line to North Carolina would be cut. Possibly this move would force Lee to recall Early from the Valley or at least not send him reinforcements from the Petersburg-Richmond line. Warren's corps of infantry could also aid Kautz's cavalry in strikes on the railroad farther to the south. To help counter these possible moves, Rooney Lee's division moved to the extreme right of the Confederate line near the railroad.[30]

By August 18 Warren had taken a portion of the Weldon Railroad and had begun the destruction of the track. The Confederates under Henry Heth made an assault that at first pushed the Federals back, but a counterattack brought the men of V Corps back to their earlier position. Warren's success led Grant to begin calling segments of Hancock's II Corps from their positions at Deep Bottom to the south side of the James to aid Warren. The next day there was severe fighting around Globe Tavern. V Corps lost heavily in prisoners during this engagement. August 20 was spent in maneuvering and consolidating positions with little fighting. On August 21 A. P. Hill assaulted Warren's lines at Globe Tavern. Lee's Virginia Brigade was positioned on the left flank of Confederate infantry as they made a "bloody assault" on the Federal line. For a couple of hours they endured the sharpshooters' fire without receiving much damage. The North Carolina Brigade was on the extreme right of the infantry on a path from Poplar Spring Church to the railroad. The Third and Fifth North Carolina Cavalries charged "in the most gallant and heroic manner" to within a few yards of the railroad itself but were obliged to withdraw when the infantry on their left faltered. The First and Second North Carolina formed on either flank of the attacking force as they withdrew and checked the enemy advance. The whole brigade withdrew at dark having lost sixty-eight men killed, wounded, or missing. Rooney Lee was with this portion of his command as they attacked.[31]

Grant now had a hold on the Weldon Railroad, which soon became a part of his entrenchments and fortifications. His next move would be to destroy more track toward the south. Lee's army was inconvenienced in its supply line, but the flow of supplies was not completely stopped. They merely ran the supplies up the rail line to Stony Creek, loaded them on wagons, and then on to Petersburg.[32]

During this time Robert Lee sent a note to Hampton "to have out your scouts to ascertain their position and the best point to attack them." The use of "scouts" for obtaining information was a common occurrence in the Confederate cavalry. On August 22 Major Tiernan Brien, Rooney Lee's assistant adjutant-general, sent a report to army headquarters "in the absence of General Lee at the front." In it he detailed the findings of Isaac Custis, "one of our best scouts," who had been within the Union lines the night before and had conversed with many Yankees. He pinpointed the positions of generals' head-quarters, the extent of fortifications, the position of pickets, artillery, and reserve ordnance, and other details. Later that day, when Rooney Lee read a copy of this report, he sent a note to his father correcting a slight error that Brien had made and making a personal request: "It was a very daring feat and I think a little note from you to him would be pleasant." Evidently Rooney could not conceive of his father having limitations of patience or time. However, intelligence of this importance would be most welcome by Lee. Because a scout rarely received public congratulations for his exploits, perhaps a thank-you note was in order. Later on, Rooney Lee lost some of his scouts. The office of Grant's provost-marshal reported: "Four of W. H. F. Lee's scouts were captured near Sycamore Church last night; found lurking within our lines. They freely confess that they came in for information, and have been in sundry times before. They are regularly detailed scouts, and are attached to General Lee's headquarters, belonging to the Ninth Virginia Cavalry."[33]

At some point between the engagement on August 21 and the next Confederate attack on August 25, Rooney Lee became acutely ill and was forced to turn over command of the division to General Barringer. On August 22 he was "at the front" and capable of reading Major Brien's report and sending the correction to his father. At 10 A.M. on August 24 Barringer sent a report to Calbraith Butler as the commander of the division. Later Barringer wrote that "Gen. Wm. H. F. Lee being ill and absent, the command of the division devolved on myself while that of the brigade fell to Col. W. H. Cheek of the First North Carolina." In the Union Army there were reports of Rooney Lee being mortally wounded as early as August 21. One report read: "W. H. F. Lee's cavalry division was also engaged this A.M., and General Rooney Lee badly wounded through lungs. So say prisoners from above commands." A captain in the Federal provost-marshal department questioned prisoners—privates as well as officers from Lee's division—who said "that General W. H. F. Lee was badly wounded in the lungs in the action this A.M." A subsequent report at 11:30 P.M. on August 21 from that office stated that "prisoners from Fifth North Carolina Cavalry confirm report that General W. H. F. Lee was severely wounded in the lungs today." The same night Meade sent a dispatch to Grant stating that "prisoners say that General W. H. F. Lee was mortally wounded today."

The Union high command reported this information on August 22 in a report from Meade to Grant. The interrogators in the provost-marshal's department questioned more recent prisoners from Chambliss's brigade who said "they heard that General W. H. F. Lee died from wounds received yesterday." This same day Grant forwarded the news of Lee's death to Lee's former jailer, Ben Butler. The reports were also forwarded to Washington on August 23 and presumably confirmed by a Richmond paper in Federal hands the night of August 24.[34]

Actually he had not been shot, and the rumors spread from the captured troopers were due to active imaginations or outright lies. He was suffering from poison oak on his face. The sap from poison oak is even worse when it is burned and carried on the air, and Lee possibly got it this way. At any rate his whole head was swollen "about the size of a half bushel" and his eyes nearly closed. His aide, Frank Robertson, escorted him to Richmond, where he was a guest with Robertson's family for a few days. Robertson wrote, "I have most earnestly cited several instances of relapse occurring from too early exposure of poison oak sufferers, but it availed nothing." Lee was anxious to return to duty as soon as he could. Robertson also mentioned "numerous lady visitors—Gen. Lee seems to be quite a favorite among them and several times there have been four or five in the parlor at a time." Among the visitors was Rooney's oldest sister, Mary, who checked in on him two or three times a day. On August 27 he was recuperating in Richmond when Robert Lee wrote to his son Custis sending news and adding: "I am glad that F, R and Bev are doing well. . . . He [Rooney] should not have gotten poisoned." Custis wrote him the same day, which Lee acknowledged in a letter to his wife on August 28: "A letter from Custis yesterday reported the invalids (Rooney and Rob) doing well. . . . I am very grateful that Rob's injury was slight & Fitzhugh unhurt."[35]

Rooney Lee missed the fight at Ream's Station, but his division fought magnificently there. Hancock's II Corps had marched down from its former position at Deep Bottom and went immediately to work tearing up the Weldon track. On the night of August 24 they were camped at Ream's Station. The Confederate attack on Hancock was proposed by Hampton after a personal study of the situation. He was to attack with his cavalry—two divisions in all—in conjunction with the infantry under A. P. Hill. The attack began at 5 A.M. on August 25. Lee's division, under the command of Rufus Barringer, moved up toward Malone's Crossing and soon encountered enemy pickets. These were all driven in by 9 A.M. The Federal cavalryman Gregg realized that the approaching force was too powerful for his cavalry alone, and he called on the infantry of Major General John Gibbon for help to reestablish their line. Hancock's men were positioned in a rough U-shaped position with the open end to the east. Hampton temporarily withdrew and notified Hill that it was time to attack. At 5 P.M. Hill's artillery opened, and soon the attack began. Hampton ordered his entire line to advance. The Federals "were driven to their works near Reams Station giving up several positions which they had fortified." Colonel Roberts with the Second North Carolina carried a line of rifle pits and took about seventy-five prisoners. Hampton, realizing that Hill's infantry was driving the enemy back toward the station, withdrew his force and realigned it. He put Lee's Virginia Brigade on the left, Barringer's Brigade in the middle, and Brigadier General P. M. B. Young's brigade on the right, with Brigadier General Thomas Lafayette Rosser in reserve in a second line. All were dismounted except for a couple of regiments kept in reserve on their horses. Hampton ordered his line to advance, with the left moving slowly and the right moving faster in a swing to gain the Federal rear. The ground they had to cross was covered with trees felled as abatis. A member of the Ninth Virginia remembered: "Never marched men over worse ground than we on this occasion. For fifty yards at times my feet did not touch the ground. We had to walk over felled trees or crouch down to get through them. No man seemed to think of danger. We were all zeal and enthusiasm." Hampton later recalled: "In spite of this & under a heavy fire of artillery & musketry the line advanced steadily, driving the enemy into his works. Here he made a stubborn stand & for a few moments checked our advance. But the spirit of the men was so fine that they charged the breastworks with the utmost gallantry, carried them & captured the force holding them." A Rebel trooper saw how "the enemy surrendered for a hundred yards at a time, many of them running towards us empty-handed, appealing for mercy." That night Hancock gave the order to withdraw.[36]

The Confederate victory was a very rewarding one for the cavalry. They captured 781 prisoners and buried 143 enemy dead. They also captured several stands of colors. The loss in Lee's division was ten killed, fifty wounded, and one missing. Hampton praised their efforts: "General Barringer commanded Lee's division to my satisfaction, whilst his brigade commanders, Colonel Davis and Colonel Cheek, performed their parts well. Chambliss' brigade was in advance when we met the enemy, and it was engaged all day, displaying through the whole fight marked gallantry." In Barringer's mind, "Never was success more complete." He also mentioned the small arms, tools, and artillery taken in the fight. Robert Lee wrote Custis to tell his recuperating brother that "his division did splendidly on the 25th, charging the enemy's breastworks on foot, as if they were armed with bayonets." Furthermore he had "just received three stand of colors taken by Chambliss' brigade." He echoed this praise in a letter to his wife: "On the 25th Fitzhugh's division behaved splendidly, charging on foot the enemy's works on the right & capturing the men at their posts with their arms, etc. The North Carolina brigades signalized themselves, & behaved most handsomely."[37]

Lee's division remained on picket at the station for a few days. Under a flag of truce the enemy dead (i.e., those the Confederates had not already buried) were buried in a hurry. A witness to the burial described how "the deep ditch or trench beside the breastworks was used for the reception of the dead bodies, and these having been laid in it were covered with earth, thus offering a melancholy illustration of how often brave men in making works for their protection literally dig their own graves." Rooney Lee rejoined the division, which moved to another camp about six miles to the west of Reams Station around September 1. On August 27 Lee had visited the camp of the Tenth Virginia. Major Clement later wrote, "Genl. Cmdg. the Division came to my camp day before yesterday to compliment me upon the gallant manner in which my men conducted themselves during the fight." The major continued in his letter, "Our Regt. has suffered severely in the late fights. I only had about two hundred fighting men for duty and have lost fifty-five of them in killed and wounded since the 15th of August, less than two weeks over one fourth loss." On September 6, 1864, The Sentinel listed the casualties in the Ninth Virginia Cavalry for the period of May 12 to September 1 as 151 killed and wounded. All of the men must have been exhausted, as they had been pushed to the limits of human endurance in marching and fighting for some time. General Barringer summed it up, "Thus in ten days our division had crossed and recrossed the James River . . . making nearly 100 miles night and day marching, and in the meantime fighting eight severe actions." The soldiers in both armies were worn out and virtually unable to do anything else for several days.[38]

CHAPTER **13**

"The slickest piece of cattle stealing"

After the engagement at Reams Station, the Confederate cavalry continued to picket while recuperating and refitting as best they could. On August 26, 1864, the commanding general sent a directive to Hampton "to rest the two divisions as much as practicable and to take such position as would enable you most speedily to intercept and punish any party which they might send out against our communications." He feared forays by Gregg's cavalry and urged the pickets to be vigilant. Lee also suggested "to let Dearing's Brigade do all the picketing if practicable so as to give the rest of the cavalry a good period of repose for refreshing their horses."

The cavalry remained relatively quiet until September 14, with Butler's division ten miles south of Petersburg near the Quaker Meeting House and Rooney Lee's division on Butler's right near the Stage Road. The brigade of James Dearing was to the right of the infantry with pickets extending down the Jerusalem Plank Road.[1]

There was a difference in the nature of the war between the area of trenches with their labyrinths of salients, tunnels, bombproofs, ditches, and abatis and the more open area to the south of the trenches. There the line was less static and the boundaries between blue and gray less obvious. There the "scouts" on both sides could slip back and forth in their efforts to glean important information. A Confederate general recalled that "the daring scouts of both armies often passed each other at night and found hiding places during their adventures" in the dense pines. One of these scouts was "Shake" Harris of the Fifth North Carolina, a man of "daring, desperate deeds" who "every night and often in the day in Federal uniform with his life in his hand" prowled the Federal territory.[2]

Another scout, Sergeant George Shadbourne, was attached to the Jeff Davis Legion and reported directly to Wade Hampton. His report of September 5, 1864, had one item in particular that interested Hampton: "At Coggins Point are 3,000 beeves, attended by 120 men and 30 citizens, without arms." These cattle could provide Lee's half-starved men with meat for weeks. Hampton formulated a plan to take the cattle and set the time for the raid to coincide with a visit by Grant to Sheridan in the Shenandoah Valley. Robert Lee gave his approval for the foray, reminding Hampton only to be careful.[3]

Hampton moved out on September 14 with Rooney Lee's division, Rosser's brigade, Dearing's brigade, and a detachment of 100 men from the brigades of P. M. B. Young and Brigadier General John Dunovant. Riding with them was a detail of forty hand-picked men and two officers serving as a "mounted engineer troop." These men were chosen for their expertise with an axe. Those from Rooney Lee's division were ordered to report to Lee's headquarters, where the tools were issued to them.

The troopers had no idea of their destination when they saddled up on the morning of September 14. An artilleryman recalled: "We waited, seated on our horses, for a long time—all waiting seems long—and while we waited we speculated upon where we were going and what we were going for. So little do soldiers know of the intention of their officers that . . . we had no intimation nor idea that beeves had any place in the picture at all."

The column moved down the Boydton Plank Road to Dinwiddie Court House. There they turned southeast, crossed the Weldon Railroad, and continued to Rowanty. After a march of twenty miles they bivouacked. At daybreak the next morning the column marched northeast to the Jerusalem Plank Road. Later that day they moved to the rear of the Federal force on backroads until arriving at Blackwater. This day's march covered eighteen more miles.

Cooke's Bridge, spanning Blackwater Creek, had been destroyed. Hampton had chosen this route "on that account that the enemy would not look for an approach from that quarter." While the engineers worked on rebuilding the bridge, the men rested and fed their

Robert Edward Lee and
W.H.F. "Rooney" Lee—This
daguerreotype was done in
New York City, possibly in Brady's
studio. Lee was thirty-eight and
Rooney was eight at the time.
The position of Rooney's hands
indicates that this photo was taken
after the accident to his fingers.
Michael Miley copied the original
in Lexington during the late 1860s.

Rooney Lee at Harvard College.

W.H.F. "Rooney" Lee—Lt. 6th
Infantry, Regular U.S. Army.
VIRGINIA HISTORICAL SOCIETY,
©1857–1858.

W.H.F. "Rooney" Lee in
Confederate uniform—All
portraits of Rooney Lee show
the three stars of a Confederate
colonel on his uniform collar,
just as his father wore. The
braid on the sleeve and the
configuration of buttons indicate
a rank of general, however.
LIBRARY OF CONGRESS.

W.H.F. "Rooney" Lee—This is the only standing portrait of Rooney Lee. It is interesting that he chose to be photographed without any accoutrements. WASHINGTON AND LEE, BY VANNERSON IN RICHMOND.

W.H.F. "Rooney" Lee—Postwar caption reads "Genl. W.H.F. Lee." WASHINGTON AND LEE.

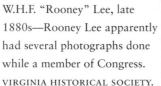

W.H.F. "Rooney" Lee, late 1880s—Rooney Lee apparently had several photographs done while a member of Congress. VIRGINIA HISTORICAL SOCIETY.

W.H.F. "Rooney" Lee— portrait late 1880s. VIRGINIA HISTORICAL SOCIETY.

W.H.F. "Rooney" Lee with family—Mary Tabb Bolling Lee, her sister, George Bolling Lee, and Robert Edward Lee III on the porch of Ravensworth, late 1880s. VIRGINIA HISTORICAL SOCIETY.

W.H.F. "Rooney" Lee with his
brothers, George Washington
Custis Lee and Robert Edward
Lee Jr. VIRGINIA HISTORICAL
SOCIETY, late 1880s.

Mary Ann Randolph Custis Lee—
1838 portrait by William E. West.
VIRGINIA HISTORICAL SOCIETY.

Robert Edward Lee—1838 portrait
by William E. West. These companion
portraits were done when Rooney
was less than one year old.
VIRGINIA HISTORICAL SOCIETY.

Henry Light Horse Harry Lee—Although Henry Lee died years before Rooney Lee was born, his legacy had quite an effect. The first two companies of cavalry under his command were "Lee's Rangers" and "Lee's Light Horse." VIRGINIA HISTORICAL SOCIETY, painting by Robert Edge Pine.

George Washington Parke Custis—This grandson of Martha Washington and adopted son of George Washington built Arlington as a repository of the Washington relics. Rooney Lee grew up in a home with the museumlike quality that this grandfather created. VIRGINIA HISTORICAL SOCIETY.

Mary Lee Fitzhugh Custis—
Portrait as a young woman
by Cephas Thompson.
Rooney Lee was very close
to his grandmother Custis
even though she died when
he was fifteen years old.
VIRGINIA HISTORICAL SOCIETY.

George Washington Custis Lee in
Confederate uniform. VIRGINIA
HISTORICAL SOCIETY.

Robert Edward Lee Jr.—
In Confederate uniform
as an aide to his brother
W.H.F. Lee. COURTESY OF
THE LEE FAMILY.

Mildred Lee—VIRGINIA
HISTORICAL SOCIETY, by
Michael Miley.

Mary Tabb Bolling Lee and her two sons George Bolling Lee and Robert Edward Lee, III.—VIRGINIA HISTORICAL SOCIETY.

J.E.B. Stuart—LIBRARY OF CONGRESS.

Wade Hampton—LIBRARY
OF CONGRESS.

Fitzhugh Lee—LIBRARY
OF CONGRESS.

John R. Chambliss—Photograph in Confederate uniform. LIBRARY OF CONGRESS.

Rufus Barringer—Although he had no military training prior to the war, this commander of the North Carolina Brigade proved to be a very competent cavalryman. NORTH CAROLINA MUSEUM OF HISTORY.

Arlington—WASHINGTON AND LEE.

White House—W.H.F. Lee's home on the Pamunkey River. Photographed May 17, 1862, by James Gibson during Federal occupation. LIBRARY OF CONGRESS.

The White House—Arsonists torch the Lee Home. *HARPER'S WEEKLY.*

White House—Ruins of house during Federal occupation. LIBRARY OF CONGRESS.

The Death of Latane—The Ninth Virginia charges the 5th U.S. Cavalry at Old Church near Tunstall's Station on June 13, 1862. Sketch by William Waud. *FRANK LESLIE'S ILLUSTRATED NEWSPAPER*, July 19, 1862.

Stuart's Raid—Rebel cavalry capture and burn Federal wagons near Garlick's Landing June 13, 1862. *FRANK LESLIE'S ILLUSTRATED NEWSPAPER*, July 19, 1862. Sketch by William Waud.

White House Landing, 1862—Rooney Lee's home on the
Pamunkey River served as a commissary and ordnance depot
for McClellan's army during the Peninsula Campaign. This
view from across the river shows the first home of Martha and
George Washington. *FRANK LESLIE'S ILLUSTRATED NEWSPAPER.*

Burning of the White House—This view shows the departure
of the Union flotilla after the raid by Stuart on Garlick's
Landing and Tunstall's Station on June 25. As the stores
were being hastily embarked at the wharves, arsonists set fire
to the house. *FRANK LESLIE'S ILLUSTRATED NEWSPAPER.*

Confederate Cavalry returning from Pennsylvania—On Sunday, October 12, 1862, Stuart's cavalry crossed into Virginia at White's Ford after a successful raid into Pennsylvania. *FRANK LESLIE'S ILLUSTRATED NEWSPAPER.*

The Office at Hickory Hill—Original pen and ink by Isabel Finch. Rooney Lee was convalescing in the office of the Hickory Hill plantation of the Wickham family when he was taken prisoner.

Fort Lafayette—Fort Lafayette was located in New York harbor on a shoal about 400 yards from Long Island. It served as a prison for state prisoners early in the war. Later Confederate officers were also housed there. *FRANK LESLIE'S ILLUSTRATED NEWSPAPER.*

Fort Lafayette—Casemate No. 2 in Fort Lafayette after the war. This would be identical to Casemate No. 3 in which Rooney Lee was held. It was fourteen feet wide and twenty-four feet long. *HARPER'S WEEKLY,* April 15, 1865.

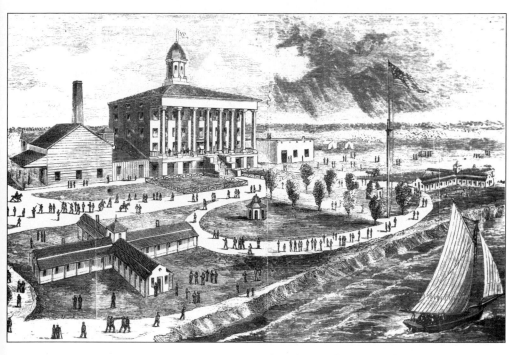

The Chesapeake Hospital at Fortress Monroe, VA—Lee was first sent to the Hampton Hospital, which was used for Confederates, then transferred to this hospital, which was reserved for Union officers. FORT MONROE CASEMATE MUSEUM.

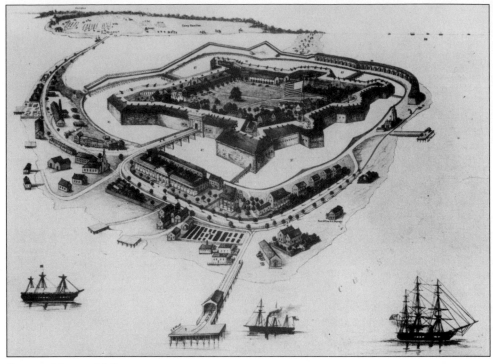

Fortress Monroe 1862—FORT MONROE CASEMATE MUSEUM.

The Bolling Residence on Sycamore Street in Petersburg, VA—Rooney Lee courted Mary Tabb Bolling at this house across from Poplar Lawn park.

St. Paul's Episcopal Church, Petersburg, VA—W.H.F. Lee and Mary Tabb Bolling were married in this church on November 28, 1867. Their wedding was a huge social occasion with throngs of people around the crowded church. The church was built in 1856, and this picture indicates how it would have appeared at the time of the wedding.

St. Paul's Episcopal Church, Petersburg, VA.—Another view.

Ravensworth, Fairfax County, VA, built about 1800 by William Henry Fitzhugh—Anne Carter Lee was nursed during her final illness here and was buried in the family cemetery. The house burned in 1926, and the entire estate was obliterated in the 1960s by a housing development. VIRGINIA HISTORICAL SOCIETY.

horses. They also took this opportunity to dig some sweet potatoes from nearby fields (they were eaten raw, as no fires were permitted). All civilians were detained so that no news of their position would reach the Yankees. At night the horsemen silently crossed the newly finished bridge. One of them described the crossing: "Several times the musical men of the column were cut short in attempted songs, which they thoughtlessly began. Nothing was heard but the steady tread of the horses and the rattling of sabres. The guns of the artillery had been muffled by grain-sacks being inserted between the elevating screws and the guns." About 3:30 A.M. they halted, and "everything was as still as death." The men dismounted, sleepy and overcome by fatigue, and "soon most if not all were dozing on the ground with our bridle reins around our elbows." The horses also rested and "showed no disposition to move or disturb their sleeping masters."

While at the bridge Hampton gave his orders to his subordinates. It would be a three-pronged movement. Rooney Lee, with the largest force, was to move on the left and serve as a screen between the main part of the Union Army and the rest of Hampton's command. He was to follow Lawyer's Road as far as the Stage Road. There he was to drive in the enemy pickets and hold the roads leading from the enemy's position to Sycamore Church. Dearing provided the same service on the right. Hampton, with Rosser's men, marched directly to Sycamore Church. This was the force that was to actually take the cattle. All three segments of the command reached their jump-off points without alerting the enemy.

To draw attention from the raiding party, diversions were carried out on the main line. Major General William Mahone's infantry demonstrated along the line between the Boydton Plank Road and the Weldon Railroad. For three days the men of Dunovant's brigade not on the raid harassed the pickets of II Corps. P. M. B. Young's cavalry covered the line vacated by the raiders and "kept up a constant show of force" with bands, fires, and artillery.

Rosser attacked the Federals at 5 A.M. After a stiff, though short, fight with a part of the First District of Columbia Cavalry, his men rounded up the cattle before they could be stampeded by the guard. Besides the beeves, there were commissary and sutlers' stores for the taking. The forces of Dearing and Lee moved at the same time as Rosser's attack. Dearing blocked the roads on the right and cut the telegraph lines to prevent the news of the raid from spreading.[4]

To the west the men of Lee's division were facing the camps of the Third New York Cavalry and components of the Eleventh Pennsylvania Cavalry and the First District of Columbia Cavalry. As soon as the shots from Rosser's attack were heard, Lee's troopers charged. Most of the Federals were "cozily sleeping in their tents and quite unprepared for so early a visit," an officer of the Ninth Virginia remembered. Some were captured while others "with white flags fluttering in the rear, sought the protecting cover of the woods." Another characterized the Yankees as "unsuspecting creatures" who "had barely time to escape, and that without waiting to put on their clothing." In the camps Lee's men eagerly gathered up the tents, horses, baggage, and some sixteen-shot carbines. Some of those who escaped sent word to General Kautz that Confederate cavalry was in the area. Others of the three Federal units rallied and began to counterattack. Lee took up position behind temporary works between Mount Sinai Church and the Stage Road. He also made effective use of the horse artillery. While the cattle were being driven back to the crossing of the Blackwater, Lee's men held their ground. Then they withdrew slowly, acting as a rear guard.

The Confederate rustlers counted their cattle as they crossed the makeshift bridge over the Blackwater. The total was 2,486. The elongated column continued with Rosser in the lead and Lee still acting as rear guard. Once the rebels were across the river the bridge was destroyed so that the pursuing Federals could not cross.[5]

From the first shots that morning, all was confusion in the Union camps with reports of Confederate cavalry everywhere. At 8:45 A.M. Meade's chief of staff reported that the "enemy's cavalry have broken through our line . . . and may make a dash toward City Point." As the facts were sorted out, the high command realized that the Rebels would have to make a circuitous route to regain their lines, whereas the Union cavalry could drive straight down the Jerusalem Plank Road to intercept them. At 12:30 P.M. more than 2,000 Federal cavalry under the command of Brigadier General Henry Davies Jr. raced down the road.[6]

Hampton sent the herd along on a route two miles south of his main line. The cattle crossed the Nottoway River at Freeman's Ford. The head of the column under Rosser reached the Jerusalem Plank Road and ran into Davies's force at about 2 P.M. The fighting escalated as more men came up. Dearing joined Rosser first, then Lee. A member of the Ninth Virginia recalled that headlong race to the battle: "We made haste to reach him the enemy, sometimes at a trot, sometimes at a gallop, for fifteen miles, and at full speed came into line of battle just as the sun went down. The enemy was lavishing profuse attention upon us in the way of solid shot and shells; but we faced him resolutely and sent back screaming and glittering-like meteors at night shot for shot, seemingly to say: 'Come take your beeves if you can.'" Hampton toyed with the idea of sending Lee around to take Davies in the flank, but night was fast approaching. Instead he ordered Lee to reinforce Rosser's right. "These orders were promptly carried out in the midst of an attack from the enemy, who were repulsed along the whole line," Hampton reported. Davies made several assaults. From Davies's viewpoint, he found the Confederates "strongly posted behind earthworks, and having in their front an impassible swamp." From this position it was "impossible to dislodge them." In his report he stated that "the force on my front was W. H. F. Lee's division."

With the steers safely across the river, Hampton decided to withdraw, fearing that the Union cavalry might try a flanking maneuver. He ordered four squadrons to remain on picket, and the rest of the command turned to their earlier camp on the Rowanty. The Federals also withdrew during the night, and the gray cavalry completed the raid with a return to the lines of the army. In three days they had ridden almost 100 miles. Besides the cattle they had taken 304 prisoners, three guidons, wagons, and property. The military stores that they could not carry off were destroyed. The Confederate loss was "10 killed, 47 wounded and 4 missing." Most of the casualties were among Rosser's men, as there were none killed in Chambliss's or Barringer's brigades and only two or three wounded. Officially Hampton reported: "I beg to express my entire satisfaction at the conduct of the officers and men. Maj. Gen'l Lee & Brig. Gen'l Dearing carried out my orders and wishes most skilfully protecting the flanks & covering the main attack thus contributing greatly to the successful issue of the expedition. . . . In the fight on the plank road the conduct of these officers was equally satisfactory & I beg to acknowledge my obligations to them."

For some time after this raid the Confederates taunted those in the Union lines "by bawling and bellowing like cattle" and asking "Hello, Yanks! Want any fresh beef?" On his return to the army Grant was asked, "When do you expect to starve out Lee and capture Richmond?" to which he answered, "Never, if our armies continue to supply him with beef-cattle." Lincoln characterized the raid as "the slickest piece of cattle stealing."[7]

Many Confederate inspection reports were lost or destroyed, but there are reports extant for Lee's division near the end of September 1864. On September 25 Barringer's brigade was stationed near Petersburg. This brigade still was composed of the First, Second, Third, and Fifth North Carolina Cavalries and could count 1,221 "effective for field." The report was "good" overall, although there were many officers listed as captured or wounded—two were absent without leave. One interesting point was that there were only sixty-six sabers in the First North Carolina and seventy-one in the Third, an indication of the decline of its use in changing cavalry tactics. Chambliss's brigade, now commanded by Colonel J. Lucius Davis, was inspected on September 27. It still comprised three Virginia regiments—the Ninth, Tenth, and Thirteenth—and was located near Stony Creek. Out of an aggregate of 2,560 there were 1,019 "effective for the field." This number represented "only those . . . who are actually available for the line of battle. . . ." This brigade also rated "good" in nearly every aspect. All of the inspection reports mention that the division commander visited the men "frequently."[8]

The cavalry remained in the old camps until September 27 when the Federals began simultaneous thrusts at the Confederate lines both north and south of the James. Benjamin Butler planned and led an assault on the lines near Richmond that culminated in the taking of Fort Harrison, while at nearly the same time another attempt was made to cut the Southside Railroad below Petersburg. Lee again shuttled troops back and forth across the James to reinforce the threatened sectors. In addition to infantry reserves and artillery, he ordered Rooney Lee's division once again north of the James.

A review had been planned for the entire division on September 27 before any action was contemplated. Lee's division had been basically in reserve for several days with Colonel J. Lucius Davis's brigade on Gresham Farm and Chappell Farm about two miles to the northeast of Dinwiddie Court House and Barringer's men on Stony Creek to the east. All were drawn up in a field on Chappell Farm for what was to be "a very pretty sight" for Hampton to review. Another trooper remembering the heyday of the cavalry thought it would be "not so grand as those we had in Culpeper as there will not be so much cavalry present." However, before the review could commence Robert Lee's orders came for Rooney Lee to ride to the north side of the James. The men fell into columns and immediately set out with the Second Stuart

Horse Artillery accompanying. They had not even reached Petersburg when these orders were countermanded.[9]

On September 29 the line held by Butler's brigade was attacked and his pickets were pushed back to Hatcher's Run. There dismounted cavalry held and repulsed the Federals. Hampton considered the attack "a serious one" and ordered Rooney Lee "to bring one of his brigades up the Vaughn Road." Lee came with his Tarheels, and they attacked "promptly and most successfully." The Union force that had attacked and been repulsed by the Confederate cavalry was the cavalry of Gregg making an attempt to threaten the railroad as a preliminary to a more sustained drive by infantry. About 9 P.M. Hampton ordered a pullback to his earlier picket lines, and men of Barringer's brigade rejoined the Virginians in a camp on the Plank Road. The day belonged to the cavalry in gray, for they had held their lines, protected the supply line, and inflicted more casualties than they had sustained. However, this day was only a prelude, as Gregg was repositioning and reinforcing his command for another try.

Gregg's cavalry was supporting two divisions of V Corps and two from IX Corps under Major General Gouverneur Warren in their attempt to turn the Confederate right near Poplar Springs Church. If successful, their goal was the Southside Railroad. Before Warren could attack he was himself attacked, and the men of IX Corps disgracefully ran for the rear, losing many killed, wounded, and taken prisoner. The Confederate infantry attempted to break through Warren's lines but was repulsed by artillery.

As the infantry lines became engaged, Hampton saw an opportunity for a strike on the Union left. He ordered Lee's division to move along the Harmon Road and occupy some works there. In Hampton's words, "As the enemy moved up to reinforce, he exposed his flank to me. I at once ordered Gen. Lee to attack, which he did with the 9th and 10th Va. Regiments in the handsomest style, leading his men in person. These regiments went in, in the line of battle, dismounted and reserved their fire until very near the enemy. Delivering it regularly, they charged, routing the enemy completely, capturing about nine hundred prisoners and ten standards." Captain John W. McGregor moved his guns with the battle line delivering "a steady & accurate fire." Faced with this fire a segment of the Forty-Fifth Pennsylvania attempted a stand but was overrun by fleeing Federals. Only a few Yankees escaped, including the brigade commander on a fast Kentucky thoroughbred.

His regimental commanders were not so lucky, as all were taken prisoner. Besides the men and flags, the Rebels had taken more than a thousand rifles that they could put to good use. One of Lee's men remembered "scooping in more prisoners than we had men."[10]

That night Hampton stationed Lee's division in the works near Fort McRae with the expectation of attacking the next morning. October 1 dawned a "miserable, cold disagreeable day," and the "bugle sounded to horse very early" among Lee's troopers. The line held by Butler's cavalry was attacked, and Hampton led two of Lee's regiments—the Ninth and Thirteenth Virginia—to his aid. They "charged the enemy in the rear." The bluecoats withdrew to a "very strong position near McDowell's house." Hampton sent orders for Lee to join him with two additional regiments. The remainder of Lee's men held the line along the Boydton Plank Road. The fighting began before Rooney Lee could reach the scene. Hampton planned a pincers movement, but as the two segments closed they ran into each other instead of bluecoats. One of Lee's men wrote that night, "We have mistaken Butler's pickets for those of the enemy" but "discovered the mistake just in time to prevent them firing into us & we into them." The Federals heard the shouting and pulled back, thus spoiling Hampton's surprise attack.

Hampton regrouped for another try, and the Virginians moved ahead. The same diarist described this action: "Suddenly a masked battery opens with grape & canister & we charge within 50 yds. of this battery under most terrible fire of carbines in addition to the grape & canister which rattled through the underbrush like hailstones." Then there were rumors of being outflanked. Before finding out that the report was false, Hampton began to make arrangements to meet the threat. By the time he knew this report was groundless it was too late to renew the attack, and he withdrew at nightfall.[11]

At the end of the day after the fighting had ceased, Rooney Lee, his two brigadiers, and their staffs formed a group just to the rear of the lines. All were "dismounted and reclining on the ground," resting themselves and their horses. A member of Barringer's staff recalled the scene:

> Each one of us with his bridle rein over his arm, ready to remount instantly, if the battle should be renewed. We had been there but a few minutes when at brief intervals a bullet would strike very near us but coming from so great a distance that no report of a gun could be heard. Directly the bridle rein of Lieut. Phil Dandridge of General Lee's staff,

was cut by a bullet. It became evident that a sharpshooter from some place of eminence was trying to pick some of us off. A little later a soldier in the lines a few yards from us threw up his hands and fell back with a stream of blood as large as one's finger gushing out of his jugular vein. He was dead in less than five minutes.

The sharp-shooter had found one victim. Some of our Staff Officers took out their field glasses and scanned the whole horizon and soon saw a small curl of smoke ascending from the top of a tall tree, fully a mile off, quickly followed by a bullet whistling near us. We had located him but there was not a small arm in the Division that would carry effectively one-fourth the distance. He had a long-range rifle, doubtless with a telescopic sight by which he could both discern objects at a great distance and draw a close bead. It so happened that McGregor's Battery was in the woods near us, unseen by Mr. Sharp-shooter. McGregor carefully measured the distance, trained one of his six-pound guns upon the object, loaded with a shell with the fuse cut to a nicety and sighted by his most skillful gunner, exploded the shell at the sharp-shooter's feet. The Staff Officers, through their field-glasses, watching the effect of the shot, saw him fall out of the tree.[12]

The next day Lee's men remained in line of battle with skirmishers out in advance and the battery of McGregor in the center. Soon the Federals fell back slowly from the field. After remaining in line for some time, the Rebels also withdrew in the direction of Malone's and encamped on the military road. Lee's troopers remained there for several days, "drilling and doing picket duty."[13]

In Hampton's report of the fighting he stated, "I am under special obligations to Maj. Genl. Lee, & Brig. Genl. Butler, both of whom rendered me great assistance & behaved most gallantly." Indirect praise for the Confederate cavalry came from the Union Army and Navy Gazette of October 8, 1864: "The 'thin-line' which we are told that Warren found on the left on Friday appears to have been rapidly augmented. At all events the flanking column, which burst in between two divisions of our troops and swept off so many men, shows the enemy to have been in anything but desperate straits."

During this period there were some changes in the cavalry of the Army of Northern Virginia. Brigadier General Thomas Rosser left for the Shenandoah Valley of Virginia on September 27 to augment the force against Sheridan. In Lee's division there were some changes of command. Colonel J. Lucius Davis had commanded the Virginia Brigade since Chambliss's death in August. On October 17 R. L. T. Beale, the colonel of the Ninth Virginia, assumed command of the brigade when Davis took a leave of absence. Davis was later assigned to court-martial duty. Thomas Waller then became colonel of the Ninth.[14]

The field returns of October 20, 1864, listed 148 officers and 2,834 men for a total of 2,982 "present for duty" in Lee's division. The part of Hampton's old division that still remained with the army near Petersburg numbered 1,444; Dearing's brigade counted 1,288. Including artillery Hampton had a total of 5,714 men on paper, more than half of them being commanded by Rooney Lee. Hampton had also put about 800 dismounted men together in one force to fight as infantry. On October 24 Hampton reported to the commanding general on his activities and the positions of his troops. The cavalry had helped the infantry to complete "a new line of works" that ran to Hatcher's Run. There were 700 men in the works with the right of the line on the creek itself about "one mile and a half above Armstrong's Mill." Butler's men occupied the line from here to Monk's Neck Bridge. Lee's men were stretched out to the Halifax Road. Hampton had dammed the creek in five different places and considered the line to be "very secure." He also reported, "My command is growing stronger every day, and it is in good condition for a fight." If all of his men could be concentrated, Hampton thought he could put nearly 5,000 into a fight. He continued, "Butler received 275 horses today and Lee can mount 2,500 men."

Hampton also asked for new recruits for the cavalry, pointing out that some men who wanted to join the cavalry and owned horses had been put into the infantry. He noted that "the Tenth and Thirteenth Virginia are small" but that the officers had assured him "that they could be filled up if the new men were allowed to choose their arm of the service." It seems the Ninth Virginia still had the aura of the preeminent cavalry regiment, for it was "already full, though many desire to join it still." When new conscripts did appear, one veteran trooper pronounced them "a sick looking set of fellows." The Virginians continued to search for new horses to replace lost ones. One trooper who lived nearby just "walked home to obtain another horse." Another private, obviously from a wealthy family, rode home with a slight wound in the company of his servant. When recuperated, he returned to his regiment with a new colt for himself and a fresh horse for his servant while their old ones were left home to recover.[15]

Hampton expected his part of the line to be hit by a Federal advance, and on October 22 he reported his position to A. P. Hill, commanding the infantry on the line. The positions were the same as he had outlined for the commanding general, and he gave Hill his plan for several exigencies, mentioning that "General Lee will picket the creek to the Halifax road, his division being held ready to move to any point." On October 26 there was a review of the division.[16]

The attack for which Hampton was preparing was not long in coming, for the Union Army of the Potomac needed to score a victory to help the Republicans win a second term on November 8. There was some sentiment in this army for George B. McClellan, the former commander and now the presidential candidate of the Democrats. The Rebels, of course, were hoping that McClellan would win and bring peace. A trooper in the North Carolina Brigade voiced these sentiments in a letter: "I hope this war will soon end now and I think it will if McClellan is elected, and I hope he will be." Grant felt the pressure as he wrote to his wife, "Time is passing and Richmond is still not ours." Meade suggested the movement, which Grant approved. Meade's proposed plan of attack involved four columns made up of a good part of three Yankee corps (II, V, and IX) as well as Gregg's cavalry. IX Corps was to attack the supposedly unfinished Confederate line and, if successful, penetrate to the inner defenses of Petersburg. If not successful, they were to attack strongly enough to keep the graycoats in their front from moving to other parts of the line. Warren's V Corps would be in support on the left of IX Corps. Hancock's II Corps was to cross Hatcher's Run and hit the railroad from the southeast. Gregg's cavalry moved on the extreme left of the Federal attack force and in support of Hancock. This force numbered approximately 40,000 while the Confederates waited with about half as many men.

The Federals were already moving when October 27 dawned cold and rainy. IX Corps soon discovered that the Confederate lines were complete and manned strongly enough to block their progress. Warren also made little progress in his sector while Hancock forged ahead and reached the Boydton Plank Road by noon. In so doing, however, he had created a gap between his men and those of V Corps. Meade ordered this mistake to be rectified, but the troops that were supposed to bridge the gap had problems in the dense forest. Gregg's cavalry crossed at Monk's Neck Bridge, pushing back the South Carolina cavalry picketed there. Then Gregg learned that Lee's camp was to his left about three miles and that Butler's division was in his front. Gregg moved to the west, then turned north on the Quaker Road. Hampton checked him there with Butler's division and sent orders to Lee to attack Gregg's rear.[17]

Lee's division had been up and mounted since 7 A.M. when a courier brought news that the enemy was advancing. Lee marched for a while, then halted in a field. One of Lee's men remembered, "We are halted in an old field the brigade drawn up in line, ordered to dismount & remain in line holding our horses by the bridle evidently awaiting orders." By 10 A.M. some began to think it was a "false alarm" and "to speculate upon the possibilities of our not seeing the Yankees much less have a fight." One cocky soldier even bet his horse that they would not see any action that day. However, at ten o'clock the orders were issued to march towards Burgess's Mill by the Military Road. As they marched off the same diarist recalled: "Gen. Wm Lee has just moved to the head of the command loading his pistol as he passed. It would seem as if he was expecting to have use of it." Lee and his men definitely had need of their pistols before long.[18]

Before Lee could attack the rear, Hampton realized that the Federals were advancing and menacing his own rear with both infantry and cavalry. Therefore he ordered Butler to withdraw from the Quaker Road to the White Oak Road and Lee to attack on the Plank Road. Once in position Butler attacked the front and Lee "attacked with great spirit driving the enemy rapidly and handsomely to Revel's House." Butler's right then connected with Lee's left and Hampton's force and enveloped the enemy from a position on the Quaker Road to Burgess's Mill Pond.

As Lee's division was moving to the attack, a force of Yankee cavalry attacked the head of the Confederate column where Rooney Lee was riding with the Ninth Virginia. Lee saw the Federals charging and thought there was time to dismount the regiment and give them a "warm reception with the carbines." When he realized there was not enough time he countermanded his orders. The blue troopers closed—with the lead fours "cutting & slashing with their sabres & emptying their pistols"—and caught some men mounted and others dismounted. For a while "a general stampede seemed inevitable." Other units of the Ninth moved quickly to the rescue of those in front, and

soon they were pouring in "a murderous volley" through the fences
that lined the road. The Yankees then retired rapidly. Lee advanced
another half-mile and struck the enemy in force—infantry this time—
and had a "pretty sharp fight." Night put an end to the engagement,
and Lee left a skirmish line out to occupy the newly won ground. The
bulk of the command pulled back and encamped for the night, certain
that "they would be called upon to renew the struggle" in the morning. By the close of day the Federals were "massed in the fields," with
the men of Lee and Butler on three sides. A heavy rain began to fall,
which precluded further movement, and Hampton proposed an attack at daylight the next morning.[19]

During the night Hancock met with Gregg to ascertain the conditions in his sector. Gregg's report was not encouraging. He was out of
ammunition for his breechloaders, and it was doubtful he could issue
new supplies by morning—if they could be obtained. Hancock met
with others and decided reluctantly to withdraw. The mud and poor
roads made withdrawal difficult, and Hancock was forced to leave
some of his wounded behind.[20]

Lee's men moved forward early the next morning. "At dawn the
bugle sounded to horse & the command moved cautiously upon
the position of the enemy the previous evening," one recalled. "To
our surprise we find the enemy had retreated hurriedly in the night
leaving the ground strewn with dead men, guns, wagons & ambulances, some of which contained dead & wounded men." The Virginians took prisoners who told them that they had been "so hard
pressed that they stood back to back, one line firing upon the infantry
& the other on our Division of Cav. while another portion of their
command held Hampton in check in front & but for the rain & darkness they would have been forced to surrender." As they moved behind the withdrawing Federal troops the Rebels found the field
"strewed with plunder abandoned in the flight." "The Slaughter Pen"
was the pejorative used by the captured Yankees to describe this fight.
Some of the Tarheels found a particularly unnerving sight as they
crossed over the battlefield of the day before—the Union dead "partially eaten up by hogs."[21]

"A decided success" was Grant's description in his report of the
operation; those closer to the action did not share this view. "A well-
conducted fizzle" summed it up for one of Rooney's old Harvard
classmates now serving on Meade's staff. Hampton reported 239

prisoners taken by his men in addition to the Federal dead and wounded. The casualties in Gregg's cavalry alone totaled 271. Still, the Confederate casualties were light, although Hampton suffered two personal losses—one son wounded and another killed. The engagement had little effect on the election; Lincoln was elected to a second term.[22]

The monthly returns for October 31, 1864, of the Army of Northern Virginia listed 3,046 officers and men effective and present for Rooney Lee's division. Butler's brigade numbered 1,547, that of Dearing 1,316. This number was very close to the inspection report of Lee's division of November 1, 1864, that listed a total of 3,035. Besides numbers, this inspection report gives an interesting look at the condition of the command. The inspection noted that the men carried guns by Sharp, Burnside, Spencer, Merrill, Smith, and Enfield. The ammunition needed for these guns ranged from .52 caliber to .58 caliber. The division also needed 320 carbines at least, for there were "men who are entirely without arms of any kind." Another 400 were needed to replace the "long infantry arms" in service. This shortage in weapons was due partially to an "increase of nearly 600 men" since the summer inspection report. "Sabres have become an obsolete arm as none can even be found," the inspection noted. Saddles, bridles, and halters were also needed for the horses. One particularly interesting detail was the mention of officers on "detached service by order of W. H. F. Lee." Were these some of the scouts that combed the area behind Union lines for information? Under the heading "Division commanders visit and inspect their commands," the column for "frequently" was checked.[23]

On November 6 Robert Lee wrote to his youngest daughter after seeing his sons in the field. He assured Mildred that Rob would never "neglect" her school friends because "he equipped himself with a new uniform from top to toe and, with a new and handsome horse, is cultivating a marvelous beard and preparing for conquest." Lee had ridden down the lines past Rowanty Creek and camped only six miles from Rooney Lee's headquarters. Rob rode over and spent the night with his father, and Rooney appeared early the next day. They rode with him all day. Rob later remembered: "Everything was quiet, and we greatly enjoyed seeing him and being with him. The weather, too, was fine, and he seemed to delight in our ride with him along the lines." Rob would see his father only one other time before war's end.

Hampton also rode with Lee during his visit and described the battle to his commander. Lee included this also in his letter to Mildred: "General Hampton in describing it said there had not been during the war a more spirited charge than Fitzhugh's division made that day up the Boydton plank road, driving cavalry and infantry before him, in which he was stopped by night. I did not know before that his horse had been shot under him."[24]

Rob Lee wrote his sister Agnes also on November 6 to describe a division review held recently. The young lieutenant only wrote about the glamorous side of the war and his newfound social graces: "I wish you could have been down to our review the other day, it was very fine. After it was over all the officers & a great many ladies came to dine with us. It was a beautiful day, warm & clear. We had two very fine bands playing during the stay of the ladies & you just ought to have seen your brother handing around the apples & cider. A very sumptuous dinner was served in camp—meeting style & everyone I believe had a plenty to eat which in itself you know in these hard times is 'fun.'"[25]

As winter moved in there was less pasture for grazing the horses; forage had to be brought in or the horses dispersed for better grazing. Army field returns for November 10, 1864, noted that out of a total of 1,832 in Butler's brigade 381 men were dismounted. In Lee's division 401 men were without horses among the total of 3,870 troopers. In Dearing's brigade the percentage was the worst—442 men dismounted out of 1,675. One officer noted that the "horses of the Confederacy were, owing to the miserable mismanagement of the Quartermaster's Department, almost always half-starved." In spite of their poor condition they were obliged "to perform the most arduous service that it was impossible for the cavalry commanders of the Southern army to keep their troops in a good state of discipline." The Federals, by contrast, had an abundance of horses and forage, and "drills were but exercise for them."[26]

One trooper of the Ninth Virginia later recalled the difficulty of obtaining horses in the winter of 1864. He wanted to go home to exchange his horse for another, and there was "no chance for getting a furlough through the regular channels." The alternative for him and many others was to "run the blockade," or "run the block," as they called it. Some men had passes that would take them by sentinels or pickets when passing through the army. The trick was to attach oneself to one of these men or details and travel with them. If caught, they had to pay the consequences of being absent without leave. Many of those without horses "were always willing to run the risk and it was very seldom that any were nabbed." A key to success was to arrange beforehand with company officers so as not to be reported missing to the regimental headquarters. This trooper, along with several others, successfully ran the gauntlet of pickets from below Petersburg to King William County. After a few days at home and with fresh horses, they returned to the regiment.[27]

Another possibility for procuring a remount was considerably more dangerous: stealing a Yankee horse from cavalry pickets. "These dismounted cavalrymen would prowl around the picket lines, causing considerable annoyance," vowed one Pennsylvania trooper. Union General August Kautz ordered his men to stand watch without their horses and declared that "dismounted cavalrymen, seeking to obtain horses to remount themselves . . . if captured, are not to be sent in as prisoners."[28]

The problem of dismounted men again was evident in the army returns for November 30. Out of 1,506 men in Butler's brigade, 705 were dismounted. In Lee's division 453 were without horses out of a total of 3,605 men. Dearing's brigade had dropped to 995 men with 127 dismounted. The end-of-November inspection reports noted that Chambliss's (Beale's) brigade was camped at Stony Creek in Dinwiddie County while Barringer's brigade was at Thompson Farm. The inspector reported that the men were "unsoldierly" in appearance but well instructed in drill and picket duty. In Dearing's brigade he noted that the horses needed forage as "one to three die every two days" and "93 horses condemned and sent to Lynchburg from this brigade within the last month."[29]

On November 29, 1864, Rooney Lee sent a letter to the War Department about the problems facing the cavalry and ended with an ominous and prophetic statement:

Richmond, November, 29, 1864
SIR:
I have the honor to acknowledge the receipt of your letter of the 23d instant. As to the requirements and principles to be observed in the reorganization of the cavalry, and to-day comply as succinctly as possible with your wishes relative to my ideas on the subject.

The cavalry of the Army of Northern Virginia is composed of the best material for troopers in the world. They are intelligent men, naturally excellent riders, and mounted on good horses, and require only, to make them more efficient, organization. First, more horse feed; second, to be more thoroughly and constantly drilled mounted; third, to be better armed. As far as my observation extends, the cavalry are well drilled on foot and with sabre, as far as laid down in the cavalry tactics, but could not be perfected in the mounted drill for the reason that the horses, from want of a sufficient supply of food, cannot stand the required work. The enemy, on the contrary, being supplied in greater abundance, their mounted drills are mere exercise for the horses; and, in this respect only (save in numbers,) is their cavalry superior to ours. Here is the advantage. Badly drilled squadrons charge, the men scatter in every direction; opposing squadrons, well drilled, moving in compact mass, fall upon the isolated fragments and overwhelm them in detail. Experience teaches the proper arm for cavalry to be—a pistol, (Colt's navy size the best,) a breech-loading carbine, (Sharp's preferred,) and a sabre. The Government has never been able to supply the demand for cavalry arms: they ought to be imported. Our most efficient arms have been captured from the enemy, but of course not in sufficient quantities to meet the demand.

The Government ought to furnish horses, at least to meritorious troopers who are no longer capable of furnishing their own; and next, to all cavalry serving out of their own States. Existing orders now require permanently dismounted men to be transferred to infantry, which is manifestly unjust to the deserving, well-trained trooper, whose circumstances are reduced, in many instances, by the enemy's incursions and depredations. Cases exist, however, sometimes requiring the transfer of cavalrymen to infantry organizations; for such men, soldiers, particularly distinguished for feats of courage, should be exchanged as an equivalent. The military axiom, that in all well disciplined, drilled commands, one soldier is as good as another, approximates to a nearer degree of truth with references to infantry than cavalry; for whilst the former admit of a higher state of discipline, the latter fight more detached and scattered, and individual dash has a greater influence. It generally requires, too, more courage to go into a fight on horseback than on foot. Should this principle be observed, the infantry soldier would have an incentive to deeds of valor, viz: the reward of putting him on horseback—and the cavalry be composed of men who would ride up to and over almost anything.

There should be prompt and just legislation to provide payment for all horses killed or permanently disabled in the line of duty, whether in action or otherwise, as long as the ownership remains with individuals. The regimental quartermaster ought to have the authority, with the approval of the Colonel, and upon the necessary certificates, to pay all such accounts in his regiment.

Now soldiers are paid for horses only when killed in battle, and the accounts have to pass through so many hands, that an unnecessary delay is produced even in that payment. A courier riding his horse a given number of miles in a given time, bearing important dispatches, breaks his horse down and has to abandon him, receives nothing, although he is ordered to make the time. A soldier has his horse permanently disabled by a wound, probably necessitating it being left in the enemy's hands, receives nothing, and, unless he can purchase another, is transferred to infantry.

I have written very hastily, but I think you will see what is really wanting. Whilst cavalry cannot play the important part in large combats, owing to the improved range of arms, nature of country, and &tc., it formerly has done in European wars, still the demand for it everywhere is very great, and unless Congress takes the matter in hand, and legislates more liberally on the subject, the enemy next spring will ride rough-shod over the whole State.

I am, sir, your obedient servant,

W. F. Lee, Major-General[30]

Winter was close at hand, however, and Grant wanted to make one last attempt to stop the supplies from North Carolina from reaching Petersburg. The Federal forces held about twenty miles of the Weldon Railroad, but the Confederates merely unloaded the trains at Stony Creek and sent the supplies on to Petersburg by wagon. The objective of the movement was to destroy the railroad "as far south as Hicks-ford, or farther south if practicable." Warren was to command the expedition. He had at his disposal three divisions of his own V Corps, one division from II Corps, and Gregg's cavalry division—a total of 22,000 infantry and 4,200 cavalry.

On December 7 Warren's infantry moved down the Jerusalem Plank Road and crossed the Nottoway at Freeman's Ford after building a pontoon bridge. Gregg's cavalry forded the river five miles to the west at Sussex Court House. Hampton was soon aware of the movement and moved his cavalry to intercept. He went to Stony Creek Depot in person and ordered Butler to cross the Nottoway that night, with Lee's division following the same route. At sunrise on the morning of December 8 Butler ran into the Federals near Field's House. Lee's men also ran into enemy troops. The command was drawn up in line of battle and skirmishers sent out. Soon shots were exchanged, but the bluecoats did not move to attack. The first squadron of the Ninth Virginia was sent out to reconnoiter. They were to move to the Sussex Court House Road and find the enemy. They were soon involved in a fight in which they were almost surrounded. Their only hope was to fight their way out, losing several men and horses before returning to the regiment.[31]

Once Hampton was aware of the strength and destination of Warren's force, he decided to move to Belfield to block the movement. A. P. Hill was also on the march with his infantry to join forces with Hampton. Meanwhile Warren's infantry had reached the railroad, but he waited until his entire command was up and deployed before beginning to destroy the track. They began the task about dark, and the fires soon lit up the night. The weather turned bitter that night, with cold rains and high winds followed by hail and sleet. Hill's men found that the weather, along "with execrable roads and worn out shoes," made for miserable marching. Many were barefoot, and "in some places the snow bore the marks of their bleeding feet."

The horsemen of Lee's and Butler's commands moved out at 2 A.M. and were near Belfield by daylight on December 9. Hampton planned to defend the town and the railroad bridge over the Meherrin River. While the Federal infantry continued the business of destroying track and nearby buildings, Gregg's cavalry pushed on toward the Hicksford-Belfield area. His advance was slowed by skirmishers, blocked fords, and one burned bridge.

There was a Confederate post at Hicksford of mixed elements under Lieutenant Colonel John J. Garnett that included some boys of the North Carolina Junior Reserves sent up from Wilmington by train. These men were already manning the redoubts and rifle pits on both sides of the Meherrin River. The Fifth North Carolina was sent to support Garnett's force, the Second North Carolina was stationed at a nearby ford, and the Jeff Davis Legion was ordered to guard another ford four miles away. The remainder of the cavalry was held in reserve and awaited the arrival of Federal troops.[32]

A member of the Ninth Virginia remembered how they were welcomed by the residents of Hicksford: "Never did I see people so glad to see soldiers & friends as those poor people seemed to see us. They rushed out of their houses & shouted with joy & I must confess that for my part, I never felt more enthusiasm or more eager for the fight."[33]

Gregg did not reach Belfield until 3:00 P.M. He then attacked with both mounted and dismounted troops, who managed to take the rifle pits near the river in spite of artillery fire and heavy musketry from the other side. The Confederates set fire to the bridge to further block the Federal advance. Warren came up at this time and conferred with Gregg on the strength of the defensive position they faced. Warren decided to return to the main Union lines early the next morning. Hampton considered Gregg's attack "a feeble one" that was "not renewed, though a sharp fire was kept up until after night."

That night freezing rain fell again. Many Federals, however, were heedless of the weather, as they had stolen nearly all the liquor in the area. Whole brigades were drunk, and "the night was one of wild hilarity and mirth."

Hampton and Hill conferred that night, and it was decided that Hampton would move on the left flank of Warren's force while Hill struck at Jarrat's Station. The next morning the Confederate cavalry was already moving when the Federal retreat was discovered. Hampton ordered Rooney Lee "to push after the enemy to develop his movements." On the road from Jarrat's Station to Sussex Court House Lee's men found the Federals "in full retreat." Lee charged with one regiment and met the cavalry. This was "driven in rapidly with loss & in confusion." They also "gallantly charged" the rear guard of the infantry. Hampton reported that "the pursuit on our part continued the remainder of the day, the enemy blocking the roads, destroying the bridges & only fighting at the obstructions he had placed in the road." One company of the Third North Carolina rode into an ambush. Three Federal regiments waited unseen as their cavalry made "a show of resistance, quickly retired, pursued by the rebels, fifteen or twenty of whom came within the ambush." More would have been killed had not the damp weather caused the guns to misfire.

When Hampton came up on the main body of Federal infantry preparing to camp for the night, he withdrew two miles and also went into bivouac. From there he sent word to A. P. Hill of the enemy position. Hill meantime had given up the chase due to the condition of his own men. Hampton was reluctant to quit, and he continued to harass Warren's rear guard the next day. "The enemy followed us closely all day," one soldier in the rear guard observed. "During the day we formed into line ten different times to keep the enemy in check." Hampton at last withdrew to Stony Creek.[34]

The military success of Warren's movement was limited to several miles of track destroyed and some small bridges burned. His losses were in excess of 300, whereas the Confederate losses are unknown. There was another aspect to the raid that marked it as different— more malevolent than others during this campaign. "I never knew the enemy more destructive of property than they were on this raid, they burned houses, barns, hay stacks & destroyed everything on their line of march, turning families out in order that the houses might be burned," wrote one of Lee's troopers. He also found that "some of the prisoners were very drunk." Another Confederate wrote, "It is distressing to see the ruin and desolation these columns inflict upon inoffensive citizens." Reports reached Union lines of stragglers being killed by the Rebels. The reaction was even more destruction. "We fired every building on the route," one Yankee boasted. "Every home, barn, and building, hay stack, corn crib, and granary, were burned to the ground." After finding the unclad bodies of other Union stragglers, several civilians of Sussex Court House were hung in retaliation. The Confederates also reported other atrocities at the hands of the Yankees, and one later recalled, "We killed everything we got our hands on that day."[35]

After this engagement the cavalry returned to their old camps at Malone's. Soon they were ordered to new camps near Belfield in order to get better forage for the horses and so the men could rebuild the railroad track destroyed by Warren. On the march to Belfield, Rooney Lee issued strict orders that all men should remain in ranks. Three

young men from the Ninth Virginia decided even so to find their own
crossing at a stream. Before long Rooney Lee rode up and found these
three out of place. He questioned them, then ordered them as punishment to walk to Belfield leading their horses—a distance of fifty miles.
When Lee moved on, General Beale countermanded the order and allowed the men to ride. Once the command reached Belfield the men
began to build shelters and cabins and make themselves as comfortable as possible. General Barringer remembered that "we enjoyed a
fair degree of rest and recreation, disturbed however, by long marches
for picket duty and occasionally some severe fighting. The winter was
a hard one; forage and other supplies were in very limited quantities
and sometimes wholly insufficient, often exposing the men to some
trials and temptations in otherwise securing necessaries for man and
beast." One private from the Thirteenth Virginia later remembered
being on picket duty that winter for eight days and nights while receiving as rations only one pound of "'Nassau pork' and three hoe
cakes of flour bread without any salt or grease in them." One Tarheel
later wrote: "We suffered unspeakably, the ration was not enough to
keep a man in vigor, even if regularly issued. It frequently was not so
issued, and we of the cavalry would parch corn and eat it."[36]

    In the field return abstract of December 20, 1864, Rooney Lee's divi-
sion numbered 3,770 officers and men "present for duty." Hampton's
division, consisting of the brigades of Butler, Young, and Dearing, totaled 2,591. The inspection reports issued in Belfield in December 1864
brought marks of "good" in all areas except hospital supplies and ac-
commodations for Barringer's brigade. However, the Virginia Brigade
received uncustomarily low marks in some areas such as discipline
("lax") and condition of equipment ("bad"). They received better
marks for "officers and men instructed in drill." Barringer himself
noted the difference between the two brigades at this time: "The N.C.
brigade gradually grew in strength and numbers, while as a matter of
fact, most of the cavalry commands in Virginia were greatly reduced in
both efficiency and numbers." This was partially due to the difficulty
men from Virginia and South Carolina found in securing remounts.
North Carolina, however, by the use of "'horse details' and the thorough discipline of her brigades," kept most of her regiments in good
condition. Barringer concluded with some pride, "We came to be relied
upon, not only to do the ordinary picket duty, but, in close quarters

and hot contests, the superior officers almost invariably looked to the North Carolina commands for the hard fighting."[37]

On December 24 Rooney Lee led his command to Burgess's Mill to counter a demonstration by the Federals there. They saw no action and marched back to Belfield. Rooney Lee was afforded a brief respite on Christmas Day in the form of a dinner in the "hospitable mansion of Mrs. Gilliam." Among the guests was Brigadier General Robert D. Johnston, a young North Carolinian whose brigade of infantry had just returned from the Shenandoah Valley. Six other gentlemen and five ladies were also present. The dinner party was "a most agreeable one," and one guest, as he recalled, "remained all night and helped to make a jolly bowl of eggnog before breakfast next morning." This was in stark contrast to the Christmas season of one year ago for Rooney Lee, when he spent the holiday in prison while mourning the loss of his wife. It was well to enjoy these few hours, for with the new year approaching there was little prospect of a bright future.[38]

CHAPTER 14

"Furl that banner"

New Year's Day 1865 was to be a day to celebrate in Robert E. Lee's Army of Northern Virginia. The ladies of Richmond were sending food—a veritable feast—to the nearly starved soldiers. An informal truce along the picket lines was agreed upon, similar to the one the Federals had enjoyed in November for their Thanksgiving Day. In stark contrast to the many turkeys, hams, and luxuries that the Union soldiers had enjoyed, the Confederates received very meager sandwiches of bread and ham. It was not much, but it was all the ladies could spare to honor their boys in gray. These two holidays symbolized the condition of the two armies. The Union Army of the Potomac could count on mountains of food and supplies as well as unending trains of ammunition. New recruits filled the ranks daily. On the other side of the trenches it was "starvation, literal starvation." Even the amusements in Richmond and Petersburg were called "starvation parties" because no food was served, only water.[1]

The military news on other fronts was terribly disheartening for the Confederates. On January 15 Fort Fisher had fallen and the last seaport closed; Wilmington had been the vital link between the outside and the Confederate capital. Shortly before Christmas 1864 William Sherman had taken Savannah after a devastating march through Georgia. His next move would be north through the Carolinas until he and Grant had the Confederate armies caught in a vise. Desertions continued to deplete the thinning gray ranks.

Robert Lee was forced to send some of his cavalry to the south to meet the threat of Sherman. He decided to send the two brigades of

M. C. Butler's division so they could serve in their native state and hopefully obtain new horses when they reached home. The orders were issued on January 19, and Butler's men were soon en route for South Carolina. Wade Hampton was also ordered to accompany this command. This was a temporary assignment that proved to be a permanent one. In Hampton's absence Rooney Lee was "charged with the conduct of the Cavalry on the right of the army." He was "responsible for the picket line" and was to report directly to the army headquarters. Major James F. Hart's battery of horse artillery was also assigned to Lee. At this time the only cavalry with the army besides Rooney Lee's division was Dearing's brigade and another unattached brigade under Martin Gary. The troops of Lee and Dearing were still in winter quarters at Belfield on the right flank of the army while Gary's brigade was north of the James on the left flank. Fitz Lee, Major General Lunsford Lomax, and Major General Rosser were still in the valley.[2]

The men in Lee's division made themselves as comfortable as possible under the conditions at Belfield. On January 5 a private in the Tenth Virginia described their quarters: "We have at last completed our quarters and begin to feel quite at home. I have been busy building a stable for my horse since we finished our shanty, and now have a dry and comfortable place for him. . . . It would surprise you to see what a large town we have built, it covers many acres of ground, and is laid off by streets with some pretension of regularity. The houses vary in size & structure as much as the building of any town you have ever visited. But unlike other towns you can form but little idea of the different classes of the inhabitants by the style in which they live; many of those who live in the most comfortable style at home, occupy the smokyest and most ordinary looking huts here, while those who are laborers at home, and live in ordinary style, have the neatest looking portion of the city." He also described going on picket duty: "Our duties in camp are light besides having to get wood, cook, attend to our horses, etc. We have to go on picket in 12 or 13 days and will remain eight days. I dread the picket duty as we will be without shelter and there is no telling what kind of weather we may have. . . . Our coarse rations are rather slim now, but we do not suffer." The cavalry was encamped mainly at Belfield to obtain forage, but the picket line was miles away on the flank of the army. Detachments would leave the winter quarters, ride to the main lines, and remain on picket for several days. Then they would be relieved and return to their camps.

The monotony of this life was interrupted by occasional dress parades, and a general review that was supposed to be held on January 30 was canceled due to rain. The Tenth Virginia received new shoes, uniforms, tents, and equipment during the winter. Also, Virginia governor William Smith presented this regiment with a new flag to replace the old one, which had been lost not on the battlefield but to a cantankerous army mule who had shredded it.[3]

In an attempt to boost morale a "grand tournament" was organized. Lee "promised to recommend the man who could crown his lady love for a 30 day furlough" and soon "a good many knights entered the list." The final two were both men from the Ninth Virginia, and the contest was finally won by Major John Lee.[4]

Rooney Lee mentioned the tournaments in a letter to his sister Agnes in mid-January. He informed her: "Several of the regiments have been having tournaments. The 9th Va. had a coronation party on Thursday last after their tournament." He also reported that they all were "pretty well just now" and that the "Cavalry has lately been pretty quiet." The rest of the letter dealt with family gossip, including Custis's inclinations toward a certain young lady. Rooney also indicated that clothing was a problem for everyone in the army, regardless of rank, when he told his sister to "tell Ma that the drawers were just in time."[5]

The war-weary soldiers in gray were beginning to think of peace by January 1865. One diarist of the Ninth Virginia recorded after a furlough: "Everyone at that time seemed to think that our cause was almost hopeless & I was sorry to hear soldiers in the camp talk as if they were not disposed to fight anymore. . . . There was much talk of truce & a great many were disposed to accept almost any terms. It was while here [Belfield] a vote was taken in the Regt. in front of H.Q. to ascertain what the feeling was among the men in regard to the continuance of the war. When the vote was put as to whether we were willing to prosecute this war until we could obtain peace upon such terms as we desired, or accept such terms as the enemy was willing to give us, only 5 or 6 men responded in favor of the war."[6]

A conference was held on February 3, 1865, on the River Queen off Fort Monroe, Virginia, between Abraham Lincoln and Alexander Stephens—vice president of the Confederacy—and others. The object of the talks was to ascertain on what grounds peace might be obtained. Neither side was willing to agree to the demands of the other, and the conference concluded. The war would continue. The same diarist from the Ninth Virginia related the reaction of the men of the cavalry to the news of this peace conference: "While we were encamped here [Belfield], the peace commissioner went to Fortress Monroe & the night that the news was brought to our camp that they had gone, most of the men seemed wild with delight, hundreds of guns could be heard in every direction about the camp & men were shouting peace! peace: which showed plainly they were for peace upon any terms. Such was the tumult & disorder that Gen. Beale had to order out a guard to suppress it."[7]

The inspection reports for late January paint a dismal picture of the cavalry stationed at Belfield. Beale's brigade could count only 958 "effective for field" while Barringer's effectives numbered 1,356. Dearing's brigade, also camped at Belfield, counted 710. In the North Carolina Brigade it was noted that "a large number of the men in this command are bare-footed." Weapons were still a problem, as they were "of a very mixed character including all kinds of breechloaders as well as rifled muskets and muzzle-loading carbines." Even of these there was not enough. Some of the captured guns, such as Spencers, required "particular ammunition which [was] not . . . made in the Confederacy." The horses were receiving forage but in some cases were unserviceable due to a lack of horseshoes. Another problem among the horses of Dearing's brigade was "scratches." (This disease was due primarily to standing in wet, muddy areas. The skin above the hoof would become hard, inflamed, and swollen. The skin developed oozing cracks, hence the name "scratches," or, as it was sometimes called, "greased heel." The best treatment was dry stabling and washing with soap and water followed by a variety of drying elements. A dry stable and the recommended castile soap were luxuries that the Confederate horses would not be afforded.) Rooney Lee commented on the inspection report: "The condition of my division is generally good. The discipline is improving & the wants of the command have been comparatively well supplied. The horses are in fair condition & are being well supplied with forage. . . . Mounted drills are ordered unless the state of ground prevents & dismounted drills & saber exercise once a day. Brigade commanders have been instructed to bring before the proper boards all inefficient officers."[8]

Less than a week after these inspections Lee's division mounted up and rode to its segment of the line on the far right of the army. This was in response to a Federal offensive, the first of the new year. The Weldon Railroad had been cut in 1864, which caused the Confederates to bring in supplies to Petersburg from the end of the line, now at Hicksford, via wagons. Grant believed that these wagons were moving north on the Boydton Plank Road. He ordered Colonel J. Irvin Gregg to take his cavalry southwest to Dinwiddie Court House to locate and destroy the purported wagon trains. Warren's V Corps moved also in the direction of Dinwiddie Court House in support of Gregg. General A. A. Humphreys, now in command of II Corps, pulled out of the Federal trenches to confront the Confederates along Hatcher's Run. Meade knew that Hampton and Butler's division had departed for South Carolina. He wrote Grant, "This would leave only one division, W. H. F. Lee's, to oppose Gregg." As Gregg's cavalry moved in there was at first only a small contingent of cavalry on the right, the bulk of the command being camped at Belfield. The Federal cavalry attacked the picket post at Malone's and scattered it, almost capturing Rooney Lee, who just happened to be there inspecting the lines. Companies F and H of the Thirteenth Virginia were on picket there, and a private described the fight: "The Sussex and Prince [George] companies were on Picket at the bridge, the Yanks crossed over, and [we] had nearly all of the planks taken off when the Yankees charged and found the bridge taken up, fell back and then came both mounted and dismounted. Our boys fought them in thirty yards gallantly (so says Genl. Lee who witnessed the fight) until they finished putting down the bridge." Lee regrouped his men on the other side of the stream and posted sharpshooters. John Esten Cooke recounted a humorous tale of this incident that occurred as he rode up to Lee: "After a few moments' conversation with General Lee—that brave and courteous gentleman whom I am glad to call my friend—I found that the reports of the cavalrymen were correct. The enemy's horse, in strong force, had driven him back to Dinwiddie, and were then at the Court-House. General Lee informed me, laughing, that in the charge he had been very nearly stampeded for the first time in his life, his horse, 'Fitz Lee,' an unruly animal of great power, having whirled round at the first volley from the enemy, and nearly carried his rider off the field! In great disgust at this unmilitary conduct, the General had mounted a more manageable courser." At a later time it can be assumed that the bellicose cousin Fitz also enjoyed a laugh at the behavior of his cowardly namesake.

Robert Lee Jr. and Phil Dandridge, of Rooney Lee's staff, also narrowly missed capture. Rob was cut off by the Federal advance but kept to the woods until he saw a chance to get through. At an interval between the regiments in the Federal column "he had put spurs to his horse, charged the opening, and cut through."

Rooney Lee waited for a short time at Roney's Bridge in expectation of an enemy advance. When none came "he sounded to horse, placed himself at the head of his small column of about eighty or a hundred men, and pushed out toward Dinwiddie Court House to attack the raiders." They had not ridden far before hearing that the Federal cavalry were pulling back toward Cattail Creek. Lee and his band followed and caught up with the rear at Cattail. There was a brief skirmish at nightfall. They had come up on the Federal infantry and consequently retired to Dinwiddie.[9]

The rest of the division had been ordered up as soon as the Federal advance was noticed. They rode forty miles in one day to join the division commander. On the night of February 6 it became very cold and snow fell, "covering the sleeping men under a white mantle." When the bugle sounded early the next morning it "roused them from their resting places on the ground, where, like occupants of so many graves in the snow, they threw it aside and came forth as in a resurrection."

Lee's command was up and mounted early the next morning and began to look for the enemy. The order was given to the Ninth Virginia "to find the enemy and charge him." A member of the advance company remembered the day as very cold with hail mixed with the falling snow. The snow was blinding and kept them from seeing the enemy until very close. They rode down into a small valley and flushed up several mounted pickets who hurriedly retired to a line of skirmishers. The Confederates pushed on as these skirmishers retired to a "long line of Federal entrenchments." There they received a volley that hit several men and horses. A lieutenant, wounded in this volley, rode back to the grove of pines where the first skirmish line was formed and met Rooney Lee and his staff. Lee "expressed regret" at his wounding and had the division surgeon dress it.[10]

A member of the Tenth Virginia wrote in his diary that on February 7 they "met the enemy formed dismounted, threw up breastworks &

fought until dark." Also on this day it snowed, which then turned to sleet until "the earth was now one solid sheet of ice & our clothes frozen on us."[11]

The cavalry fight on the edge of this engagement was minor compared to the clash of infantry. Both sides had rushed in reinforcements, and the fighting escalated. In the final analysis the Confederates suffered about 1,000 casualties while the Federals lost about 2,000. However, the blue line had extended another three miles to where the Vaughan Road crossed Hatcher's Run. With the Confederates already stretched so thin, three more miles could not make much difference. On February 8 Robert Lee sent a blistering report to the Confederate secretary of war: "All the disposable force of the right wing of the army has been operating against the enemy beyond Hatcher's Run since Sunday. Yesterday, the most inclement day of the winter, they had to be retained in line of battle, having been in the same condition the two previous days and nights. I regret to be obliged to state that under these circumstances, heightened by assaults and fire of the enemy, some of the men had been without meat for three days, and all were suffering from reduced rations and scant clothing, exposed to battle, cold, hail, and sleet." Without changes he could only "apprehend dire results." Very poignantly Lee predicted, "The physical strength of the men, if their courage survives, must fail under this treatment." He also mentioned the dispersing of the cavalry: "I had to bring William H. F. Lee's division forty miles Sunday night to get him in position. Taking these facts in connection with the paucity of our numbers, you must not be surprised if calamity befalls us."[12]

Late in February a trooper of the Ninth Virginia wrote home expressing optimism for the future of the Confederacy, in stark contrast to others in his outfit: "I do firmly believe we will gain our independence & that the day is not far distant." He was ready to fight and did not object to the idea of blacks serving in the Confederate Army, as he considered slavery "a dead letter in Va."[13]

On February 28, 1865, the organizational reports of the army indicated two divisions of cavalry. Fitz Lee, still operating in the Shenandoah Valley, had three brigades under Brigadier General Williams Carter Wickham (under the command of Colonel Thomas Munford), Brigadier General William Payne, and Brigadier General Martin Gary. Rooney Lee's division was actually with the army and stationed on the far right, almost as an outpost. It comprised three brigades under Beale, Barringer, and Dearing.[14]

Rooney and Rob spent some time with their father at the end of February. Robert Lee wrote to his wife of seeing their sons: "We got down in good time yesterday & Fitzhugh & Rob continued their journey in the afternoon. They only expected to go as far as the first cav. camp last night."[15]

Desertions continued to plague the Confederate Army, including the cavalry. Federal reports of March 12, 1865, noted the desertion of a corporal and seven men from the Fourth North Carolina Cavalry "with their horses, arms and accoutrements." Colonel Savage of the Thirteenth Virginia tried to stop this from happening by enforcing orders that one trooper called "the stricktest & most absurd."[16]

Early in March Robert Lee began to formulate an idea for breaking through the blue cordon around Petersburg. He turned to John B. Gordon, his youngest commander on the corps level, to implement a plan of attack. In his words to Gordon, "There seemed to be but one thing that we could do—fight. To stand still was death." Gordon's plan was complicated and relied on specialized groups of men to complete their assigned tasks on a rigid schedule. Their object was Fort Stedman and its surrounding batteries. The Confederates planned to move in the dark to remove the sections of abatis and other obstructions in order to clear paths through to the Union defenses. Other commandolike parties were to clear out the pickets in front of Fort Stedman. Then the axemen would tear openings in the wooden spikes or fraises, which would allow room for the soldiers who would actually storm the fort. The main body of Gordon's infantry would then exploit the break and move in both directions along the Federal trenches to widen the gap. If all went well to this point, a division of cavalry would also ride through the break, slashing for the enemy rear to raid, destroy supplies, and cut communications links. Rooney Lee brought up his division from Stony Creek Depot as part of this plan.

Gordon implemented his plan early in the morning of March 25. All went well for a while. Three batteries and Fort Stedman were soon in Confederate hands. However, some of the specific targets were missed; also, the Federals did not panic but launched defensive actions along the line. The Confederates were pushed back with heavy losses in a relatively short time.[17]

Rooney and Rob Lee, riding in advance of the division, met their father returning from Gordon's lines. Rob remembered their father's sadness, the "careworn expression" of his face. "When he caught sight of his two sons, a bright smile at once lit up his countenance, and he showed very plainly his pleasure at seeing us. He thanked my brother for responding so promptly to his call upon him, and regretted that events had so shaped themselves that the division would not then be needed, as he had hoped it would be." The boys apparently visited for a while, as Lee wrote his wife on March 28, "I saw Fitzhugh & Rob yesterday. They dined with me. I had been on the lines & returned late & found them here. They returned to their bivouac last night & this morning will resume their former position."[18]

Meanwhile the noose was tightening around the Confederacy. On March 20 and 21 the battle of Bentonville was fought between the Confederates, now under General Joseph E. Johnston again, and the Union Army under Sherman. This was a decisive Union victory, which led Johnston to telegraph Lee: "Sherman's course cannot be hindered by the small force I have. I can do no more than annoy him." Sherman then advanced to Goldsboro, North Carolina, where he joined another Federal force under Major General John McAllister Schofield that had moved up from New Bern on the coast. Johnston withdrew in the direction of Raleigh. Sherman then traveled to City Point to confer with Grant and Lincoln. The men discussed what would have to be the final campaign and the restoration of peace.[19]

Grant formulated his plan for the big offensive. The Army of the James, now under E. O. C. Ord, was to move into the line held by II Corps, and II Corps, under the command of Humphreys, was to move into position between Hatcher's Run and the Quaker Road. Once Humphreys was in position, Warren's V Corps was to proceed along the Boydton Plank Road into position on Humphrey's left, with the left of its line at an angle to prevent its being turned. These two corps, once in position, were to move against the Confederate outposts. The Union's VI and IX Corps remained in the line as before. The cavalry under Sheridan was to form a mobile strike force designed to go around to the Confederate flank and rear. Phil Sheridan's men were to ride past the extreme left of Warren's line and proceed to Dinwiddie Court House. Grant opted for this cavalry threat rather than a frontal assault on established lines. Once he reached Dinwiddie Court House, Sheridan would be in position to strike toward the South Side Railroad, or even the Richmond and Danville Railroad. To maintain the appearance of business as usual along the lines once Ord's men pulled out, the bands played, and squads kept numerous fires burning.[20]

Sheridan's cavalry first rode south and then west, crossing the Rowanty at Malone's Bridge. In the advance was George Crook's division, followed by the divisions of George Custer and Brigadier General Thomas Casimir Devin; the cavalry numbered approximately 9,000. Recent rains and the heavy traffic of many horses soon turned the roads into bogs. The Rebels also had burned the bridge over the Union cavalry's anticipated crossing spot, which further impeded their progress.

Robert Lee was soon informed that a general movement was under way and correctly surmised that the main Federal thrust would come through Dinwiddie Court House and Five Forks to the South Side Railroad. It was impossible to extend his lines of infantry far enough to cover an attack from this direction. He therefore decided to employ his own mobile strike force.

The bulk of Rooney Lee's division still was encamped near Stony Creek Station while segments took turn on picket on the extreme right of the army. To meet the menace of Sheridan, the division was ordered up to the Five Forks area. Thomas Rosser's cavalry division, recently arrived from the Valley, also joined this force. Robert Lee also committed his only reserve infantry unit, Major General George Pickett's infantry division. On March 28 Fitz Lee's mounted men rode from their position north of the James to the south side. This command numbered approximately 5,400 cavalry (2,400 in Rooney Lee's division) and 5,000 infantry.

The cavalry converged at Sutherland Station on the South Side line, and Fitz Lee was given over all command with orders to attack Sheridan, now en route to Dinwiddie Court House. While the cavalry of both sides gathered and marched toward each other, the infantry of V Corps became embroiled in battle as they approached the Boydton Plank Road. The ensuing fight on Lewis Farm resulted in the Federals taking possession of part of the Plank Road. Because of this success on March 29, Grant sent orders to Sheridan to "push around the enemy . . . and get on his right rear" rather than strike at the railroad itself. Furthermore if Sheridan thought he could "turn the enemy's right with the assistance of a corps of infantry," then Grant would place V Corps under Sheridan's command for the operation. On the other side, Lee ordered Pickett to take five brigades to Five Forks. There they would meet with the cavalry and proceed to Dinwiddie Court House.

On the morning of March 31 the infantry engaged in battle again as the Federals moved against the Confederates along the White Oak Road. While they were forming for the attack, the Rebels boldly attacked first and forced the bluecoats of V Corps to retreat. Warren requested reinforcements from II Corps, and the Confederates pulled back to earthworks south of the White Oak Road that the Federals had held earlier. In the early afternoon the Federals returned to the attack after regrouping. This time they reached the White Oak Road. Warren's move had precluded any help from the main part of Lee's army from reaching Pickett. At about 5 P.M. Meade ordered Warren to consolidate his current position and to send a part of his command toward Dinwiddie Court House in an effort to communicate with Sheridan.

At the same time that Warren's V Corps was fighting for control of the White Oak Road, there was another battle brewing to the southwest. Sheridan ordered patrols to be sent up several roads that led toward Five Forks—the Court House Road itself, the Crump Road, and the Ford Station Road. This last one turned off the Court House Road at an angle and crossed Chamberlain's Bed at Fitzgerald's Crossing. This swampy creek was also known as Chamberlain's Run and was somewhat swollen on account of recent rains. Pickett's combined force of cavalry and infantry moved south on Scott's Road. At the intersection of that road and Ford's Station Road (known as Little Five Forks) the graycoats took a southeasterly turn toward Chamberlain's Bed. Sheridan learned of this move from prisoners and hurriedly sent Charles H. Smith's brigade to Fitzgerald's Ford and Henry Davies's brigade to Danse's Ford. Pickett's plans were for the infantry to cross at Danse's Ford at the same time that the cavalry of Rooney Lee and Tom Rosser moved across at Fitzgerald's.

The Confederate cavalry attacked before their infantry counterparts. Rosser's and Rooney Lee's men moved up to the ford. Smith made preparations for the defense of the ford as soon as his advance units were engaged. Dismounted men from the Second New York and the Sixth Ohio took positions on the opposite bank and fired at the coming Rebels, who momentarily recoiled. Smith then ordered a battalion of the First Maine to cross the run. They crossed without any problem and started to advance. They quickly met the Confederates, both mounted and dismounted, in a very strong line of battle.[21]

Rooney Lee ordered the men of Barringer's brigade (only the First, Second, and Fifth North Carolina—the Third was with the wagon

train) to dismount and meet the advance of the First Maine. The Fifth
North Carolina was in front, supported by the First and Second. In
addition a battery of horse artillery was in position, and Beale's
brigade was in reserve. Naturally the bluecoats were "speedily
checked" and driven back "across the stream over waist deep, all in
the wildest haste and confusion." Lee's cavalry in turn charged across
the stream, and the Confederates advanced. Smith brought in his reserves from the Thirteenth Ohio and the First Maine. They were
quickly dismounted and positioned on the right of the road in some
woods and on the left of the road in an open field. Once in position
these two units were ordered to attack, and as they advanced the men
of the Second New York and Sixth Ohio joined them. They in turn
pushed the Confederates back across the ford. A member of the Sixth
Ohio described the Confederate crossing and repulse, according to the
report of the forty-sixth annual reunion of the Sixth Ohio Veteran
Volunteer Cavalry Association:

> The enemy's cavalry mounted, crossed the stream, and formed along
> the south east bank of the creek, partly covered by a strip of woods
> along the bank. The Sixth kept up a fire at them from our partly shel-
> tered position in the woods. Finally they made a charge up through this
> open space, which had been in corn the year before, making it soft un-
> derfoot, particularly so as there had been much rain in the last few
> days. Our regiment fired into their right flank as they passed in the di-
> rection of the First Maine, which was lying down in the double rank
> formation. As soon as the enemy's cavalry got within close range, the
> First Maine opened upon them with their repeating (Henry) carbines,
> which held sixteen shots. The enemy were at a great disadvantage, as
> they had made a long charge up the hill through the soft ground. Their
> horses were exhausted, their lines badly broken, many saddles emptied,
> not only by the First Maine, but also from the Sixth Ohio firing at close
> range as they passed up the hill. There was nothing for them to do but
> fall back towards Chamberlain's Bed. The First Maine followed them
> while the Sixth continued their fire on the flank as the enemy passed to-
> ward the stream, our Regiment falling in on the left of the First Maine,
> and charging with them until the enemy were driven across the stream.
> Many of the enemy were killed and wounded, and a considerable num-
> ber were taken prisoner.

A member of the First Maine who witnessed the charge later recorded: "It was a sight at once startling and awful, and yet joyous to us, to see the heavy column of the enemy melt away. It was forced back, swept down the hill and across the creek. It is due the rebel soldiers to say that their behavior was that of cool, brave soldiers. . . . They fought like men, and if they were unsuccessful in this charge, it was because our men fought like lions." The colonel of the Fifth North Carolina drew special praise from this same Maine man, who wrote that he "commanded their highest admiration, by his bravery, charging at the head of his regiment, animating his men by his intrepid bearing, keeping to the field to the last, and falling almost alone." Rooney Lee personally directed this charge by the North Carolina troops and had ordered the Virginia Brigade to charge also to follow their lead. Contrary to his wishes only one squadron of the Thirteenth Virginia made it through the ford, losing two-thirds of its men. In Barringer's words, "General Lee, seeing the advantage of the enemy, both in numbers and position, quickly ordered his whole command to recross the run, and hold the West bank." The Confederate loss was high. In Barringer's brigade the loss was twenty officers, including Colonel James H. McNeil and Lieutenant Colonel Elias F. Shaw of the Fifth North Carolina, and more than 100 men killed and wounded.

Cavalrymen on both sides began now to throw up breastworks and fortify their lines. The Confederates had a well-protected line of works some distance behind the stream on a hill. From this vantage point they had the range of an open space between the Yankee front lines and their source of supply. One Ohio trooper recorded that "it was dangerous for us to even stand up at our breastwork." With the constant skirmishing, the ammunition began to run short for General Smith's men. Smith finally had to ask for volunteers to cross the open space with the needed ammunition. These volunteers raced across to the front line, dropped the boxes, and rode hard for the safety of the woods. Those on the front line did not bother with screwdrivers to open the boxes; rather they used their sabers and quickly passed out the ammunition.[22]

Scattered firing continued throughout the early part of the afternoon. During lulls in the firing, the men in the front lines could hear commands being given on the other side of the run. Sheridan was jubilant

over Smith's repulse of the gray cavalry at Chamberlain's Bed and sent
the following message to headquarters: "W. H. F. Lee attacked Smith's
brigade, of Crook's division, on Chamberlain's Creek, and got cleaned
out." Crook, reacting to the cavalry threat at Fitzgerald's Ford, ordered
Davies to send reinforcements to Smith from his position at Danse's
Ford. Davies's troopers marched on foot toward Fitzgerald's Ford, as
the road was impassable for men on horseback. Just as Davies reached
Smith's position, he learned that Smith and his men had things under
control. He rode back to his men and ordered them to turn back. As
they returned, they could hear heavy firing from the direction of
Danse's Ford.[23]

Confederate infantry had crossed in Davies's absence after over-
coming stiff opposition from the battalion Davies had left behind to
guard the ford. The Confederate impetus almost led to the capture of
the led horses of Davies's brigade. Pickett ordered four more infantry
brigades across the run. Davies retreated and regrouped near the farm
of J. Boisseau. There they briefly checked the gray tide, but Colonel
Thomas Munford's division came down the Dinwiddie Road to add
pressure. Pickett's infantry continued to advance in the direction of
Dinwiddie Court House. At about 3 P.M. Rooney Lee received an order from Fitzhugh Lee to charge again across Fitzgerald's Ford in order to push the Federals all along the line. Lee passed the order on to
Barringer and the North Carolina Brigade. Barringer at first demurred
because of the losses of the morning attack and asked Lee to withdraw the order. In deference to Barringer, Rooney Lee wrote to
Fitzhugh Lee but received again the order to attack. Barringer then
asked Lee to substitute the Virginia Brigade for his. Lee "kindly considered" the request but offered "their reduced strength as a reason
why he should not wish a change." Lee left the details of committing
his regiments to Barringer. "Every effort was made to conceal and
screen all these preliminary movements" as the regiments moved into
position. The First North Carolina was to cross the stream dismounted about 150 yards above the ford while the Second crossed
mounted at the ford. The Fifth was to follow the Second and charge
to its right after crossing.[24]

At the command to advance, the veterans of the First "rose to their
feet, dressed their line, and stepped defiantly forward." The bluecoats
on the other side "heard a tramping in the woods across the creek,
and the cry, 'there they come.'" The butternuts waded across in water

"almost up to their necks." The Yankees near the ford could plainly hear the Rebel command "Forward, Trot, March" as the mounted troops splashed across the stream. As they charged, the Rebel bands began to play "Dixie." Smith defiantly sent the band of the First Maine to the front to counter with "Yankee Doodle" and other patriotic airs, thereby losing several band members. A member of the First Maine Cavalry later described the charge: "One heavy body of infantry crossed well up on our right. Another in front of the right of our line, forded the stream neck deep while the cavalry crossed at the ford. Right in the face of the hottest fire those brave fellows came on. Many never reached the shore, but enough did reach it unharmed to outnumber our little force. . . . They were now too strong to be successfully resisted long." The Federal repeating carbines made "fearful havoc" in the gray lines. Another trooper in the same regiment left this impression: "The boys fought bravely—the enemy advanced as bravely, keeping up a heavy fire and taking our fire without being checked in the least. They had a piece or two of artillery in position, and were throwing shot and shell into the woods, rattling down among us twigs and large limbs as well as their iron hail, while above all the noise and confusion, the rattling of the carbines, the roar of the artillery, the screaming and bursting of shells, the commands of officers and shouts of men, rose the shrieking, whining, rebel charge yell." The Federals were pushed back, slowly at first, then with gaining momentum. Soon they were "retreating as fast as possible." Rooney Lee's reaction to the bravery of the troops under his command was recorded later by Barringer: "As the 1st regiment crossed the Run—advancing through water over waist deep, with a steady step and an unshaken front, under a galling and deadly fire—General W. H. F. Lee, no mean judge, and usually as stern as the Iron Duke, broke forth in a strain of enthusiastic admiration, 'Sir! the world never saw such fighting!'"

The retreat continued for more than a mile. Barringer remembered: "The enemy still fought with dogged obstinacy. . . . The Federals would rally and re-form, only to be broken and dispersed." As they pressed toward Dinwiddie Court House, Beale's brigade took over for the Tarheels.[25]

The fighting stopped at dark with the opposing forces in close proximity. The Confederate infantry was along the Adams Road with Munford's cavalry on its left and that of Rooney Lee and Rosser on the right. The Federals were massed closer to Dinwiddie Court House with two of Custer's brigades in front in case of further attack. Sheridan must have felt that another attack was imminent, as he wrote headquarters that the force under Pickett was "too strong for us. I will hold on to Dinwiddie Court House until I am compelled to leave." In the battle of Dinwiddie Court House the Federal losses were approximately 450. Confederate losses are estimated at 360 for the cavalry alone. Of these, 230 were in Barringer's brigade. At about 3 A.M. Lee's division was ordered to pull back to their former position north of the run as Pickett moved his line. Pickett knew that Federal infantry (from V Corps) was to his rear and wanted to avoid being cut off. While his force was moving, he received the following message from Robert Lee: "Hold Five Forks at all hazards. Protect road to Ford's Depot and prevent Union forces from striking the Southside Railroad. Regret exceedingly your forced withdrawal, and your inability to hold the advantage you gained."

Pickett posted his force along the White Oak Road, the main east-west artery of Five Forks, with the five infantry brigades holding the middle. On the left was one regiment of Munford's cavalry, which was to keep in touch with the small cavalry brigade of William P. Roberts. This cavalry command was between Pickett and the main Confederate lines at Claiborne Road Junction. Rooney Lee's division held the right of the line on Gilliam Farm. Artillery from Pegram's battery was placed in areas where there was an adequate field of fire. Three guns were at Five Forks, and three more were on the right end of the infantry line between Brigadier General Montgomery Dent Corse's brigade and Rooney Lee's men. Four guns of McGregor's battery were placed on the extreme left of the infantry line. The rest of Munford's division was on the Ford's (Church) Road while Rosser's division was held in reserve north of Hatcher's Run. The graycoats began to put up works as was their custom.[26]

With his division in reserve, Tom Rosser finally had time to bake some shad that he had caught earlier in the Nottoway River. While the fish were being cooked Rosser invited his superiors, Fitz Lee and George Pickett, to share this delicacy. Both accepted the invitation and lost no time in heading toward the rear. After 2 P.M., as Fitz Lee was just leaving for the shad bake, General Munford rode up with what should have been disturbing news. Munford had a dispatch from the Eighth Virginia Cavalry, which was posted on the left of Pickett's line between the infantry and Roberts's brigade of cavalry. It contained the news that Roberts's brigade had been overrun by Yankee cavalry. The remnants of the small brigade had fled to the main Confederate line that Anderson's Corps held, and their departure opened a gap in the line next to the Eighth Virginia. If correct, this meant that the Federals had penetrated between Robert Lee's main army and Pickett's force. For some reason, Fitz Lee chose to ignore the importance of this news. He rode off after telling Munford to personally check on the situation and to send in his division, if necessary. When Fitz Lee and Pickett departed, this left Rooney Lee as the senior officer of the entire line. However, he was far off on the right end of the line (where he should have been), and no one apprised him of the situation or of the attack on the left.

On the morning of April 1 the Federals had not remained idle long. Custer followed the Confederates once he had learned that their camps were deserted. Devin followed Custer while Crook guarded the cavalry's trains, the Court House, and Little Five Forks. As Custer and Devin moved toward Five Forks they encountered the first two divisions of the Federal V Corps moving into position. The Federal line took shape with Custer on the far left near Gilliam Farm. Colonel William Wells's brigade held the extreme left, then Colonel Henry Capehart and Colonel Alexander Pennington. Next came Devin's cavalry division and the infantry divisions of Brigadier General Ayers, Brigadier General Samuel Wylie Crawford, and Brigadier General Simon Goodell Griffin. On the extreme Federal right was a newly arrived and undersized cavalry division under Ranald Mackenzie. Sheridan's plan called for Custer to make a feint against the Confederates in his front while V Corps attacked the Confederate infantry line where it was refused on the end. The other cavalry would attack all along the line. As the infantry was getting into place, Sheridan fumed impatiently over what he considered Warren's tardiness. Warren received orders to move at about 1 P.M., but it was almost 4 P.M. before Warren had his 12,000 men in position to begin the attack. While these movements were under way, Mackenzie attacked and scattered Roberts's small brigade.

Warren made no secret of his corps massing to attack. Munford watched these preparations and sent one messenger after another to his superiors to inform them of the impending attack. All his efforts were to no avail. Fitz Lee and Pickett had told no one of their destination

and had made no contingency plans for forwarding news from the
front. Munford and Ransom prepared for the onslaught with little or
no cooperation between the two of them. Munford's men dismounted
and threw up some rail breastworks to the left of the angle of the infantry line.

The Union assault began at about 4:15 P.M. Warren and Sheridan
rode with the troops. After some realignment of the divisions the Federals closed on Munford's position and the angle. To complete the
sweep Sheridan sent Mackenzie's troopers out on Warren's right to
range as far north as Hatcher's Run. The Federal battle line extended
past the end of the refused angle, which was approximately 150 yards
long. The blue tide was overwhelming. The butternuts who were not
killed or captured fled. McGregor's battery just barely escaped with its
four guns and flowed with the retreating infantry.

Two of Warren's divisions had missed the angle and had to be
brought back into line with some difficulty, confusion, and loss of
time. The initial attack and subsequent retreat by Ransom's North
Carolina Brigade had uncovered the remainder of the Confederate
line. In turn, the brigades of Wallace and Stewart were dislodged. The
remnants of these three brigades fell back and formed a new line in
some woods at a right angle to the original line.

The strong Federal force also overran this position, though with
some difficulty. Crawford's Federal division had made a rather circuitous route and finally reached the Ford's (Church) Road that came
down to Five Forks from the north. He turned his men south along
the road. At this point the remaining Confederates in the immediate
vicinity of Five Forks were almost surrounded. As Crawford made his
move against Munford, the noise of the fighting finally reached the
generals at the shad bake. Pickett raced through a gauntlet of Union
fire to reach Five Forks. Fitz Lee was unable to reach his men by the
same route. Instead he tried to lead the reserve division of Rosser
down the Ford's (Church) Road. They were repulsed. Then Fitz Lee
and Rosser's division fell back to the northern side of Hatcher's Run
on either side of the road leading to the South Side Railroad.

At Five Forks Pickett attempted to establish a line paralleling the
Ford's (Church) Road. McGregor's battery was on this road facing
north to meet Crawford. A good part of Colonel Robert M. Mayo's
brigade (Mayo has assumed command of Terry's brigade when Terry
was injured) was deployed on either side of the road with the battery

of four guns near the road. Although Crawford's men took casualties, they were too strong for Mayo's brigade. Those who were not killed or captured fled to the northwest and then were ordered on to the South Side Railroad. Part of the battery was also taken. With this roadblock out of the way, Warren ordered Crawford to turn off Ford's (Church) Road and attempt to reach the White Oak Road west of the junction at Five Forks. This move would cut off the Rebels at the crossroads. At this point Crawford could hear the fighting off to the southwest between Rooney Lee and Custer. Pickett ordered his one remaining infantry brigade, that of Corse, to form a battle line at the edge of the Gilliam field at a right angle to the White Oak Road. Corse was to hold as long as he could to give the remnants of the other commands a chance to escape.[27]

After the losses the day before, Rooney Lee's command was down to approximately 1,400, less one regiment sent to Hatcher's Run to guard the wagon trains. This regiment was the North Carolina regiment that had suffered the most casualties in crossing Chamberlain's Bed. Beale's brigade was posted dismounted to the right of Corse's infantry brigade on Gilliam Farm. On the extreme right of the Confederate line was Barringer's brigade, mounted. The dismounted men were behind light breastworks. Earlier in the day a trooper noticed Rooney Lee as he "rode up and down the line, talking in a quiet tone to officers as he passed." "He was ready to fight and so were we," the soldier added.[28]

The fight on Lee's end began at the same that V Corps began its move. Sheridan had ordered "that the cavalry must co-operate" with the infantry attack. The cavalry all along the line was to make a coordinated assault. Custer's orders were to engage the enemy while keeping one brigade mounted "to make the most of a pursuit when the enemy was dislodged from his works." Union cavalry helped carry key positions all along the White Oak Road.

Custer ordered the Fifteenth New York to charge Corse's infantry brigade and the three guns placed with it. This attempt was twice repulsed. At the same time that the New Yorkers charged Corse's position, Custer sent in the mounted brigades of Capehart and Wells. He wanted to gain the rear of Corse's line. Lee's pickets fell back before Custer's men. As they reached Lee's lines, they reported: "Boys, we are going to catch hell. The whole earth is covered with cavalry."[29]

Another participant later wrote, "The voices of Custer and his officers rang out in clear, clarion tones, orders that every old cavalryman in that little field distinctly heard and knew to mean our utter destruction if executed." The Rebels were ordered to hold their fire. The Second and Third North Carolina "sat still in their saddles, every man with his sword or his pistol in his hand." As the Federal cavalry approached, the command "Fire!" loosed "an awful volley" from the rifles of the Fifth North Carolina, followed by "one continuous fire." The two mounted regiments then charged and closed with the bluecoats. A veteran described the clash: "The shock of the collision was terrible. Orders rang out on both sides clear-cut and loud. Sabers rang on each other with a cold steel ring that only the bravest veterans can stand. Pistol shots here and there and everywhere emptied saddles and burnt, with powder flashes, faces with death's pallor on them. Each side knew what was at stake, and this saber slashing lasted longer than I ever saw one." While the Confederates were being pushed back every where else on the line, Rooney Lee's men held their position. Custer was not able to cut his way through, even with superior numbers. General A. A. Humphreys summed up this operation: "With his two other brigades General Custer made a charge upon General W. H. F. Lee's right. One of Lee's brigades was with Corse, dismounted. With the other General Lee advanced to meet Custer's charge, when a brilliant encounter took place. Lee, however, maintained his position on the right."[30]

Early in the day, as the fighting neared Burnt Quarter, the Gilliam house, Rooney Lee sent an ambulance to take the ladies to safety. Three young ladies left the house at dusk in the ambulance and traveled to Ford's Depot, where they passed the night. The next morning they took the train to a safer place.[31]

As the blue tide rolled on from the east, Beale's dismounted brigade was in jeopardy. Beale rode to Rooney Lee and informed him that the enemy was 100 yards to the rear of the brigade. Years later Rooney Lee remembered this moment on the battlefield: "I had dismounted this brigade—something we did not like to do—but as they requested it I yielded; and he was very much concerned, because in that kind of woods he was afraid he could not get his led horses. At the same time this cavalry (Custer) commenced to make this move on my right. I told him to do the best he could to hold the enemy in check, and get his men withdrawn by degrees to his horses, and I would take Barringer's brigade and try and protect that flank, and hold the enemy there until they could get out." Lee summed up the operation: "I insisted on holding on as long as possible, so as to give my men a chance to get out. I held on until it was so dark that we could hardly see."[32]

Rooney Lee carried out a masterful delaying action, and the "retreat was slow and deliberate." A lieutenant who took part in this action described how it was accomplished: "We were quickly engaged from all three directions, our front and right by cavalry and our left by infantry. One squadron would charge and check the enemy in their efforts to surround us and rally and reform in the rear. That uncovered another squadron, formed and ready for instant action which shortly repeated the same operation, charging, rallying in the rear, always presenting in each of the three directions, an effective fighting front to the enemy. It was grand! It was magnificent!"

With the collapse of Corse's infantry brigade, Lee's men were the only Confederate unit still holding. Still fighting as well, they withdrew more quickly without having whole segments of the command cut off by Custer's troopers. It was now becoming dark. The same lieutenant recalled that "after a while we had charged and rallied and reformed so often that we had lost all cohesiveness and were in a veritable melée."

Rooney Lee and his command followed a woods road to the north, crossed a branch of Hatcher's Run, then followed the Ford's (Church) Road. There he reported to Fitz Lee. Custer's men pursued a ways in the dark, then returned to the battlefield to camp for the night.[33]

There is an interesting vignette of Rooney Lee early on the morning of April 2. It is provided by one of the men of his division who, with two others, had become separated from his artillery command the day before. One of the "three boys" had managed to save the battle flag from one of Lee's regiments. While trying to find their unit, they came upon Lee: "Before we had gone far, however, we came upon a group of mounted men, and in their midst we soon made out Maj. Gen. William Henry Fitzhugh Lee. It was now broad daylight, and we could see things plainly. But I must say that in the darkest part of that forest at the darkest period of the night we could have made out General Lee. He was six feet three or four and weighed not an ounce less than three hundred pounds. He was mounted on his brown war horse, 'Frantic,' a horse he always had his saddle changed to before going into a fight. The two together, man and horse, made one of the largest establishments I ever saw." The three sat their horses near Lee, "feeling very much at home with our division commander." Lee was trying to sort out the elements of his command. "The General would call out, for instance: 'Is there any officer here from the 1st North Carolina Regiment. Is Colonel Cowles here?' No reply. 'Is Lieut. Col. So and So here?' No reply. 'Is there any officer of this regiment here?' Some captain or lieutenant would ride up and say: 'I am here, General. I am Captain So and So, of Troop B.' 'Well, Captain, form the 1st Regiment out there and take command.' And so he went through the whole list of his regiments and formed what was left of that once splendid division." Next he turned his attention to the "three boys" still sitting behind him. Lee "turned in his saddle and in a sweet, soft, courteous voice said: 'Well, young gentlemen of the artillery, what is your battery?'" They answered proudly, "McGregor's." Lee then said, "Well, permit me to inquire why you are not with your battery." They told him their story and showed the flag they had rescued. Lee "answered with more harshness than [they] thought him capable of" and told them to return to their command.[34]

When Robert Lee received the news of the near destruction of Pickett's force, he ordered reinforcements from Anderson's corps to the South Side Railroad. This shift stripped the defenses of Petersburg along the bend of Hatcher's Run. Grant's reaction to the news was to order "an immediate assault along the lines." Pickett had lost at least 2,500–3,000, killed, wounded, and captured compared to 830 on the Federal side.[35]

Pickett had high praise for Rooney Lee in his report of the battle: "One of the most brilliant cavalry engagements of the war took place near Mr. Gilliam's residence. The enemy made a most determined attack in heavy force of cavalry, but were in turn charged by W. H. F. Lee and driven completely off the field. This with the firm stand made by Corse's brigade enabled many to escape capture. Had the cavalry on the left done as well as that on the right, the day might have been ours." He echoed this praise in a letter to his wife: "A rally and stand of Corse's Brigade and W. H. F. Lee's Cavalry, who made one of the most brilliant cavalry fights of the war, enabling many of us to escape capture."

Even Custer gave Lee a compliment of sorts in his battle report, as he stated, "The gradual nearing of the firing indicated that the enemy's left was being forced back. This fact had its influence on the position of the enemy with whom we were engaged, and aided us in effecting a total rout of the entire force of the enemy."[36]

Yet another erroneous report of the death of Rooney Lee was carried in the New York Herald. A brief summary of his life accompanied the claim that he was killed in the fighting before Petersburg on April 2.[37]

Dawn of April 2 brought a series of Federal assaults all along the Confederate defensive line. VI Corps under Brigadier General Horatio Gouverneur Wright formed a wedge that drove through the right of the gray line past the Boydton Plank Road to the South Side Railroad. They joined with Gibbon's XXIV Corps to assail the city of Petersburg. Fighting was desperate as Gordon's butternuts cut down hundreds of bluecoats trying to take Fort Mahone, or "Fort Damnation," as the soldiers called it.

Early that morning A. P. Hill had met with Robert Lee then ridden out to try to patch his lines and stop VI Corps. He was killed as he approached the firing line. The news of Hill's death was brought to Robert Lee. The situation facing him was dismal. The remnant of Pickett's command and the cavalry were cut off from the rest of the army. Anderson's men, who had been sent to help Pickett late on April 1, were now unable to reach Pickett or return to their former positions. Two divisions of Hill's corps had been cut off by the Union VI Corps and were in retreat. Only Gordon's section of line still held. The elements of Lee's army that had been cut off reformed at Sutherland Station on the South Side Railroad about seven miles from Petersburg. Other segments moved into the interior line of defense just outside the city. With Federals in sight of his headquarters, Robert Lee telegraphed to the secretary of war, "I advise that all preparation be made for leaving Richmond tonight."

The remnants of the divisions of Heth and Wilcox that had assembled at Sutherland Station were attacked by II Corps. For the first two attacks they held. On the third the line was taken, with approximately half the defenders taken prisoner. Those who escaped formed a "weary, mortified angry stream of men" as they retreated toward the Appomattox River.

Lee's plan for the evacuation of Richmond and Petersburg and the withdrawal to Amelia Court House, located on the Richmond and Danville Railroad, was complicated. The different units would have to pull out of the lines and move by various routes to the assigned rendezvous point thirty-five miles northwest of Petersburg. To buy Lee time, the defenders of Fort Gregg and Battery Whitworth made a desperate defense against the overwhelming tide of blue. Their heroism gave Longstreet's men, just brought in from north of the James, enough time to man the inner perimeter of works around Petersburg. The Union forces were content to rest on their laurels won that day.[38]

In the city of Petersburg that night it was all "commotion and bustle," recalled Kyd Douglas. The sky was lit by mortar shells as he took leave of friends. The last person he spoke to in the city was Mary Tabb Bolling, who "uttered not a word of fear or complaint: the infinite sadness of her silence was pathetic beyond words."[39]

Sheridan's force was also moving on April 2. V Corps, now commanded by Griffin, moved east along the White Oak Road until it met II Corps, headed toward Sutherland Station. V Corps then retraced its steps and turned north on Ford's (Church) Road from Five Forks. It eventually came within a mile of Sutherland Station in time to hear the last of the fight there. V Corps continued north and camped for the night at the intersection of Namozine Road and River Road. The cavalry of Sheridan moved behind V Corps and came up on the South Side Railroad at Crowder's (Church Road) Crossing. There it ran into Rooney Lee's troopers and began a running fight as Lee fell back and the Federal cavalry pursued. After advancing for five miles, the bluecoats came upon the rebels "dug in along the ridge of Namozine Road." Rooney Lee's division formed the rear guard of the Confederate force that had survived Five Forks.

Lee had procured a guide in a manner that demonstrated "the rigors and severities of war." He had asked for a man who knew the area to serve as a guide. No one answered. Lee then told a courier, "Go up to that house, rouse them, and say that I want a man that can guide me." The occupants of the house protested, "but General Lee ordered the man to come out at once and guide the command." The man came while his wife "wept bitterly." Lee had the man ride a led horse and "guide him as he directed."

Rooney Lee's division continued to act as rear guard for Anderson's infantry column as it moved toward Bevill's Bridge on the Appomattox River. The Confederates marched northward and reached Namozine Road near the intersection of the road and Namozine

Creek. When news of approaching Federal cavalry reached the column, the men began to put up barricades on high ground approximately one and a half miles southeast of Namozine Creek. About 5 P.M. the Federals arrived. Sheridan's cavalry attacked the rebel works about 6:30 P.M. and were thrown back. They charged twice more and were twice repulsed. Dark brought an end to the fighting on April 2.

The Confederate infantry continued their march toward the Appomattox that night. General Roberts with three regiments (the Fourth and Sixteenth North Carolina and a Virginia regiment) was in charge of putting up works on the western bank of Namozine Creek to delay any pursuing Federals. They also destroyed the bridge.

On the morning of April 3 Custer's division was in the front of Sheridan's advance. Custer brought up artillery, and under its fire a flanking force managed to cross the creek upstream from Roberts's position. The Confederates retired to keep from being taken in flank. Custer's men crossed the stream and followed the retreating Rebels. Along the road they encountered felled trees and other obstructions left to delay the pursuit. Another delaying tactic was discarded ammunition and shells left along the route along with deliberately set fires in the woods and fences. The resulting explosions slowed but did not stop the Federals. This continued for five miles until the command reached the area of Namozine Church.[40]

At about 9 A.M. on April 3 a council was held near Namozine Church between Fitz Lee, Rooney Lee, and Rufus Barringer. They, along with staff members, were mounted at the intersection of the Green Road and the Cousins Road. Fitz Lee, the overall commander of cavalry, turned to Rooney Lee and said: "General Lee, you must leave our best brigade here and hold this position to the last. The safety of our army depends upon it, and I will move on in rear of the retreat with the rest of the cavalry." Rooney Lee then turned to Barringer and said, "General Barringer, you have heard the orders; you must do that duty here." At once the three North Carolina regiments moved into position. The Fifth was dismounted on a ridge along the Green Road. The regiments' led horses were taken down the road to a position near the last of McGregor's guns. The Second remained mounted on the Cousins Road. The First, also mounted, was in a woods to the left and somewhat ahead of the Second. Barringer had less than 800 men in the battle line. In front of it was a large open field, then some woods. It was not long before they could see the lead elements of Custer's division emerging from the woods.

The Eighth New York charged the Confederate line near the church and drove in the pickets before retiring. Another regiment came to the aid of the New Yorkers, who tried to turn the flank of the First North Carolina. Barringer ordered the First to charge, but it was not successful. Ammunition was running low for Barringer's men and, "seeing the inevitable," he ordered the Fifth to retire to their horses. The courier who carried these orders found the commander of the fifth squadron of this regiment still exhorting his men to "give them hell, boys, give them hell." The majority of this regiment retreated along a line forming what one trooper called "a compact, irresistible movement, like a glacier's." A few rallied long enough to fire their last shots at Custer's pursuing troopers. Just at this moment Rooney Lee rode up and asked Private Paul B. Means where General Barringer was. Obviously concerned about his men, Lee had apparently ridden to the front to try to extricate as many as possible. The private later expressed his amazement that he had been able to get through. "How on earth he got there past that left flanking column I have never been able to conceive," he recorded. The private could only point in the direction Barringer had taken. Their conversation took place near the position of McGregor's last gun, which was still firing at the bluecoats while McGregor was "raving like a mad man."[41]

Where Lee went from there is not known. Barringer had himself ridden over to the position of the Fifth North Carolina to guide it through the woods. Many escaped along this route, although they could not get to their horses. Barringer was not so fortunate. He was surrounded by a squad of Sheridan's "Jessie Scouts" dressed in Rebel gray and was captured. The survivors of the Fifth North Carolina escaped by following the path Barringer had indicated. Commanded by Captain J. R. Erwin, they walked "all day, all night and all the next day, almost without stopping." They "never rejoined the army." Many more of Barringer's men were captured, as well as McGregor's last gun and the led horses of the Fifth. Confederate casualty figures are not known.

Rooney Lee's division, or what was left of it, moved along the Green Road with Bushrod Johnson's infantry division. Fitz Lee's division followed a different route but in the same general direction. They crossed Winticomack Creek shortly after leaving the area of Namozine Church and continued toward Amelia Court House. Custer split his command at this point. He sent Capehart after Rooney Lee and Wells after Fitz Lee. Pennington sent regiments with both these contingents with reserves at Namozine Church. The infantry under Johnson had to change direction because Deep Creek was unfordable in the direction they were heading. They, along with Fitz Lee's cavalry, fought with Capehart's brigade as they proceeded to another crossing place. When the Federals went into camp on the night of April 3 Sheridan's headquarters were near Namozine Church.[42]

On April 4 the different segments of Robert Lee's army were converging on Amelia Court House. Food and supplies had been ordered to this point to replenish the army. However, once the army reached the courthouse, only ordnance supplies were to be found. There was no food for the ravenous soldiers. This caused Lee to lose the advantage of a full day's march over Grant because the army had to be fed somehow. He also had to await Lieutenant General Richard Stoddart Ewell's command from Richmond. Forage wagons were sent out into the countryside with an appeal from Lee for food. He also ordered rations to be sent by rail from Danville. The majority of the cavalry was still with Anderson's corps about five miles southeast. They had been hampered by skirmishing during the day.

The next day the army moved on toward Jetersville and Burkeville. Rooney Lee's men were in advance, screening the infantry column. Following him were the divisions of Field, Mahone, Heth, and Wilcox, then Anderson's corps. Soon Lee was skirmishing with Sheridan's cavalry. Robert Lee and Longstreet rode to the front to see what was ahead. "With the diligence he always displayed," Rooney had fully reconnoitered the area and gave his report to the commanding general and Longstreet. They were facing dismounted cavalry, for sure, and possibly infantry. Infantry was no doubt on its way. It appeared that the bulk of the Union Army was converging on Burkeville. Breastworks were visible on the Confederate line of retreat. Robert Lee studied the land in front of them with his field glasses and asked his son many questions. Farmers living nearby were called in to add details to the inadequate maps of the vicinity that showed only roads and streams. Lee finally decided that the route was blocked and the

Federals too strong to attack. Besides Crook's cavalry, V Corps was also in position, with II Corps arriving and VI Corps not far off. Indeed, the way to Burkeville was blocked.[43]

Lee's army had to march west toward Farmville—"a race for life or death" in the words of one soldier. For the first few miles to Deatonville the roads were filled only by infantry and artillery, as the wagon train had been sent from Amelia Court House by a circuitous route. But from Deatonville on the wagons and foot soldiers used the same clogged roads. On into the night they marched. Hungry, exhausted, nervous, and sleepy, they continued. Many were unable to keep up and fell out by the roadside or strayed to forage for food. By morning the column had dwindled appreciably in numbers. The strongest units, those under Longstreet and Gordon, marched at the head and in the rear. In the middle were the weakest units, the remnants of the Third Corps, Anderson, and Ewell. At first Rooney Lee was still in the vanguard.

April 6 brought fighting on several fronts. As Longstreet approached Rice's Station, he received word of a Federal party sent to destroy the High Bridge on the South Side Railroad. Immediately he sent Rosser's and Munford's cavalry to deal with the bridge-burners. This was accomplished, although with losses among the Confederates' high-ranking officers, notably General James Dearing and Colonel Reuben Boston of the Fifth Virginia. Gordon, bringing up the Confederate rear, had to halt and fight on numerous occasions as he was attacked by II Corps. This fighting continued for fourteen miles, from Amelia Springs to Little Sailor's Creek. Part of this time Rooney Lee's cavalry "boldly had covered Gordon's retreat," but late in the afternoon it was withdrawn, leaving Gordon to fight on his own. This he successfully did even though losing about 1,700 men.

On this same day catastrophe fell on the middle segment of Lee's army. A gap in the marching column had occurred as some wagons were sent behind Longstreet while Anderson and Ewell waited. When these wagons were attacked by Union cavalry, Ewell sent the remaining wagons by another road off to the north. Gordon, uninformed of the change, continued to follow the wagons as he had been doing earlier. This left Anderson's and Ewell's commands cut off from the rest. Soon they found themselves with Sheridan's cavalry to the left and VI Corps to the rear. After savage fighting in many corners, the outnumbered Confederates caved in, and thousands surrendered. Eight Confederate generals, including Ewell and Rooney's older brother Custis, were taken prisoner. As Robert Lee watched the end of this debacle from an overlook of Big Sailor's Creek and the retreating mob, he was heard to exclaim, "My God! Has the army dissolved?" In response, Mahone established a line to face the enemy and to rally the remnants of Ewell's and Anderson's commands.

On the night of April 6 Lee's army was realigned into two corps, one under Longstreet and the other under Gordon, with the survivors of the smashed units being absorbed. The destination of the march was Farmville. The next morning they arrived in Farmville, and some received the rations they so sorely needed.[44]

Back at City Point the prisoners taken along the route of retreat were being tallied. From these records of prisoners of war, 226 were from Rooney Lee's division—100 from Beale's brigade, with the Ninth Virginia losing the most, and 126 from Barringer's brigade. They had been captured during April 2–5 at various places such as Dinwiddie Court House, Amelia Court House, Sutherland's Station, Ford's Depot, Burkeville, Jetersville, and so on. This command, like the rest of the army, was fast dwindling.[45]

Many of Lee's veterans had barely received their rations when they were called upon to repulse the pursuing Federals. Quickly they moved out of Farmville, heading north for several miles. For some reason one of the four key bridges was not completely burned to stop the Federal pursuit. The Union soldiers had put out the fires on the wagon bridge below High Bridge and crossed easily. Soon they were harassing Gordon's rear guard. Fitz Lee's men repulsed a cavalry attack on the wagons and captured a Federal brigade commander of Sheridan's cavalry, brevet Brigadier General J. Irvin Gregg. The threats to Lee's army were in every direction. They were being pressed from the rear by infantry, and from the south the cavalry could strike. Blue infantry was also marching to get ahead of Lee's army. While many Confederates still believed that the Army of Northern Virginia was invincible with Lee at its head, anyone rationally assessing the situation must have had some doubts. Possibly Lee was reacting to the look on his son's face when he told Rooney shortly after Gregg's capture, "Keep your command together and in good spirits, General—don't let them think of surrender—I will get you out of this." Late on April 7, however, the first of the flags of truce arrived from the Federal lines with a letter addressed to Lee. Although several officers were aware of the letter and could guess its purpose, only Longstreet was allowed to read it. His answer was, "Not yet."

On the morning of April 8 the army resumed its march. The prospects somehow seemed brighter that morning. Some of the cavalry had been reunited with their wagons and had some food. For the most part the march was unimpeded by Federal attacks. The destination was Appomattox Station, located about twenty-five miles west of Farmville on the South Side Railroad. Supplies were waiting for the worn-out, hungry Rebels at this point. The march for the infantry was relatively quiet that day. At about 3 P.M. it was learned that a force of Federal cavalry was on the Southside Railroad, twenty miles east of Appomattox Station, and could reach that place early on April 9. Fitz Lee ordered Rooney Lee and Martin Gary to push on to Appomattox as quickly as possible; he would soon follow. It was therefore a race to see which side's cavalry could get to Appomattox first. The Confederates arrived at the station first. Rooney Lee reached the station early on the morning of April 9 with about 400 men—all that was left of his division.[46]

However, that night, as it grew dark, there was an ominous red glow from the east, the south—and the west. It was the campfires of the encircling Union Army. To the north only was there the normal darkness of night undisturbed. Lee's army was at or nearing its destination—Appomattox Court House—and was almost completely surrounded. Also, after dark Lee received yet another letter from Grant. Lee answered that he did not propose to surrender his army but that he would meet Grant the next day to discuss "the restoration of peace." At about 9 P.M. Union troops cut in from the south and took some Confederate artillery as well as trains from Rooney Lee's division. Lee ordered all the cavalry to the front and requested Fitz Lee to attend a council, which also included Gordon and Longstreet. Lee summed up the position of the army, told them of Grant's letter, and asked for advice. It was decided to make an attempt to cut through in front. If only cavalry was blocking the way, then that just might be possible. If, however, the way was blocked by infantry, then there was nothing left to do but surrender. The corps commanders worked out the details of the morrow's assault and went to their respective commands.[47]

Rooney Lee spent the night of April 9 in the village of Appomattox Court House. During the night William Thomas Poague of the

Rockbridge Artillery arrived in the village looking for Longstreet. A cavalry picket informed him that Rooney Lee was occupying the village, and he went to Lee for information about Longstreet's position. "I know nothing of his whereabouts," Lee answered—"Where are you going?" Poague replied, "I had orders to move at 2:00 A.M. and follow Longstreet on the road to Lynchburg. I am hunting him." Lee responded: "I don't think you'll find him ahead of you, but you will find the enemy not far beyond the village. Don't you think it would be well not to go any further, but wait until daylight and see how things look?" In Poague's words, "This last sentence was accomplished with a smile and a slight twinkle of the eye as much to say, 'O, how innocent these artillerymen are.' Of course, I took the hint, dismounted the drivers and all hands went to sleep."[48]

On the evening of April 8 Lieutenant Colonel Augustus Root of the Fifteenth New York Cavalry charged into the village of Appomattox itself accompanied by a small force. They were repulsed by Lee's men, and Root was killed within a few paces of the courthouse.

Early on the morning of April 9 Gordon formed his infantry into line of battle with the Confederate cavalry to his right. Rooney Lee's men were next to the infantry, then Rosser's and Munford's divisions. The cavalry numbered approximately 2,400, the infantry less than 2,000. The cavalry was formed in "columns of squadrons" to the right of the Stage Road about a half-mile from the courthouse. There was a large open field in front of them. The Federal cavalry facing them were on a ridge and in a wooded area to the west. As they began to move forward, Rooney Lee's men went straight ahead while Rosser and Mumford attempted to flank the enemy and reach the Lynchburg Stage Road. Within Lee's division, Beale's brigade was closest to the infantry, then the North Carolinians of Barringer's brigade (remnants) and Roberts's brigade. As Lee's men charged, Federal guns opened but caused little damage due to the undulating nature of the terrain. The color-bearer of the Fourteenth Virginia was killed in this action—one of the last casualties of the war. A Virginia trooper described the charge: "Across the field we dashed right up to the guns, shooting the gunners and support down with our Colt's Navies. Just as our colors were planted on the guns, out of the woods on our left flank came a regiment of Yankee Cavalry in fine style. With empty pistols and disorganized as we were, every man wheeled his horse to the left, and we drew sabers and went at them with steel."[49]

During this charge a number of Federal prisoners were taken and herded back across the open field. The Rebel guards were "lost in the crowd," and to the Confederate artillerists it seemed to be an attack. They fired two quick shells into their midst before the mistake was rectified. One officer described this mistake: "Was sitting my horse, by Rooney Lee, when one of our batteries opened upon what looked like a charging regiment of the enemy's infantry. I saw in a moment they were prisoners being driven toward us by a few of our cavalry & called the Gen's attention to it. He sent me at once to stop the battery's fire." [50]

The Federal cavalry under General Charles H. Smith held the position long enough for infantry to move into place behind them. As Smith's men fell back, however, a path of escape along the Oakville Road opened up for the Confederate cavalry. Fitz Lee, along with the divisions of Munford and Rosser, made good his escape and headed in the direction of Lynchburg. In his report, he stated, "I rode out in person with a portion of W. H. F. Lee's Division, the nearest to me at the time." Rooney Lee, with the remainder of his men, retired to the main Confederate line. [51]

As this action closed, Gordon sent Robert Lee word, "Tell General Lee I have fought my corps to a frazzle, and I fear I can do nothing unless I am heavily supported by Longstreet's Corps." Lee's response to the finality of this news was to utter, "Then, there is nothing left me to do but to go and see General Grant, and I would rather die a thousand deaths." Lee then rode off to meet Grant and sent word to Gordon to cease fighting. Gordon arranged for a flag of truce to be sent into the Union lines.

Rooney Lee also sent staff members with orders to cease firing. One later wrote, "Gen. Rooney ordered me to ride the infantry line and tell them to 'stop firing and fall back.' Waving my hat, I galloped down the line giving this order. The men stopped, apparently as surprised as I was, but promptly turned on their tracks and marched back. I carried this message of stirring import until I met an infantry staff officer carrying the same order." [52]

A private of the Fourteenth Virginia found himself guarding some of the prisoners just taken in the last charge and not knowing where his command was. Later he remembered: "General W. H. F. Lee came along my way as I stood with the prisoners, and I asked him where the command was. He answered me: 'It has gone; you turn them fellows aloose and come with me,' and I came. As I looked over my shoulders, as I went down the hill we had charged up, I saw a regiment of Yanks riding by front of line with their carbines slung, and carrying a white flag in the middle of the regiment and gradually expanding around our camp."[53]

After the truce had been established and before the actual meeting of Lee and Grant, an impromptu meeting of the ranking generals on both sides took place at the courthouse. Most versions do not mention Rooney Lee as being in attendance. However, one Federal version lists "Runy" Lee as being among the Confederate generals. He recorded that "these gentlemen exchanged such simple courtesies as might be expected between officers of rank who had fought in opposing armies through many campaigns, and whose troops had, as a consequence, come to regard each other with no little respect."[54]

When the commander of the Army of Northern Virginia returned to his headquarters after the surrender proceedings, the men rushed to greet him and show their love and respect. One of Stuart's old staff members became a participant and witness to the scene:

As soon as he entered this avenue of these old soldiers, the flower of his army, the men who had stood to their duty through thick and thin in so many battles, wild heartfelt cheers arose which so touched General Lee that tears filled his eyes and trickled down his cheeks as he rode his splendid charger, hat in hand, bowing his acknowledgments. This exhibition of feeling on his part found quick response from the men, whose cheers changed to choking sobs. As with streaming eyes and many cries of affection they waved their hats as he passed. Each group began in the same way with cheers and ended in the same way with sobs, all the way to his quarters. Grim bearded men threw themselves on the ground, covered their faces with their hands and wept like children. Officers of all ranks made no attempt to conceal their feelings, but sat on their horses and cried aloud and among these I remember seeing Gen. W. H. F. Lee, Gen. R. E. Lee's son, much moved.[55]

This indicates the most probable reason that Rooney Lee did not ride out with Fitz Lee, Munford, and Rosser: He had made up his mind to accept the inevitable fate if the army could not break through and share it with his father.

About this time the two Lees caught the eye of an Irish paymaster in Longstreet's corps. Francis Potts described a group of Confederate generals: "There were present General R. E. Lee, looking grander than I ever saw him before, in full uniform . . . the handsomest man I ever saw, my old chief . . . and Major General W. F. Lee, soldier-like and imposing, inferior in personal appearance only to his father. A crowd of staff officers made up the party and a sadder one I have seldom seen."[56]

By Grant's order rations were issued to the Confederates in Lee's army, now technically prisoners of war. Benjamin Crowninshield, Rooney Lee's old rowing mate from Harvard, was Sheridan's provost-marshal. Therefore Lee was in his direct jurisdiction as a prisoner of war in the cavalry. Crowninshield's son later recalled that it was "a truly embarrassing position for both of them," and the "young General Lee preferred to be a regular prisoner rather than accept any of the privileges my father sought to bestow upon him."[57]

The Federal printing presses began to churn out parole papers, and the lists were compiled for those to be paroled. The designated day for the cavalry was April 10. General Ranald Mackenzie's command received the accoutrements of the cavalry. It seems that Rooney Lee did not take part in this final stacking of arms, although he was still in the vicinity. Colonel Alexander Haskell of the Seventh South Carolina Cavalry "was designated by General Lee to lead the cavalry" to the appointed place. The number of cavalry paroled at Appomattox seems high at 1,559, but this number reflects many who were not actually at the surrender but rode in later. The official totals for Rooney Lee's division at Appomattox were:

	Officers	Enlisted Men	Aggregate
Maj. Gen. W. H. F. Lee & Staff	7	1	8
Barringer's Brigade	2	21	23
Beale's Brigade, Capt. S. H. Burt	22	152	174
Roberts' Brigade, Brig. Gen. W. P. Roberts	5	88	93
Totals	36	262	298[58]

A trooper from the Thirteenth Virginia Cavalry recorded in his diary the events of that day: "Our regiment stacked arms on the hill east of the C.H. Monday P.M. There were no noisy exultations of the 'Feds' over our disaster. We marched slowly and sadly out to the appointed spot, and formed with the balance of the cavalry in column of regiment in one rank. Capt. Burt gave the order 'Prepare to Dismount!'—'Dismount!'—'Stack arms!'—'Mount!'—'By twos to the right—March!' and 'the end was to all our greatness.' Every heart was oppressed with the deepest gloom, and not a word was spoken as the bronzed veterans marched back to our camp." They received their paroles the next day, and on April 13 the regiment was disbanded.[59]

At the stacking of arms throughout the army, the flags of the various regiments were also placed on the piles. In some instances the color-bearers could not think of this ultimate humiliation. The flag of the Tenth Virginia was removed from its staff when the final orders to cease fire were heard. A trooper who "never surrendered and was never paroled" carried it to the house of some kind ladies when it appeared he might be captured. Before leaving it, he tore out a star for himself and others as souvenirs for friends. This flag was later given in safekeeping to another man, and the original keeper could not find it after the war. In the Ninth Virginia, a soldier took the flag from the staff, "wrapped it around his body beneath his clothes and made his escape." It became a priceless family heirloom.[60]

In the two days following the surrender, Rooney Lee aided the Federals in preparing exact parole lists for the cavalry. George Sharpe, assistant provost marshal general, reported that "the paroling of the artillery and the cavalry command of General William H. F. Lee was personally superintended by the commanding officers thereof, and the papers are methodical to a considerable extent." He also wrote his final report on April 11. It covers little more than two handwritten pages and covers operations from March 29 to April 9. As usual, this report is laconic and to the point and offers his indebtedness to his staff and subordinates. In Fitz Lee's later, and much longer, report of the same period, he called attention "to the marked and excellent behavior of Generals W. H. F. Lee, Rosser and Munford."[61]

Robert Lee left Appomattox for Richmond on April 12. Rooney Lee and his cousin John Lee, formerly a staff officer, joined him on the morning of April 15. The procession, about twenty horsemen, rode through Powhatan and Chesterfield Counties and entered Richmond during a downpour. One officer who accompanied Rooney Lee on part of this ride later wrote that they had "journeyed by easy stages during each day, at night bivouacking by the wayside." By the time they reached the house where Mary Lee awaited, the party had dwindled to Robert Lee and five more, including Rooney Lee, and Taylor and Marshall of headquarters staff. They all still carried their sidearms, and the horses were in poor condition. Throngs of people came out to greet them and to cheer and pay respects to Robert Lee. One of the first things they did in Richmond was to find forage for the horses.

For the next few days Rooney Lee remained in Richmond with his family, acting almost as a social secretary to his father along with the other young Lees. Strangers came to the door to catch a glimpse of the South's idol; veterans seeking advice, other friends, and well-wishers stopped by. Rooney Lee was still in Richmond as late as April 19, as he is mentioned in an official report from E. O. C. Ord, the commander of the newly designated Department of Virginia, to Secretary of War Stanton. Ord listed his many problems, then stated, "Generals W. H. F. Lee, Heth, Pickett, Alexander and others, and many prominent and formerly wealthy citizens, are asking me what they shall do to make their bread, expressing their great desire to co-operate with this Government if they can have peace and protection."[62]

A short time later, on or before April 23, Rooney rode to his home at the White House, primarily to see if a safe haven could be found there for his mother. He found everything there in ruins. The house itself had been burned in 1862, and the landing had served as a Federal supply depot off and on during the war. The only thing left was the land itself, and at this point Rooney Lee decided to return to his former occupation of farmer. In this way he could provide food for himself and his cousin John Lee, who joined him, and make an honorable living. He could also eventually provide a place for his parents and sisters if necessary. Rooney and John put up a shanty and began to break the ground for a crop of corn with their former cavalry horses pulling the plows. They also put in a vegetable garden. By mid-May Rooney took a load of vegetables to the market in Richmond to sell. To most of the former Confederate generals, this type of subsistence living, which included driving a load of vegetables to sell in the market, would have been a fate worse than death. However, for Rooney

Lee, a man with no false sense of pride, he was merely doing what had to be done to survive. By mid-May Rooney Lee had taken the oath of allegiance as a step toward renewing citizenship and keeping his land.

Rob Lee also joined Rooney on the farm at the White House. He had become separated from his command in one of the engagements on April 2 or 3 when his horse was shot. The Federal cavalry got between him and the retreating Confederates as he tried to get himself and his horse off the field. He left the horse at the home of a farmer to recuperate and borrowed another. As he rode toward Appomattox he ran into General Rosser, who told him that the army was surrendered. He refused to believe the news until all his friends assured him it was true. He accompanied his friends to Lynchburg, where he found the divisional headquarters wagons complete with horses and servants. Still refusing to give up, he made his way with other officers to Greensboro, North Carolina. He was with Jefferson Davis when the Confederate president received news of the surrender of Lee's army. At this point Rob headed to Richmond with his entourage of wagons and horses. The family was "much relieved" to finally see him. He stayed a few days in Richmond and rejected the idea of returning to college. Instead he rode to the White House to help Rooney farm. Rob was "hailed with delight" on his arrival there with "three servants and about eight horses" to aid in the farming. Years later he wrote, "The crop of corn which we planted that summer, with ourselves and army servants as laborers and our old cavalry horses as teams, and which we did not finish planting until the 9th of June, was the best I ever made."[63]

CHAPTER 15

"A practical life"

All during the spring and summer months of 1865 Rooney Lee, Rob, and the others worked the soil of the White House to get in a crop of corn. Mary Lee described her sons' life in a letter to a friend during this time: "[Rob] & Roon are down at the White House working hard with their own hands. They staid there a week without any shelter save the sky & slept on their blankets on the ground for which their military life for the last 4 years had well fitted them. Now they have put up a shanty. The enemy had destroyed every vestige of a habitation." She was optimistic for their success, however, as she continued, "They are young & hearty & able to struggle with their destiny." Mary Lee was correct in her statement about the advantage of youth. Rooney Lee was only twenty-seven years old at Appomattox. He had already accomplished much, but there was more yet to be accomplished.[1]

Farming problems were not the only ones confronting Rooney Lee during this time. In June 1865 indictments of treason were passed naming Robert Lee and other Confederate generals, including Rooney Lee, as traitors. Lee felt that their position as paroled prisoners of war exempted them from such indictments as long as they adhered to the provisions of the paroles. Grant upheld this view against the Radicals in Congress. The indictments remained in effect for some time, although no one was actually arrested or prosecuted. Robert Lee wrote to his son on June 13 regarding the indictments: "I have been told that thirty persons were indicted by the Grand Jury at Norfolk & that myself & sons were of the number. I presume that Robert is not included.

Fitzhugh, who is here, says he understands he is of the number which I think probable. I have no intimation what action will be taken on the subject. If I am to be prosecuted I cannot make the application [for pardon] under the proviso in Pres. Johnson's proclamation, but will let the Gov't take its course. If I am not to be prosecuted, I will do so. I do not know at present that you can do other than you have done." This last reference is to the fact that Rooney Lee had already taken the oath of allegiance and applied for pardon.[2]

The work on the farm continued, and the crops flourished. Rooney wrote this news to his father on June 22 and received the following reply: "We had all been quite anxious to hear from you, and were much gratified to learn that you were all well, and doing well. It is very cheering to me to hear of your good prospects for corn and your cheerful prospects for the future. God grant they may be realised, which, I am sure, they will be, if you will unite sound judgment to your usual energy in your operations." The indictments were still on their minds. Lee continued: "As to the indictments, I hope you, at least, may not be prosecuted. I see no other reason for it than for prosecuting all who ever engaged in the war. I think, however, we may expect procrastination in measures of relief, denunciatory threats, etc. We must be patient, and let them take their course."[3]

By fall the corn crop was harvested, and Rooney realized that even with all their hard work it was barely enough to meet their immediate needs. If his sisters' legacies were ever to be met, and the farm brought to its full potential, another way had to be found to increase the yield at the White House. At this time James Black, from Scotland, proposed to lease a part of the White House for the next year. He guaranteed a set sum of money for the use of the land as well as improvements. He would also initiate "modern farming" and provide his own labor. Rooney explained fully his situation in regard to the indictments and parole. Black in turn stated that he was certain that the existing paroles included the security of owning property. Rooney had apparently agreed to the lease already but wrote to his father to inform him and ask for approval. Naturally he would have to consult the executor of the Custis estate before finalizing any deals. He wrote: "I am sure that you will see the advantage of the lease to myself. Without expending a considerable amount of money, I could not cultivate the land to advantage & believe this to be a very advantageous arrangement." Rooney also planned to build a sawmill and cut the timber as a further means of making a living. Robert Lee apparently had sent him money, as he continued, "I propose to put up a saw mill & saw the timber & desire to pay you fully for everything & the rents of the farm will be placed at your disposal." If he could break even on the current crops of corn and wheat, he wanted to give his mules to Rob so that he could make a start at Romancoke the next year. At some time during the year Rooney had at least two attacks of the "chills" (malaria) but by November was well again.[4]

Father and son exchanged letters again in November concerning the lease. Rooney presented more arguments for the lease. He definitely did not want to deal with the carpetbaggers that were spreading through the South; neither was he in favor of sharecropping. At any rate, he was willing to take the risk unless, of course, his father disapproved. Although the White House belonged to Rooney and Romancoke to Rob by their grandfather's will, that same will left several encumbrances on the land. Therefore final approval had to come from Robert Lee as the will's executor.[5]

In May 1866 Rooney traveled to Lexington, Virginia, to visit his parents. His mother thought he had gained a little weight since she last saw him after Appomattox and confided to a friend, "Fitzhugh . . . in spite of all his afflictions & they have been very great, has still a gay light heart." Also, probably on this same visit, an amusing incident occurred in the president's house at Washington College. It was the Lees' custom to entertain young men from the two schools in Lexington. One young cadet from the Virginia Military Institute was calling on the Lee girls and, for lack of something better to say, remarked, "Do you know this is the first civilian's house I have entered in Lexington." Robert Lee was in the room as well as Custis and Rooney. All had a good laugh over the lad's use of the word "civilian" in referring to three generals.

Custis met Rooney in Richmond on August 6, and they journeyed to the Warrenton White Sulphur Springs in Warrenton, North Carolina. The people of the community had raised the money to erect a monument over their sister Annie's final resting place, and the two brothers were on hand to see it dedicated.[6]

The dedication of this monument must have brought back memories of Charlotte and the two babies who died during the war. They were all buried in Shockoe Cemetery in Richmond with some haste and little fanfare. Charlotte died and was buried while Rooney was still a prisoner of war, and it was almost three months later when he was finally released that he could even visit her grave and attain a certain closure over her death. He was also not present at the burials of the two children due to the exigencies of the war. He apparently wrote his concerns to his father in a letter that no longer exists. Robert Lee's reply is poignant: "I consulted with your mother in reference to your desire to erect a monument over our sweet Charlotte, & I presume she told you our opinion in the letter she wrote at the time. Nothing is requisite to retain her living image in my memory, nor could a column be built high enough to record my affection for her. Still a stone to mark her resting place is proper & whenever most convenient, I should be pleased that a suitable monument be erected. If you have not sufficient funds for the purpose at the time, let me know & I shall be glad to contribute, that you may procure such as you may desire." Apparently more immediate concerns consumed what little money Rooney had at the time, and the proposal was put on hold.

In that same letter was a reference to Rooney's sawmill, which was "progressing satisfactorily," and to improvements at the White House. Rooney was still living in the "shanty" they first put up, which had withstood several storms.[7]

In November 1866 Rooney made a visit to Essex County to identify a sorrel mare named Lucy Long. The mare was presented to Robert Lee by Jeb Stuart after the Maryland campaign as an easygoing alternate to Traveller. She had been sent to recuperate in Henry County in the spring of 1864, and Lee had arranged for her return in the spring of 1865. In the confusion of the last days of the Confederacy, the mare was mixed in with a group of government horses and ended up in North Carolina. William Campbell of Essex County had bought the mare, and several neighbors thought they recognized her as belonging to Lee. Rooney made the trip to identify her and paid the man $125 for the mare. She stayed with Rob until he was ready to go to Lexington for his Christmas visit. Robert Lee was delighted to be reunited with his horse.[8]

Much of what is known of Rooney Lee from this period is through his father's letters, as he was never a prolific letter-writer, and many of those he did write are now lost. In February 1867 Robert Lee wrote to his son expressing his desire to see him "re-established at your home and enjoying the pleasure of prosperity around you." He thanked Rooney for his Christmas present but chided, "I . . . do not think you ought to spend anything, except on your farm, until you get that in a prosperous condition." Apparently the lease to the Scot had lasted only one year, and Rooney was again managing the farm with plans to expand. Lee wrote, "While you are your own manager you can carry on cultivation on a large scale with comparatively less expense than on a small scale, and your profits will of course be greater. I would commence a system of progressive improvement which would improve your land and add steadily to your income." Robert Lee had asked Rooney to write an account of his cavalry division's operations from the winter of 1863–1864 until the surrender. "How are you progressing with it?" he hopefully asked. "I know the difficulties of making such a narrative at this time; still, by correspondence with your officers, and by exerting your own memory, much can be done, and it will help me greatly in my undertaking. Make it as full as you can, embracing all circumstances bearing on the campaigns affecting your operations and illustrating the conduct of your division." Rooney apparently never wrote this narrative.[9]

By the spring of 1867 he had other things on his mind. He had become reacquainted with Mary Tabb Bolling of Petersburg. Tabb, as she was known to her friends, was one of the most beautiful belles in the city of Petersburg. Her father, George W. Bolling, had been most considerate and kind to Robert Lee during the months of siege. Tabb had visited him often, and she was "a great favourite of his." The White House was close enough to Richmond for Rooney to become involved in the social gatherings of that city, as well as of Petersburg. The social circle of that element of Virginia society was very close and tightly knit. After four years of war and one year of drudgery on the farm, he was ready to attend social gatherings. Also, after nearly four years of mourning, he was ready to fall in love again. He began corresponding with Tabb on May 24, 1867, and lost no time in declaring his love: "Everything looks peculiarly bland here now. A few weeks ago I thought my present establishment all I required and imagined myself a contented man but now everything seems constricted. I believe I even appear smaller myself. The truth of it is a serpent has stolen into my garden and invites me to eat of the tree of knowledge. I follow willingly her advice and think her more beautiful then the one that brought sin into the world." He was greatly concerned by his sense of propriety, however, as her father was at that time unaware of their love. He asked her: "Don't you think that your father's wishes about my seeing you ought to be ascertained as soon as possible? I felt so badly when I was there in thinking of his ignorance of the relations existing between us. You might find out certainly whether my attentions would be agreeable."[10]

Rooney wrote to his parents on his thirtieth birthday and mentioned his prospects for a good crop and the fact that the railroad to the White House from Richmond, which had been destroyed during the war, had been rebuilt. There was no mention, however, of his love for a certain young lady in Petersburg.[11]

Rooney seems to have wasted no time in his courtship, as the tone in his letter to Tabb dated June 12 was much more intense. He could not believe that one "so beautiful and young" (ten years younger) could love him. He had been in Richmond to see about building a new house on the farm. He wrote of it: "I hope it may soon be in process of construction, and that 'my mistress' will appear as soon as possible to take charge. I hope you will love your new home, and I am sure if you do, that I will." This former cavalryman also felt that the truest way to win a girl's heart was to offer his horse. He was spending much time training his gray horse with the idea of turning his cavalry steed into a proper lady's mount.[12]

All summer and fall he continued his courtship by letters between visits to Richmond and Petersburg. In one dated July 1, he wrote: "I have just come from my friends the builders and they promise to build you a nice house and have it ready by the 1st of November. What then? I long for that time to arrive and hope that I may be able to see you often before this. Why is it that you are so necessary to my happiness? I feel that I should be miserable without you." Tabb had still not informed her father, and Rooney felt that "it would not be right . . . to go again to Petersburg until he is informed." He strongly felt that "it is the proper course to be pursued."[13]

Three days later he wrote again. "How entirely you have taken possession of my thoughts!" he confessed. He informed her that his mother had written and wanted to know "the facts of the case" instead of rumors of his courtship. As in everything else, Rooney was candid and open in his professions of love, as he wrote, "We have made up our minds and only await the sanction of our Parents to acknowledge our mutual love before the world, and why should we not give to each other our full confidence." He also promised to "punctually obey all orders from 'my general.'"[14]

After Tabb finally talked with her father, she evidently asked Rooney to write her father a formal letter of his intentions to court her. It was easy enough for him to pour out his affections for her, but the letter to George Bolling was more difficult. "I tried to unbend as much as possible, but fear that I appeared awkward," he told Tabb. At any rate it was sent, and he anxiously awaited for "G. B." to decide "the fate of nations." The house was progressing, and Rooney hoped to "carry water all through it," which was a very modern marvel of the time. Of it he wrote, "You don't know how anxious I am that you should be pleased, and become attached to your new home. Imagine it what you like and let us try to realize it in your wishes. We can dig and plant, and cause the flowers to grow in a very short time." Almost all the trees around the old house had been cut down during the war, and Rooney was anxious to cover the old scars on the land as well as rebuild a house. His love for flowers is also evident in this letter, a love inherited from, or at least shared by, his grandmother Custis and his parents. Another pastime that he shared with his father—that of socializing with and corresponding with women—seems to have met with some early remonstrances from Tabb. "Why do you always mention Lotte Haxall to me. You certainly do not suffer from 'The Monster'?" he teased. This was a trait to which Tabb would have to become accustomed, as Rooney throughout his life preferred the company of women and enjoyed socializing with them. This in no way lessened his love for his wife or his complete dedication to her.[15]

In late July Tabb became ill and asked her sister Anna to write to Rooney for her. He wrote her back immediately and urged her to take good care of herself. "You must be assured of my entire sympathy during your confinement, and my anxiety to hear that you are out again." This was the second time she had been sick since their courtship began, which made him very anxious over her health. Throughout their life together, he was almost paranoid over her health, due probably to losing his first wife and two babies so quickly. Also, the medical practices were so limited during this time that everyday illnesses that are no longer fatal today could lead to death in very little time.[16]

In August Tabb's father finally gave his blessing to the marriage, and their engagement was publicly announced. On returning from a visit to Tabb, Rooney found several letters (all from women) inquiring about Tabb. One was from his mother, and he shared it with Tabb:

"Mama writes that she is glad to hear that I am engaged to one who is represented as so sweet and amiable and sends you her love. Agnes also writes her congratulations and says she is prepared to love you very dearly. Mary Lee also writes to the same effect."[17]

By mid-September Rooney was sick himself with the chills again. His workmen had assured him the house would be ready to move into by the last of November. He suggested a wedding date of "any day after the 15th November" and told her to proceed with the arrangements. His mother and Mildred had written again expressing their love for Tabb and joy over the marriage and asking for a photograph of Tabb. "I will be obliged to tell them that I have none to send," he lamented.[18]

Robert Lee wrote a very gracious letter to his son at this time: "I have been anxious for some time to write to you, to express the pleasure I have felt at the prospects of your marriage with Miss Bolling. But sickness has prevented, & I am still so feeble that I cannot attend to the pressing business connected with the exercises of the college. As you know how deeply I feel all that concerns you, you may feel assured of the pleasure I derived from your letter to your mother informing her of your engagement. I have the most pleasing recollections of Miss Tabb, & of her kindness to me, & now that she has consented to be my daughter, the measure of my gratitude is filled to overflowing. . . . You must present her my warm love & you both must accept my earnest prayers & most fervent wishes for your future happiness & prosperity."[19]

The entire Lee family welcomed Tabb, and in response to a letter from Mildred, Rooney wrote: "I hope you may love your new sister for her own sake, as well as for mine. I know that she will love you all dearly and think she will suit the fastidious tastes of my sisters, as 'The Oracle' of the family [Rob] has said as much." Rooney felt the same of Tabb's family, as he requested news of Tabb's brother George: "Do write me fully about my brother George who as you say is a bird, and a very dear one to me."[20]

For Rooney Lee this entire year had been spent on farming, courting, building a house, and wedding plans. Other former Confederate officers, however, had begun to write their personal narratives of the war while the memories were fresh. One of these was Rufus Barringer, the former commander of the North Carolina Brigade. Barringer had written an account of the battle of Chamberlain Run of March 31,

1865, and it had recently been published. He sent a copy to Lee, who at once wrote to Barringer to express his pleasure. He praised the accuracy of the report, except on one detail: "From my recollection I think the second charge across the run was made by Beale and yourself, and you stated that you made the attack supported by Beale." He continued, "It is a matter of no importance, and, although you try to do full justice to your gallant command, I do not think you have said half enough in their praise for their conduct that day." In this account Barringer referred to Rooney Lee as being as "stern as the Iron Duke," to which Lee jokingly took exception: "I must be permitted to complain of injustice done to our person in your very graphic account and that is in attributing sternness to your humble servant. I have to learn, for the first time, that there is such a trait in my character."[21]

The construction of the house was delayed in October because a pile of timber that had been drying was accidentally burned. This would not change the wedding date, however, which had been set for November 28. Tabb was planning a trip to Baltimore to see her new furniture that had been ordered. Then she was to go on to New York to shop for her trousseau and other items. Rooney would have liked to join her, but he had pressing "business engagements" and planned to visit Lexington during that time. In a letter to Tabb, he sighed, "But just think that in another six weeks we will have no more separations!"[22]

Before she left he informed her that his "trousseau" had arrived and received the approval of those at the White House. "I hope you have as little trouble with yours as I have had with mine," he dryly commented. Tabb was hoping that his parents would attend the wedding. Mary Lee's invalidism prevented her attending, and Robert Lee also did not want to attend. This was not due to any concerns over their marriage but rather a reluctance to return to Petersburg, the scene of the terrible siege and final defeat. Rooney gave Tabb this news: "Pa writes that he fears he will not be able to come down but I fancy he will change his mind." He planned to travel to Lexington as soon as the winter wheat was sowed.[23]

On October 25 Robert Lee wrote to his son expressing every reason, except the real one, why he was not planning to attend. Instead he proposed a visit to Lexington after the ceremony. He also wanted some advice on a suitable wedding present for Tabb "to remind her hereafter of her Papa." After receiving this letter Rooney traveled to Lexington. Where his letters had failed to produce the results he desired, his personal charm when face to face with his father won easily. On his return to Richmond he brought his father's measurements for a new suit to be made for the wedding. Once he was talked into attending the wedding, Robert Lee began to make his travel plans. He and Custis would travel together to Richmond just before the wedding and spend several days visiting afterward. They arrived in Richmond on November 25 and checked into the Exchange Hotel. Rooney joined them there. Well-wishers thronged Robert Lee whenever he appeared in public. He managed some social visits, and for the next two days he was involved in the indictment hearing of Jefferson Davis.[24]

William Wickham, kin to Rooney's first wife, also joined the wedding party in Richmond. On October 26 Rooney rode out to Hickory Hill, Charlotte's family home, to "pay his adieux" to the family and urge them to attend the wedding. Fitz, Rob, Agnes, and Mildred joined the rest of the family in Richmond also. The wedding party boarded the train and traveled to Petersburg. There Robert Lee was surprised to see throngs of cheering people, bands playing, and a carriage with four white horses to carry him to the residence of his host, General William Mahone.

That afternoon he called on Miss Bolling at her request. The Bolling home near Poplar Lawn was located on Sycamore Street within easy walking distance of the Mahone residence. Tabb greeted her father-in-law and was delighted with the necklace that the Lees had chosen as a wedding present.[25]

That evening Rooney and the groomsmen dined at the hotel while all the ladies flocked to the Bolling home. After dinner the men also went to the Bolling home to form the wedding party. The crowd was huge. One guest estimated that 2,000 were packed inside the church, and the police outside said there were another 1,000 who could not get in. Robert Lee entered first and stopped to kiss some little girl as he entered. Tabb had ten bridesmaids, for whom Rooney had found ten friends to serve as groomsmen. One of those in attendance in the reserved pews near the altar later said, "I did not hear the sound of Fitzhugh's voice, but the bride responded, tho' in a low tone, with perfect distinctness." The ceremony itself was short. Afterward all returned to the Bolling home for a spectacular party considering the hard times just past. The same guest and his escort were charmed by Tabb: "The bride looked magnificently, a perfect figure, a very handsome face, sweet & easy in her manner." He described the dresses of the ladies as "rich & showy" with "very long trains." A "sumptuous" dinner was served at midnight. The party went on into the wee hours.[26]

Before breakfast the next morning Robert Lee wrote a letter to Mary describing the wedding: "Our son was married last night and shone in his happiness. The bride looked lovely and was, in every way, captivating. The church was crowded to its utmost capacity, and the streets thronged." He left the details until he could see her. The couple's plans originally included starting on "their travels" the morning after the ceremony, but Robert Lee thought he "saw indications of a change of purpose." Indeed they stayed in Petersburg until December 2 and then went to Baltimore and other places. On one day Rooney went to the White House to check on the farm and the progress of the house. The other Lees parted company and paid social visits to several places. Robert Lee invited the new couple to include Lexington in their travel plans, but Rooney preferred to wait. Lee commented on this decision: "I do not think she will come at this time, for she is in that happy state which causes her to take pleasure in doing what she thinks he prefers, and he, I think, would like to go to the White House and arrange for the winter."[27]

After an extensive wedding trip through Virginia to Baltimore and New York, the newlyweds were back in Richmond by December 18. They planned to spend the Christmas season in Petersburg. Robert Lee wrote to his son again on December 21 to express the pleasure and feeling of renewal his trip to Petersburg had brought: "My visit to Petersburg was extremely pleasant. Besides the pleasure of seeing my daughter and being with you, which was very great, I was gratified in seeing many friends. In addition, when our armies were in front of Petersburg I suffered so much in body and mind on account of the good townspeople, especially on that gloomy night when I was forced to abandon them, that I have always reverted to them in sadness and sorrow. My old feelings returned to me, as I passed well-remembered spots and recalled the ravages of the hostile shells. But when I saw the cheerfulness with which the people were working to restore their condition, and witnessed the comforts with which they were surrounded, a load of sorrow which had been pressing upon me for years was lifted from my heart." The bad winter weather was now hindering the completion of the house, but Lee was confident that "it will soon pass away, and your sweet helpmate will make everything go smoothly." He again extended an invitation to come to Lexington.[28]

Actually Robert Lee visited the White House before they ever went to Lexington. In May 1868 he was summoned to Richmond to testify in the trial of Jefferson Davis, but once he arrived in Richmond he found that the proceedings had been deferred. He took this opportunity to visit Rob at Romancoke and Rooney and Tabb at the White House. He praised the new house as "convenient, well-arranged and well-built." Soon after his return to Lexington he wrote to Tabb, telling her how much he enjoyed seeing them and renewing his invitation to come to Lexington.[29]

In June Tabb went to Petersburg for the social activities before her sister's wedding. Rooney managed the house as well as the farm in her absence and informed her of his progress: "I have had the house scoured from top to bottom and will have the carpets whipped as soon as I can spare the hands. . . . Miller works in the garden every day and the two Mrs. Christians do the rest." He closed with "I miss you terribly."[30]

During the year of 1868 another loose end of the Custis estate was settled. Smith's Island had been sold for taxes in 1864, but in April 1868 it was returned to the Custis estate. The island was located off Cape Charles in the Atlantic and included more than 4,000 acres of land. Rooney went to the island to see what shape it was in and reported to his father. He found it "considerably pillaged" and much of the timber cut. He thought it would be a nice "sea-bathing establishment," as it had "the best beach I have seen on the Atlantic." This would require a large capital outlay, however. A public sale was arranged, and Rooney and Rob bought the island for $9,000 on December 22. Their father took their note for this sum, without interest.[31]

In November 1868 Rooney Lee and his father were called to Richmond to testify in the ongoing Davis trial. That same month, Rooney and Tabb finally made the trip to Lexington and stayed for three weeks. Mary Lee found her new daughter-in-law charming, and "the entire community vied in paying her attention." Tabb fit in well with the Lee family and was very attentive to Mary Lee. Family prayers were led every morning by Robert Lee just before breakfast, which was served at seven o'clock. Although Tabb was not accustomed to such early hours, she impressed everyone by not being late a single time. Rooney had warned her that she must be punctual. Later she said "that she did not believe General Lee would have an entirely high opinion of any person, even General Washington, if he could return to earth, if he were not ready for prayers!" When she was packing to leave, Robert Lee filled the top of her trunk with pecans.

General amnesty was proclaimed in December 1868 for the former Confederates. In February 1869 the indictments for treason against Robert, Custis, Rooney, and Fitz Lee and other former Confederate generals were dropped. The Fourteenth Amendment barred those who had served in the regular army and taken the oath to uphold the Constitution, then subsequently served in the Confederate Army, from holding any state or federal office. This right could be restored only by a two-thirds vote of Congress.

On February 11, 1869, Tabb gave birth to a son, an event that caused great joy in the Lee family. The baby was christened on August 1 in St. Peter's Church not far from the White House. This small church was the one in which George Washington had married the widow Custis, according to family tradition. They definitely attended services there while in residence at the White House. In this church with such strong family ties, the baby was baptized Robert Edward Lee. His grandfather was in attendance and served as the godfather as well.

The baby had just had a bout with the whooping cough, and Tabb was not well. Robert Lee decided a stay in the mountain air would do wonders for both. It was decided to travel to the Rockbridge Baths. Robert Lee wrote to a friend of his undertaking, "I shall travel up in a capacity that I have not undertaken for many years—as escort to a young mother and her infant, and it will require the concentration of all my faculties to perform my duties." Their stay continued for weeks. The summer months were the ones that brought the mosquitoes and the subsequent chills to those who could not escape. Rooney remained on the farm and oversaw the harvesting of wheat and the preparation of the land. He missed them a great deal but put their health before pleasure. He wrote to Tabb: "Always keep in view the object of your trip and spare no means to regain perfect health. I am very much concerned about the baby." The weather was "hot and disagreeable" on the Pamunkey, but he assured Tabb that her "domestics" were filling up the jars and making butter. Rooney regretted that he could not accompany Custis on a round of visits due to the harvest. He assured his wife "that while you are present I have no desire to gad about but it is only during your absence when everything is so black & dreary that I long for a change."[32]

While Tabb was in Lexington she frequently went for carriage rides with her father-in-law. On one of these the mare Lucy Long choked and lost consciousness due to the harness being too tight. Robert Lee hurriedly jumped down and removed the harness. Naturally he was extremely upset that his carelessness had caused the accident. Fortunately the mare was soon up, and no harm was done.[33]

Rooney, Tabb, and the baby spent the Christmas season of 1869 at the White House. Mildred was a house guest at that time. Robert Lee ordered his son to tell Tabb that Mildred was "modest and backward in giving advice, but that she has mines of wealth on that subject, and that she [Tabb] must endeavor to extract from her views on the management of a household, children, etc. and the proper conduct to be observed toward husbands and the world in general." He wished his son and daughter-in-law a "pleasant Christmas and many, many Happy New Years" and added, "I shall think of you and my daughter and my grandson very often during the season when families are generally united, and though absent from you in person, you will always be present in mind, and my poor prayers and best wishes will accompany you all wherever you are."[34]

Both Robert and Mary Lee visited the White House in the spring of 1870. Robert Lee and Agnes made an extended tour through the South, which included visiting Annie's grave in North Carolina. He was traveling on the advice of his doctors to go to a warmer climate. Mary Lee went straight to the White House on April 20. Robert Lee and Agnes joined them on May 12. Everyone enjoyed a very pleasant stay, and the grandparents doted on the youngest Robert Lee. Robert Lee paid some other visits, then returned to Lexington. Mary remained at the White House a while longer. She took many carriage rides over the property and noted to Mildred later that there was only one tree left of those Charlotte had planted earlier. Robbie, as the grandson was called, referred to her as "Ban Mama."[35]

Tabb remained at the White House during the summer of 1870 and became sick with the chills. The baby's health remained good. The work of the farm continued as usual with the harvesting of crops. On September 28 Robert Lee fell gravely ill with his recurrent heart disease. Although Rob and Rooney were notified of the illness, they were not called to his bedside until the very last. Recent floods caused them delays in reaching Lexington. They were already in Richmond waiting for a train when Custis telegraphed them that their father was worse.

Rooney wrote to Tabb, "I pray that God in his mercy may spare him to us, but I am very anxious." Robert Lee died before Rooney and Rob were able to reach Lexington. Two days later the eulogies were delivered by three clergymen. The entire town of Lexington put on mourning for their hero, and all due respect and dignity surrounded the funeral procession. Robert Lee was laid to rest in the vault beneath the chapel of Washington College. All of the other members of the Lee family that were present at the funeral would eventually join him there.[36]

Not long after Robert Lee died the Association of the Army of Northern Virginia was formed. The founders planned to include officers and men from all the former Confederate states, and the members of each state would form a "division." The organizational meeting was held on November 4, 1870, in Richmond, and Rooney Lee was a lifelong member of the association. Their aim was "the preservation of the friendships that were formed in that army, the perpetuation of its fame, and the vindication of its achievements." Rooney Lee became president of the Virginia Division in 1875, succeeding Fitz Lee and George Pickett. He served in that capacity for ten years.[37]

The second child of Rooney and Tabb, a girl named Mary Tabb Lee, was born during the winter. Her uncle Rob described her to his mother: "The little girl is so very small that an old bachelor like myself can't form much of an idea as to her merits. She has beautiful gray eyes and cries remarkably well for one so young." Tragically this little girl died in infancy.[38]

As his life stabilized after the war, Rooney Lee became more and more involved with his civic responsibilities. A first indication of this is a letter from him to W. W. Corcoran of Washington, D.C., written in May 1872. St. Peter's Church, the one in which George Washington married the widow Custis, was in need of renovation. At the request of the rector Lee wrote to Corcoran, a man known for his philanthropy. The very modestly worded request worked, and the money was granted.[39]

On his thirty-fifth birthday he wrote to his mother in Lexington about Tabb's plans to join her at the springs. After the usual gossip, he teased his mother, "You possibly have forgotten that this is my birthday—35th at that. Just think what a wonder appeared in the world this day thirty five years ago!!" More seriously he continued: "I hope that, during this long stretch of time, of the pleasure and pain which my existence has caused you, that the pleasure has outweighed the pain. I am certain of one thing you must have already been well aware of—that I have never had toward you but one emotion; that of the warmest and deepest love—which has grown with my growth and strengthened with my strength."[40]

Another child was born on August 31, 1872, the third child and second son. He was named George Bolling Lee after his maternal grandfather. This child and the firstborn son, Robbie, would live to adulthood. Rooney and Tabb had two more children, Annie Agnes Lee and William Henry Fitzhugh Lee Jr. They died in infancy in 1874 and 1875, respectively. What anguish this must have caused the young couple, especially Rooney. Being a father was probably the most important aspect of his life, and out of the seven children he fathered (two by Charlotte and five by Tabb) only two survived infancy. The way in which Rooney dealt with these losses is found in a letter to Tabb after the last child died: "The grief which you feel for our lost darling is natural but you must strive to submit with humblest humility to the will of Him who controls everything for our eventual good. It is not only useless but wicked to encourage or harbor feelings against those who used every skill known to man to save her. My consolation at her loss is that she is free from all pain. . . . Only the most unshakable of faiths could have helped him through the hard times of his life."[41]

In September 1872 Rooney went to visit Rob and his wife. Rob had married Charlotte Haxall only ten months earlier, and when Rooney saw her she was on her deathbed. He described her to Tabb as "much wasted" and "her eyes are like ice." He feared correctly that it would be the last time he saw her.[42]

Lee's interest in farming and the improvement of agricultural skills and techniques led him into two more organizations. In December 1872 he became president of the state agricultural society and also became a member of the board of directors of the Virginia Agricultural and Mechanical College in Blacksburg, Virginia (now known as Virginia Polytechnic Institute). Remembering his own education at Harvard and its lack of relevance in his life, Lee was against a move to change the school into a liberal arts college. "We want a school for farmers & mechanics—men who will have to labor with their own hands for a livelihood," he expressed to a professor there. He continued: "I am more convinced than ever that unless the college is made a practical school, it will fail. Everything about it, in my opinion, should be subordinated to the agricultural department & also the mechanical."[43]

In the fall of 1873 Rooney's younger sister Agnes became ill from a "debilitating intestinal disorder." She died on October 15. The death of this daughter and Mary Lee's recent visit to Arlington, which she found almost unrecognizable due to the changes made during the war, weighed heavily on the matriarch. She spent her time sitting and petting her favorite cat and wept whenever Agnes's name was mentioned. Her physical and mental state began to deteriorate. She thought she was again at her beloved Arlington with her "little children." Mildred described her last weeks as "cruel tortures." Rooney and Rob were called to Lexington, but by the time they arrived their mother was already unconscious.

Rooney left his mother's bedside to write Tabb, "Ma is now dying. . . . She has been unconscious since Saturday last. Her last gleam of intelligence was in reply to some question about her opinion of 'Bolly' [Rooney's second son]. She said 'bless his little heart.'" Then Rooney summed up his mother's life: "Thus passes from this earth a devoted wife—a self-sacrificing mother and a pure Christian and one of the most intellectual women of her day." Mary Lee died on November 5. The three sons and Mildred attended the funeral and saw her laid to rest between the graves of Agnes and Robert Lee.[44]

In 1874 Rooney and his brothers and sisters received inheritances from their great-aunt, Mrs. Anna Maria Fitzhugh, the widow of William Henry Fitzhugh. He was the brother of Mary Lee Fitzhugh Custis, Mary Custis Lee's mother. He was Rooney's great-uncle and the man for whom he was named. The land was divided into five lots among the surviving children of Mary Custis Lee. Rooney's lot included more than 500 acres of land and the Fitzhugh home of Ravensworth situated in Fairfax County. Ravensworth was closely linked to the Lee family. Robert Lee's mother had died at Ravensworth and was buried in an old graveyard covered with ivy. Mrs. Fitzhugh had no children of her own and was especially close to her niece and her niece's children.[45]

Rooney and Tabb then moved from the White House to Ravensworth. A cousin of Mrs. Fitzhugh's wrote to a friend that she was "glad to know that sunshine is admitted there, the brightness revived" to replace the gloom. She continued, "I am sure you find the present family as kind & agreeable as possible. I have known dear Rooney from his early boyhood." Rooney had taken Tabb to meet this lady while in Baltimore on their honeymoon, and they made a lasting, favorable impression on her. She asked her friend, "Please give my love to 'Rooney' and 'Tabb' (just what he told me to call them) & tell them it is with inexpressible comfort that I think of them as fixed at dear 'Ravensworth'."[46]

The move to Ravensworth in Fairfax County brought Rooney Lee close to the hub of politics in Washington, D.C. In 1875 he was elected to serve in the Virginia state senate representing his district. He served in that capacity for three years and for a while was the presiding officer of that body. He evidently considered it his civic duty to serve as an elected official, but he missed his wife and young family while separated from then. He also frequently went down to the White House to oversee the farming operations there.[47]

His letters of this period are very reminiscent of those his father wrote to his mother when Lee was stationed apart from the family. From the White House he wrote to Tabb, "I am grieved to hear that you are not so well and regret that I cannot be near you to nurse you and comfort you. But we must hope for the best and both try and do our duty. My work is very much behind now and it will require my utmost exertions to get my crops in this fall in time." He also talks of clearing up any debts: "I will write today & enclose the money you ask for & more besides. If this is not sufficient, let me know & I will send you more, but please do not leave a cent's obligation behind you." He also kept abreast of the social gossip that was current. On more than one occasion he played the host to visiting relatives and friends. One of the novelties that made the rounds at social gatherings was Planchette, a type of Ouija board. Another pastime was playing euchre or whist. Rooney was very much involved in household chores and the education of the boys. In one letter he echoed his father by writing, "Virtue and common sense generally bring content and happiness in this world." In another he recommended a switching for Bolly if he continued to spit at anyone.[48]

Rooney Lee was much more outspoken in professing his love for his wife than his father had been. In one letter he wrote, "The boys are constantly talking of you and your husband is constantly thinking of you—and counting the moments which drag heavily along in your absence!!" In another quick note he expressed his love: "My angel wife, how I miss you. Oh, that I were at old Ravensworth tonight. It is piping hot—but not too hot to prevent my thoughts longing to you. Take care of yourself, my own precious, and know that 'your own' is longing for you."[49]

As for his political involvement, there is rarely a mention in his letters. In one he mentioned an acquaintance who was "much cast down about the election." He continued, "I tell him that I am used to such little upsets up in old Fairfax." Rooney learned to make speeches on the political circuit, and on one occasion he wrote home, "My speech was all right & we have won the fight." Another time he reported: "I am this far on my tour and will speak at Middleburg tomorrow, at Union today. So far we have had a success."[50]

Another area of involvement that frequently required making speeches was that of the Virginia Division of the Army of Northern Virginia Association. As its president, Rooney called the annual meetings to order and introduced the main speakers. At one banquet he welcomed those in attendance and "concluded . . . that the people still cherished the memory of the brave men who during the four years of the unequal contest bore themselves nobly, and proved themselves worthy of the land that gave them birth and the cause for which they fought." The rhetoric of his speeches was in vogue at that time, and although it may seem flowery and verbose to the modern ear, it was then heralded as "graceful and appropriate." Lee believed wholeheartedly in the aims of the association: "General Lee then gave the audience a hearty and cordial welcome, and said that these reunions were not only for the pleasure of comradeship which they afford, but also to perpetuate the heroic deeds of the mighty men who composed our grand old army. . . . He eloquently and earnestly insisted that although the battle had finally been lost, it is our privilege and duty to perpetuate the fame of our great army."

Lee also attended the reunion and banquet of the Society of Confederate States Army and Navy in the State of Maryland on February 21, 1882, in Baltimore. As the various branches of the service were toasted, Rooney Lee rose to respond to the toast offered to the cavalry. As he did, "He was greeted with enthusiastic cheers, frequently repeated as he proceeded to make the speech of the occasion." After he expressed his great pleasure at seeing the old soldiers, he noted that he was probably "too partial to the cavalry, since it had been his proud privilege to 'follow the feather' of Jeb Stuart and the leadership of Wade Hampton on so many glorious fields." Lee stated that all branches of the army had "done their duty and won their share of the glory of that grand old army." He wanted to speak not only as a cavalryman but also as a Confederate to express his appreciation of the "importance and value of these reunions." He continued: "We have kept inviolate our paroles—we have no purpose of renewing the war—we do not expect to vote pensions to even needy Confederates—to decorate the graves of our dead at the public expense—or to tax the people to establish 'homes' for our maimed veterans. But it does behoove us to see to it that the graves of our dead are kept green—that the memories of our heroic endeavor are kept fresh—and that the true story of our struggle is put upon the page of history and transmitted to coming generations." Lee's speech was "rapturously received," and as he took his seat there were "three rousing cheers."[51]

Although Rooney never wrote his own memoirs of the war, he read with interest the narratives of others. In October 1877 he wrote to Colonel Walter Herron Taylor to tell him how impressed he was with Taylor's account of the battle of Gettysburg. It is interesting how he defended Stuart, even though he was not present during the Gettysburg Campaign. "I can not sympathize with you, in your gentle, it is true, strictures upon Gen. Stuart, but upon the whole, yours is, as it ought to be, the clearest and fairest account of that great battle that I have read."[52]

Rooney Lee traveled to Charleston, South Carolina, in February 1878 to present a new flag to an old organization that had seen service in the American Revolution and the Civil War—the Washington Light Infantry. Governor Wade Hampton introduced him and stated that it was appropriate for Lee to present the flag, as he was a descendant of both Light Horse Harry Lee and Robert Edward Lee. In his speech Lee said that they were honoring "the heroes of two revolutions—one crowned with victory, the other with defeat." He felt both "sorrow and joy" in rejoining old comrades in arms and remembering the dead. Of those who gave their lives he asked "who can believe that they died in vain?" Then he continued: "In commemorating the deeds of the heroes of '76, we must not forget, my friends, the valor of those who for long and wearying years conducted a defensive warfare unparalleled in history, until overwhelmed by superior numbers and resources, and who furled their banners only when resistance ceased to be possible. Ours was a lesson often taught in the world's history.

Right may succumb to might, but this need not work dishonor. Our lands were laid waste, our houses burned, and our sufferings were great; and yet, moved by the ennobling ambition to preserve our honor untarnished, we live today in the good esteem of all fair-minded people, and our deeds will descend in history, and burn to our imperishable credit on its pages." The reporter who wrote down his words said it was "impossible to catch many eloquent passages amid the enthusiasm and applause."[53]

Lee's involvement with politics moved up a level as he was elected to serve in the U.S. House of Representatives beginning on March 14, 1887. He served in the Fiftieth and Fifty-First Congresses and was reelected to serve in the Fifty-Second, but he died before the first session began. Before he could serve, a bill had to be passed "to remove the political disabilities" under the provisions of the Fourteenth Amendment. This bill (S.2759) was passed during the Forty-Ninth Congress after he was elected. During the first session of the Fiftieth Congress Lee served on three committees—the District of Columbia, Expenditures in the State Department, and Accounts. During this session he asked for a short leave due to illness and personal obligations. In the next Congress Lee continued on the Committee on Accounts. He again had to ask leave for a day on account of illness. Representative Charles T. O'Ferrell left a vivid pen portrait of Rooney Lee during his years in Congress as well as an anecdote that certainly sums up the man:

General Lee was a very large man, much larger than his illustrious father. He was a born gentleman, and had of course been reared in an atmosphere of culture and refinement. He was a strikingly handsome man, tall, erect, and in height several inches over six feet. He was a lovable man, and the people of his district, which was immediately opposite Washington, were devoted to him. He was faithful to every duty, and to such an extent as to break down his health by overwork, causing his premature death.

He was a pleasant talker, and there was not a member on the floor who would have made a caustic reply to anything he might have said; in fact, he was so gentle and moderate in speech as never to irritate or provoke a sharp retort. He had in his district an Episcopal Seminary, from which a vast number of young ministers had walked forth to become in after years distinguished divines. The Seminary suffered severely in the destruction of, or damage to, its buildings during the war.

General Lee introduced a bill to reimburse it for its losses, and the bill came up for consideration upon a favorable report; the Democrats generally favored it, but the General, fearing that the Republicans would oppose it, quietly and with dignity walked to the center of their side, and made his speech in behalf of his bill directly to them.

They listened attentively and with profound respect. Finally there came an interruption from behind him. A faint voice was heard: "Will the gentleman from Virginia yield to a question?" The General turning his head, said in the most winning manner, "Why certainly." "Was this school continued during the Rebellion?" "Yes, as far as possible. Most of the professors remained there," said the General. "For whom did those professors pray? Did they pray for the Unionists or for the Confederates?" The General's reply was instant, "I do not know; I never heard them pray, but they were saintly men, and I presume they prayed for all sinners, and left the good Lord to say who were the sinners."

The whole House applauded, the General continued his speech to the end without further interruption, and his bill passed.[54]

Lee worked as diligently at being a public servant as he had at being a soldier. A fellow congressman once wrote that in his service he was "faithful, conscientious, and painstaking—ever alert to the interests of his constituents and seeking only how he could serve them." Another stated that he held "in the greatest degree the confidence of his constituents and the people of his entire State. No one who ever knew him could fail to implicitly trust him." Furthermore he represented all the people and associated "freely and unrestrainedly" with them. To Lee "public office was a public trust" that he carried out for all his constituents regardless of "race, color or party affiliation." He spoke on the floor of the House only when necessary to promote a bill he thought beneficial to his constituents. His influence was felt more in committees; indeed it "was irresistible, because his judgment and integrity were above dispute." Although he served as a Democrat, he was not a slave to party politics. He always put the people's good above partisanship. Because the district he represented was so close to Washington, it was fairly easy to reach him. Often as he came in from Ravensworth to the depot in Washington several petitioners would wait for him. He patiently listened to all. It was also a custom for a page to bring a card to the floor of the House whenever anyone wanted to meet with a congressman. One colleague whose seat was near Lee's remembered: "Often have I known him to be carded out a dozen times a day; and if he ever expressed himself to me as worried by these interruptions he never failed to show by what he said that his annoyance arose not so much from the importunities of his friends as from his inability to serve them." In 1890 a Republican came to Lee with the case of a black man who had a pension claim and was suffering because of delays in the bureaucracy. This man asked Lee to expedite the case as only a congressman could. When he told Lee that the suffering man was also a Republican and had probably voted against him, Lee replied, "Smith, don't hesitate to call on me to help any of my constituents. I represent all of the people of my district, and will serve them all alike."[55]

One of Lee's customs while serving in Congress may seem odd by modern norms, but it is as refreshing as it is indicative of the man. In the spring when his roses were blooming, Rooney Lee brought in baskets of flowers and gave them to his friends on the floor of the House, some delivered personally, some with the help of a page. One recipient later recorded: "Who is there among his associates on this floor that will ever cease to remember him as, morning after morning in the springtime, he came into this Hall, bringing from his home a basket of roses to distribute among his friends? He was not seeking popularity. Such a thought had not occurred to him, nor did it enter into the mind of anyone here. He simply loved his friends, and he loved flowers just as he loved all things beautiful and true."

Lee found time somehow for other interests as well. He was a trustee for Washington and Lee University for many years before his death. He was also a member of the Harvard Club in Washington and on at least one occasion was an after-dinner speaker at one of its banquets. In the summer of 1888 he traveled to Cambridge for the first time since leaving Harvard. He visited the campus and met many old friends. After the class supper he spoke briefly, and he attended the commencement exercises. One old classmate of Lee's who lived for a while in Washington was Benjamin Crowninshield, who had rowed with Rooney Lee at Harvard. He spoke at local observances such as the one on Decoration Day in 1887 near Arlington. A man who accompanied him that day was impressed by the esteem in which the audience held him. There were many old veterans in attendance, and he was immediately surrounded by an eager throng when he descended from the podium. "Admiration and affection were expressed upon their countenances for the brave man before them, whose gallant deeds had been told at every fireside in the country around, and who was loved and honored," this observer recorded. As a speaker Rooney was certainly not the orator Light Horse Harry Lee had been, but he spoke from the heart and reached his audiences. One who heard him speak on several occasions found him "graceful in delivery, persuasive in manner, and forcible in argument. His diction was pure, unpretentious, and simple." Rooney was a member of the Lee Memorial Association and was present at the unveiling of the Lee Monument in Richmond on May 29, 1890.[56]

On February 11, 1890, Rooney Lee wrote a letter to his son Robbie, who was turning twenty-one. It is truly reminiscent of his father's letters to him at the same age, preaching to a certain extent and then stopping when he realized he had overdone the advice: "Well! You have today arrived at 'Man's Estate' and I will send you a Father's love and blessings, and my hopes for your being a successful, good and distinguished man. Above all I pray for your being distinguished as a good man. . . . I really believe that a proper ambition is satisfied with nothing less than honorable success. To accomplish that with proper habits and behavior you must have economy, patience and perseverance. Well, you have had enough advice."[57]

By the summer of 1891 he was too ill to attend Robbie's final school oration. Tabb went on a trip through New York, and in a letter to her Rooney wrote mostly of social gossip and his concern for her health. He also hinted at his own state of health: "Bolly has given you day by day the news. I am certainly no worse and upon the whole, some days I feel stronger." Bolly, or George Bolling Lee, the second son, already had plans to become a doctor and waited on his father during his illness. Rooney added, "He is very attentive and promises to make a good Dr."[58]

Lee had been in declining health for some time with what was then called "valvular disease of the heart," or possibly congestive heart failure. He had been sick since the past winter, and when Congress adjourned he went to the Virginia mountains, long a refuge for the Lee family. His health continued to deteriorate, and he came back to his home at Ravensworth to die. He could not lie down but rather rested in a sitting position. During the last thirty-six hours of his life he was unconscious and had difficulty breathing. The doctor in attendance administered digitalis, whiskey, and strychnia every two hours. At

9 A.M. on October 15 the doctor informed the family that death was imminent. It was felt that he "suffered but little" and that the death was "absolutely painless." Tabb remained by her husband's side until the last, which came at two-thirty that afternoon. Lee's sons Robbie and Bolly were also present, as were Custis, Rob, Mary, Mildred, Tabb's sister, and family servants. As soon as the news of his death reached Alexandria, the mayor ordered the fire bells and the church bells to be tolled for one hour.[59]

The mayor also called for a public meeting at the opera house in Alexandria that night in order to express the bereavement of the citizenry. A committee was appointed to attend the funeral and to prepare proper resolutions in memory of the deceased. It was also decided to toll the bells of Alexandria during the funeral service. The Lee Camp of the Confederate Veterans also decided to board special cars that would take them to Ravensworth for the ceremony. The pallbearers were Colonel Arthur Herbert, General William H. Payne, Captain A. D. Payne, Dr. S. G. Gordon, Captain James Love, and Mr. John W. Burke.[60]

The funeral service was held on October 17 at Ravensworth at 4 P.M. Approximately 500 people attended, including family, friends, congressmen, veterans, and neighbors. Two special cars left Washington earlier in the day, and two more were added at Alexandria before going on to the depot at Ravensworth. There the mourners disembarked and walked through the woods to the residence. The house was a large two-story building on a hill with a magnificent view of the remainder of the estate. Lee's coffin was located in the hall of the house and was draped in black and covered with flowers. The simple silver inscription plate stated "William Henry Fitzhugh Lee. Born May 31, 1837. Died October 15, 1891." After those who wished to do so had viewed the body, the casket was closed. The Episcopal burial service was read by the Reverend Dr. Randolph H. McKim, rector of the church Lee attended in Washington, and the Reverend J. Cleveland Hall, rector of the Fairfax County church of which Lee had been a vestryman. Those present sang the hymn "Jesus, Lover of My Soul." Then the coffin was carried out through the south door of the house onto the lawn where the Confederate Veterans of the Lee Camp were lined up. The coffin was actually carried to its resting place by hands on the estate while the pallbearers acted in an honorary position. Lee was interred in the Fitzhugh burial ground, which was surrounded by a

low brick wall with an iron railing on top. Ivy, myrtle, and honeysuckle
draped the wall and the ground. The circling trees were just turning to
their autumn colors. The family, clergy, pallbearers, and General Wade
Hampton were the only ones to enter the walled area. Dr. McKim read
the committal service, and a chorus of women sang the hymn "Asleep
in Jesus." The family returned to the house, and the hands began to fill
the grave. This task was quickly taken up by the veterans, who completed the work "as a last token of respect for the general." Flowers
blanketed the ground. A newspaper reported that the "service had been
completed with a simplicity equal to that which had characterized the
life of Gen. Lee." Three generations of the family were represented in
that burial plot—Ann Carter Lee and the Fitzhughs; the two infant
daughters and infant son of Rooney and Tabb; and now Rooney Lee.
One of those present left a poignant vignette of the ceremony: "White
and colored, rich and poor, high and low, soldiers, citizens, and states-
men, all were there. . . . In the presence of that vast throng, with uncovered heads, his comrades, who had followed him on many a hard-
fought battlefield, performed the last sad rites, and with their own
hands filled his grave and planted upon it the 'immortelles' of their affection and devotion. Faces that never blanched amid the storm of battle paled, hearts that never quailed in the presence of an enemy broke in
the presence of the last enemy of us all."

Rooney's youngest sister Mildred later wrote an account of the death
of her "warm & loving-hearted brother." Rooney had died on the same
day as Agnes nineteen years ago and on the anniversary of the burial of
their father. As Mildred looked out of the window of Ravensworth's library, she viewed "the same golden sunshine [and] changing foliage as
on those other fall days" and felt "the same tears & pain at parting. . . .
Dear, dear Fitzhugh—Goodnight."[61]

Soon after, tributes were prepared by Washington and Lee, the Virginia Division of Army of Northern Virginia Association, and the U.S.
Congress, among others. Cards and letters of sympathy also poured in
to the family. Among these was one from William B. Lightfoot, which
was representative: "The morning papers convey to me the sad, sad
news of the death of my dear General. I feel as if I had lost one of my
oldest & dearest friends. Pardon me for asking you to allow me to
share your sorrow and mingle my tears with those who loved him. As
a member of his favorite regiment the 9th Va. Cavalry. I was with him
in many a trying scene. We parted at Appomattox, his parting words

to me were, 'We have done our best. Go home and work out an honest living.' A braver soldier never drew sabre. He loved his men and his men loved him. I feel his loss deeply but I know he is enjoying that everlasting rest which he deserves. Accept my sympathy & good wishes for the sake of one whom I loved and admired." Another man who knew him only after the war and who had received advice from him, as from "an elder brother," shared his thoughts with the family: "I think he had the greatest control over himself of any man I ever knew and I believe few men who held as high political office were as pure." So ended the life of Rooney Lee—not only a practical life as he had wished but also a good life.[62]

The remains of Rooney Lee were reinterred in the Lee Mausoleum beneath the Lee Chapel at Washington and Lee, Lexington, Virginia, in September 1922.[63]

Ravensworth was left to Lee's sons and eventually became the property of George Bolling Lee. The house was destroyed by fire in 1925. A shopping center stands on its site today.[64]

Mary Tabb Bolling Lee outlived her husband by many years and continued to live at Ravensworth. Robert Edward Lee III became a lawyer, and George Bolling Lee became a doctor. When Custis Lee retired from the presidency of Washington and Lee in 1897 due to ill health, he moved to Ravensworth. He lived there in "scholarly seclusion" until his death in 1913.[65]

In Lee's will he wanted his executors to "erect a suitable monument and to cost not less than one thousand dollars over the grave of my wife whose remains lie buried with her two children in the old cemetery at Richmond, Virginia." This was never done.[66]

CHAPTER 16

"Rooney Lee"

William Henry Fitzhugh Lee was known as Rooney throughout his life. His father gave him the nickname, which means "darling" in Gaelic, when he was barely three months old. The only ones who called him Fitzhugh were Charlotte, his first wife, and his father beginning at the time of his first marriage. His mother called him Fitzhugh generally but occasionally slipped back to Roon. In the army he was known as Rooney. It has been supposed that Fitz Lee and Rooney Lee were known as such to avoid confusion, as both their real names were Fitzhugh Lee. In official correspondence Fitz was Fitzhugh Lee and Rooney was W. H. F. Lee. In fact they were known as Fitz and Rooney because that is what they had always been called. At Harvard he was known as Rooney. Tabb, his second wife, called him Rooney. On at least one occasion, in later life, he told a new acquaintance to call him Rooney. A colleague in Congress wrote after his death that "Rooney was his father's term of endearment, which all who knew him, without distinction of age, race or sex, delighted to apply to him when absent. When present it was always 'general.'" Certainly in his case the nickname fit the man.[1]

Physically Rooney Lee was a big man. Many who described him noted his size and physique. In 1935 his son George Bolling Lee, in answer to a Lee biographer's question of actual size, replied: "My father, Gen. W. H. F. Lee, was six foot two in stocking feet. As a young man he was tall and slender, later in life he became stout due to lack of exercise, heart and kidney trouble. He weighed in the neighborhood of 220 pounds." Rooney had his father's dark hair and eyes.

One veteran said of him: "To see him once was to remember him forever. His image is as distinct before me this moment as if he stood in the flesh with his eye beaming forth the goodness of his nature and his hand outstretched, as was his wont, to receive mine."

Lee is primarily remembered as a soldier. He served in the Confederate cavalry from the outset of the war until the surrender at Appomattox. His first rank was that of captain, and his first assignment was in the camp of instruction for cavalry near Richmond. By war's end his rank was that of major general—the youngest in the Confederate service. His worth as a soldier may best by decided by those who fought alongside him—his superiors, his subordinates, and those of equal rank. Jeb Stuart relied heavily on Lee and on several occasions trusted him to take care of whatever might arise on his front. Two notable examples of this were the Stoneman Raid and the battle of Brandy Station. Stuart also chose Lee and his men to accompany him on all his famous raids. This was due to Lee being a very capable subordinate, as well as the high state of readiness and discipline of Lee's troops. Wade Hampton wrote of Lee: "He was a zealous, conscientious, brave, and intelligent soldier, who fully discharged all of his duties. He was one of those safe, sound, judicious officers, and you always felt when you sent instructions to him that they were going to be obeyed promptly and to the letter."

M.C. Butler served "side by side" with Lee and had "the best opportunities of forming a correct estimate of him as a soldier and a man." In Butler's opinion Lee "never aspired to be what is sometimes called a 'dashing' soldier. He was quite content with the serious, earnest, steady performance of his duties." His courage was without question but "was not that frothy, noisy kind so often paraded to attract attention." Butler continued: "In battle he was as steady, firm and immovable as any soldier who ever wielded a sword or placed a squadron in the field. In his relations to his subordinates he was the perfection of military propriety, always considerate and kindly, but firm and impartial in the enforcement of discipline."

A fellow Virginian, in a memorial address, said of Lee after his death:

> It was my privilege and pleasure to form his acquaintance in the army and to watch his flashing blade amid the carnage of battle, observe his cool courage and intrepid bearing and the love and confidence of his

men upon more than one sanguinary field. He was as calm when the leaden hail was rattling and as cool when the shells were shrieking and bursting as he was upon this floor [of Congress]. He was a leader, not a follower of his men; if they went into the jaws of death, he was at their head. He fared as his men fared; if their haversacks were empty, his was empty; if they laid down in the mud, he laid there too; if they sweltered in the summer heat or shivered in the winter blast, he sweltered or shivered too; and thus it was he kindled in the breasts of his men intense love for himself and secured their implicit confidence in his leadership.

An officer of the First North Carolina Cavalry, W. H. H. Cowles, thought that Rooney Lee was so "gentle and tender" that an observer might think he was best suited for "the paths of peace." However, in Cowles's estimation, "upon the battlefield he was brave as the bravest. Whenever and wherever duty called him his personal safety was by him never considered." He recalled: "Often have I seen him in the thickest of the fight, by his presence and personal direction cheering and encouraging both officers and men. Though the son of the general in chief of the army, he took no favor by it. He never took advantages of his rank to keep to the rear and send his regiments in."[2]

W. T. Robins, who had served as an officer in the Ninth Virginia Cavalry as well as on Lee's staff, described "General Rooney" as "one of the bravest men that ever lived and always at his post." Furthermore he "would not take foolish chances or expose his men simply for the sake of fighting, but when the necessity arose and it was incumbent upon him to protect anything in his rear, cover a retreat, hold a position, or when a point was to be gained by fighting, he was a rough rider, concentrated every faculty of mind and body upon the work before him, and was stubborn to the last degree. He understood the game of scientific warfare and played it well."

Although he could be "as stern as the Iron Duke," as Barringer said, Lee was "universally beloved by the soldier" because he "always carefully considered the welfare of his men and was extremely particular about exposing them to any unnecessary hardships." One of his old troopers recalled that he never forgot a name or a face. He had not been the colonel of the Ninth Virginia long "before he knew the name of every man in the regiment." Another of the privates who served under him gave this description: "General 'Rooney' Lee was universally beloved. He was a thoroughly kind-hearted gentleman, always approachable, and never gave an order even to the humblest private save in a gentle manner. He was a disciplinarian, and believed in thorough drilling, carrying this idea to the extent that he never lost an opportunity to exercise the men even if he could do nothing else but put them through the saber drill. Yet he never enforced discipline in a harsh way." This man did not consider Lee to be a "dashing cavalryman"; rather he was "consummately cool, always kept his men well in hand, kept his own head and the boys had perfect confidence in him." He continued: "They knew that when 'Rooney' gave an order he had the whole thing mapped out. He never played for personal reputation. His game was to win and take the best care of his men. He maneuvered for position and when he got it, it meant stubborn fighting. Don't you make any mistake about that. He was as tenacious as a bull dog." Yet another trooper emphasized his accessibility: "He had not a particle of pretentious pride, but to all men, privates in the ranks as well as officers . . . he always found 'time enough for courtesy.'"[3]

William P. Roberts, at one time the colonel of the Second North Carolina Cavalry and later a brigadier general, left a personal anecdote that shows the mutual esteem held by Lee and his troopers. Roberts remembered: "That courteous gentleman and splendid soldier, General W. H. F. Lee, the division commander, said to me, 'Roberts, I think my division equal, if not superior, to any division in the army, but let me tell you that I think I am growing a little partial to your regiment, because I feel more secure and my sleep is less disturbed when the gallant "Two Horse" is in my front.'" Roberts emphasized that these were "his exact words" and that he felt "it was the most splendid compliment ever paid the regiment."[4]

Lee's competence—indeed excellence—as a cavalry officer was demonstrated in many ways. He could read the lay of the land and use topography to the utmost in the positioning of troops. He was equally adept in both offensive and defensive maneuvers. His part of the battlefield or picket line was always secure, and he worked well in a subordinate role or on his own. Like his father, he was good at working with others and never let any personal ambition get in the way of achieving the goal at hand. Considering some of the prima donnas in the Confederate service, this was no small task. The welfare of his men was of the highest priority with him, and he never sacrificed his men unnecessarily. He paid attention to the details—discipline, forage, drill, and picket duty. Frequently he was seen riding his picket line with perhaps one aide accompanying him. In the last month of the war along the lines below Petersburg, one trooper remembered Lee riding the picket line: "It was a dark, rainy night . . . at the midnight hour, the tramp of horses was heard and the visitors were found to be General Lee, an aide, and an orderly, wrapped in rubber coats, inspecting the line to see that a sharp outlook was observed. His command was never taken unawares." He himself was always at his post. He did what he was supposed to do when he was supposed to do it.[5]

As the war progressed, cavalry tactics changed. Early in the war lightning raids were the norm, and battles were waged with monumental charges and flashing sabers. By 1864 all that had changed. The cavalry moved on horseback but usually fought on foot. The lines were more static and picket duty more important. Lee was able to adapt to these changing tactics. Along with the change came the use of scouts. Many of Lee's scouts were men from the Ninth Virginia who were assigned to headquarters, but they ranged far behind enemy lines to gather useful information. The most daring of these was a man named Curtis. He was remembered as "Gen. Rooney's scout" and wore "a coat blue on one side, gray on the other." Wearing the blue side out, he was "a frequent visitor to the Yankee camps." Just before Appomattox one trooper ran into Curtis, who had been riding with Sheridan's cavalry for some time and was returning to report to Lee. The trooper told him that he had given him a fright with that blue uniform and he had almost claimed to be a Yankee himself. Curtis replied by tapping his gun and saying, "It is well you did not. I am taking no prisoners this trip." After the battle of Five Forks one of Lee's scouts, "a Confederate soldier disguised in Yankee uniform," made his way through the lines to Burnt Quarter to let the widow Gilliam know that her daughter had reached safety. He coolly sat on the front porch in the midst of Custer's men and chatted with the mother.[6]

In one other respect Lee adapted to the change in tactics by organizing a "pioneer company." This consisted of seventy mounted men who were supplied with axes, shovels, picks, and the like. It was under the command of a second lieutenant, and it was their job to build abatis, destroy or repair bridges as the case may be, and cut through enemy works.[7]

Rooney Lee had a temper, although most of the time he kept it under control. One thing that could cause him to lose it was if the officers of his command did not do their duty. Soon after he became colonel of the Ninth Virginia Cavalry he suspected that a surgeon had been remiss in his duties. Lee called in a sergeant to question him. This man remembered: "Colonel Lee, with a flush on his cheek and fire in his eye, wished to know if two men of my company had not been left ill and uncared for in an outhouse near our former camp. I replied that I did not really know; that the men had been reported as ill to the surgeon and turned over to him." The surgeon was then questioned and shortly afterward dismissed. In another instance Lee "removed from command" a major of the Thirteenth Virginia Cavalry who had "allowed himself to be captured" and later returned to the regiment.

All the attributes of a good officer were apparent in Lee from the beginning. One lieutenant who first met him in May 1862 described him as follows: "As commander of the regiment, he began at once to display the alertness, watchfulness, disciplinary power, and minute care as to details characteristic of a good military leader. The interests of the men and horses alike engaged his jealous care. The choice of a good camping ground, the careful arrangement of his picket lines, the inspection of the camp, the soldiers' arms and accouterments, the quartermaster's commissary and medical department of the regimental services all received his watchful supervision." At this time Lee was twenty-four years old. His military career was over at the age of twenty-seven, long before the age that many gained prominence.[8]

There was much more to Rooney Lee's personality and character that seemed to shine even more under adverse conditions. During the war, when he was exchanged after nine months as a prisoner of war, he refused to speak harshly of his captors. One of the first things he did when he reached Richmond after being exchanged for Union General Neal Dow was to go to Libby Prison to meet the two captains for whom he had been held hostage for so long. Lee had lost virtually everything during the war—wife, children, home. When the war was over he accepted the fact of defeat and the changes in society. "He liked the old manners and customs of Virginia, but tried to conform to the new order of things with no audible complaint and no useless repinings," a newspaper editor noted.

He enjoyed being a farmer and was "proud of his occupation." As such he "mingled freely and congenially" with all other tillers of the soil. A fellow Virginian said of Lee's character: "He practiced from his earliest childhood a scrupulous regard for the rights and feelings of others, and an indulgence to all faults except his own. With a self-control and equipoise which were never disturbed under the most trying circumstances, and a graciousness of manner which broke down all barriers, giving to the humblest as well as the highest the assurance of his friendly consideration."

Like his father, adherence to duty was a salient aspect of Lee's character. "It was the star by which his life was guided," a friend said of his dutifulness. "Once persuaded that a certain measure or certain line of policy was right, and he was unflinchingly firm in its support. No burden was too heavy, no privation too severe, if only they were borne along the path of duty," this friend continued.

Many who knew Lee remarked on his modesty. He was certainly not reticent or shy but rather unpretentious in his approach to others. Throughout his adult life Rooney Lee demonstrated that he possessed the "substance" rather than the "show" that his father had wished for him at Harvard. A congressman from Alabama spoke of this: "He never put himself forward except when duty prompted, and then he did nothing for display." Another wrote that he was a "simple, kindly, unaffected, modest gentleman" who always had a "sweet, calm smile." Yet another put it quite simply: "He sought to be useful rather than to shine."

Lee's faith was just as the man himself was—simple, unaffected, and strong. It permeated his entire being. A fellow Virginian noted this faith in his tribute to Lee after his death: "As gentle as a child and as tender as a woman, with the courage of a hero and a faith that never faltered." Through the trials of war and the loss of one wife and five children, his faith remained strong. He was brought up to believe in Christ, and his mother and his grandmother Custis served as his early spiritual guides. No matter how hard it may have seemed, he was always willing to submit to the will of God.

Lee was a model husband and father. One who knew him well declared that "it was in the home circle, as husband and father, and not on the battlefield, in civil life, or in the halls of legislation, that the beauty and loveliness of his character drew a halo around him." Another expressed this opinion: "He seemed to me an ideal specimen of true American manhood. His wife was a lady whose appearance at once attracted attention and whose qualities of head and heart charmed and delighted friends and associates. He was a devoted husband. His tender and gentle bearing toward his wife were natural and

unaffected. The daily life and conduct of both were a conspicuous example of the benign influence of a husband and wife who love, honor
and respect each other." When Rooney was in Washington for sessions of Congress, Tabb also came, and they lived at the Ebbitt House.
During the winter they held weekly receptions there. One visitor remembered that these were "most popular" and that "as a hostess
Mrs. Lee was without a rival and her every effort had always been en-
thusiastically seconded by her husband, who was never so happy as
when by the side of his handsome helpmeet extending a cordial welcome to all." Lee was also a devoted father, and one can only guess at
the pain he must have felt in his lifetime to lose five children in infancy. He often carried treats for children in his pockets and delighted
in handing these out. One who knew him wrote that "his love for
little children was intense and beautiful." Perhaps his love of family
can best be expressed by Rooney Lee himself when he wrote to his
wife, "Every day from home is agony! to me!"[9]

Strength of character was emphasized by all those who paid tribute
to Lee in the halls of Congress after his death. For example, a Virginian stated, "The blameless life he had led, his high character, his gentle
and unassuming manners won for him not only the respect but the admiration of all with whom he came in contact." One who had served
with him during the war concluded: "In his private relations he was
literally without guile or deceit. Straightforward, honorable, just in all
his dealings, he was a model citizen and faithful friend." One of his
subordinates summed him up: "The soul of candor, his heart shone in
his eye."[10]

Rooney Lee was very much the product of his family lineage. As
the grandson of Light Horse Harry Lee and the son of Robert Edward
Lee, he was a third-generation general, cavalryman, and Rebel. Although he never knew his grandfather on the Lee side, the tradition of
the Revolutionary War cavalry hero had been handed down to him.
Ironically the grandfather he did know well seems to have had less effect on him. In fact, Rooney may have drawn a lesson from this
grandfather's negligence and his dilettantism in farming to map out a
life of practicality, hard work, and progressive farming. As a child
Rooney grew up with the Washington relics and tradition that Mr.
Custis had enshrined at Arlington, and this may have had more lasting effect on him than the grandfather himself.

Rooney never knew his grandmother Lee, but her precepts of duty, self-sacrifice, faith, and self-control that she inculcated in her son Robert were passed through him. His grandmother Custis was a considerable influence on him. She was known for her "warm heart, piety and kindliness." She was a "simple woman, entirely without ostentation and singularly pious." She loved to garden and kept a greenhouse. Roses were her joy and pride, and she shared this love with her grandson.[11]

Robert Edward Lee was the single most important factor in shaping the life of his son. Rooney loved and emulated him. As a young man Rooney doubted that he would ever be able to be worthy of his father, but as he matured he became more and more like his father in many ways. Mary Custis Lee was almost equally as important in the molding of the man Rooney Lee would become. She was his earliest teacher. Her faith and her total involvement with the family were traits that she passed on to her son.

A blend of all those who preceded him, Rooney Lee was also a unique individual. The very fact that he was a Lee has caused his achievements and abilities to be overlooked. His lack of self-serving ambition has also been a factor in this. There were many others in the cavalry service on both sides during the war who contributed much less to their causes but whose flamboyance and even arrogance have brought them more attention. In war and in peace, Lee sought to be "useful, rather than to shine." It is time for one who accomplished so much to finally have the recognition due him.

Notes

DU   Duke University, Perkins Library
HL   Huntington Library, San Marino, CA
HSP   Historical Society of Pennsylvania
LOC   Library of Congress
NA   National Archives
SCL   University of South Carolina, South Caroliniana Library
SHC   University of North Carolina, Southern Historical Collection
SHSP *Southern Historical Society Papers*
UOC   University of Chicago
UVA   University of Virginia, Alderman Library
VHS   Virginia Historical Society
VSL   Virginia State Library
W&L   Washington and Lee University, Leyburn Library

CHAPTER 1

1. Douglas Southall Freeman, *R.E. Lee* (New York, 1934–1935) I, 137; Clifford Dowdey, *Lee* (New York, 1965), 42, 96.

2. R.E. Lee to Captain Talcott, June 29, 1837, Lee Family Papers, Virginia Historical Society (hereafter VHS); Emory Thomas, *Robert E. Lee* (New York, 1995), 86; R.E. Lee to Mary Custis Lee, August 21, 1837,

Lee Family Papers, University of Virginia, Alderman Library (hereafter UVA); R.E. Lee to Jack Mackay, October 12, 1837, Lee Family Papers, VHS.

3. Thomas, *Robert E. Lee*, 92–93; R.E. Lee to Harriet Talcott, May 29, 1838, Lee Family Papers, VHS.

4. R.E. Lee to Cassius Lee, August 20, 1838, J.W. Jones, *Life and Letters of General Robert E. Lee* (New York, 1900), 35; R.E. Lee to G.W.P. Custis, August 25, 1838, Lee Family Papers, VHS; Mary Custis Lee to G.W.P. Custis, August 25, 1838, Lee Family Papers, VHS.

5. R.E. Lee to Carter Lee, December 24, 1838, Lee Family Papers, UVA; Mary Custis Lee to Harriett Talcott, January 1, 1839, Lee Family Papers, VHS; R.E. Lee to Carter Lee, January 7, 1839, Lee Family Papers, UVA; R.E. Lee to Mary Lee Fitzhugh Custis, March 20, 1839, Lee Family Papers, VHS; Margaret Sanborn, *Robert E. Lee: A Portrait* (Philadelphia, 1966), I, 124.

6. Thomas, *Robert E. Lee*, 96; R.E. Lee to Mary Custis Lee, June 5, 1839, from Jones, *Life and Letters*, 34–35.

7. Thomas, *Robert E. Lee,* 97; R.E. Lee to Colonel Talcott, April 27, 1840, Lee Family Papers, VHS; Sanborn, *Robert E. Lee: A Portrait*, I, 139.

8. Thomas, *Robert E. Lee*, 101; R.E. Lee to Henry Kayser, September 27, 1842, *Glimpses of the Past: Letters of Robert E. Lee to Henry Kayser* (Missouri Historical Society, St. Louis, 1936); R.E. Lee to Mary Lee Fitzhugh Custis, October 31, 1843, Lee Family Papers, VHS.

9. R.E. Lee to Mary Lee Fitzhugh Custis, April 13, 1844, Lee Family Papers, VHS.

10. R.E. Lee to G.W.C. Lee, June 1, 1844, Lee Family Papers, VHS; R.E. Lee to Carter Lee, September 1, 1844, Lee Family Papers, UVA.

11. R.E. Lee to Henry Kayser, October 15, 1845, *Glimpses of the Past*; R.E. Lee to Martha Williams, September 17, 1845, Avery Craven, ed., *To Markie: The Letters of Robert E. Lee to Martha Custis Williams* (Cambridge, 1938), 14; Mary Custis Lee to Mary Lee Fitzhugh Custis, October 27, 1844, Lee Family Papers, VHS.

12. Freeman, *R.E. Lee*, I, 196; R.E. Lee to G.W.C. Lee, November 30, 1845, Lee Family Papers, VHS.

13. R.E. Lee to Henry Kayser, December 19, 1845, *Glimpses of the Past*, 40–41.

14. R.E. Lee to G.W.C. Lee, November 30, 1845, Lee Family Papers, VHS; R.E. Lee to Henry Kayser, December 19, 1845, *Glimpses of the*

Past, 40–41; W.H.F. Lee to G.W.C. Lee, December 18, 1845, Lee Family Papers, UVA; R.E. Lee to G.W.C. Lee, December 18, 1845, Lee Family Papers, UVA; Mary Custis Lee to Mary Lee Fitzhugh Custis, December 25, 1845, Lee Family Papers, VHS.

15. R.E. Lee to Mary Custis Lee, January 21, 1846, Lee Family Papers, VHS; Robert E. Lee Jr., *Recollections and Letters of General Robert E. Lee* (Garden City, New York, 1924), 9.

16. R.E. Lee to Mary Custis Lee, March 24, 1846, Lee Family Papers, VHS; R.E. Lee to Mary Custis Lee, February 5, 1846, Lee Family Papers, VHS; R.E. Lee to Henry Kayser, July 4, 1846, *Glimpses of the Past*.

17. Thomas, *Robert E. Lee*, 112; R.E. Lee to Mary Custis Lee, December, 1846, Lee Family Papers, VHS.

18. R.E. Lee to W.H.F. Lee and G.W.C. Lee, December 24, 1846, Lee Family Papers, Library of Congress (hereafter LOC); R.E. Lee to W.H.F. Lee, April 11, 1847, Lee Family Papers, VHS.

19. Freeman, *R. E. Lee*, I, 309; Sanborn, *Robert E. Lee: A Portrtrait*, I, 199.

20. Freeman, *R. E. Lee*, I, 309–310; Mary Custis Lee to G.W.C. Lee, December 1, 1851, Lee Family Papers, VHS; Sanborn, *Robert E. Lee: A Portrait*, I, 209.

21. R.E. Lee to G.W.C. Lee, December 28, 1851, from Jones, *Life and Letters*, 76–77.

22. R.E. Lee to G.W.C. Lee, January 12, 1852, Lee Family Papers, VHS.

23. Sanborn, *Robert E. Lee: A Portrait*, I, 207–208.

24. R.E. Lee to Mary Custis Lee, August 22, 1852, Lee Family Papers, VHS; R.E. Lee to W.H.F. Lee, February 2, 1853, Lee Family Papers, Washington and Lee University, Leyburn Library (hereafter W&L); R.E. Lee to W.H.F. Lee, March 3, 1853, Lee Family Papers, VHS; Mary Custis Lee de Butts, ed., *Growing Up in the 1850's: The Journal of Agnes Lee* (Chapel Hill, 1984) 16, 43.

25. Thomas, *Robert E. Lee*, 153; R.E. Lee to Martha Williams, September 16, 1853, from *To Markie*, 35–37; G.W.C. Lee to Mary Lee Fitzhugh Custis, March 19, 1853, Lee Family Papers, VHS; R.E. Lee to W.H.F. Lee, March 3, 1853, Lee Family Papers, VHS; R.E. Lee to Mary Custis Lee, May 21, Lee Family Papers, VHS; R.E. Lee to W.H.F. Lee, June 15, 1853, Lee Family Papers, UVA.

26. Thomas, *Robert E. Lee*, 159; de Butts, ed., *Growing Up in the 1850's*, 13; W.H.F. Lee to Mary Custis Lee, May 13, 1853, Lee Family Papers, VHS.

27. de Butts, ed., *Growing Up in the 1850's*, 18; W.H.F. Lee to Mary Custis Lee, May 13, 1853, Lee Family Papers, VHS; R.E. Lee to Martha Williams, September 16, 1853, from Craven, ed., *To Markie*, 37.

28. de Butts, ed., *Growing Up in the 1850's*, 33; R.E. Lee to Anna Maria Fitzhugh, April 3, 1854, Lee Family Papers, VHS; Sanborn, *Robert E. Lee: A Portrait*, I, 229.

CHAPTER 2

1. Sanborn, *Robert E. Lee: A Portrait*, I, 227.

2. Edward Chalfant, *Both Sides of the Ocean: A Biography of Henry Adams His First Life* (Hamden, Connecticut, 1982), 55; N. L. Anderson, *Journal and Letters of N. L. Anderson*, 13, 15, 129–131.

3. Chalfant, *Both Sides of the Ocean*, 55; Anderson, *Journal*, 14, 129–131.

4. Anderson, *Journal*, 16–17, 22, 25.

5. Archives, HU; Anderson, *Journal*, 36, 106.

6. Anderson, *Journal*, 21, 33–34, 36, 41, 52, 53–54, 56; Benjamin W. Crowninshield, *A Private Journal, 1856–1858* (Cambridge, 1941), 2–3, 6, 381.

7. Henry Adams, *The Education of Henry Adams* (Boston, 1918), 57; Anderson, *Journal*, 31, 48–49, 57, 65.

8. Mary Custis Lee to John R. Peters, February 2, 1855, Lee Family Papers, VHS.

9. de Butts, ed., *Growing up in the 1850's*, 47, 59.

10. Anderson, *Journal*, 39, 50–52, 54.

11. de Butts, ed., *Growing up in the 1850's*, 72; Freeman, *R. E. Lee*, I, 361; R.E. Lee to Mary Custis Lee, August 5, 1855, Lee Family Papers, VHS; R.E. Lee to Mary Custis Lee, August 20, 1855, Lee Family Papers, VHS.

12. R.E. Lee to Mary Custis Lee, September 13, 1856, Lee Family Papers, VHS.

13. R.E. Lee to Mary Custis Lee, September 3, 1855, Lee Family Papers, VHS; R.E. Lee to Mary Custis Lee, September 9, 1855, Lee Family Papers, VHS.

14. R.E. Lee to Mary Custis Lee, September 3, 1855, Lee Family Papers, VHS; Anderson, *Journal*, 35, 73, 76; Chalfant, *Both Sides of the Ocean*, 63–65.

15. Anderson, *Journal*, 114–115.

16. Anderson, *Journal*, 85–86.

17. R.E. Lee to Mary Custis Lee, March 28, 1856, Lee Family Papers, VHS.

18. W.H.F. Lee to Mary Custis Lee, March 30, 1856, Lee Family Papers, VHS.

19. Dr. Johnson to Mary Custis Lee, May 30, 1856, Lee Family Papers, VHS; R.E. Lee to Mary Custis Lee, July 28, 1856, Lee Family Papers, VHS; R.V. Pierce, *The People's Common Sense Medical Advisor* (Buffalo, 1886), 405–406; de Butts, ed., *Growing Up in the 1850's*, 94–95.

20. R.E. Lee to Mary Custis Lee, August 4, 1856, Lee Family Papers, VHS; R.E. Lee to Mary Custis Lee, September 13, 1856, Lee Family Papers, VHS.

21. Mary Custis Lee to R.E. Lee, September 6, 1856, Lee Family Papers, VHS.

22. R.E. Lee to W.H.F. Lee, November 1, 1856, Lee Family Papers, LOC.

23. R.E. Lee to Mary Custis Lee, January 31, 1857, Lee Family Papers, VHS; R.E. Lee to Mary Custis Lee, December 10, 1856, Lee Family Papers, VHS.

24. R.E. Lee to Mary Custis Lee, January 31, 1857, Lee Family Papers, VHS; R.E. Lee to Mary Custis Lee, March 7, 1857, Lee Family Papers, VHS.

25. Crowninshield, *A Private Journal*, 53, 56; *Dictionary of American Biography*, Vol. 6.

26. R.E. Lee to Mary Custis Lee, March 13, 1857, Lee Family Papers, VHS.

27. R.E. Lee to Mary Custis Lee, May 18, 1857, Lee Family Papers, VHS; R.E. Lee to Mary Custis Lee, May 25, 1857, Lee Family Papers, VHS.

28. Sanborn, *Robert E. Lee: A Portrait*, I, 263; Charles B. Hall, *Generals of the C. S. Army, 1861–1865* (New York, 1898), 78; W.H.F. Lee to Mary Custis Lee, June 2, 1857, Lee Family Papers, VHS.

29. Jones, *Life and Letters,* 127–128.

30. Adams, *The Education of Henry Adams*, 59; Crowninshield, *A Private Journal*, 59.

31. Adams, *The Education of Henry Adams*, 58.

32. *Memorial Addresses on the Life and Character of Gen. William Henry Fitzhugh Lee* (Washington, D.C., 1892), 76–78.

33. Crowninshield, *A Private Journal*, 20; Adams, *The Education of Henry Adams*, 57; Patricia O'Toole, *The Five of Hearts: An Intimate*

Portrait of Henry Adams and His Friends, 1880–1918 (New York, 1990), 387; Chalfant, *Both Sides of the Ocean,* 57; *Memorial Addresses,* 41, 46, 70, 89.

34. Adams, *The Education of Henry Adams,* 58; Anderson, *Journal,* 27, 77; R.E. Lee to W.H.F. Lee, May 30, 1858, Lee Family Papers, VHS.

35. Worthington Chauncey Ford, ed., *Letters of Henry Adams, 1858–1891* (Boston, 1930), 98, 109.

CHAPTER 3

1. Mary Custis Lee to R.E. Lee, June 24, 1857, Lee Family Papers, VHS; Mary Custis Lee to Helen (friend), July 3, 1857, Lee Family Papers, W&L.

2. R.E. Lee to Mary Custis Lee, July 5, 1857, Lee Family Papers, VHS.

3. Mary Custis Lee to R.E. Lee, July 7, 1857, Lee Family Papers, VHS; Mary Custis Lee to R.E. Lee, July 25, 1857, Lee Family Papers, VHS; Annie Lee to R.E. Lee, July 30, 1857, Lee Family Papers, VHS.

4. R.E. Lee to Mary Custis Lee, New York, 1857, Lee Family Papers, VHS; R.E. Lee to Mary Custis Lee, August 12, 1857, Lee Family Papers, VHS.

5. Mary Custis Lee to R.E. Lee, August 4, 1857, Lee Family Papers, VHS.

6. Freeman, *R.E. Lee,* I, 389.

7. R.E. Lee to Mary Custis Lee, August 12, 1857, Lee Family Papers, VHS.

8. R.E. Lee to Mary Custis Lee , August 22, 1857, Lee Family Papers, VHS; R.E. Lee to Mary Custis Lee, October 10, 1857, Lee Family Papers, VHS.

9. R.E. Lee to Mary Custis Lee, August 22, 1857, Lee Family Papers, VHS; Mary Custis Lee to R.E. Lee, October 2, 1857, Lee Family Papers, VHS.

10. Mary Custis Lee to R.E. Lee, October 2, 1857, Lee Family Papers, VHS; R.E. Lee to Charlotte Wickham Lee, October 10, 1857, Lee Family Papers, LOC.

11. Jones, *Life and Letters,* 87; de Butts, ed., *Growing Up in the 1850's,* 99–100; Mary Custis Lee to R.E. Lee, October 11, 1857, Lee Family Papers, VHS.

12. R.E. Lee to G.W.C. Lee, January 17, 1858, Lee Family Papers, Duke University, Perkins Library (hereafter DU); Annie Lee to Helen Bratt, February 10, 1858, Lee Family Papers, W&L; R.E. Lee to G.W.C. Lee, February 15, 1858, Lee Family Papers, DU; R.E. Lee to W.H.F. Lee, February 24, 1858, Lee Family Papers, VHS.

13. R.E. Lee to G.W.C. Lee, March 17, 1858, Lee Family Papers, DU; R.E. Lee to G.W.C. Lee, May 17, 1858, Lee Family Papers, DU.

14. Henry Heth, *The Memoirs of Henry Heth* (Westport, Connecticut, 1974), 142.

15. R.E. Lee to W.H.F. Lee, May 30, 1858, Lee Family Papers, VHS.

16. Charles P. Roland, *Albert Sidney Johnston: Soldier of Three Republics* (Lexington, KY, 2001), 211–214, 218–219, 224–228.

17. R.E. Lee to W.H.F. Lee, August 7, 1858, Lee Family Papers, VHS.

18. R.E. Lee to W.H.F. Lee, January 1, 1858, Lee Family Papers, VHS.

19. Annie Lee to Helen Bratt, February 15, 1859, Lee Family Papers, W&L.

20. R.E. Lee to W.H.F. Lee, February 5, 1859, Lee Family Papers, VHS; R.E. Lee to Anna Maria Fitzhugh, February 17, 1859, Lee Family Papers, DU; Freeman, *R. E. Lee*, I, 389.

21. Freeman, *R. E. Lee*, I, 9, 389; Sanborn, *Robert E. Lee: A Portrait*, I, 281; Hall, *Generals of the C. S. Army, 1861–1865*, 78.

22. R.E. Lee to G.W.C. Lee, May 30, 1859, Lee Family Papers, VHS.

23. R.E. Lee to G.W.C. Lee, August 17, 1859, Lee Family Papers, VHS; C. Vann Woodward, ed., *Mary Chesnut's Civil War* (New Haven, 1981), 116.

24. R.E. Lee to W.H.F. Lee, January 1, 1860, Lee Family Papers, VHS.

25. Mary Custis Lee to Ladies at Arlington, March 10, 1860, Lee Family Papers, LOC; R.E. Lee to W.H.F. Lee, April 2, 1860, Lee Family Papers, VHS.

26. Mary Custis Lee to Ladies at Arlington, March 10, 1860, Lee Family Papers, LOC; R.E. Lee to W.H.F. Lee, January 29, 1861, Lee Family Papers, VHS; Sanborn, *Robert E. Lee: A Portrait*, I, 302; R.E. Lee to Mildred Lee, March 15, 1861, Lee Family Papers, VHS; Mary Custis Lee to a daughter, April 10, 1861, Lee Family Papers, VHS.

27. R.E. Lee to G.W.C. Lee, December 14, 1860, Lee Family Papers, VHS; R.E. Lee to G.W.C. Lee, January 23, 1861, Lee Family Papers, VHS.

28. Jones, *Life and Letters*, 125; R.E. Lee to Mary Custis Lee, May 13, 1861, Lee Family Papers, VHS; S. L. Lee, "War Time in Alexandria, Virginia," *South Atlantic Quarterly* (July 1905), 235.

CHAPTER 4

1. W.H.F. Lee to Governor John Letcher, April 20, 1861, Greer Collection, Historical Society of Pennsylvania.

2. Hall, *Generals of the C.S. Army, 1861–1865*, 78; "The Famous Lee Rangers," *SHSP*, Vol. 23, 290.

3. Military Service Records, National Archives.

4. G. W. Beale, *A Lieutenant of Cavalry in Lee's Army* (Boston, 1943), 220; "The Battle of Five Forks," *Confederate Veteran*, Vol. 22, 119.

5. R.E. Lee to Mary Custis Lee, July 8, 1861, Lee Family Papers, VHS; R.E. Lee to Mary Custis Lee, August 9, 1861, Lee Family Papers, VHS; *The War of the Rebellion: A Compilation of the Official Records of the Union and Confederate Armies*, 128 volumes (Washington, 1880–1901), Series II, Vol. 3, 25 (hereafter cited as *OR*).

6. R.E. Lee to Mary Custis Lee, September 1, 1861, Lee Family Papers, VHS; R.E. Lee to Mary Custis Lee, September 9, 1861, Lee Family Papers, VHS; R.E. Lee to G.W.C. Lee, September 3, 1861, Lee Family Papers, VHS.

7. Freeman, *R. E. Lee*, I, 489, 568; W.H.F. Lee to Colonel John Levering, June 8, 1889, Levering Correspondence, UVA; W.H.F. Lee to Colonel John Levering, June 25, 1889, Levering Correspondence, UVA.

8. R.E. Lee to Mary Custis Lee, October 7, 1861, Lee Family Papers, VHS; R.E. Lee to daughters, November 15, 1861, Lee Family Papers, VHS; R.E. Lee to Mary Custis Lee, November 18, 1861, Lee Family Papers, VHS.

9. R.E. Lee Jr. to a sister, December 1, 1861, Lee Family Papers, VHS; R.E. Lee to daughters, December 8, 1861, Lee Family Papers, VHS; R.E. Lee to daughters, December 27, 1861, Lee Family Papers, VHS; R.E. Lee to W.H.F. Lee; December 23, 1861, Lee Family Papers, VHS.

10. R.E. Lee to W.H.F. Lee, December 21, 1861, Lee Family Papers, VHS; R.E. Lee to Charlotte Wickham Lee, December 29, 1861, Lee Family Papers, VHS.

11. R.E. Lee Jr. to Mildred Lee, January 5, 1862, Lee Family Papers, VHS.

12. R.E. Lee to W.H.F. Lee, February 16, 1862, Lee Family Papers, VHS.

13. W.H.F. Lee to Charlotte Wickham Lee, February 27, 1862, Lee Family Papers, VHS.

14. W.H.F. Lee to Charlotte Wickham Lee, Lee Family Papers, VHS.

15. Robert Krick, *Ninth Virginia Cavalry* (Lynchburg, 1982), 3–4; William L. Royall, *Some Reminiscences* (New York, 1909), 11; Richard

B. Armstrong, ed., *The Journal of Charles R. Chewning Company E 9th Virginia Cavalry C. S. A.,* 1.

16. Krick, *Ninth Virginia Cavalry,* 4.

17. R.L.T. Beale, *History of the Ninth Virginia Cavalry* (Richmond, 1899), 15; H.R. McIlwaine, ed., *Two Confederate Items* (Richmond, 1927), from the *Bulletin of the Virginia State Library,* Vol. 16, Numbers 2 and 3, 16–17; Armstrong, ed., *The Journal of Charles R. Chewning,* 2; W.H.F. Lee to Charlotte Wickham Lee, April 21, 1862, Lee Family Papers, VHS.

18. *OR,* Vol. 24, 438–439.

19. *OR,* Vol. 24, 430–431.

20. Armstrong, ed., *The Journal of Charles R. Chewning,* 2; R.L.T. Beale, *History of the Ninth Virginia Cavalry,* 13; Krick, *Ninth Virginia Cavalry,* 4.

21. Krick, *Ninth Virginia Cavalry,* 1; Armstrong, ed., *The Journal of Charles R. Chewning,* 2; Hall, *Generals of the C. S. Army;* 78; National Archives; Mark Mayo Boatner III, *The Civil War Dictionary* (New York, 1959), 53.

22. Krick, *Ninth Virginia Cavalry,* 1–2; R.L.T. Beale, *History of the Ninth Virginia Cavalry,* 16; Armstrong, ed., *The Journal of Charles R. Chewning,* 2–3.

23. Freeman, *R. E. Lee,* II, 80; R.E. Lee to Charlotte Wickham Lee, June 2, 1862, Lee Family Papers, VHS.

24. W.H.F. Lee to Charlotte Wickham Lee, Lee Family Papers, VHS.

CHAPTER 5

1. Emory M. Thomas, *Bold Dragoon: The Life of J.E.B. Stuart* (New York, 1986), 110–111.

2. H. B. McClellan, *I Rode with Jeb Stuart* (Bloomington, 1958), 52–53.

3. John W. Thomason Jr., *Jeb Stuart* (New York, 1930), 141.

4. R.L.T. Beale, *History of the Ninth Virginia Cavalry,* 16–17.

5. Thomas, *Bold Dragoon,* 113; Thomason, *Jeb Stuart,* 14.

6. John Esten Cooke, *Wearing of the Gray* (Bloomington, 1959), 167.

7. G.W. Beale, *A Lieutenant of Cavalry in Lee's Army,* 24–25; Armstrong, ed., *The Journal of Charles R. Chewning,* 4.

8. *OR,* Vol. 11, Part 1, 1037.

9. R.L.T. Beale, *History of the Ninth Virginia Cavalry,* 17; G.W. Beale, *A Lieutenant of Cavalry in Lee's Army,* 25–26.

10. Cooke, *Wearing of the Gray*, 169, Thomas, *Bold Dragoon*, 116–117; *OR*, Vol. 11, Part 1, 1043–1044.

11. Armstrong, ed., *The Journal of Charles R. Chewning*, 4.

12. Cooke, *The Wearing of the Gray*, 169.

13. John S. Mosby, *Mosby's War Reminiscences: Stuart's Cavalry* (New York, 1958), 224; *OR*, Vol. 11, Part 1, 1038.

14. G. W. Beale, *A Lieutenant of Cavalry in Lee's Army*, 27; W.T. Robins, "Stuart's Ride Around McClellan," *Battles and Leaders of the Civil War* (New York, 1887), Vol. 2, 272.

15. McClellan, *I Rode with Jeb Stuart*, 59–60.

16. Cooke, *The Wearing of the Gray*, 170–171; Robins, "Stuart's Ride Around McClellan," 273.

17. Thomason, *Jeb Stuart*, 147.

18. Robins, "Stuart's Ride Around McClellan," 273; R.L.T. Beale, *History of the Ninth Virginia Cavalry*, 19–20.

19. Cooke, *Wearing of the Gray*, 174; McClellan, *I Rode with Jeb Stuart*, 61.

20. McClellan, *I Rode with Jeb Stuart*, 62; Cooke, *The Wearing of the Gray*, 174–175.

21. Robins, "Stuart's Ride Around McClellan," 273; R.L.T. Beale, *History of the Ninth Virginia Cavalry*, 20; Cooke, *Wearing of the Gray*, 175; George A. Townsend, *Rustics in Rebellion* (Chapel Hill, 1950), 118; Mosby, *Reminiscences*, 229.

22. Robins, "Stuart's Ride Around McClellan," 273.

23. McClellan, *I Rode with Jeb Stuart*, 63; Robins, "Stuart's Ride Around McClellan," 273; Richard E. Frayser, "Stuart's Raid in Rear of the Army of the Potomac," *Southern Historical Society Papers* (hereafter *SHSP*), Vol. 11, 1883, 510.

24. Cooke, *Wearing of the Gray*, 177.

25. G. W. Beale, *A Lieutenant of Cavalry in Lee's Army*, 30.

26. McClellan, *I Rode with Jeb Stuart*, 64–65; Cooke, *The Wearing of the Gray*, 178–179.

27. G. W. Beale, *A Lieutenant of Cavalry in Lee's Army*, 31; Cooke, *Wearing of the Gray*, 179.

28. G. W. Beale, *A Lieutenant of Cavalry in Lee's Army*, 31; McIlwaine, ed., *Two Confederate Items*, 69.

29. Armstrong, ed., *The Journal of Charles R. Chewning*, 4.

30. John S. Mosby, "The Ride Around General McClellan," *SHSP*, Vol. 26, 1898, 254.

31. *OR*, Vol. 11, Part 1, 1040–1041.

32. R. E. Lee to Charlotte Wickham Lee, June 22, 1862, Lee Family Papers, VHS.

33. W.H.F. Lee to Charlotte Wickham Lee, June 25, 1862, Lee Family Papers, VHS.

34. G. W. Beale, *A Lieutenant of Cavalry in Lee's Army*, 33.

35. McClellan, *I Rode with Jeb Stuart*, 73; G.W. Beale, *A Lieutenant of Cavalry in Lee's Army*, 34; R.L.T. Beale, *History of the Ninth Virginia Cavalry*, 23.

36. G. W. Beale, *A Lieutenant of Cavalry in Lee's Army*, 34–36.

37. Freeman, *R. E. Lee*, Vol. 2, 159–161.

38. Stephen W. Sears, *To the Gates of Richmond: The Peninsula Campaign* (New York, 1992), 28, 104; James I. Robertson Jr., ed., *The Civil War Letters of General Robert McAllister* (New Brunswick, 1961), 156–157; Charles N. and Rosemary Walker, ed., "Diary of the War by Robert S. Robertson," *Old Fort News*, Vol. 28, 27.

39. Francis Colburn Adams, *A Trooper's Adventures in the War for the Union* (New York, 1863), 455–456, 464; Sears, *To the Gates of Richmond*, 104.

40. W. W. Blackford, *War Years with Jeb Stuart* (New York, 1945), 7 4–75.

41. Walker, ed., "Diary of the War by Robert S. Robertson," 36–38, 220–222, 226.

42. Armstrong, ed., *The Journal of Charles R. Chewning*, 6.

43. McClellan, *I Rode with Jeb Stuart*, 75–76; G.W. Beale, *A Lieutenant of Cavalry in Lee's Army*, 36, 38–39.

44. R.L.T. Beale, *History of the Ninth Virginia Cavalry*, 29.

45. *Registry of St. Paul's Episcopal Church, 1862–1875*; W. H. F. Lee to Charlotte Wickham Lee, July 11, 1862, Lee Family Papers, VHS.

46. Mary Custis Lee to Charlotte Wickham Lee, July 11, 1862, Lee Family Papers, VHS.

47. Mary Custis Lee to Annie Lee, July 27, 1862, Lee Family Papers, VHS.

CHAPTER 6

1. Blackford, *War Years with Jeb Stuart*, 87; R.E. Lee to Charlotte Wickham Lee, Lee Family Papers, VHS; Mary Custis Lee to Lee Girls, August 4 and 6, 1862, Lee Family Papers, VHS.

2. McClellan, *I Rode with Jeb Stuart*, 86–87; Thomas, *Bold Dragoon*, 139–140.

3. R.L.T. Beale, *History of the Ninth Virginia Cavalry*, 29; Krick, *Ninth Virginia Cavalry*, 8; Armstrong, ed., *The Journal of Charles R. Chewning*, 7: McClellan, *I Rode with Jeb Stuart*, 87–88.

4. John J. Hennessy, *Return to Bull Run: The Campaign and Battle of Second Manassas* (New York, 1993), 40.

5. Freeman, *R.E. Lee*, Vol. 2, 264

6. R.L.T. Beale, *History of the Ninth Virginia Cavalry*, 29.

7. Thomas, *Bold Dragoon*, 143–144.

8. Hennessy, *Return to Bull Run*, 12, 67; Blackford, *War Years with Jeb Stuart*, 100.

9. R.L.T. Beale, *History of the Ninth Virginia Cavalry*, 31.

10. Blackford, *War Years with Jeb Stuart*, 100–101.

11. R.L.T. Beale, *History of the Ninth Virginia Cavalry*, 32; Blackford, *War Years with Jeb Stuart*, 103.

12. Blackford, *War Years with Jeb Stuart*, 107; Armstrong, ed., *The Journal of Charles R. Chewning*, 9, 102, 104.

13. R.L.T. Beale, *History of the Ninth Virginia Cavalry*, 32.

14. Blackford, *War Years with Jeb Stuart*, 104, 108.

15. *OR*, Vol. 12, Part 2, 731–732

16. Thomas, *Bold Dragon*, 152, 154.

17. R.L.T. Beale, *History of the Ninth Virginia Cavalry*, 34–37; G.W. Beale, *A Lieutenant of Cavalry in Lee's Army*, 42.

18. R.E. Lee to Charlotte Wickham Lee, August 26, 1862, Lee Family Papers. VHS.

19. Thomas, *Bold Dragoon*, 162.

20. R.L.T. Beale, *History of the Ninth Virginia Cavalry*, 37–38; Stephen W. Sears, *Landscape Turned Red: The Battle of Antietam* (New York, 1983), 83.

21. G.W. Beale, *A Lieutenant of Cavalry in Lee's Army*, 44–45.

22. McClellan, *I Rode with Jeb Stuart*, 125; Maps of Boonsboro.

23. G.W. Beale, *A Lieutenant of Cavalry in Lee's Army*, 45.

24. McClellan, *I Rode with Jeb Stuart*, 126.

25. Sears, *Landscape Turned Red*, 175, 291; G.W. Beale, *A Lieutenant of Cavalry in Lee's Army*, 49.

26. Henry Kid Douglas, *I Rode with Stonewall* (Chapel Hill, 1940), 159–160; Alexandra Lee Levin, *This Awful Drama: General Edwin Gray Lee, C.S.A., and His Family* (New York, 1987), 45.

CHAPTER 7

1. R.L.T. Beale, *History of the Ninth Virginia Cavalry*, 43–44; OR, Vol. 19, Part 2, 10, 13.

2. Thomas, *Bold Dragoon*, 171; OR, Vol. 19, Part 2, 11–12; R.L.T. Beale, *History of the Ninth Virginia Cavalry*, 45.

3. OR, Vol. 19, Part 2, 11–14, 55.

4. McClellan, *I Rode with Jeb Stuart*, 136–137; OR, Vol. 19, Part 2, 56; Blackford, *War Years with Jeb Stuart*, 164.

5. McClellan, *I Rode with Jeb Stuart*, 138–139; OR, Vol. 19, Part 2, 31–33, 36–38.

6. Blackford, *War Years with Jeb Stuart*, 166–168; McClellan, *I Rode with Jeb Stuart*, 140–141.

7. Blackford, *War Years with Jeb Stuart*, 165.

8. OR, Vol. 19, Part 2, 52–53; McClellan, *I Rode with Jeb Stuart*, 149; Blackford, *War Years with Jeb Stuart*, 170–171, 173.

9. Blackford, *War Years with Jeb Stuart*, 174–175; OR, Vol. 19, Part 2, 40, 42, 59; McClellan, *I Rode with Jeb Stuart*, 152; *Harper's New Monthly Magazine*, 573–574.

10. OR, Vol. 19, Part 2, 53; McClellan, *I Rode with Jeb Stuart*, 155–158, 160–161; Blackford, *War Years with Jeb Stuart*, 176.

11. OR, Vol. 19, Part 2, 42; *Harper's*, 574; Russell Duncan, ed., *Blue-Eyed Child of Fortune: The Civil War Letters of Colonel Robert Gould Shaw* (Athens, 1992), 253; Sears, *Landscape Turned Red*, 328; William R. Brooksher and David K. Snider, "A Piece of Rebel Rascality," *Civil War Times Illustrated* (April 1973), 48.

12. Blackford, *War Years with Jeb Stuart*, 180–181; OR, Vol. 19, Part 2, 669, 712; OR, Vol. 21, 544.

13. R.E. Lee to Charlotte Wickham Lee, October 19, 1862, Lee Family Papers, VHS.

14. Mary P. Coulling, *The Lee Girls* (Winston-Salem, 1987), 108–110; R.E. Lee Jr. to Mary Custis Lee, October 30, 1862, Lee Family Papers, VHS.

15. Mary Custis Lee to Mary Lee, November, 1862, Lee Family Papers, VHS; R.E. Lee to Mary Custis Lee, November 13, 1862, Lee Family Papers, VHS.

16. R.E. Lee Jr., *Recollections and Letters of General Lee*, 81, 84.

17. OR, Vol. 21, 1013–1014, 1020, 551.

18. G. W. Beale, *A Lieutenant of Cavalry in Lee's Army*, 59–61; OR, Vol. 21, 37.

19. Samuel N. Mason to home, October 9, 1862, North Carolina Museum of History.

20. *Registry of St. Paul's Episcopal Church,* Richmond, VA; R.E. Lee to Charlotte Wickham Lee, December 10, 1862, Lee Family Papers, VHS.

21. G. W. Beale, *A Lieutenant of Cavalry in Lee's Army,* 65–66; OR, Vol. 21, 558; Freeman, *R.E. Lee,* II, 472.

22. Thomas, *Bold Dragoon,* 195–197; McClellan, *I Rode with Jeb Stuart,* 196–197; OR, Vol. 33, 733.

23. OR, Vol. 33, 733–735, 742; McClellan, *I Rode with Jeb Stuart,* 200, 202.

CHAPTER 8

1. R.E. Lee to Mary Custis Lee, January 8, 1863, Lee Family Papers, VHS.

2. R.E. Lee Jr. to his sisters, January 18, 1863, Lee Family Papers, VHS; R.E. Lee to Mary Custis Lee, January 21, 1863, Lee Family Papers, VHS.

3. R.L.T. Beale, *History of the Ninth Virginia Cavalry,* 60.

4. OR, Vol. 25, Part 1, 20; *Naval OR,* Series I, Vol. 5, 256.

5. Blackford, *War Years with Jeb Stuart,* 203; John Bigelow Jr., *The Campaign of Chancellorsville* (New Haven, 1910), 136, 25; OR, Vol. 31, 983.

6. Daniel T. Balfour, *13th Virginia Cavalry* (Lynchburg, 1986), 12; McClellan, *I Rode with Jeb Stuart,* 260; Walter Clark, ed., *Histories of the Several Regiments and Battalions from North Carolina in the Great War, 1861–1865,* rpt. (Wendell, NC, 1982), Vol. II, 79; R.E. Lee to Mary Custis Lee, February 23, 1863, Lee Family Papers, VHS.

7. W.H.F. Lee to Major Fitzhugh, March 4, 1863, Historical Society of Pennsylvania (hereafter HSP); R.E. Lee to Charlotte Wickham Lee, March 3, 1863, Lee Family Papers, VHS; R.E. Lee, to Mary Custis Lee, March 27, 1863, Lee Family Papers VHS.

8. R.L.T. Beale, *History of the Ninth Virginia Cavalry,* 60; Bigelow, *The Campaign of Chancellorsville,* 134, 136.

9. William K. Goolrick, *Rebels Resurgent: Fredericksburg to Chancellorsville* (Alexandria,VA, 1985), 105; Bigelow, *The Campaign of Chancellorsville,* 142–143, 145–146; R.L.T. Beale, *History of the Ninth Virginia Cavalry,* 60; Balfour, *13th Virginia Cavalry,* 14.

10. Bigelow, *The Campaign of Chancellorsville,* 147–148; OR, Vol. 37, 85.

11. Heros von Borcke, *Memoirs of the Confederate War for Independence* (Dayton, 1985), Vol. II, 196–197.

12. Bigelow, *The Campaign of Chancellorsville,* 148.

13. OR, Vol. 37, 85–86; R.L.T. Beale, *History of the Ninth Virginia Cavalry*, 61.

14. Bigelow, *The Campaign of Chancellorsville*, 152; OR, Vol. 37, 86.

15. Bigelow, *The Campaign of Chancellorsville*, 160, 183.

16. OR, Vol. 37, 1074–1075, 1078; G.W. Beale, *A Lieutenant of Cavalry in Lee's Army*, 70; Bigelow, *The Campaign of Chancellorsville*, 257.

17. OR, Vol. 37, 1076, 1080, 1073; Bigelow, *The Campaign of Chancellorsville*, 268–269.

18. OR, Vol. 37, 1098, 442–443; Bigelow, *The Campaign of Chancellorsville*, 441–442.

19. OR, Vol. 37, 1060–1061; Bigelow, *The Campaign of Chancellorsville*, 443.

20. OR, Vol. 37, 1097–1098, 1085; G.W. Beale, *A Lieutenant of Cavalry in Lee's Army*, 73.

21. Bigelow, *The Campaign of Chancellorsville*, 450, OR, Vol. 37, 1089, 1098–1099.

22. Bigelow, *The Campaign of Chancellorsville*, 454, 457, 459.

23. OR, Vol. 37, 1069, 1090; Charles Frances Adams to his mother, May 12, 1863, from Worthington Chauncey Ford, ed., *A Cycle of Adams Letters* (Boston, 1920), Vol. 2, 5; Bigelow, *The Campaign of Chancellorsville*, 459.

24. *Richmond Sentinel*, May 16, 1863, reprinted in the *New York Herald*, May 18, 1863.

25. OR, Vol. 37, 804, 1047; Bigelow, *The Campaign of Chancellorsville*, 456.

26. G.W. Beale, *A Lieutenant of Cavalry in Lee's Army*, 74; W.H.F. Lee to R.E. Lee, May 1863, Lee Family Papers, VHS.

27. W.H.F. Lee to Mary Custis Lee, May 17, 1863, Lee Family Papers, VHS.

CHAPTER 9

1. Thomas, *Bold Dragoon*, 215–216; Krick, *Ninth Virginia Cavalry*, 18.

2. W.H.F. Lee to Mary Custis Lee, May 17, 1863, Lee Family Papers, VHS; Heros Von Borcke and Justus Scheibert, *The Great Cavalry Battle of Brandy Station* (Winston-Salem, 1976), 11, 28; Blackford, *War Years with Jeb Stuart*, 207–208.

3. R.E. Lee to Mary Custis Lee, May 23, 1863, Lee Family Papers, VHS; R.E. Lee to W.H.F. Lee, May 1863, Lee Family Papers, VHS.

4. Thomas, *Bold Dragoon*, 216; R.E. Lee to Mary Custis Lee, May 31, 1863, Lee Family Papers, VHS.

5. von Borcke, *Memoirs of the Confederate War*, Vol. 2, 263.

6. Thomas, *Bold Dragoon*, 215.

7. *OR*, Vol. 27, Part 3, 3, 8; G.W. Beale, *A Lieutenant of Cavalry in Lee's Army*, 80.

8. Blackford, *War Years with Jeb Stuart*, 211–212; Edward Longacre, *The Cavalry at Gettysburg* (Rutherford, 1986), 39.

9. von Borcke, *Brandy Station*, 20; Blackford, *War Years with Jeb Stuart*, 212; "The General's Tour," *Blue and Gray* (October 1990), 56.

10. *OR*, Vol. 27, Part 3, 14, 32; *New York Herald*, June 8, 1863.

11. Longacre, *The Cavalry of Gettysburg*, 40–41; John N. Opie, *A Rebel Cavalryman with Lee, Stuart, and Jackson* (Dayton, 1972), 145–146; Blackford, *War Years with Jeb Stuart*, 212–213.

12. R.E. Lee Jr., *Recollections and Letters of General Lee*, 95–96.

13. R.E. Lee to Mary Custis Lee, June 9, 1863, Lee Family Papers, LOC; R.E. Lee to Colonel Josiah Gorgas, June 8, 1863, National Archives (hereafter NA).

14. G. W. Beale, *A Lieutenant of Cavalry in Lee's Army*, 81–82.

15. *OR*, Vol. 27, Part 3, 16–17; *OR*, Vol. 27, Part 1, 168–170; Longacre, *The Cavalry at Gettysburg*, 41–42, 63.

16. *OR*, Vol. 21, Part 3, 32; Gary W. Gallagher, "Brandy Station: The Civil War's Bloodiest Arena of Mounted Conflict," *Blue and Gray* (October 1990), 11–12.

17. Longacre, *The Cavalry at Gettysburg*, 65–66; George M. Neese, *Three Years in the Confederate Horse Artillery* (New York, 1911), 171.

18. Report of John Buford, June 13, 1863, Huntington Library, San Marino, California (hereafter HL); Longacre, *The Cavalry at Gettysburg*, 67; Boatner, *The Civil War Dictionary*, 97; Daniel Oakey, *History of the Second Massachusetts Regiment of Infantry* (Boston, 1884), 7; *OR*, Vol. 27, Part 2, 749.

19. Clark, ed., *North Carolina Regiments*, Vol. 2, 90; *OR*, Vol. 27, Part 2, 749; *OR*, Vol. 27, Part 3, 38.

20. Report of John Buford, June 13, 1863, HL; Gallagher, "Brandy Station," 18; Henry C. Whelan letter, June 11, 1863, Cadwalader Collection, HSP.

21. Clark B. Hall, "Long and Desperate Encounter: Buford at Brandy Station," *Civil War* (July–August 1990), 17.

22. Gallagher, "Brandy Station," 19–20; Report of John Buford, June 13, 1863, HL; Clark, ed., *North Carolina Regiments*, Vol. 2, 91.

23. McClellan, *I Rode with Jeb Stuart*, 280–281; Hall, "Long and Desperate Encounter," 17; Gallagher, "Brandy Station," 50 (map).

24. *OR*, Vol. 27, Part 1, 903; Report of John Buford, June 13, 1863, HL; Oakey, *History of the Second Massachusetts Regiment of Infantry*, 9, 13; *OR*, Vol. 25, Part 2, 823; Longacre, *The Cavalry at Gettysburg*, 60.

25. Gallagher, "Brandy Station," 48, 50.

26. McClellan, *I Rode with Jeb Stuart*, 282; G.W. Beale, *A Lieutenant of Cavalry in Lee's Army*, 95–96; William L. Royall, *Some Reminiscences* (New York, 1909), 13.

27. G. W. Beale, *A Lieutenant of Cavalry in Lee's Army*, 96; Oakey, *History of the Second Massachusetts Regiment of Infantry*, 13; Longacre, *The Cavalry at Gettysburg*, 84–85.

28. G. W. Beale, *A Lieutenant of Cavalry in Lee's Army*, 96; Clark, ed., *North Carolina Regiments*, Vol. 2, 91–92.

29. R.L.T. Beale, *History of the Ninth Virginia Cavalry*, 68; G.W. Beale, *A Lieutenant of Cavalry in Lee's Army*, 223.

30. McClellan, *I Rode with Jeb Stuart*, 283; Report of John Buford, June 13, 1863, HL; Gallagher, "Brandy Station," 50; Longacre, *The Cavalry at Gettysburg*, 86.

31. Clark B. Hall, "The Battle of Brandy Station," *Civil War Times Illustrated* (May–June 1990), 45; Report of John Buford, June 13, 1863, HL; G.W. Beale, *A Lieutenant of Cavalry in Lee's Army*, 97; *OR*, Vol. 27, Part 2, 684.

32. Gallagher, "Brandy Station," 51–52; McClellan, *I Rode with Jeb Stuart*, 293–294; Hall, "The Battle of Brandy Station," 42.

33. McClellan, *I Rode with Jeb Stuart*, 281; *OR*, Vol. 27, Part 2, 682–683; Adele H. Mitchell, ed., *The Letters of Major General James E. B. Stuart* (Stuart Mosby Historical Society, 1990), 324; Willard Glazier, *Three Years in the Federal Cavalry* (New York, 1870), 221; von Borcke, *The Battle of Brandy Station*, 106; Von Borcke, *Memoirs of the Confederate War*, Vol. 2, 278.

34. *New York Herald*, June 11, 1863, June 14, 1863, and June 16, 1863.

CHAPTER 10

1. R.E. Lee to Mary Custis Lee, June 11, 1863, Lee Family Papers, LOC; R.E. Lee to Charlotte Wickham Lee, June 11, 1863, from Jones, *Life and Letters*, 245–246; *Historic Culpeper* (Culpeper, 1974), 17; Conversation

with Miss Lucy Wiltshire, October 1985, owner of the Hill Mansion at that time. Note: This brick Victorian mansion, built circa 1855, still stands at 501 S. East Street in Culpeper.

2. R.E. Lee Jr., *Recollections and Letters of General Lee*, 97; R.E. Lee to W.H.F. Lee, June 10, 1863, from Jones, *Life and Letters*, 245.

3. R.E. Lee to Charlotte Wickham Lee, June 11, 1863, from Jones, *Life and Letters*, 245–246.

4. R.E. Lee to Mary Custis Lee, June 14, 1863, Lee Family Papers, VHS.

5. R.E. Lee Jr., *Recollections and Letters of General Lee*, 98.

6. OR, Vol. 39, Part 2, 795–796; *History of the Eleventh Pennsylvania Cavalry* (Philadelphia, 1902), 76–77.

7. R.E. Lee Jr., *Recollections and Letters of General Lee*, 98–99.

8. *History of the Eleventh Pennsylvania Cavalry*, 76–77; Boatner, *The Civil War Dictionary*, 781; R.E. Lee Jr., *Recollections and Letters of General Lee*, 99; Arthur Fremantle, *Three Months in the Southern States* (London, 1863), 295; *New York Herald*, June 30, 1863.

9. R.E. Lee Jr., *Recollections and Letters of General Lee*, 100.

10. *Richmond Daily Dispatch*, June 27, 1863; *Daily Richmond Enquirer*, June 29, 1863; *New York Times*, June 29, 1863; *New York Herald*, June 30, 1863.

11. R.E. Lee to Mary Custis Lee, July 7, 1863, Lee Family Papers, LOC; Justus Scheibert, *Seven Months in the Rebel States* (Tuscaloosa, 1958), 102; Freeman, *R.E. Lee*, Vol. 3, 90–91; OR, Vol. 27, Part 1, 76–77.

12. OR, Vol. 39, Part 2, 794; Military Records, NA; Correspondence with R. Cody Phillips, Curator, Casemate Museum, Fortress Monroe, Virginia, November 22, 1983; John Gardner Perry, *Letters from a Surgeon of the Civil War* (Boston, 1906), OR, Series II, Vol. 6, 69.

13. Roger Long, "Johnson's Island Prison," *Blue and Gray* (March 1987); Harry E. Neal, "Rebels, Ropes, and Reprieves," *Civil War Times Illustrated* (February 1976), 30; Frederic Denison, *Sabres and Spurs* (First Rhode Island Cavalry Veteran Association, 1876), 246–247; C.E. Godfrey, *Sketch of Major Henry Washington Sawyer* (Trenton, 1907), 6

14. George E. Lippincott, "Lee-Sawyer Exchange," *Civil War Times Illustrated* (June 1962), 39–40; Godfrey, *Sketch of Major Henry Washington Sawyer*, 7–8; Neal, "Rebels, Ropes, and Reprieves," 35; OR, Series II, Vol. 6, 104, 108–109.

15. Carl Sandburg, *Abraham Lincoln* (New York, 1936), Vol. 4, 351–352, 354; OR, Series II, Vol. 6, 118, 1127.

16. Military Records, NA; Correspondence with R. Cody Phillips, Curator, Casemate Museum, Fortress Monroe, Virginia, November 22, 1983; *OR*, Series II, Vol. 6, 364.

17. Godfrey, *Sketch of Major Henry Washington Sawyer*, 9; *OR*, Series II, Vol. 6, 219, 647–648; R.E. Lee to G.W.C. Lee, August 7, 1863, Lee Family Papers, DU.

18. R.E. Lee to Mary Custis Lee, November 25, 1863, Lee Family Papers, VHS; R.E. Lee to Mary Custis Lee, December 29, 1863, Lee Family Papers, LOC.

19. R.E. Lee to Mary Custis Lee, July 12, 1863, Lee Family Papers, LOC; R.E. Lee to Charlotte Wickham Lee, July 26, 1863 from Jones, *Life and Letters*, 277–278; R.E. Lee to Mary Custis Lee, August 2, 1863, Lee Family Papers, LOC; R.E. Lee to Mary Custis Lee, August 23, 1863, Lee Family Papers, VHS; R.E. Lee to Mary Custis Lee, September 8, 1863, Lee Family Papers, VHS; R.E. Lee to Mary Custis Lee, September 10, 1863, Lee Family Papers, VHS.

20. *OR*, Series II, Vol. 6, 69, 364, 522.

21. R.E. Lee to Mary Custis Lee, December 25, 1863, Lee Family Papers, LOC; Judith W. McGuire, *Diary of a Southern Refugee During the War* (New York, 1867), 233; Mary Custis Lee to Mildred Lee, August 16 and 19, 1863, Lee Family Papers, VHS; R.E. Lee to Charlotte Wickham Lee, July 26, 1863, from Jones, *Life and Letters*, 277–278; R.E. Lee to Mary Custis Lee, August 2, 1863, Lee Family Papers, LOC; R.E. Lee to Mary Custis Lee, September 8, 1863, Lee Family Papers, VHS; George Bolling Lee to Henry St. George Tucker, Lee Family Papers, W&L; R.E. Lee Jr., *Recollections and Letters of General Lee*, 117; Woodward, ed,. *Mary Chesnut's Civil War*, 450.

22. William Best Hesseltine, *Civil War Prisons: A Study in War Psychology* (New York, 1978), 96, 110; R.E. Lee to Mary Custis Lee, August 2, 1863, Lee Family Papers, LOC; R.E. Lee to Mary Custis Lee, October 28, 1863, Lee Family Papers, LOC; R.E. Lee to Mary Custis Lee, November 25, 1863, Lee Family Papers, VHS; William J. Jones, *Personal Reminiscences, Anecdotes and Letters of Gen. Robert E. Lee* (New York, 1875), 184; R.E. Lee to Mary Lee Fitzhugh Custis, March 17, 1852, Lee Family Papers, VHS; *OR*, Series II, Vol, 6, 691.

23. *OR*, Series II, Vol. 6, 358, 362, 488.

24. *New York Times*, November 6, 1863; *Richmond Enquirer*, July 28, 1863; *OR*, Series II, Vol. 6, 161, 192–193, 510–511, 513–514, 523–524.

25. Hesseltine, *Civil War Prisons*, 102; *OR*, Series II, Vol. 6, 484–485, 495, 500, 515, 576; W.H.F. Lee to G.W.C. Lee, November 12, 1863, Lee Family Papers, VHS; R.E. Lee to Mary Custis Lee, November 21, 1863, Lee Family Papers, VHS.

26. "Fort Hamilton at the Narrows." Note: Fort Lafayette was razed in 1959 to make way for the Verrazano Bridge over the Narrows. It was located near the Brooklyn side, where the bridge tower now rises. Correspondence with Phillip A. Melfi, Curator, Harbor Defense Museum of New York City; Clifford Dowdey, *Lee* (New York, 1965), 60, 73; R.E. Lee to W.H.F. Lee, November 1, 1856, Lee Family Papers, VHS; Military Records, NA; Charles J. Faulkner to Abraham Lincoln, October 8, 1861, Manuscripts, DU; *Fort Lafayette Life* (London, 1865), 8–14.

27. *Fort Lafayette Life*, 7–12, 14, 29–31, 33, 37–40, 42; *OR*, Series II, Vol. 6, 654.

28. *Fort Lafayette Life*, 28, 37–39, 42–43, 57, 59–60, 62–64, 70–72; *OR*, Series II, Vol. 6, 688, 911.

29. Mary Custis Lee to Margaret Stuart, December 31, 1863, Lee Family Papers, W&L; R.E. Lee to Mary Custis Lee, December 27, 1863, Lee Family Papers, LOC; R.E. Lee to Mary Custis Lee, December 29, 1863, Lee Family Papers, LOC; R.E. Lee to Margaret Stuart, December 29, 1863, from Jones, *Life and Letters*, 297; McGuire, *Diary of a Southern Refugee During the War*, 233; R.E. Lee to Mary Custis Lee, January 24, 1864, Lee Family Papers, VHS; R.E. Lee to Mary Custis Lee, February 14, 1863, Lee Family Papers, VHS.

30. Neal Dow, *The Reminiscences of Neal Dow* (Portland, 1898), 731–733; Herbert Adams, "Enemy of Rebels and Rum Lovers," *Civil War Times*, March, 1986.

31. *Fort Lafayette Life*, 72, 82–84, 89.

32. Military Records, NA; *Daily Press*, December 1957; R.E. Lee Jr., *Recollections and Letters of General Lee*, 100.

33. Woodward, ed., *Mary Chesnut's Civil War*, 586, 589; R.E. Lee to Mary Custis Lee, March 18, 1864, Lee Family Papers, VHS; R.E. Lee to Mary Custis Lee, March 20, 1863, Lee Family Papers, VHS.

34. J.E.B Stuart to Agnes Lee, September 11, 1863, Lee Family Papers, VHS; J.E.B. Stuart to W.H.F. Lee, March 16, 1864, Lee Family Papers, VHS.

35. R.E. Lee to Mary Custis Lee, March 30, 1864, Lee Family Papers, VHS; R.E. Lee to W.H.F. Lee, April 24, 1864, Lee Family Papers, VHS; R.E. Lee to Mary Custis Lee, April 30, 1864, Lee Family Papers, VHS.

CHAPTER 11

1. Cooke, *War Diaries*, April 1, 1864, DU.

2. J.E.B. Stuart to R.E. Lee, May 27, 1863, Manuscript Collection, VHS; *OR*, Vol. 25, Part 2, 836–837.

3. *OR*, Vol. 27, Part 3, 1068–1069; *OR*, Vol. 29, Part 2, 707–708; *OR*, Vol. 41, 902.

4. J.E.B. Stuart to Samuel Cooper, October 23, 1863, Manuscript Collection, VHS; William C. Davis, ed., *The Confederate General* (National Historical Society, 1991), Vol. 1, 173; *OR*, Vol. 51, Part 2, p. 817.

5. J.E.B. Stuart to Samuel Cooper, March 23, 1864, Records Division, National Archives.

6. Ezra J. Warner, *Generals in Gray* (Baton Rouge, 1981), 381–382.

7. G.W. Beale, *A Lieutenant of Cavalry in Lee's Army*, 220; Krick, *Ninth Virginia Cavalry*, 34; R.L.T. Beale, *History of the Ninth Virginia Cavalry*, 116; Daniel T. Balfour, *13th Virginia Cavalry* (Lynchburg, 1986), 30; R.E. Lee Jr., *Recollections and Letters of General Lee*, 119–120; Diary of John W. Chowning, April 30, 1864, Mary Ball Washington Library; Diary of Byrd C. Willis, May 2, 1864, Virginia State Library.

8. Dowdey, *Lee*, 51, 71.

9. Roy Morris Jr., *Sheridan: The Life and Wars of Phil Sheridan* (New York, 1992), 155, 157–159; Dowdey, *Lee*, 173.

10. Gary W. Gallagher, ed., *Fighting for the Confederacy: The Personal Recollections of General Edward Porter Alexander* (Chapel Hill, 1989), 346; David Crawford to his mother, April 30, 1864, Crawford Family Papers, University of South Carolina, South Caroliniana Library (hereafter SCL); R.E. Lee to Mary Custis Lee, May 2, 1864, Lee Family Papers, LOC: Gordon C. Rhea, *The Battle of the Wilderness, May 5–6, 1864* (Baton Rouge, 1994), 18–21, 25.

11. Dowdy, *Lee*, 61; Rhea, *The Battle of the Wilderness*, 63–65, 82–84; R.L.T Beale, *History of the Ninth Virginia Cavalry*, 116; *OR*, Vol. 36, Part 2, 961–963.

12. Rhea, *The Battle of the Wilderness*, 435–436, 440.

13. *OR*, Vol. 51, Part 2, 898; *OR*, Vol. 36, Part 2, 970–971.

14. R.L.T. Beale, *History of the Ninth Virginia Cavalry*, 117–118; Krick, *Ninth Virginia Cavalry*, 34.

15. R.L.T. Beale, *History of the Ninth Virginia Cavalry*, 119; *OR*, Vol. 51, Part 2, 916–917.

16. Morris, *Sheridan*, 164; Gordon C. Rhea, *The Battles for Spotsylva-nia Court House and the Road to Yellow Tavern, May 7–12, 1864* (Baton Rouge, 1997), 194, 209–210; G.W. Beale, *A Lieutenant of Cavalry in Lee's Army*, 142–143; OR, Vol. 36, Part 2, 1001.

17. William D. Matter, *If It Takes All Summer: The Battle of Spotsyl-vania* (Chapel Hill, 1988), 283–286; OR, Vol. 51, Part 2, 930; G.W. Beale, *A Lieutenant of Cavalry in Lee's Army*, 143–144.

18. Matter, *If It Takes All Summer*, 296; R.L.T. Beale, *History of the Ninth Virginia Cavalry*, 125; OR, Vol. 51, Part 2, 937, 942; Robert J. Driver, *14th Virginia Cavalry* (Lynchburg, 1988), 54; Gallagher, ed., *Fighting for the Confederacy*, 430; Krick, *Ninth Virginia Cavalry*, 35.

19. OR, Vol. 36, Part 3, 801; Matter, *If It Takes All Summer*, 331; G.W. Beale, *A Lieutenant of Cavalry in Lee's Army*, 146–149.

20. Diary of John W. Chowning, May 21, 1864; OR, Vol. 36, Part 3, 44–45; R.L.T. Beale, *History of the Ninth Virginia Cavalry*, 120.

21. Gordon C. Rhea, *To the North Anna River: Grant and Lee, May 13–25, 1864* (Baton Rouge, 2000), 267, 287; R.L.T. Beale, *History of the Ninth Virginia Cavalry*, 121–123.

22. Rhea, *To the North Anna River*, 266.

23. Clark, ed., *North Carolina Regiments*, Vol. 3, 608; *Richmond En-quirer*, June 4, 1864.

24. Wade Hampton, *Connected Narrative*, Hampton Family Papers, SCL, 38; Clifford Dowdey, *Lee's Last Campaign* (Wilmington, 1988), 273–274; *Richmond Enquirer*, June 4, 1864.

25. Hampton, *Connected Narrative*, 39; R.L.T. Beale, *History of the Ninth Virginia Cavalry*, 124; OR, Vol. 57, Part 2, 970.

26. Hampton, *Connected Narrative*, 40; *Richmond Enquirer*, June 4, 1864; Balfour, *13th Virginia Cavalry*, 32.

27. Robert J. Trout, ed., *Riding with Stuart: Reminiscences of an Aide-de-Campe* (Shippensburg, 1994), 74–75, 120.

28. Rufus Barringer, "The First North Carolina," reprint from articles written for the Confederate Veterans Association, 8.

29. *Richmond Enquirer*, June 4, 1864; Hampton, *Connected Narra-tive*, 42; R.E. Lee to Mary Custis Lee, June 4, 1864, Lee Family Papers, LOC; R.E. Lee to Mary Custis Lee, June 7, 1864, Lee Family Papers, LOC.

30. Mary B. Daughtry, "Lincoln Finds a Rebel General," *Blue and Gray* (October 1988), 45; R.L.T. Beale, *History of the Ninth Virginia Cavalry*, 127; Balfour, *13th Virginia Cavalry*, 33; Krick, *Ninth Virginia*

Cavalry, 36; OR, Vol. 51, Part 2, 997–998; *Daily Confederate*, February 22, 1865; OR, Vol. 36, Part 3, 889.

31. Dowdey, *Lee's Last Campaign*, 317, 320; R.E. Lee to Mary Custis Lee, June 12, 1864, Lee Family Papers, LOC.

32. OR, Vol. 51, Part 2, 1009, 1018; Diary of W.A. Curtis.

33. OR, Vol. 40, Part 2, 663; OR, Vol. 51, Part 2, 1080, 1020.

34. Diary of W.A. Curtis.

35. R.E. Lee to Jefferson Davis, June 18, 1864, Virginia State Library (hereafter VSL).

36. Edward G. Longacre, *From Union Stars to Top Hat: A Biography of the Extraordinary General James Harrison Wilson* (Harrisburg, 1972), 134.

37. Boatner, *The Civil War Dictionary*, 930; Morris, *Sheridan*, 158; Longacre, *From Union Stars to Top Hat*, 134–135; OR, Vol. 40, Part 1, 620.

38. Davis, *The Confederate General*, Vol. 2, 55–56; OR, Vol. 40, Part 2, 669.

39. Barringer, "First North Carolina," 9.

40. OR, Vol. 40, Part 1, 621, 645, 731; *History of the 11th Pennsylvania Volunteer Cavalry* (Philadelphia, 1902), 127; Longacre, *From Union Stars to Top Hat*, 135; Barringer, "First North Carolina," 10; Diary of W.A. Curtis.

41. Barringer, "First North Carolina," 10; *Macon Daily Telegraph*, July 14, 1864; A.B. Cummins, *The Wilson-Kautz Raid* (Nottoway, 1959), 5–6; Clark, ed., *North Carolina Regiments*, Vol. 3, 613–614; Diary of W.A. Curtis, DU; OR, Vol. 40, Part 1, 645;OR, Vol. 63, Part 1, 272.

42. *Macon Daily Telegraph*, July 14, 1864; OR, Vol. 63, Part 1, 272; Barringer, "First North Carolina," 10–11; Noah Andre Trudeau, *The Last Citadel* (Boston, 1991), 88; OR, Vol. 40, Part 1, 622, 731; Diary of W.A. Curtis; Longacre, *From Union Stars to Top Hat*, 138–139.

43. *History of the 11th Pennsylvania Volunteer Cavalry*, 130–131, 133. Hampton, *Connected Narrative*; R.L.T. Beale, *History of the Ninth Virginia Cavalry*, 133; Longacre, *From Union Stars to Top Hat*, 139–140.

44. Trudeau, *The Last Citadel*, 90; Frederick H. Dyer, *A Compendium of the War of the Rebellion* (New York, 1959), Vol. 2, 947; *History of the 11th Pennsylvania Volunteer Cavalry*, 132, 135; *Macon Daily Telegraph*, July 14, 1864; Marguerite Merrington, ed., *The Custer Story: The Life and Intimate Letters of Gen. George A. Custer and His Wife Elizabeth* (New York, 1950), 110–111.

45. *OR*, Vol. 40, Part 3, 758; J. William Jones, ed., *Army of Northern Virginia Memorial Volume* (Dayton, 1976), 145–146; Lloyd Halliburton, ed., *Saddle Soldiers: The Civil War Correspondence of General William Stokes of the 4th South Carolina Cavalry* (Orangeburg, 1993), 153; Diary of W.A. Curtis; Longacre, *From Union Stars to Top Hat,* 143.

46. Diary of Leiper Moore Robinson, VHS.

CHAPTER 12

1. Driver, *14th Virginia Cavalry,* 58–59; Report of McGregor's Battery, December 7, 1864, USMHI; Barringer, "Cavalry Sketches," 11.

2. R.E. Lee to Jefferson Davis, July 2, 1864, Manuscripts, VSL; R.E. Lee to Jefferson Davis, July 5, 1864, Manuscripts, VSL.

3. *OR*, Vol. 40, Part 2, 707; *OR*, Vol. 40, Part 3, 762.

4. R.E. Lee Jr., *Recollections and Letters of General Lee,* 131–132.

5. John Sergeant Wise, *The End of an Era* (New York, 1965) 328–329, 333–334.

6. Trudeau, *The Last Citadel,* 17, 146; William C. Davis, ed., *Death in the Trenches* (Alexandria, 1986), 69.

7. R.L.T. Beale, *History of the Ninth Virginia Cavalry,* 136–137; Diary of John W. Gordon, July 28–29, 1864, North Carolina Collection, MOC; Davis, ed., *Death in the Trenches,* 70; Bryce Suderow, unpublished manuscript on Deep Bottom, chapter 9.

8. Diary of W. A. Curtis, DU.

9. Diary of John W. Gordon, July 31–August 14, 1864, North Carolina Collection, MOC; *OR*, Vol. 40, Part 3, 693.

10. R.E. Lee to his sisters, August 12, 1864, Lee Family Papers, VHS.

11. Davis, ed., *Death in the Trenches,* 94–95; Hampton, *Connected Narrative,* 166; Trudeau, *The Last Citadel,* 146–147.

12. John Horn, *The Destruction of the Weldon Railroad: Deep Bottom, Globe Tavern, and Reams Station* (Lynchburg, 1991), 9, 11–12; Trudeau, *The Last Citadel;* 147.

13. *OR*, Vol. 42, Part 2, 1177; Major W.H. Taylor to General Charles W. Field, August 15, 1864, Manuscripts, MOC; Diary of Byrd Willis, VSL; Trudeau, *The Last Citadel,* 151.

14. Diary of Byrd Willis, VSL.

15. Clark, ed., *North Carolina Regiments,* Vol. 3, 619; Horn, *The Destruction of the Weldon Railroad,* 21–22; Diary of John W. Gordon, August 15, 1864, North Carolina Collection, MOC.

16. Horn, *The Destruction of the Weldon Railroad*, 26.

17. G. W. Beale, *A Lieutenant of Cavalry in Lee's Army*, 166–168; Horn, *The Destruction of the Weldon Railroad*, 27; James C. Mohr, *The Cormany Diaries: A Northern Family in the Civil War* (Pittsburgh, 1982), 465.

18. Diary of Byrd Willis, VSL; R.L.T. Beale, *History of the Ninth Virginia Cavalry*, 137–138; Clark, ed., *North Carolina Regiments*, Vol. 3, 619.

19. R.E. Lee to Jefferson Davis (telegram), August 16, 1864, Manuscripts, DU; Horn, *The Destruction of Weldon Railroad*, 27–29.

20. Barringer, "First North Carolina," 11; Clark, ed., *North Carolina Regiments*, Vol. 3, 104.

21. R.L.T. Beale, *History of the Ninth Virginia Cavalry*, 139; Diary of Byrd Willis, VSL.

22. Horn, *The Destruction of the Weldon Railroad*, 29; Diary of W.A. Curtis, DU; Clark, ed., *North Carolina Regiments*, Vol. 3, 619, Diary of John W. Gordon, August 16, 1864, North Carolina Collection, MOC; *Daily Confederate*, February 22, 1865.

23. R.L.T. Beale, *History of the Ninth Virginia Cavalry*, 139–140.

24. Hampton, *Connected Narrative*, 67, SCL.

25. Davis, ed., *Death in the Trenches*, 99; Horn, *The Destruction of the Weldon Railroad*, 48; G.W. Beale, *A Lieutenant of Cavalry in Lee's Army*, 169–170; R.L.T. Beale, *History of the Ninth Virginia Cavalry*, 141.

26. R.E. Lee Jr., *Recollections and Letters of General Lee*, 137.

27. Diary of Byrd Willis, VSL.

28. Hampton, *Connected Narrative*, 68, SCL.

29. OR, Vol. 51, Part 2, 1036; OR, Vol. 42, Part 2, 218–220.

30. Horn, *The Destruction of the Weldon Railroad*, 50, 56; R.L.T. Beale, *The History of the Ninth Virginia Cavalry*, 141; Clark, ed., *North Carolina Regiments*, Vol. 3, 619.

31. Davis, ed., *Death in the Trenches*, 101, 103; Horne, *The Destruction of the Weldon Railroad*, 90; R.L.T. Beale, *The History of the Ninth Virginia Cavalry*, 141; Clark, ed., *North Carolina Regiments*, Vol. 3, 619–620; *Daily Confederate*, February 23, 1865.

32. Davis, ed., *Death in the Trenches*, 104; R.E. Lee to Jefferson Davis, August 22, 1864, Manuscripts, VSL.

33. OR, Vol. 42, Part 2, 1011, 1202; OR, Vol. 51, Part 2, 1036–1037.

34. Barringer, "First North Carolina," 11; OR, Vol. 51, Part 2, 1037, OR, Vol. 42, Part 2, 358–360; 393–394, 410, 418, 441–442.

35. Frank Robertson to sister Kate, August 28, 1864, Manuscripts, University of Chicago (hereafter UOC); R.E. Lee to G.W.C. Lee, August

27, 1864, from Jones, *Life and Letters*, 306; R.E. Lee to Mary Custis Lee, August 28, 1864, Lee Family Papers, LOC.

36. Davis, ed., *Death in the Trenches*, 104–105, 107; Hampton, *Connected Narrative*, 74, SCL; G. W. Beale, *A Lieutenant of Cavalry in Lee's Army*, 184–185.

37. *OR*, Vol. 42, Part 1, 944; Barringer, "First North Carolina," 11; R.E. Lee to G. W. C. Lee, August 27, 1864, Lee Family Papers, VHS; R.E. Lee to Mary Custis Lee, August 28, 1864, Lee Family Papers, LOC.

38. R.L.T. Beale, *History of the Ninth Virginia Cavalry*, 145; G. W. Beale, *A Lieutenant of Cavalry in Lee's Army*, 187; Krick, *Ninth Virginia Cavalry*, 40; Driver, *14th Virginia Cavalry*, 62; *The Sentinel*, September 6, 1864; Barringer, "First North Carolina," 12.

CHAPTER 13

1. Hampton, *Connected Narrative*, 77, SCL.

2. Trudeau, *The Last Citadel*, 194; Clark, ed., *North Carolina Regiments*, Vol. 3, 626.

3. Hampton, *Connected Narrative*, 86, SCL; Davis, ed., *Death in the Trenches*, 111.

4. Hampton, *Connected Narrative*, 78–79; David Cardwell, "Gen. Hampton's Cattle Raid," *SHSP*, Vol. 22, 1894, 149–150; Richard W. Lykes, "The Great Civil War Beef Raid," *Civil War Times Illustrated*, Vol. 5, No. 10 (February 1967), 5–9; Barringer, "First North Carolina," 12.

5. Trudeau, *The Last Citadel*, 198, 200; R.L.T. Beale, *History of the Ninth Virginia Cavalry*, 145–146; G.W. Beale, *A Lieutenant of Cavalry in Lee's Army*, 195; Lykes, "The Great Civil War Beef Raid," 10–11.

6. *OR*, Vol. 42, Part 2, 858; Trudeau, *The Last Citadel*, 200.

7. G.W. Beale, *A Lieutenant of Cavalry in Lee's Army*, 195–196; Hampton, *Connected Narrative*, 80–82; *OR*, Vol. 42, Part 2, 869; Trudeau, *The Last Citadel*, 201; William R. Brooksher and David K. Snider, "A Piece of Rebel Rascality," *Civil War Times Illustrated* (June 1984), 18.

8. Inspection Reports, September 25 and 27, 1864, NA.

9. Davis, ed., *Death in the Trenches*, 150; Richard J. Sommers, *Richmond Redeemed: The Siege at Petersburg* (Garden City, 1981), 110, 196–197; Diary of John W. Gordon, September 29, 1864, North Carolina Collection, MOC.

10. Hampton, *Connected Narrative*, 88–89; Sommers, *Richmond Redeemed*, 205, 289; Davis, *Death in the Trenches*, 152–153; Fred Foard, "Reminiscences," University of North Carolina, Southern Historical Collection (hereafter SHC), 6.

11. Hampton, *Connected Narrative*, 90; Diary of Byrd Willis, VSL; Sommers, *Richmond Redeemed*, 327, 343.

12. Foard, "Reminiscences," SHC, 6–7.

13. Diary of Byrd Willis, VSL.

14. Hampton, *Connected Narrative*, 91, 93; Edward L. Wells, *Hampton and His Cavalry in '64* (Richmond, 1991), 321; Driver, *14th Virginia Cavalry*, 63; Krick, *Ninth Virginia Cavalry*, 41.

15. OR, Vol. 42, Part 3, 1156, 1161; Balfour, *13th Virginia Cavalry*, 39; Diary of Byrd Willis, VSL.

16. OR, Vol. 42, Part 3, 1159–1160; Diary of John W. Gordon, North Carolina Collection, MOC.

17. Trudeau, *The Last Citadel*, 220–221, 230–231, 233; Davis, ed., *Death in the Trenches*, 154–155, Hampton, *Connected Narrative*, 96.

18. Diary of Byrd Willis, VSL.

19. Hampton, *Connected Narrative*, 96–97, 101; Diary of Byrd Willis, VSL.

20. Trudeau, *The Last Citadel*, 249–250.

21. Diary of Byrd Willis, VSL; Clark, ed., *North Carolina Regiments*, Vol. 3, 541.

22. Trudeau, *The Last Citadel*, 251; George R. Agassiz, *Meade's Headquarters 1863–1865: Letters of Theodore Lyman from the Wilderness to Appomattox* (Freeport, 1970), 251; Hampton, *Connected Narrative*, 102; OR, Vol. 42, Part 1, 160.

23. OR, Vol. 42, Part 3, 1187; Inspection Report, W.H.F. Lee's Division, November 1, 1864, NA.

24. R.E. Lee to Mildred Lee, November 6, 1864, Lee Family Papers, VHS; R.E. Lee Jr., *Recollections and Letters of General Lee*, 140.

25. R.E. Lee Jr. to Agnes Lee, November 6, 1864, Lee Family Papers, VHS.

26. OR, Vol. 42, Part 3, 1209; James D. McCabe Jr., *Life and Campaigns of General Robert E. Lee* (Atlanta, 1866), 646.

27. Diary of Leiper Moore Robinson, VHS, 30–33.

28. Trudeau, *The Last Citadel*, 194.

29. OR, Vol. 42, Part 3, 1236; Cavalry Inspection Reports, November 30, 1864, NA.

30. W.H.F Lee to War Department, November 29, 1864, from James D. McCabe Jr., *Life and Campaigns of General Robert E. Lee* (Atlanta, 1866), 647–649.

31. Trudeau, *The Last Citadel*, 263–264, 268; Hampton, *Connected Narrative*, 108; Diary of Byrd Willis, VSL.

32. Trudeau, *The Last Citadel*, 271–274; Wells, *Hampton and His Cavalry in '64*, 287.

33. Diary of Byrd Willis, VSL.

34. Trudeau, *The Last Citadel*, 276–278, 280–282; Hampton, *Connected Narrative*, 109–111.

35. R.E. Lee to G.W.C. Lee, December 13, 1864, Lee Family Papers, DU; Trudeau, *The Last Citadel*, 280, 282–284; Diary of Byrd Willis, VSL; Foard, "Reminiscences," SHC, 10.

36. Hampton, *Connected Narrative*, 112; Diary of Byrd Willis, VSL; Barringer, "First North Carolina," 13; Balfour, *13th Virginia Cavalry*, 40–41; Clark, ed., *North Carolina Regiments*, Vol. 3, 541.

37. OR, Vol. 42, Part 3, 1285, 1369; Inspection Reports, December 28 and 30, 1864, NA; Barringer, "First North Carolina," 13.

38. Hampton, *Connected Narrative*, 112; Davis, ed., *The Confederate General*, Vol. 3, 198–199; Douglas, *I Rode with Stonewall*, 321.

CHAPTER 14

1. Jerry Korn, *Pursuit to Appomatox* (Alexandria, 1987), 16–17.

2. Hampton, *Connected Narrative*, 112–115; OR, Vol. 46, Part 2, 1101.

3. Driver, *14th Virginia Cavalry*, 67–69.

4. Diary of Byrd Willis, VSL.

5. W.H.F. Lee to Agnes Lee, January 15, 1865, Lee Family Papers, VHS.

6. Diary of Byrd Willis, VSL.

7. Trudeau, The Last Citadel, 310–311; Diary of Byrd Willis, VSL.

8. Inspection Reports, W.H.F. Lee's Division, January 28–31, 1865, NA; Robert Jennings, V.S., *The Horse and His Diseases* (Philadelphia, 1862), 284–285.

9. Korn, *Pursuit to Appomatox*, 27; OR, Vol. 46, Part 2, 368; Cooke, *Wearing of the Gray*, 535, 537; Balfour, *13th Virginia Cavalry*, 43, 539–540.

10. G.W. Beale, *A Lieutenant of Cavalry in Lee's Army*, 198–199.

11. Driver, *14th Virginia Cavalry*, 69.

12. Korn, *Pursuit to Appomatox*; OR, Vol. 46, Part 2, 1209–1210.

13. Krick, *Ninth Virginia Cavalry*, 43.

14. *OR*, Vol. 46, Part 2, 1273.

15. R.E. Lee to Mary Custis Lee, March 1, 1865, Lee Family Papers, VHS.

16. *OR*, Vol. 46, Part 2, 937; Balfour, *13ᵗʰ Virginia Cavalry*, 43.

17. Trudeau, *The Last Citadel*, 334–336, 342–343.

18. R.E. Lee Jr., *Recollections and Letters of General Lee*, 146–147; R.E. Lee to Mary Custis Lee, March 28, 1865, Lee Family Papers, VHS.

19. Korn, *Pursuit to Appomatox*, 76.

20. Ed Bearss and Chris Calkins, *The Battle of Five Forks* (Lynchburg, 1985), 2, 4.

21. Chris Calkins, "The Battle of Five Forks: Final Push for the South Side," *Blue and Gray* (April 1992), 8; Bearss and Calkins, *The Battle of Five Forks*, 8–13, 15, 37.

22. Barringer, "The First North Carolina," 13–14; Bearss and Calkins, *The Battle of Five Forks*, 37; *Report of the Forty-Sixth Annual Reunion of the Sixth Ohio Veteran Volunteer Cavalry Association* (Warren, OH, 1911), 40–41; Samuel H. Merrill, *The Campaigns of the First Maine and First District of Columbia Cavalry* (Portland, 1866), 334.

23. Edward P. Tobie, *Service of the Cavalry in the Army of the Potomac* (Providence, 1882), 47; Clark, ed., *North Carolina Regiments*, Vol. 2, 7.

24. Bearss and Calkins, *The Battle of Five Forks*, 38, 41; Barringer, "The First North Carolina," 14; Rufus Barringer, "Cavalry Sketches," *The Land We Love*, Vol. 4, No. 1, November, 1867, 4.

25. Tobie, *Service of the Cavalry in the Army of the Potomac*, 47–49; Clark, ed., *North Carolina Regiments*, Vol. 2, 8; Barringer, "Cavalry Sketches," 4, 6; *Report of the Forty-Sixth Annual Reunion of the Sixth Ohio Veteran Volunteer Cavalry Association*, 41; Merrill, *The Campaigns of the First Maine and First District of Columbia Cavalry*, 335.

26. Bearss and Calkins, *The Battle of Five Forks*, 45–46, 77–78; Calkins, "The Battle of Five Forks," 17–18; Barringer, "Cavalry Sketches," 5; Barringer, "The First North Carolina," 15.

27. Bearss and Calkins, *The Battle of Five Forks*, 81, 92, 95, 102–104; Calkins, "The Battle of Five Forks," 19, 22, 41, 45.

28. *Court of Inquiry in the Case of Gouverneur K. Warren* (Washington, 1883), 532, 534, 615; David Cardwell, "The Battle of Five Forks," *Confederate Veteran*, Vol. 22 (March 1914), 118.

29. Bearss and Calkins, *The Battle of Five Forks*, 104–105, 107–108; Cardwell, "The Battle of Five Forks," 118.

30. Clark, ed., *North Carolina Regiments*, Vol. 3, 646–647; Bearss and Calkins, *The Battle of Five Forks*, 108; Andrew A. Humphreys, *The Virginia Campaign 1864 and 1865* (New York, 1995), 351.

31. *The Progress Index*, January 31, 1925.

32. *Court of Inquiry in the Case of Gouverneur K. Warren*, 535.

33. Bearss and Calkins, *The Battle of Five Forks*, 109; Foard, "Reminiscences," SHC, 18; Calkins, "The Battle of Five Forks," 49.

34. Cardwell, "The Battle of Five Forks," 119.

35. Bearss and Calkins, *The Battle of Five Forks*, 111, 113; Calkins, "The Battle of Five Forks," 51.

36. Thomas Munford, "Five Forks," DU; Arthur Crew Inman, ed., *Soldier of the South: General Pickett's War Letters to His Wife* (Boston, 1928), 130; *Court of Inquiry in the Case of Gouverneur K. Warren*, 1075.

37. *New York Herald*, April 10, 1865.

38. Korn, *Pursuit to Appomattox*, 92–93, 95–97, 99; Chris Calkins, "With Shouts of Triumph and Trumpets Blowing: George Custer Versus Rufus Barringer at Namozine Church, April 3, 1865," *Blue and Gray* (August, 1990), 27.

39. Douglas, *I Rode with Stonewall*, 330.

40. Calkins, "Namozine Church," 32–33; Cardwell, "The Battle of Five Forks," 119.

41. Clark, ed., *North Carolina Regiments*, Vol. 3, 650–653; Calkins, "Namozine Church," 34.

42. Barringer, "The First North Carolina," 15–16; Clark, ed., *North Carolina Regiments*, Vol. 3, 653; Calkins, "Namozine Church," 35–36.

43. Freeman, *R.E. Lee*, Vol. 4, 66–67, 69; Freeman, *Lee's Lieutenants*, Vol. 3, 693; Korn, *Pursuit to Appomattox*, 113.

44. Freeman, *Lee's Lieutenants*, Vol. 3, 694–696, 708–712, 715; Korn, *Pursuit to Appomattox*, 125–126.

45. Record of Prisoners of War received at City Point, April 13, 1865, NA.

46. Freeman, *R.E. Lee*, Vol. 4, 91, 101, 111; Freeman, *Lee's Lieutenants*, Vol. 3, 717–720; Report of W.H.F. Lee, April 11, 1865, Georgia Callis West Papers, VHS.

47. Freeman, *Lee's Lieutenants*, Vol. 3, 723–725.

48. Monroe F. Cockrell, ed., *Gunner with Stonewall: Reminiscences of William Thomas Poague* (Jackson, TN, 1957), 122.

49. Korn, *Pursuit to Appomattox*, 135; Freeman, *Lee's Lieutenants*, Vol. 3, 726; Chris Calkins, *The Battles of Appomattox Station and Appo-*

mattox Court House, April 8–9, 1865 (Lynchburg, 1987), 58, 60, 62; E.E. Bouldin, "Charlotte Cavalry," *SHSP*, Vol. 28, 75; Burke Davis, *To Appomattox: Nine April Days*, 1865 (New York, 1959), 347–348.

50. Theodore S. Garnett, "Last Fighting at Appomattox," *Times Dispatch*, April 16, 1905; Frank S. Robertson, "Memoir," from *Bulletin of the Washington County Historical Society*, 1986, 2.

51. Calkins, *The Battles of Appomattox*, 76; Report of Fitzhugh Lee, April 22, 1865, Lee Family Papers, VHS.

52. Freeman, *R.E. Lee*, Vol. 4, 120; Freeman, *Lee's Lieutenants*, Vol. 3, 733; Robertson, "Memoir," 2.

53. W. L. Moffett, "The Last Charge," *SHSP*, Vol. 36, 14–15.

54. Calkins, *The Battles of Appomattox*, 135; Henry Edwin Tremain, *Last Hours of Sheridan's Cavalry* (Providence, 1882), 259.

55. Blackford, *War Years with Jeb Stuart*, 294–295.

56. Kelly J. O'Grady, *Clear the Confederate Way: The Irish in the Army of Northern Virginia* (Mason City, Iowa, 2000), 200.

57. Crowninshield, *A Private Journal*, 1.

58. Chris Calkins, *The Final Bivouac: The Surrender Parade at Appomattox and the Disbanding of the Armies April 10–May 20, 1865* (Lynchburg, 1988), 9; *OR*, Vol. 46, Part 1, 1278.

59. Diary of J. Armfield Franklin, April 13, 1865, Douglas Freeman Papers, MOC.

60. N. B. Bowyer, "Last Fighting at Appomattox," *The Times Dispatch*, July 12, 1908; Krick, *Ninth Virginia Cavalry*, 44.

61. *OR*, Vol. 46, Part 3, 852; Report of W.H.F. Lee, April 11, 1865, Georgia Callis West Papers, VHS; Report of Fitzhugh Lee, April 22, 1865, Lee Family Papers, VHS.

62. Freeman, *R.E. Lee*, Vol. 4, 158, 161, 163–164, 190; Driver, *14th Virginia Cavalry*, 74; *OR*, Vol. 46, Part 3, 835.

63. Freeman, *R.E. Lee*, Vol. 4, 198; R.E. Lee Jr., *Recollections and Letters of General Lee*, 155–161; Adam Badeau to James Harrison Wilson, May 27, 1865, *The Ulysses S. Grant Association Newsletter*, Vol. 3, No. 1 (October 1965).

CHAPTER 15

1. Mary Custis Lee to a friend, Lee Family Papers, W&L.

2. Freeman, *R. E. Lee*, Vol. 4, 202, 206–207; R.E. Lee to W.H.F. Lee, June 13, 1865, Lee Family Papers, VHS.

3. R.E. Lee to W.H.F. Lee, July 29, 1865, Lee Family Papers, VHS.

4. W.H.F. Lee to R.E. Lee, November 1, 1866, Lee Family Papers, W&L.

5. W.H.F. Lee to R.E. Lee, November 21, 1865, Lee Family Papers, W&L; R.E. Lee Jr., *Recollections and Letters of General Lee*, 236.

6. Mary Custis Lee to Caroline Stewart, May 4, 1866, Lee Family Papers, W&L; R.E. Lee Jr., *Recollections and Letters of General Lee*, 241–242, 245–246.

7. R.E. Lee to W.H.F. Lee, October 15, 1866, Lee Family Papers, VHS.

8. *Richmond Times Dispatch*, August 1, 1915; R.E. Lee Jr., *Recollections and Letters of General Lee*, 252.

9. R.E. Lee to W.H.F. Lee, February 26, 1867, from R.E. Lee Jr., *Recollections and Letters of General Lee*, 258–259.

10. R.E. Lee Jr., *Recollections and Letters of General Lee*, 284; W.H.F. Lee to Mary Tabb Bolling, May 24, 1867, Lee Family Papers, VHS.

11. R.E. Lee to W.H.F. Lee, June 8, 1867, Lee Family Papers, VHS.

12. W.H.F. Lee to Mary Tabb Bolling, June 12, 1867, Lee Family Papers, VHS.

13. W.H.F. Lee to Mary Tabb Bolling, July 1, 1867, Lee Family Papers, VHS.

14. W.H.F. Lee to Mary Tabb Bolling, July 4 and 6, 1867, Lee Family Papers, VHS.

15. W.H.F. Lee to Mary Tabb Bolling, July 27, 1867, Lee Family Papers, VHS.

16. W.H.F. Lee to Mary Tabb Bolling, July 30, 1867, Lee Family Papers, VHS.

17. W.H.F. Lee to Mary Tabb Bolling, September 5, 1867, Lee Family Papers, VHS.

18. W.H.F. Lee to Mary Tabb Bolling, September 19, 1867, Lee Family Papers, VHS.

19. R.E. Lee to W.H.F. Lee, September 20, 1867, Lee Family Papers, VHS.

20. W.H.F. Lee to Mildred Lee, September 22, 1867, Lee Family Papers, VHS.

21. W.H.F. Lee to Rufus Barringer, October 13, 1867, Lee Papers, DU.

22. W.H.F. Lee to Mary Tabb Bolling, October 20, 1867, Lee Family Papers, VHS.

23. W.H.F. Lee to Mary Tabb Bolling, October 22, 1867, Lee Family Papers, VHS.

24. R.E. Lee to W.H.F. Lee, October 25, 1867; Lee Family Papers, VHS; R.E. Lee to W.H.F. Lee, November 15, 1867, Lee Family Papers, VHS; Freeman, *R.E. Lee*, Vol. 4, 335–336.

25. R.E. Lee to Mary Custis Lee, November 26, 1867, Lee Family Papers, VHS; Freeman, *R.E. Lee*, Vol. 4, 338–339.

26. William F. Wickham to his nieces, December 4, 1867, Wickham Family Papers, VHS; Freeman, *R.E. Lee*, Vol. 4, 339–340.

27. R.E. Lee to Mary Custis Lee, November 29, 1867, Lee Family Papers, VHS; R.E. Lee to Mary Custis Lee, December 1, 1867, Lee Family Papers, VHS.

28. R.E. Lee to W.H.F. Lee, December 21, 1867, Lee Family Papers, VHS.

29. Freeman, *R.E. Lee*, Vol. 4, 363–364; R.E. Lee to Mary Bolling Lee, May 29, 1868, from R.E. Lee Jr., *Recollections and Letters of General Lee*, 312–313.

30. W.H.F. Lee to Mary Bolling Lee, June 30, 1868, Lee Family Papers, VHS.

31. Freeman, *R.E. Lee*, Vol. 4, 388–389; W.H.F. Lee to R.E. Lee, September 22, 1868, Lee Family Papers, VHS.

32. Freeman, *R.E. Lee*, Vol. 4, 365, 381–382; R.E. Lee Jr., *Recollections and Letters of General Lee*, 330–331, 341, 364–365; W.H.F. Lee to Mary Bolling Lee, August 19, 1869, Lee Family Papers, VHS.

33. R.E. Lee Jr., *Recollections and Letters of General Lee*, 371.

34. R.E. Lee to W.H.F. Lee, December 18, 1869, Lee Family Papers, VHS.

35. Freeman, *R.E. Lee*, Vol. 4, 460–461, 463; Mary Custis Lee to Mildred Lee, May 9, 1870, Lee Family Papers, VHS.

36. R.E. Lee to W.H.F. Lee, August 20, 1870, Lee Family Papers, VHS; R.E. Lee Jr., *Recollections and Letters of General Lee*, 426–427, 433; W.H.F. Lee to Mary Bolling Lee, October 12, 1870, Lee Family Papers, VHS; Marshall W. Fishwick, *Lee After the War* (New York, 1963), 220–221.

37. *SHSP*, Vol. 2, 159; *SHSP*, Vol. 13, 1885.

38. R.E. Lee Jr. to Mary Custis Lee, January 9, 1871, Lee Family Papers, VHS; Inscription on stone in Lee Family Vault, Lee Chapel, Washington and Lee University.

39. W. W. Corcoran, *A Grandfather's Legacy* (Washington, 1879), 390.

40. W.H.F. Lee to Mary Custis Lee, May 31, 1872, Lee Family Papers, VHS.

41. Inscription on stone in Lee Family Vault, Lee Chapel, Washington and Lee University; W.H.F. Lee to Mary Bolling Lee, August 20, 1875.

42. W.H.F. Lee to Mary Bolling Lee, September 20, 1872, Lee Family Papers, VHS.

43. Lyle Kinnear, *The First Hundred Years: A History of Virginia Polytechnic Institute* (1972), 44; W.H.F. Lee to Professor J.W.C. Davis, July 4, 1873, Beale-Davis Papers, SHC.

44. Coulling, *The Lee Girls*, 179–180; Sanborn, *Robert E. Lee: A Portrait*, 494; W.H.F. Lee to Mary Bolling Lee, Lee Family Papers, VHS.

45. *Yearbook of the Historical Society of Fairfax County, Virginia*, Vol. 3, 24–27; W.H.F. Lee to Mr. Gratz, April 10, 1878, Gratz Collection, HSP; R.E. Lee Jr., *Recollections and Letters of General Lee*, 349–350.

46. Mrs. Fitzhugh's cousin to Mrs. E.A. Pickins, January 20, 1875, Francis Asbury Dickins Papers, SHC.

47. *Biographical Directory of the American Congress, 1774–1971*, 1278.

48. W.H.F. Lee to Mary Bolling Lee, July 26 (no year given), Lee Family papers, VHS; W.H.F. Lee to Mary Bolling Lee, January 19, 1884, Lee Family Papers, VHS; W.H.F. Lee to Mary Bolling Lee, February 7, 1875, Lee Family Papers, VHS; W.H.F. Lee to Mary Bolling Lee, December 21, 1875, Lee Family Papers, VHS.

49. W.H.F. Lee to Mary Bolling Lee, March 26, 1881, Lee Family Papers, VHS; W.H.F. Lee to Mary Bolling Lee, June 25, 1875, Lee Family Papers, VHS.

50. W.H.F. Lee to Mary Bolling Lee, May 28, 1886, Lee Family Papers, VHS; W.H.F. Lee to Mary Bolling Lee, March 22, 1877, Lee Family Papers, VHS; W.H.F. Lee to Mary Bolling Lee (no date), Lee Family Papers, VHS.

51. *Minutes of Proceedings of Southern Historical Society*, *SHSP*, Vol. 8, 1880, 44; *SHSP*, Vol. 12, 1884, 500; *SHSP*, Vol. 6, 1878, 283; *SHSP*, Vol. 10, 1882, 94–95.

52. W.H.F. Lee to Walter Herron Taylor, October 6, 1877, Walter H. Taylor Papers, Stratford Hall.

53. *Ceremonies Attending the Presentation of the Courtenay Flag* (Walhalla, South Carolina, 1903), 21–27.

54. *Biographical Directory of the American Congress, 1774–1971*, 1278; *Congressional Record*, Vol. 17, Part 7, 6708; *Congressional Record*, Vol. 19, Part 1, 280, 2847; *Congressional Record*, Vol. 21, Part 1, 115, 782; Charles T. O'Ferrell, *Forty Years of Active Service*, 320–321.

55. *Memorial Addresses on the Life and Character of General William Henry Fitzhugh Lee* (Government Printing Office, 1892), 10, 13, 39, 43, 46, 50–51; *The Washington Post*, October 16, 1891.

56. *Memorial Addresses*, 18–20, 79, 85; Crowinshield, *A Private Journal*, 1; Archer Anderson, *Robert Edward Lee An Address delivered at the Dedication of the Monument to General Robert Edward Lee at Richmond Virginia, May 29, 1890* (Richmond, 1890).

57. W.H.F. Lee to R.E. Lee III, February 11, 1890, Lee Family Papers, VHS.

58. W.H.F. Lee to Henry St. George Tucker, June 21, 1891, Tucker Papers, SHC; W.H.F. Lee to Mary Bolling Lee, July 30, 1891, Lee Family Papers, VHS.

59. *Alexandria Gazette* and *Virginia Advertiser*, October 16, 1891.

60. *Washington Post*, October 17, 1891.

61. *Washington Post*, October 18, 1891; Coulling, *The Lee Girls*, 190–191; *Memorial Addresses*, 21–22.

62. William B. Lightfoot to Mrs. Gen. W.H.F. Lee, October 16, 1891, Lee Family Papers, VHS; Frank Page to Mrs. W.H.F. Lee, October 29, 1891, Lee Family Papers, VHS.

63. Biographical Directory of the American Congress 1774–1971, 1278.

64. Historical Society of Fairfax Virginia Yearbook, Vol. 3, 27.

65. Encyclopedia of Virginia Biography, Vol. 5, 774 *SHSP*, Vol. 39, 175.

66. Wayland, *Robert E. Lee and His Family*, 50.

CHAPTER 16

1. *Memorial Addresses*, 64.

2. John W. Wayland, *Robert E. Lee and His Family* (Staunton, 1951), 65; *Memorial Addresses*, 9, 26–28, 66–67, 93.

3. *Richmond Dispatch*, October 16, 1891; *Memorial Addresses*, 66.

4. Clark, ed., *North Carolina Regiments*, Vol. 2, 106–107.

5. G.W. Beale, *A Lieutenant of Cavalry in Lee's Army*, 224.

6. Frank Robertson, "Memoir," 3, Robertson Papers, UOC; Wise, *The End of an Era*, 425; *The Progress Index*, January 31, 1926.

7. Frank Robertson to his mother, November 28, 1864, Robertson Papers, UOC.

8. G.W. Beale, *A Lieutenant of Cavalry in Lee's Army*, 221; Balfour, *13th Virginia Cavalry*, 31.

9. *Memorial Addresses*, 7, 9–10, 12, 14–15, 20, 29, 42, 51, 86, 105; *Washington Post*, October 16, 1891; W.H.F. Lee to Mary Bolling Lee, undated, Lee Family Papers. VHS.

10. *Memorial Addresses*, 7, 67, 94.

11. Freeman, *R.E. Lee*, Vol. 1, 129; Sanborn, *Robert E. Lee: A Portrait*, 77, 84.

Bibliography

ARTICLES

Adams, Herbert. "Enemy of Rebels and Rum Lovers." *Civil War Times* (March 1986).

Barringer, Rufus. "Cavalry Sketches." *The Land We Love* 4 (November 1867–April 1868).

Bouldin, E. E. "Charlotte Cavalry." *Southern Historical Society Papers.* 28 (1900).

Bowyer, N. R. "Last Fighting at Appomattox." *The Times-Dispatch* (Richmond, VA) (July 12, 1908).

Brooksher, William R., and Snider, David K. "A Piece of Rebel Rascality." *Civil War Times* (June 1984).

———. "The Great Circuit Around McClellan." *Civil War Times Illustrated* 12, no. 1 (April 1973).

Calkins, Chris. "The Battle of Five Forks: Final Push for the South Side." *Blue and Gray* (April 1992).

Campbell, William. "Stuart's Ride and Death of Latane." *Southern Historical Society Papers* 39 (1914).

Cardwell, David. "The Battle of Five Forks." *Confederate Veteran* 22 (March 1914).

Cardwell, David. "General Wade Hampton's Cattle Raid." *Southern Historical Society Papers* 22 (1894).

Daughtry, Mary B. "Lincoln Finds a Rebel General: The Unusual Tale of Rufus Barringer's Encounter with the Yankee President." *Blue and Gray* (October 1988).

Davis, L. H. "Famous Cattle Raid." *Confederate Veteran* 26 (October 1918).

Foote, James H. "Scrapbook, Roll of Honor, North Carolina Troops, 1861–1865." North Carolina State Library.

Frayser, Richard E. "Stuart's Ride in Rear of the Army of the Potomac." *Southern Historical Society Papers* 11 (1883).

Gallagher, Gary. "Brandy Station: The Civil War's Bloodiest Arena of Mounted Combat." *Blue and Gray* (October 1990).

Garnett, Theodore S. "Last Fighting at Appomattox." *The Times-Dispatch* (Richmond, VA) (April 16, 1905).

Lee, Fitzhugh. "Chancellorsville." *Southern Historical Society Papers* 7 (1879).

Lee, S. L. "War Time in Alexandria, Virginia." *South Atlantic Quarterly* 4, no. 3 (July 1905).

Lippincott, George E. "Lee-Sawyer Exchange." *Civil War Times Illustrated* (June 1962).

Long, Roger. "Johnson's Island Prison." *Blue and Gray* (March 1987).

Longacre, Edward. "The Raid That Failed." *Civil War Times Illustrated* (January 1988).

Lykes, Richard W. "The Great Civil War Beef Raid." *Civil War Times Illustrated* 10, no. 10 (February 1967).

McClellan, H. B. "Address." *Southern Historical Society Papers* 8 (1880).

Moffett, W. L. "The Last Charge." *Southern Historical Society Papers* 36 (1907).

Mosby, John S. "The Ride Around General McClellan." *Southern Historical Society Papers* 26 (1898).

Neal, Harry E. "Rebels, Ropes, and Reprieves." *Civil War Times Illustrated* (February 1976).

Robertson, Frank. "Memoir." *Bulletin of the Washington County Historical Society*, 1986.

Robins, W. T. "Stuart's Ride Around McClellan." In *Battles and Leaders of the Civil War*, vol. 2. Ed. Ned Bradford. New York: Appleton-Century-Crofts, 1956.

Walker, Charles N., and Rosemary, ed. "Diary of the War by Robert S. Robertson." *Old Fort News* 28 (January–March 1965).

———. "The Battle of Greatest Lustre." *Southern Historical Society Papers* 34, paper 5. Ed. R.A. Brock. Richmond: Virginia Historical Society, 1876–1959, pp. 208–209.

———. "The Famous Lee Rangers." *Southern Historical Society Papers* 23 (1895).

_____. "Military Hospital of Fort Monroe Busy During Civil War." *Daily Press* (Newport News–Warwich–Hampton, VA) (December 29, 1957).

_____. "Personal Recollections of the War." *Harper's New Monthly Magazine.*

_____. "Two Confederate Items." *Bulletin of the Virginia State Library* 16, nos. 2 and 3 (July 1927).

NEWSPAPERS

Daily Confederate
Daily Press (Newport News, VA)
Daily Richmond Enquirer
Harper's New Monthly Magazine
Macon Daily Telegraph
New York Herald
New York Times
Progress-Index (Dinwiddie, VA)
Richmond Daily Dispatch
Richmond Enquirer
Richmond Sentinel
Richmond Times Dispatch
The Sentinel

MANUSCRIPTS

Duke University, William R. Perkins Library
Confederate Veterans Papers
John Esten Cooke War Diairies
Lee Papers
Thomas T. Munford Papers
Diary of W.A. Curtis
Fairfax City Regional Library, Virginia Room
Ravensworth File
Harvard University Library
Faculty Records
College Papers
Historical Society of Delaware
James Harrison Wilson Diary
Historical Society of Pennsylvania

Gratz Collection
Cadwalader Collection
Greer Collection
Huntington Library, San Marino, CA
Joseph Hooker Papers
Library of Congress, Manuscript Division
Lee Family Papers
James H. Drake Papers
Douglas Freeman Papers (J. Armfield Franklin Diary)
Jedediah Hotchkiss Papers
Mary Ball Washington Library
John W. Chowning Diary
Museum of the Confederacy
North Carolina Collection (John W. Gordon Diary)
North Carolina State Archives
James B. Gordon Papers
Riley W. Leonard Papers
Simpson and Biddle Family Papers
Registry St. Paul's Episcopal Church, Richmond, VA
Stratford Hall Plantation, Jessie Ball DuPont Memorial Library, Strat-
    ford, VA
Taylor Family Papers
South Carolinian Library
Crawford Family Papers
Wade Hampton's "Connected Narrative"
University of Chicago
Wyndham Robertson Papers
University of North Carolina–Chapel Hill, Southern Historical Collection
Rufus Barringer Papers
Beale-Davis Papers
Francis Asbury Dickins Papers
Fred C. Foard Papers
R. Channing Price Papers
Tucker Papers
University of Virginia Library, Manuscripts Department
Lee Family Papers
Levering Correspondence
U.S. Government Printing Office
Court of Inquiry of Gouverneur K. Warren
Congressional Record
Military Service Records
U.S. Military History Institute

Louis Leigh Papers (report from McGregor's battery)
Virginia Historical Society
Lee Family Papers
Wickham Family Papers
Virginia State Library
Byrd Willis Diary
Washington and Lee University Library, Manuscripts Division
Lee Family Papers

BOOKS

Adams, Francis Colburn. *A Trooper's Adventures in the War for the Union.* New York: Hurst, 1863.

Adams, Henry. *The Education of Henry Adams.* Boston and New York: Houghton Mifflin, 1918.

Agassiz, George R., ed. *Meade's Headquarters: 1863–1865: Letters of Colonel Theodore Lyman from the Wilderness to Appomattox.* Reprint. Freeport, NY: Books for Libraries Press, 1970.

Anderson, Archer. *Robert Edward Lee: An Address Delivered at the Dedication of the Monument to General Robert Edward Lee at Richmond, Virginia May 29, 1890.* Richmond, VA: William Ellis Jones, Printer, 1890.

Anderson, N. L. *The Letters and Journals of General Nicholas Longworth Anderson, 1854–1892.* New York: F.H. Revell, 1942.

Armstrong, Richard B., ed. *The Journal of Charles B. Chewning, Company E 9th Virginia Calvary.* Spotsylvania, VA: R.B. Armstrong, 1986.

Balfour, Daniel T. *13th Virginia Cavalry.* Lynchburg, VA: H. E. Howard, 1986.

Beale, G. W. *A Lieutenant of Cavalry in Lee's Army.* Boston: Gorham Press, 1943.

Beale, R.L.T. *History of Ninth Virginia Cavalry.* Richmond, VA: B.F. Johnson Publishing, 1899.

Bearss, Ed, and Chris Calkins. *The Battle of Five Forks.* Lynchburg: H.E. Howard, 1985.

Bigelow, John Jr. *The Campaign of Chancellorsville.* New Haven: Yale University Press, 1910.

Blackford, W. W. *War Years with Jeb Stuart.* New York: Charles Scribner's Sons, 1945.

Boatner, Mark Mayo III. *The Civil War Dictionary.* New York: David McKay, 1959.

Boykin, Edward. *Beefsteak Raid.* New York: Funk and Wagnalls, 1960.

Brown, R. Shepard. *Stringfellow of the Fourth.* New York: Crown Publishers, 1960.

Calkins, Chris. *The Battle of Appomattox Station and Appomattox Court House, April 8–9, 1865.* Lynchburg, VA: H.E. Howard, 1987.

_____. *The Final Bivouac: The Surrender Parade at Appomattox and the Disbanding of the Armies, April 10–May 20, 1865.* Lynchburg, VA: H. E. Howard, 1988.

Cavada, F. F. *Libby Life.* Reprint. Lanham, MD: University Press of America, 1985.

Chalfant, Edward. *Both Sides of the Ocean: A Biography of Henry Adams—His First Life, 1838–1862.* Hamden, CT: Archon Books, 1982.

Clark, Walter, ed. *Histories of the Several Regiments and Battalions from North Carolina in the Great War, 1861–1865.* Reprint. Wendell, NC: Broadfoot's Bookmark, 1982.

Cockrell, Monroe F., ed. *Gunner with Stonewall: Reminiscences of William Thomas Poague.* Jackson, TN: McCowat-Mercer Press, 1957.

Cooke, John Esten. *Wearing of the Gray.* Bloomington: Indiana University Press, 1959. Reprint. Millwood, NY: Kraus, 1977.

Connelly, Thomas L. *The Marble Man.* Baton Rouge: Louisiana State University Press, 1977.

Corcoran, W. W. *A Grandfather's Legacy.* Washington, DC: Henry Polkinhorn, 1879.

Coulling, Mary P. *The Lee Girls.* Winston-Salem, NC: John F. Blair, 1987.

Crowninshield, Benjamin W. *A Private Journal, 1856–1858.* Cambridge: Riverside Press, 1941.

Cummins, A. B. *The Wilson-Kautz Raid.* Blackstone, VA: Nottoway, 1961.

Davis, Burke. *To Appomattox: Nine April Days, 1865.* New York: Rinehart, 1959.

Davis, William C., ed. *The Confederate General.* National Historical Society, 1991.

_____. *Death in the Trenches.* Alexandria, VA: Time-Life Books, 1986.

Denison, Frederic. *Sabres and Spurs.* First Rhode Island Cavalry Veteran Association, 1876.

Dobbins, Auston C. *A Grandfather's Journal.* Reprint. Dayton, OH: Morningside, 1988.

Dodge, Theodore A. *The Campaign of Chancellorsville.* Boston: James R. Osgood, 1881.

Douglas, Henry Kyd. *I Rode with Stonewall*. Chapel Hill: University of North Carolina Press, 1940.

Dow, Neal. *The Reminiscences of Neal Dow*. Portland, ME: Evening Express Publishing, 1898.

Dowdey, Clifford. *Lee*. New York: Bonanza Books, 1965.

_____. *Lee's Last Campaign*. Wilmington, NC: Broadfoot Publishing, 1988.

Driver, Robert J. Jr. *14ᵗʰ Virginia Cavalry*. Lynchburg, VA: H. E. Howard, 1988.

Duncan, Russell, ed. *Blue-Eyed Child of Fortune: The Civil War Letters of Colonel Robert Gould Shaw*. Athens: University of Georgia Press, 1992.

Dyer, Frederick H. *A Compendium of the War of the Rebellion*. New York: Thomas Yoseloff, 1959.

Fishwick, Marshall W. *Lee After the War*. New York: Dodd, Mead, 1963.

Ford, Worthington Chauncey, ed. *Letters of Henry Adams, 1858–1891*. Boston and New York: Houghton Mifflin, 1930.

_____. *A Cycle of Adams Letters, 1861–1865*. Boston: Houghton Mifflin, 1920.

Freeman, Douglas Southall. *R. E. Lee: A Biography*. New York: Charles Scribner's Sons, 1934.

Freemantle, Lt. Col. *Three Months in the Southern States*. London: William Blackwood and Sons, 1863.

Furguson, Ernest B. *Chancellorsville 1863: The Souls of the Brave*. New York: Alfred A. Knopf, 1992.

Gallagher, Gary, ed. *Fighting for the Confederacy: The Personal Recollections of General Edward Porter Alexander*. Chapel Hill: University of North Carolina Press, 1989.

Garnett, Captain Theodore Stanford, and Robert J. Trout, ed. *Riding with Stuart: Reminiscences of an Aide-de-Camp*. Shippensburg, PA: White Mane Publishing, 1994.

Glazier, Willard. *Three Years in the Federal Cavalry*. New York: R.N. Ferguson, 1870.

Godfrey, C. E. *Sketch of Major Henry Washington Sawyer*. Trenton, NJ: MacCrellish and Quigley, 1907.

Goolrick, William K. *Rebels Resurgent: Fredericksburg to Chancellorsville*. Alexandria, VA: Time-Life Books, 1985.

Grimsley, Daniel A. *Battles in Culpepper County*. Orange, VA: Green Publishers, 1900.

Hall, Charles B. *Generals of the C. S. Army, 1861–1865*. New York: The Steele Company, 1898.

Halliburton, Lloyd, ed. *Saddle Soldiers: The Civil War Correspondence of General William Stokes of the 4th South Carolina Cavalry.* Orangeburg, SC: Sandlapper Publishing, 1993.

Hennessy, John J. *Return to Bull Run: The Campaign and Battle of Second Manassas.* New York: Simon and Schuster, 1993.

Hesseltine, William Best. *Civil War Prisons: A Study in War Psychology.* Reprint. New York: Frederick Ungar Publishing, 1978 [1930].

Horn, John. *The Destruction of the Weldon Railroad: Deep Bottom, Globe Tavern, and Reams Station.* Lynchburg, VA: H.E. Howard, 1991.

Humphreys, Andrew A. *The Virginia Campaign 1864 and 1865.* New York: DaCapo Press, 1995.

Inman, Arthur Crew, ed. *Soldier of the South: General Pickett's War Letters to his Wife.* Boston and New York: Houghton Mifflin, 1928.

Jennings, Robert V. S. *The Horse and His Diseases.* Philadelphia: John E. Potter, 1862.

Jones, Rev. J. William. *Army of Northern Virginia Memorial Volume.* Reprint. Dayton, OH: Morningside Bookshop, 1976.

Jones, J. William D.D. *Life and Letters of Robert Edward Lee, Soldier, and Man.* Reprint. Harrisonburg, VA: Sprinkle Publications, 1978 [1906].

Jones, J. William. *Personal Reminiscences, Anecdotes, and Letters of Gen. Robert E. Lee.* New York: D. Appleton, 1875.

Keys, Thomas Bland. *Tarheel Cossack: The Life of W. P. Roberts.* Unpublished manuscript, 1983.

Kinnear, Lyle. *The First Hundred Years: A History of Virginia Polytechnic Institute and State University.* Blacksburg, VA: Virginia Polytechnic Institute and Educational Foundation, 1972.

Korn, Jerry. *Pursuit to Appomattox.* Alexandria: Time-Life Books, 1987.

Krick, Robert. *Ninth Virginia Cavalry.* Lynchburg, VA: H. E. Howard, 1982.

Lee, Robert E. Jr. *Recollections and Letters of General Robert E. Lee.* Reprint. Garden City, NY: Garden City Publishing, 1924 [1904].

Levin, Alexandra Lee. *This Awful Drama: General Edwin Gray Lee, C. S. A., and His Family.* New York: Vantage Press, 1987.

Longacre, Edward. *The Cavalry at Gettysburg.* Rutherford, NJ: Fairleigh Dickinson University Press, 1986.

Longacre, Edward G. *From Union Stars to Top Hat: A Biography of the Extraordinary General James Harrison Wilson.* Harrisburg: The Stackpole Company, 1972.

MacDonald, Rose Mortimer Ellzey. *Mrs. Robert E. Lee.* Boston: Ginn, 1939.

Martin, David G. *The Chancellorsville Campaign*. Conshohocken, PA: Combined Books, 1991.

Matter, William D. *If It Takes All Summer: The Battle of Spotsylvania*. Chapel Hill: University of North Carolina Press, 1988.

McCabe, James D. Jr. *Life and Campaigns of General Robert E. Lee*. Atlanta, Philadelphia, Cincinnati, and St. Louis: National Publishing, 1866.

McClellan, H. B. *I Rode with Jeb Stuart*. Bloomington: Indiana University Press, 1958. Reprint. Millwood, NY: Kraus, 1981.

McGuire, Judith W. *Diary of a Southern Refugee During the War*. New York: E.J. Hale and Son, 1867. Reprint. New York: Arno Press, 1972.

Merrill, Samuel H. *The Campaigns of the First Maine and First District of Columbia Cavalry*. Portland, ME: Bailey and Noyes, 1866.

Merrington, Marguerite, ed. *The Custer Story: The Life and Intimate Letters of Gen. George A. Custer and His Wife Elizabeth*. New York: Devin-Adair, 1950.

Mitchell, Adele H. *The Letters of Major General James E.B. Stuart*. Stuart-Mosby Historical Society, 1990.

Mohr, James C., ed. *The Cormany Diaries: A Northern Family in the Civil War*. Pittsburgh: University of Pittsburgh Press, 1982.

Morris, Roy, Jr. *Sheridan: The Life and Wars of General Phil Sheridan*. New York: Crown Publishers, 1992.

Morrison, James L. Jr., ed. *The Memoirs of Henry Heth*. Westport, CT: Greenwood Press, 1974.

Mosby, John S. *Mosby's War Reminiscences: Stuart's Cavalry*. New York: Pageant Book, 1958.

Nagel, Paul C. *The Lees of Virginia*. New York: Oxford University Press, 1990.

Neese, George M. *Three Years in the Confederate Horse Artillery*. New York: Neale, 1911.

Oakey, Daniel. *History of the Second Massachusetts Regiment of Infantry*. Boston: Geo. H. Ellis, Printer, 1884.

O'Ferrell, Charles T. *Forty Years of Active Service*. New York: Neale, 1904.

O'Grady, Kelly J. *Clear the Confederate Way: The Irish in the Army of Northern Virginia*. Mason City, IA: Savas Publishing, 2000.

O'Toole, Patricia. *The Five of Hearts: An Intimate Portrait of Henry Adams and His Friends, 1880–1918*. New York: Clarkson Potter, 1990.

Opie, John N. *A Rebel Cavalryman with Lee, Stuart, and Jackson*. Reprint. Dayton, OH: Morningside, 1972.

Pierce, R. V. *The People's Common Sense Medical Adviser.* Buffalo, NY: World's Dispensary Printing Office and Bindery, 1886.

Perry, John Gardner. *Letters from a Surgeon of the Civil War.* Boston: Little, Brown, 1906.

Rhea, Gordon C. *The Battle of the Wilderness, May 5–6, 1864.* Baton Rouge: Louisiana State University Press, 1994.

_____. *The Battles for Spotsylvania Court House and the Road to Yellow Tavern, May 7–12, 1864.* Baton Rouge: Louisiana State University Press, 1997.

_____. *To the North Anna River: Grand and Lee, May 13–25, 1864.* Baton Rouge: Louisiana State University Press, 2000.

Richardson, Albert D. *The Secret Service, the Field, the Dungeon, and the Escape.* Hartford, CT: American Publishing, 1865.

Robertson, James I. Jr., ed. *The Civil War Letters of General Robert McAllister.* New Brunswick, NJ: Rutgers University Press, 1961.

Rockwell, A. D. *Rambling Recollections: An Autobiography.* New York: Paul B. Hoeber, 1920.

Roland, Charles P. *Albert Sidney Johnston: Soldier of Three Republics.* Lexington: University Press of Kentucky, 2001.

Royall, William L. *Some Reminiscences.* New York: Neal Publishing, 1909.

Royster, Charles. *Light Horse Harry Lee and the Legacy of the American Revolution.* New York: Alfred A. Knopf, 1981.

Sanborn, Margaret. *Robert E. Lee: A Portrait (1807–1861).* Philadelphia and New York: J. B. Lippincott, 1966.

Sandburg, Carl. *Abraham Lincoln.* 6 vols. New York: Charles Scribner's Sons, 1936.

Scheibert, Justus. *Seven Months in the Rebel States During the North American War, 1863.* Trans. Joseph C. Hayes. Ed. William Stanley Hoole. Tuscaloosa, AL: Confederate Publishing, 1958.

Sears, Stephen W. *Landscape Turned Red: Battle of Antietam.* New York: Ticknor and Fields, 1983.

_____. *To the Gates of Richmond: The Peninsula Campaign.* New York: Ticknor and Fields, 1992.

Sommers, Richard J. *Richmond Redeemed: The Siege at Petersburg.* Garden City, NY: Doubleday, 1981.

Stackpole, Edward J. *Chancellorsville.* 2nd ed. Harrisburg, PA: Stackpole Books, 1988.

Starr, Stephen Z. *The Union Cavalry in the Civil War.* 2 vols. Baton Rouge: Louisiana State University Press, 1979.

Thomas, Emory M. *Bold Dragoon: The Life of J.E.B. Stuart.* New York: Harper and Row, 1986.

Thomason, John W. Jr. *Jeb Stuart*. New York: Charles Scribner's Sons, 1930. Reprint. New York: Mallard Press, 1992.

Tobie, Edward P. *Service of the Cavalry at the Army of the Potomac*. Providence: N. Bangs Williams, 1882.

Townsend, George R. *Rustics in Rebellion*. Chapel Hill: University of North Carolina Press, 1950.

Tremain, Henry Edwin. *Last Hours of Sheridan's Cavalry*. New York: Bonnell, Silver, and Bowers, 1904.

Trudeau, Noah Andre. *The Last Citadel*. Boston: Little, Brown, 1991.

Tyler, Lyon Gardiner, ed. *Encyclopedia of Virginia Biography* Vol. 5. New York: Lewis Historical Publishing, 1915.

von Borcke, Heros. *Memoirs of the Confederate War for Independence*. 2 vols. Reprint. Dayton, OH: Morningside Bookshop, 1985.

von Borcke, Heros, and Scheibert, Justus. *The Great Cavalry Battle of Brandy Station*. Reprint. Winston-Salem, NC: Palaemon Press, 1976.

Warner, Ezra J. *Generals in Gray: Lives of the Confederate Commanders*. Baton Rouge: Louisiana State University Press, 1981.

Wayland, John W. *Robert E. Lee and His Family*. Staunton, VA: McClure Printing, 1951.

Weld, Stephen W. *War Diary and Letters of Stephen M. Weld*. Boston: Massachusetts Historical Society, 1979.

Wellman, Manly Wade. *Giant in Gray: A Biography of Wade Hampton of South Carolina*. Dayton, OH: Morningside Press, 1980.

Wells, Edward L. *Hampton and His Cavalry in '64*. Richmond, VA: Owens Publishing, 1991.

Wise, John Sergeant. *The End of an Era*. New York: John Yoseloff, 1965.

Woodward, C. Vann, ed. *Mary Chesnut's Civil War*. New Haven: Yale University Press, 1981.

ADDITIONAL REFERENCES

Biographical Directory of the American Congress, 1774–1971. Washington, DC: U.S. Government Printing Office, 1971.

Ceremonies Attending the Presentation of the Courtenay Flag. Walhalla, SC: Keowee Courier Presses, 1903.

Court of Inquiry in the Case of Gouverneur K. Warren. Washington, DC: U.S. Government Printing Office, 1883.

Encyclopedia of Virginia Biography. New York: Lewis Historical, 1915.

Fort Lafayette Life. London: Simpkin, Marshall, 1865.

Historic Culpeper. Culpeper, VA: Culpeper Historical Society, 1974.

The Historical Times Illustrated Encyclopedia of the Civil War. New York: Harper and Row, 1986.

History of the 11th Pennsylvania Volunteer Cavalry. Philadelphia: Franklin Printing, 1902.

Memorial Addresses on the Life and Character of Gen. William Henry Fitzhugh Lee. Washington, DC: U.S. Government Printing Office, 1892.

Report of the Forty-Sixth Annual Reunion of the Sixth Ohio Veteran Volunteer Cavalry Association. Warren, OH: W.M. Ritezel, 1911.

Yearbook of the Historical Society of Fairfax County, Virginia. Vol. 3, 1954.

The War of the Rebellion: A Compilation of the Official Records of the Union and Confederate Armies. Washington, DC: U.S. Government Printing Office, 1899.

Index